Black Pilgrimage to Islam

Black Pilgrimage to Islam

Robert Dannin

Photographs by Jolie Stahl

OXFORD
UNIVERSITY PRESS

2002

OXFORD
UNIVERSITY PRESS

Oxford   New York
Athens   Auckland   Bangkok   Bogotá   Buenos Aires   Cape Town
Chennai   Dar es Salaam   Delhi   Florence   Hong Kong   Istanbul   Karachi
Kolkata   Kuala Lumpur   Madrid   Melbourne   Mexico City   Mumbai   Nairobi
Paris   São Paulo   Shanghai   Singapore   Taipei   Tokyo   Toronto   Warsaw

and associated companies in
Berlin   Ibadan

Library of Congress Cataloging-in-Publication Data
Dannin, Robert, 1952–
Black pilgrimage to Islam / Robert Dannin ; photographs by Jolie Stahl.
   p.   cm.
Includes bibliographical references and index.
ISBN 0-19-514734-0
1. Islam—United States—History.   2. African American Muslims—United
States—History.   3. Muslim converts—United States—History.   4. Black Muslims—
United States—History.   I. Title.
BP67.U6 D34   2002
297.8'7'0973—dc21   2001036234

9 8 7 6 5 4 3 2 1

Printed in the United States of America
on acid-free paper

Preface

History is animated by a will for encounter as much as by a will for explanation.
—Paul Ricoeur

EL-HAJJ WALI AKRAM sat in a swivel chair inside the tiny study attached to his old workshop. Long ago when his wife Kareema was alive and their children still lived at home, he built an addition onto the wood frame house at the corner of Union Avenue and East 136th Street in Cleveland. It was a big room, where he could tinker day and night on his inventions. There was enough space for a two-ton printing press with shelves everywhere, now littered haphazardly with tools, lead fonts, and unfinished pamphlets.

On his lap was a book, *The Masonic Ritual for Use of the Ancient Free and Accepted Masons,* by A. Mizzardini. "The whole thing rested on the Masonic order! There's no use beating around the bush, that's how Islam came to America," he declared and then reminisced about college in Prairie View,

Texas, where he had joined a nearby fraternal lodge long before he accepted Islam.

I interrupted to mention that many orthodox Muslims object vehemently to any mention of Freemasonry.

"There are many things about the history of Islam in America that people would not like to hear," he retorted. "The Ahmadiyyas were another example, but the truth is that their missionaries performed a great service in bringing the Quran to the United States. Anyway," he said, "you don't go out and get Islam. Islam gets you!"

The old imam's remarks pertained to the religious subcultures that preceded the introduction of Islamic orthodoxy on the mean streets of depression-era ghettos. Although his days as an active *da'i* (proselytizer) were over, Akram was offering a valuable lesson in cautioning his listener not to ignore what he learned as a young man traveling the rails and highways northward from Texas. Vernacular speech and plain writing are the best ways to make a point because they disseminate information to a wide audience without exclusivity. It is best not to begin by alienating the uninitiated, those who might lose interest upon hearing too many foreign terms or reading too many inscrutable concepts. The message or meanings, if valuable, will take care of themselves. They will grab an audience spontaneously. An author is simply delivering information and ought to do it efficiently.

Originally conceived as work in the anthropological subfield called ethnohistory, my research absorbs whatever possible from these academic styles but dispenses with formalisms in order to narrate stories of Islamic conversion as accurately as possible. The main job has been to steer these biographies toward publication without encoding them in excessive jargon. These accounts are important for the depth of the personalities they reveal and for expressing the motives and desires of individuals intent on choosing their own path toward salvation. All of them are informed by the power and poetry of a sacred book, the Holy Quran.

Today there is disturbance in all latitudes of discourse, however, so the navigator who successfully guides his or her ship needs more than a reliable compass. One needs an internal gyroscope that takes into account the direction of trade winds, the cresting and falling tides, water temperatures, the habits of sea life, cloud formations, swirling fogs, the creaking of the shipboard, the crew's mood, and even the fleeting neuralgia caused by subtle changes in atmospheric pressure. Finally, one needs the confidence that comes from seeking a truth—whether by means of faith or science, whether one believes it is directed from the heavens or is deduced from observed human experience.

Nearly everyone described in this study referred to the Traditions of the Prophet Muhammad, in which he reportedly advised the curious to seek knowledge "from the cradle to grave . . . all the way to China." Some then suggested that I should not pursue this work, calling it inappropriate. Others, like El-Hajj Wali Akram, encouraged me with their generous cooperation. I wrestled with these alternatives and decided to continue on the assumption that the questions raised herein address an important challenge to those who, in the spirit of Ricoeur, wish to advance crosscultural dialogue.

From time to time, many of the individuals whose stories are represented in this book may have wondered exactly what happened to this research, some having concluded that it would never be published. Now they will have the opportunity to judge whether it was worth their participation; and their opinions, for better or worse, will be the ultimate evaluation of this work's success.

An academic book normally contains thanks to those of the scholar's mentors, colleagues, and students who have endured his or her bad temper and executed his or her orders in order to produce the work. I have no such debts here and wish only to thank a few individuals for their professional advice and friendly support. Michael Ratner provided an initial boost for the project by furnishing my wife, Jolie Stahl, and myself with his contacts in the Muslim community. In order of succession we met Sahar Abdul-Azziz, Dhoruba bin Wahad, Imam Al-Amin Latif, and Shuaib Abdur Raheem; they played key roles by helping us build a grassroots network among African-American Muslims. Utrice Leid and Andrew Cooper recognized the potential significance of this information to their readership and published early field reports in the Brooklyn weekly *City Sun*. Similarly, Noel Rubinton at *Newsday Magazine*, Francis X. Clines of the *New York Times*, Carlo Pizzati of *La Repubblica*, and Serge Halimi and Ignacio Ramonet of *Le Monde Diplomatique* reinforced the principle that an open, free press is still the best antidote to prejudice. Marc Landas serialized my prison research in his web magazine *Urban Dialogue*.

I am very grateful to Cynthia Read of Oxford University Press for her thoughtful and serious consideration of my work. Professors Barbara Metcalf, Yvonne Haddad, and Jane Smith also demonstrated kindness and patience as editors; they had confidence in the soundness of my scholarship and encouraged me to complete this book when it seemed no else would. Victoria Ebin first put me in touch with Professor Metcalf and arranged our fieldwork in Senegal. Howard Zinn generously responded to my entreaty for moral support nearly thirty years after first seeing merit in my writing. Frank Peters, Jill Claster, and John Devine offered opportunities to present our materials at New York University; the same may be said for Andrew Apter and Robin Derby at the University of Chicago. Howard Dodson, O. R. Dathorne, and Maria Diedrich invited us to conferences at home and abroad. Mohamed Abdus-Sabur introduced me to Frank Vogel at Harvard, who in turn invited me to speak to his Harvard Law School class on Islamic jurisprudence. Ricarte Echeverria read draft versions of the manuscript and gave critical opinions from the perspective of someone who has grown up in a neighborhood similar to those depicted herein. Theo Calderara and Jessica Ryan of Oxford University Press were helpful and supportive throughout the publication process.

Hailu Paris kindly shared his experiences, his optimism, and spiritual uplift.

Trix Rosen was a great friend and avid supporter who lent Jolie her dark-room and also her expertise as a printer. Dale Hoffer transcribed all the interviews which included many difficult foreign terms. Brian Young made extraordinary photographic prints that translate the depth and tension of real events. David Pryor provided a watershed of knowledge about printing and manufacturing books.

My source of strength and guiding light in this endeavor has been my wife, Jolie Stahl, who never wavered in her commitment to completing this work although it often seemed more convenient and certainly less costly in all senses to let it go. Her confidence in my skills exceeds all visible results to date, but I hope that this publication will begin to prove her wisdom.

Contents

Abbreviations

AAUAA Adenu Allahe Universal Arabic Association
AME African Methodist Episcopal Church
AMM American Muslim Mission
CUP Committee for Union and Progress
DAR Dar ul-Islam Movement
DOCS Department of Correctional Services
FCM First Cleveland Mosque
ICNA Islamic Circle of North America
IMA Islamic Mission to America
IPNA Islamic Party of North America
IRM Islamic Revivalist Movement
ISNA Islamic Society of North America
MIB Mosque of Islamic Brotherhood
MSA Muslim Students Association
MST Moorish Science Temple of Islam
NAIT North American Islamic Trust
NOI Nation of Islam
OAAU Organization of Afro-American Unity
OAU Organization of African Unity
TISO The Islamic School of the Oasis
UIB Universal Islamic Brotherhood
UISA Uniting Islamic Society of America
UNIA Universal Negro Improvement Association

Black Pilgrimage to Islam

Introduction

Whether in private or public, any attempt I made to explain how the
Black Muslim movement came about, and how it has achieved such force, was
met with a blankness that revealed the little connection that the liberals'
attitudes have with their perceptions or their lives, or even their knowledge—
revealed, in fact, that they could deal with the Negro as a symbol or a victim
but had no sense of him as a man. —James Baldwin, *The Fire Next Time*

IGNORANCE about African-American Muslims has robbed
students of an important aspect of American history. It
has also hindered a thorough understanding of the impli-
cations of slavery's nefarious legacy. At the beginning of this study in 1986,
I decided to fill in the blanks by contacting African-American Muslims and
recording their conversion narratives. I soon discovered that their testimonies often recapitulated the themes of *The Autobiography of Malcolm X.*
Upon reading the classics of conversion literature, I also found that their
ideas about symbolic death and rebirth, heroism, sacrifice, and redemption

reiterated ideas expressed by John Bunyan in *The Pilgrim's Progress*, Leo Tolstoy in *A Confession*, and Søren Kierkegaard in *Fear and Trembling*. As an immensely popular work, Malcolm X's story also captured the Gestalt of earlier slave narratives—Booker T. Washington's classic *Up from Slavery* comes to mind—and quickly became a paradigm for conversion, functioning, like its predecessors, as a template on which the believer might inscribe his or her own experiences. Malcolm's story made it socially acceptable to discuss Islam and religious conversion because, as Claude Brown wrote shortly after its publication, "the Muslims were the home team. They were the people talking for everyone."[1]

This is an ethnography about that "home team." It summarizes original, independent ethnographic research. It is the first publication to use documentary photos, interviews, unpublished archival documents, historical research, and critical commentary to explore issues of theology, religious conversion, and social transformation as they apply to the extraordinary rise of Islam as an American religion. It emphasizes a documentary approach by focusing on contemporary religious practices, including worship, ritual feasts, rites of passage, and internal family dynamics. This book also treats important contemporary issues such as identity politics, morality, educational alternatives, and entanglements between religion and the state.

I began by asking Why would African Americans fashion themselves into a double minority by converting to Islam? Was there something about the Holy Quran or Islamic morality that attracted African Americans? What could Islamic worship accomplish that was absent from the many denominations of the Black Church? How does the highly disciplined Islamic lifestyle contrast with mainstream American values?

To answer such questions, I began to explore the varieties of Islamic sects in America and discovered that the modern practice of orthodox Islam among African Americans dates from the early decades of the twentieth century. Through oral history and archival research, I reconstructed the folkways of Islamic conversion and identified individual missionaries and religious organizations who proselytized Islam to African-American communities beginning in 1913.

In the 1960s several books focused on the separatist-nationalistic Nation of Islam.[2] These works displayed sound scholarship for the most part and were widely read, too, yet they were inadequate for a clear understanding of the scope and diversity of the Muslim phenomenon in America. They did nothing to rectify the mass media's already distorted image of Islam, which was often based on a hagiography of Elijah Muhammad. They ended up portraying a single, notorious example as representative of the entire religious movement. Rather than focus on the cultlike Nation of Islam, its racialist discourse, and its conspicuous personalities, this book intends to avoid the mistakes of those authors and their epigones by looking at the religious and historical aspects of normative Islamic worship. Thus, the photos and text of this book signify the first interpretive ethnology of orthodox Islamic worship among African Americans.

As author and photographer, man and woman, we established contacts with orthodox Muslims in the New York area by frequenting several storefront mosques, learning the history of these institutions, and presenting a case for research and study. Some of our approaches were at first rebuffed. However, we eventually persuaded several key Muslim leaders of the merits to a book that would educate the public about Islam and its American-born practitioners.

Almost immediately, photography became a controversial issue. The privilege to photograph Muslim persons and their community activities was not obtained easily. It was first necessary to convince our subjects that the materials resulting from this study would be used responsibly and exclusively as educational tools. We gradually became familiar personalities in several neighborhood communities, acquired friends, and built confidence. By working with imams or the religious leaders and ordinary worshipers, both male and female, we constructed a network to various centers of Muslim worship across the country. We continued to focus on New York but also went to Atlanta, Winston-Salem, Detroit, Toronto, Cleveland, Chicago, Indianapolis, and Los Angeles, frequently coordinating travel plans to coincide with the two most important Muslim holidays, connected to Ramadan and the annual pilgrimage to Mecca. We also attended weekly prayer services in each city.

The study progressed from public rituals and events to family and individual profiles, where it became possible eventually to explore sensitive issues in depth. In Cleveland, we encountered El-Hajj Wali Akram at the celebration of his eighty-sixth birthday surrounded by his children, grandchildren, and great-grandchildren. An accomplished inventor with several important patents to his credit, Akram was born on a farm in East Texas and converted to Islam in St. Louis in 1925. He founded the First Cleveland Mosque in 1932, which is now the oldest continuously running Muslim institution in America. The First Cleveland Mosque presented an opportunity for an intensive study of extended family relationships on a daily basis. It resulted in a rich pastiche of images, narratives, and documents showing the history and sociology of four generations of African-American Muslims.

Later, we encountered a second Muslim community in Cleveland, the Universal Islamic Brotherhood. In contrast with the members of the First Cleveland mosque, this community represents first-generation converts who are working to build an ideal society governed by Islamic law. We were also the first outsiders to study Jabul Arabiyya, a Muslim village near Buffalo, New York, founded by four steel workers who converted to Islam during the Great Depression.

This book strives to convey individuals' spiritual orientation and the search for truth through personal transformation. Nowhere is this more evident than in the research concerning the role of Islam in prison. The documentation of Muslim communal worship in New York's maximum security jails is supplemented with personal narratives by Muslim inmates. These images and words are testimony to the powerful attraction of Islam for individuals in desperate situations—to how it structures broken lives and furnishes an alternative vision of the world.

Another part of our odyssey concerns Islam and the African diaspora. In West Africa, we visited Medina Kaolack, holy city of the four-million-strong Tijaniyya Muslim brotherhood, which claims members in over twenty-five countries. We traveled there to focus on the lives of a handful of resident American converts. From young boys through teens to some adults, African-American Muslims gravitate to countries like Senegal to become proficient at Quranic recitation and Islamic jurisprudence. In their peregrinations to Africa and beyond, Muslim converts seek to reconnect with a heritage of Afro-Islamic identity that was broken by the Atlantic slave trade.

Within this work, we sought to portray ethnographic reality without sacrificing biographical details that will draw readers to formulate their own critical views of the material. As a publication for general readers, scholars, libraries, and religious professionals, this book seeks crosscultural understanding. It is an effort to give image and voice to the thousands of African Americans who see themselves as returning to an old tradition from which they were violently wrenched.

The principal means for achieving this transformation is that of oral narrative. Narrative has long served as one of the main sources of folklore in the African-American community, important because it has provided a common vehicle for the expression of literary and artistic talents where no one is excluded by race or class. Early slave narratives served as testimonies to religious convictions and the vital traditions otherwise denied by the slaves' masters. After emancipation, folk tradition and the rural church were welded into a singular tradition. The greatest orators mesmerized congregants with their flair for mixing biblical allegory and personal experience. In the sermon could be found the elements of a literary form with its own aesthetic viewpoint, style, grammar, rhythm, images, and vocabulary.

In the depths of the Great Depression, the Works Progress Administration commissioned the Federal Writer's Project to record a set of narratives by former slaves who recalled their conversions to Christianity. The motivation was to rescue these folk tales, which were about to become extinct with the death of their authors. Entitled *God Struck Me Dead*, this collection served as a model for our work in eliciting from Muslims their stories about religious transformations.

The most famous of such modern conversion narratives appears in *The Autobiography of Malcolm X*, where ideas about symbolic death and rebirth, heroism, sacrifice, and commitment often repeat the archetypal themes of universal folklore. Immensely successful, this work succeeded in canonizing the life of a single man, and it continues to overshadow many tales that chronicle other lives and similar transformations. This book seeks to redress this imbalance by surveying a plurality of voices who express their philosophies, narrate their adventures, and testify to their personal religious experiences. Of the various ways of doing this, I have employed several methods here. Part I is an ethnohistorical narrative that mixes primary sources, including interviews and unpublished documents, with historical research. This approach continues at the beginning of part II in chapter 4 where the written archives of El-Hajj Wali Akram gave me the opportunity to reconstruct the early history of Islam in Cleveland. It is supplemented by individual recollections and comments. Chapter 5 is constructed similarly except that Sheik Daoud Ghani was able to provide me with a detailed narrative of the founding of the West Valley settlement in the absence of extensive documents that remain either missing or undiscovered. For chapter 6, I relied almost entirely on Shuaib Abdur Raheem's revealing personal narrative although my introduction to his story came from other eyewitness accounts, news archives, and a thorough examination of court transcripts and depositions. The sources used in chapter 7 were primarily ethnographic research and interviews in the New York State prisons supplemented by many telephone conversations with five inmates over a period of four years. I had additional access to documents generated by Muslim prisoners, their correspondence, official grievances, and also conversations with chaplains, administrators, and some of their family members. Chapter 8 gives detailed information about the family life of one particular woman, based on extensive interviews but presented in the third person. Chapter 8 is an interpretation and comparison of marriage customs where primary and textual sources serve to illustrate analytical comments. Chapter 9 combines all of the preceding approaches. Altogether these methods reflect the varying degrees of propinquity inherent in the practice of anthropology.

In most cases conversion to Islam is depicted as a return to the cosmic order. The Muslim sees this as the sine qua non for personal redemption, the road back to virtues obscured by the forces of subjugation and injustice. It is a theme reflected continually in the testimonies presented here. The narrators are mostly individuals who were familiar with the Bible though never quite affected by it the way they are by the Quran. Some were Christians; others were lapsed churchgoers, seekers of the truth, dabblers, or unbelievers. When conversion struck them, however, there was no room for compromise and hardly any sentiment to retain their former lives. Change was seen as totally positive.

The typical conversion narrative is a ritual act depicting an individual's pilgrimage from the chaos of unbelief (*fitna*) toward salvation. The ritual and also the narrative theme resolve the historical tensions of African-American society by concluding that liberation from racial domination and spiritual redemption are one and the same. The end goals require an indefatigable dedication to transform oneself and one's fellows. "Verily, Allah does not change the state of a people until they change themselves inwardly" (Quran 13:12) is by far the most frequently quoted scriptural passage among African-American Muslims.

From an ethnographic viewpoint, public recitation of this narrative is an essential ritual of African-American Muslim worship. The testimony of one's pilgrimage to the Divine Truth becomes a literary trope meant to circulate among friends, family, and even strangers. No details of the convert's previous life are too intimate to spare, no sins too ugly to describe, no transgressions too vile to repeat. A confession of these proportions defies censure because it shows the way forward and symbolizes the convert's ability to subdue his or her material desire (*nafs*, in Arabic, meaning the carnal, base tendencies). This is the *jihad al-akbar* ("the greater struggle") to which Muslims refer in describing the "fear and trembling" that overtakes the human soul as it wrestles with the satanic forces of unbelief.

In practice, requests to record these biographies generally elicited modesty. Sometimes individuals who were highly suspicious of our motives felt compelled nonetheless to take a chance that their story would circulate and become an influential device for propagating Islam among people who find themselves in similar conditions. For those who choose to speak publicly, the conversion narrative supersedes nearly every other religious attribute as a sign of Islamic authenticity. It serves as an ellipsis for the normative definition of a Muslim as one who follows the Five Pillars of Faith—profession of faith (*shahada*); daily prayer (*salat*); observance of Ramadan fasting; tithing (*zakat*), and pilgrimage to Mecca (*hajj*). It marks the spot, like an X, where one's life took a momentous detour from which there is theoretically no return.

Firmly rooted in the oral tradition, the conversion narrative signifies the will, often desperate, to renegotiate one's personal history and ethnic destiny. Ironically, it can also mean a further alienation from one's family and friends. It complicates social relations at work, in school, or in civic affairs. But the price seems worth paying for the steady few. Their sacrifice of real ties to family recapitulates symbolically the total dehumanization that vitiated African-American life for a very long time—breakup of the family, ghettoization, crime, substance dependencies, and myriad health problems. Islamic conversion promises to resolve these problems once and for all by furnishing a new genealogy (membership in the worldwide Islamic *umma*), a new moral system, and a new code of personal and social hygiene. Henceforth the believer enters a new space-time continuum that separates believers from infidels.

Suddenly, geographical space gets reorganized according to a map where Mecca is the center for all calibrations of place. Chronologically, the believer resets his or her calendar to a reckoning of time based on a new epoch that began when the Prophet formed his community-in-exile at Medina in A.D. 622, known as year I of the Hegira. The Prophetic Traditions become the superstructure for a virtuous life with divine law (*sharia*) as its governing moral code. Even the human senses are purified (*wudzu*), leading to changes in the aesthetic appreciation of sight, sound, taste, aroma, and touch, each yielding to the primacy of the recited word of Allah in the original Arabic of the Holy Quran. Socially, the narrative rejuvenates a popular imagination in the guise of a subjectivity that is neither transcendental nor romantic yet is plainly therapeutic. In these terms, conversion relates to a psychology that owes as much to Franz Fanon as to Freud because the narrative of Islamic conversion is a ritual excoriation of the old life that purifies by exposing a person's sins to the acid light of family and community. Its inward trajectory confronts the repressed trauma exclusive to African-American history: the very distortion of memory itself during slavery, the destruction of extended genealogy, enforced belief systems and modes of thought, intraethnic ambivalence and conflict, misrecognition (as in the constant denial of Islam by black chroniclers), and lack of access to scripture and truth.

Historically, the conversion narratives reported herein begin at the junction of two epic tragedies of the early twentieth century, the Great Migration (1914–19) and the Great Depression (1929–45). These were periods of profound suffering for African Americans, uprooted from the land and dumped unceremoniously into the urban miasma. Conventional religious beliefs were incapable of explaining this topsy-turvy world, where men and women died on the streets, victimized not by war or any plague indexed in the Bible but by a mysterious force called "the economy." Is it such a wonder that spiritual inspiration would arise from these dire circumstances? Or that the working poor, excluded by racism from political power, would seek redemption in an alternative faith?

It was in this context that El-Hajj Wali Akram and Sheik Daoud Ghani sought personal redemption according to their measure of suffering, rejection, homelessness, and poverty. Each story recounts a pilgrimage motivated by the need to break with a suffocating rural tradition that retained emotional, if not material, connections to slavery. Through physical displacement and eventually religious conversion, both men severed these bonds as a way of liberating themselves from extended-family responsibilities and a life of debt in the rural South. They sealed this rupture by changing their Christian names and surnames, both sources of identification with a false ancestor—the white slave master. Thus, young Walter Gregg became Wali Akram in 1926 after hearing a Muslim missionary on a St. Louis street corner, and David Duffy became Daoud Ghani in 1932 after attending several meetings held by another Islamic missionary in downtown Buffalo. Certainly there was more than one way for an urban migrant to remake himself as a modern wage laborer, but this was perhaps the most dramatic declaration of personal independence.

In considering religious conversions, I have tried to build on the theoretical work of Melville Herskovits, Peter Worsley, and Weston LaBarre. Of the many anthropologists who have investigated this general topic, Herskovits was the first to research New World "African" culture and define the concept of syncretism as the selective fusion of disparate cultures into contemporary practices and beliefs. He postulated a heterogeneous Afro-American cultural area, whose social geography was defined by the Black Diaspora of North and South America, the Caribbean, and West Africa. Within these limits, he believed, the ethnographer could excavate cultural, social and linguistic artifacts by observing contemporary rituals, linguistic patterns, and other cultural practices.[3] In the resulting debate about his ideas, Herskovits questioned E. Franklin Frazier's counterintuitive assumption that the experiences of the Middle Passage and plantation slavery had stripped from African Americans all memories of African culture.

Farther afield but still conceptually relevant, Worsley's work on Melanesian islanders and LaBarre's on Native Americans complement Herskovits's pioneering work with their documentary evidence of syncretism and the identification of revitalization movements as moments of acculturation and religious conversion. By resisting the materialist temptation to ignore belief systems as merely ideological expressions, they recognized religious conversion movements as mediation between indigenous and colonial systems, more aptly described as the struggle for hegemony between local and global forces. Since the publication of Worsley's book *The Trumpet Shall Sound* and LaBarre's book *The Ghost Dance*, anthropologists have found it necessary to adopt a more dynamic approach to the analysis of religious movements. This means describing social action according to ethnographic, historical, and psychological data.

When viewed in this light, African-American revitalization movements can be seen as the manifestation of a deep commitment to encounter history and rewrite the collective African-American experience in a global context. For individuals like Noble Drew Ali, Elijah Muhammad, and Malcolm X, Islam not only was emblematic of this imperative but also provided legitimacy to myths that had circulated for years as part of the spiritualist dogma of the eighteenth-century plantation where slave-preachers creatively transformed scripture into imagined victories for the oppressed. In their quest to learn about the belief systems of their antecedents, many African Americans have embraced Islamic pedagogy as a means for self-discovery because it opens new historical vistas and uncommon trajectories. In most cases the route leads through the Arab nations, with emphasis on the history of the Muslim caliphates in Baghdad, Cairo, and Istanbul. Other routes lead through West Africa, the Maghreb, or the Sudan. There are still others that cross neither through Africa nor the Middle East, taking instead the long way around the world from the United States to points in Southeast and Southwest Asia and then into Mecca from the east.

Faced with these competing itineraries, I wanted to keep an eye fixed on Mecca as the ultimate symbol of Islam. To maintain the *dar al-Islam* (the House of Islam) as a methodological anchor, however, demanded far more than I had realized, in terms of scholarship. Indeed, religious scholarship was the source of my own terror of displacement, loss of identity, and hesitation. My ignorance of Islam and Arabic is an aspect of this work for which I offer no excuse. The limitations of my role as ethnographer were tested often and so, too, was this project's integrity as a quest for knowledge. My sincerity in seeking to understand other persons' cherished beliefs frequently came under fire, and it was never easy to control my own reactions when shunned for who I am or when asked to profess belief in another faith.

Such are the trials of contemporary anthropology, grasping for the right descriptive tools while simultaneously absorbing a new canon. This pilgrimage is an interpretive experience; it is informed by the author's own biography and characterized by the inevitable social antagonisms of gender, race, and class. (The Quran gives credence to this hermeneutic principle when declaring that humanity is divided into innumerable tribes, so that they might know each other better.) Writing about religion or culture in modern societies is an exercise that demands a constant effort to depict individual choice and belief as consequences of many contradictory forces. Such variables as economic or historical antagonisms may be readily apparent to the reader, while theology or political ideology often defy simple explanations. The task is to clarify diverse theologies or ideologies and render them in contemporary language. It is neither an exercise in self-contemplation nor an opportunity for self-attainment. I have no obvious constituencies and believe that in such an endeavor one must be prepared to say precisely what no one, including oneself, wishes to hear.

DEMOGRAPHIC NOTE: AN INFLUENCE GREATER THAN THEIR NUMBERS Although the U.S. Census Bureau asks Americans about their race, their income, and even how many toilets there are in their homes, religion is a taboo subject for fear of entanglements between church and state. Therefore, it has been difficult to obtain real figures for religious affiliation. However, a survey characterized as "the largest and most comprehensive survey of American religions"[4] estimates that the largest percentage of Americans are Christians (86.5 percent, or 214 million). Jews represent 1.8 percent of the population, or 4.3 million, while Muslims are about 0.5 percent, or 1.4 million. Of Muslims, 40 percent, or 560,000, are black, representing less than 2 percent of the approximately 30 million African Americans.[5] A more recent survey raises the estimate to 1.6 million African-American Muslims from a total U.S. count of 4.1 million Muslims.[6] With less than a decade separating these two studies, the figures represent a nearly 200 percent increase in total Muslim and African-American Muslim population. More significant, it would raise the ratio of Muslims to total African Americans to nearly 5 percent. Whatever their discrepancies in methodology and reporting, the studies indicate growth in both immigration and conversion, although the higher estimate still falls below the inflated figures uncritically circulated by the mass media.

There are African-American Muslims in almost every major American city. New York is only one area that has experienced such enormous growth. There are 112 mosques in the state of New York, with 71 in the five boroughs of New York City. Chicago has at least 40 mosques. In addition, Los Angeles, Washington, Atlanta, Detroit, Cleveland, and Toledo are cities where one might expect to see 10,000 Muslims celebrating the 'Id al-Fitr communally. In total there are nearly 1,200 mosques nationwide.

The South-Central area of Los Angeles, scene of the 1992 uprising in reaction to the injustice at the Rodney King trial, counts dozens of small storefront mosques of various affiliations and beliefs. There was even a Shiite mosque, al-Rasul, whose black imam espoused jihad until he moved to Iran in 1989. Local Muslim activists proselytized among the notorious Crips and Bloods long before the riots gave further cause to the idea of unity. Their efforts are based on the belief that gangs represent a "primitive" stage of cultural nationalism whose logical culmination lies in adherence to Islam as the "true" religion for people of African descent. Because of the persistence of this minority of partisans in the cause of Allah throughout the past decades, it is often said that every black youth grows up in proximity to some notion of Islam.

Consequently, almost 90 percent of the converts to Islam in the United States are African Americans, a trend whose meaning has not been lost to prominent Arab- or Asian-American Muslims who desire to build a political coalition with the goal of enhancing their position in American society. The alliance of the Muslim Political Action Committee (now called the American Muslim Council) with Jesse Jackson's 1988 presidential campaign was only one example of this attitude, which envisions electing a Muslim to Congress in the coming years. One of the immediate goals of this movement has been to start people thinking of America as a Judeo-Christian-*Muslim* society.

I

Tracking the Red Fez

1

Of Masons and Moors

THE first task of this book is to describe what I call the unchurched culture of African Americans in the nineteenth and early twentieth centuries. Without any written historical narrative and owing to the deliberately obscure accounts of non-Christian religious traditions among African Americans, writing this history is difficult and fraught with great potential for error. It is nonetheless essential if one is to properly understand the complex social, political, and intellectual forces contributing to the extraordinary rise of modern Islamic conversion that is the principal subject of this work. To portray this history requires an interpretative rendering of African-American civic life, religion, and folk practices. It means discussing mystical religious themes, including Sufism, gnosis, Freemasonry, hermeticism, and Egyptology. It encompasses relations between black, red, and white Americans. It also demands an understanding of the world of international diplomacy, whose impact on race relations in America has been underestimated if ever mentioned seriously.

Finally, this work transgresses an unspoken taboo by offering evidence that the Black Church was not necessarily central to the spiritual life of all African Americans. By definition, unchurched means to be away from the influence of the institutions of Christianity, implying an existence at one remove from civil society. As it concerns one's attitude toward public life, to be unchurched is to eschew social convention, to stand apart. What is clear from my field research is that part of African-American society has always been unchurched. The unchurched person finds himself or herself to be "other than Christian" in religious matters but also opposes mass political culture. His or her persona in civil society is characterized by the rejection of all conventional sacerdotal and secular hierarchies. Part of my job here is to explain the directions taken by the unchurched in their search for meaning and inspiration.

The anthropological concept of *liminality* expresses the idea that all societies incorporate the seeds of their own denial to a greater or lesser extent. While liminal characters and their "unprincipled" behavior normally threaten the social integument, they are tolerated nonetheless and sometimes celebrated because their persistent antagonism redefines the notion of community. New forms of legitimacy and power surge forth when a community or nation recognizes beliefs and practices hitherto considered unconventional. For example, the First and Second Great Awakenings were liminal events that appeared to challenge the colonial and postcolonial order of American society. The gatherings of these movements cast their participants into an acute spiritual maelstrom from which they emerged with a radically different view of their mission in the New World. Some were converted literally overnight from obedient colonial subjects into determined agents of Manifest Destiny.

The liminality of unchurched African Americans is chronic throughout history because of slavery and brutal prejudice. The institutional mechanisms that might normally encourage the reintegration of discontents back into the society were off limits. Except perhaps for the performing arts, most life options, including the military, fine arts, and thinking professions were closed to most African Americans until the last quarter of the twentieth century. Rejected by white society and feeling isolated from their own communities, some individuals remained unchurched in the broadest sense, subscribing to political radicalism or religious cults. A few, after passing through a liminal or unchurched stage, discovered the Quran or Torah, converting to Islam or Judaism permanently. The rest were condemned to repeat the process indefinitely, cycling back and forth from conversion to liminality.

Since the end of the Civil Rights era, unchurched African Americans have been moving more rapidly toward Islam. I call this historic and spiritual transformation a Black Pilgrimage to Islam. My main challenge has been to write a narrative of this journey that describes the shared experiences, passions, and folklore of those individuals who identify themselves as Muslims.

I have conducted this research according to an inductive method taught to me by the anthropologist William Fenton, who coined the term "upstreaming" to describe his ethnohistorical approach to studying Iroquois society.[1] Briefly, this means taking information from the ethnographic present and applying it to the historical record. It is comparable to the use of a divining rod passed over dry land in search of subterranean water. My "divining rod" here is the sign of the red fez, a hat worn by men that is almost immediately recognizable as the symbol of the unchurched subculture.[2] In much the same way that many students of Afro-American Christianity have used the symbol of "the river" to draw connections between New World Baptist cults and certain riparian cults in Africa, I shall travel upstream using the fez to visit the world of the unchurched.[3]

FROM PLANTATION TO LODGE

> *"Dey waz bery puhticluh bout duh time dey pray and dey bery regluh bout duh hour. . . . Dey bow tuh duh sun an hab lil mat tuh kneel on. Duh beads is on a long string," reported Katie Brown the great-great-granddaughter of the Muslim slave Bilali Muhammad when reminiscing about his religion in Georgia in the 1930s.*

Of the millions of Africans brutally enslaved and inhumanly transported to the Americas, how many were Muslims? From what part of Africa did they come? What set them apart from other enslaved Africans?[4] Why did they play preponderant roles in rebellions throughout the seventeenth and eighteenth centuries? How were they able to persist in their faith without written scripture? Is it possible to trace lineages from enslaved African Muslims to contemporary African-American Islam? These questions are the core of a rapidly growing corpus of research that involves the work of historians, anthropologists, archaeologists and many African-American scholars.[5]

The experiences of the earliest African Muslims in America and their resistance to the fate of slavery come to us through the narratives of slaves brought to North America from Sahelian Africa. Beginning in the late seventeenth century a significant number of African Muslims were introduced into the Atlantic slave trade. Estimating on the basis of their ethnic origin, approximately 15 percent of the African slaves sold in North America came from nominally Muslim tribes.[6] The ratio was perhaps higher in South America, where African Muslims reportedly fomented antislavery rebellions.[7]

Islam figured as one amid a plurality of indigenous African religions that came to be mixed with elements of the slave-owners' Hebrew and Christian teachings.[8] The strength of Islam in this mix derived from the Arabic literary tradition and the Quran. Whereas animist slaves were divided by language and culture, Muslim slaves had a common, unifying scripture. Some of the men were *hafis*, having spent years under the tutelage of Quran teachers, mastering the

Arabic language and committing to memory each *sura*, or chapter, of the holy book. Violently separated from Africa, a few of these men kept their own memoirs in Arabic or continued to recite the Quran, creating for themselves a reputation for scholarship that set them apart from other slaves. The *almamis*, or "sheiks," as they were known in the United States, sometimes were given special treatment. Fearing them as dangerous or powerful men, most planters singled them out for rough, brutal treatment. On the other hand, some masters welcomed the opportunity to exploit these slaves' linguistic skills and forced them into positions of managerial responsibility. Muslim slaves whom the master considered closer to his own beliefs in religious matters might even be induced to convert to Christianity or Judaism.

The trail of the red fez links the slave rebellions of Latin America to the United States by the agency of Black seafarers, usually former slaves but also free men, who played an important historical role in transmitting politically subversive information among members of the African diaspora.[9] One of them was Prince Hall, a twenty-seven-year-old tanner from Bridgetown, Barbados, who arrived in colonial Boston in 1765, the date associated with the mass religious event known as the First Great Awakening. Hall was drawn from the docks along South Street to the revival meetings on the Boston Common, where he witnessed firsthand the feverish religious ecstasy sweeping the Bay Colony. He converted to Methodism and soon began to preach.[10] Five years later, when Crispus Attucks, a black man, became the first casualty of the American Revolution, Hall's sermons took a sharp political turn. He espoused the belief that emancipation from slavery was integral to American independence. Stepping down from the pulpit to join the struggle for independence, he also petitioned John Hancock of the Massachusetts Committee on Public Safety, asking him to enlist the service of slaves for the revolutionary army. Although he was quickly rebuffed, Hall volunteered for the revolutionary army when Washington opened his ranks to free blacks on December 30, 1775.

Significantly, Hall was initiated into Masonry in 1775 and established a lodge for nonwhites under the aegis of an Irish lieutenant attached to a British regiment guarding Boston. He called on fellow lodge members to join the struggle for national independence, asserting that "[the slaves] cannot but express their astonishment that every principle from which America has acted, in the course of the unhappy difficulties with Great Britain, pleads stronger than a thousand arguments in favor of the slaves."[11] First renowned for preaching and then for his public stance on abolition, Prince Hall recruited many freedmen and escaped slaves into his lodge, where they pledged to cooperate with the revolutionary American state.[12]

Hall became first grand master of African Lodge, no. 459, officially chartered in 1784 and renamed the African Grand Lodge in 1791. It was a cornerstone for the work of abolitionism and integration throughout the former colonies; immediately after his death in 1808 it was renamed the Prince Hall

Lodge.[13] One can reasonably conclude that it was the first organized abolitionist movement in the United States led by a free person of African descent.

Other free men and women of African descent followed Prince Hall's example in the eighteenth and early nineteenth century. They too were skilled, literate professionals, like the merchant sea captain Paul Cuffee and the astronomer Benjamin Banniker. James B. Dudley, grand master of North Carolina's Prince Hall Lodge, was a former slave who became a public school teacher in Wilmington, Delaware, and then an editor of the local black newspaper. He founded the first African-American insurance company, the People's Perpetual, and the first African-American bank, the Metropolitan Building and Loan Association. In 1818 "Sir Knight" Passey Benjamin organized the first "colored" Knights Templar under authorization from the duke of Sussex. The following year, Peter Ogden founded the Black Odd Fellows. Like Prince Hall, both Ogden and Benjamin were immigrants from the West Indies, seafarers who plied the route between the former colonies and Liverpool, England. These individuals and doubtless others formed a transatlantic network dedicated to the abolition of slavery. The official historian of the Prince Hall lodge wrote:

> By occupation these brethren were all seafaring men, who had received all the degrees in Masonry, including that of Knights Templars in London and Liverpool. . . . Commanderies were rapidly organized and constituted in the United States. Warrants were issued to freedmen not withstanding slavery. Its banners were unfolded in many of the slave states prior to 1865.[14]

Freemasonry was thus integral to the construction of black civil society in colonial North America. In the first half of the eighteenth century, lodges were chartered in Martinique, Jamaica, Antigua, Barbados, and Haiti. This movement spread to North America in the second half of the century, with lodges established in Albany, New York, and Charleston, South Carolina. By the beginning of the nineteenth century, Prince Hall lodges had opened in Baltimore, Philadelphia, New York, Boston, Providence, and New Orleans; much of the growth was owing to the "considerable immigration of West Indian colored people."[15]

Did the black merchant class comprise a liminal society bound by Masonic ritual and a code whose mission was the abolition of slavery? If so, the red fez survives as an artifact embracing the symbolism of that struggle.

A good lead for showing historical links between Islam and African-American Freemasonry can be found in the story of Ibrahima Abdul Rahaman, an African Muslim who suffered the misfortune of spending the last half of the eighteenth century as a slave in Natchez, Mississippi. One day, a traveling surgeon recognized him; he had doctored Ibrahima's father, a local Tukolor chieftain, after a serious hunting accident in Senegal forty years earlier. Seeing injustice in this reversal of fortune for the son who was now a slave, the physician reported his identity to a journalist. Subsequent articles in the local newspaper created a sensation about the hidden "African prince" whom everyone seemed to know as just an old slave. The story of this "wrongful" enslavement gained wide appeal east of the Mississippi and eventually caught the attention of the Department of State, whose head, Henry Clay, then persuaded President John Quincy Adams to negotiate Ibrahima's manumission. The planters around Natchez must have considered Ibrahima a dangerous character because his own slavemaster strenuously resisted the government's offer. He finally agreed to liquidate the old African's contract on the condition that he would be deported immediately!

One can imagine that something subversive about Ibrahima or his behavior had prompted the planter's demand. Could it have been his refusal to abandon his Islamic beliefs and the threat of such an example, if widely known, to the maintenance of order among slaves?

Ironically, it was precisely his identity as a Muslim that led Clay and his president to cast Ibrahima's manumission as a diplomatic gesture toward the North African sultanates, particularly Morocco. Unwittingly or not, Ibrahima played along with this strategy by traveling to the White House, where he expressed his gratitude by reciting and writing (in Arabic) *al-Fatihah*, the first verse of the Quran. Upon his arrival in Washington, Ibrahima became a ward of the American Colonization Society, a Methodist-dominated organization that was planning to send missionaries to Africa. Surmising that his exotic identity would lend an air of authenticity to their vision of civilizing Africa, they dressed him in silk robes and a fez before dispatching him on a promotional tour through the New England states.

In ignoring the warnings of the local planters, Clay apparently failed to appreciate the potential domestic consequences of his actions, for Ibrahima soon embarrassed his sponsors by stirring religious controversy everywhere. He relished the opportunity to question Christianity by arguing with religious leaders and insisted that Islam was the only true religion. Word of his notoriety spread, provoking local churches to retract their welcome and forcing him to lecture either outdoors, as he did in Niagara Falls, or in the Prince Hall lodges in Boston, Hartford, and Providence. Among freemen and slaves in his audiences, Ibrahima's attitude, as well as his exotic appearance, inspired more than passive curiosity. Some began to recall their own Islamic religious backgrounds. Several publicly reclaimed their African-Muslim names, invoking the wrath of local whites, who branded them as impostors.

Ibrahima's brief career as a public figure suggested a latent dissonance between slave beliefs and Christianity, an unchurched attitude that probably resonated forcefully within the network of Prince Hall lodges. Fortuitously chartered just before independence, the fraternal orders championed independence from not only the state but also the church. They served as mutual self-help organizations, insurance funds, and banks, thus assuring a degree of autonomy from the church that was otherwise unfeasible.

Some writers have asserted that the African-American lodges merely imitated and emulated the white fraternal orders.[16] Against this opinion, an anthropologist has hypothesized that their structure and values were more emblematic of African secret societies.[17] The Prince Hall lodges perpetuated an irrepressible spirit of rebellion against the slave regime while simultaneously rejecting Christianity as the handmaiden of racial oppression. Such evidence furnishes a compelling reason to associate Freemasonry with unchurched religious practices and beliefs.

Ibrahima's legacy of exclusion from the church pulpit and his affirmation of African-Islamic identity was one of the first publicly documented manifestations of unchurched autonomy. Shortly before sailing for Africa in 1828, Ibrahima addressed a meeting at Boston's African Lodge. Upon his arrival, he was honored by a fraternal committee led by David Walker, the young abolitionist thinker. Escorting the old Muslim through the crowd of black New Englanders who had come to bid him farewell, Walker seemed deeply affected by the old man's resiliency after four decades in slavery. Pushed out of the church into the lodge halls, he had stimulated a collective African memory among his constituents, foreshadowing a collective space for black revolt, which found its first genuine voice in Walker's manifesto of liberation.[18]

Walker's abolitionist philosophy reentered the church movement by way of the developing racial consciousness of individuals like Martin Delany, Alexander Crummell, and Henry McNeil Turner. Drawn from his own journeys in the West Indies and Nigeria, Delany began a debate about the ultimate destiny of African Americans that coincided with the great historical events of the century: Emancipation, Civil War, and Reconstruction. Coincidentally, Delany was also the earliest commentator on African-American Freemasonry.[19]

Considering the radicalization of the African-American church fathers, it is tempting to assume a significant degree of autonomy from the white Christian denominations altogether. This is a very controversial point whose examination lies beyond my scope here. However, as African-American mission work in Africa became a reality, further developments showed a will on the part of African-American clergymen to subvert church dogma, not only in its emphasis on Islam as an African religion but also in its demarcation of the African diaspora. Missionary emigrationism provided the conceptual foundation for later forms of black nationalism and Pan-Africanism.[20] These embryonic movements embraced the cause of Africans and New World blacks, Christians for the most part, whose nationalist and internationalist discourse found common cause in abolitionist and then anticolonialist propaganda.

The views about Islam held by Edward Wilmot Blyden contrasted sharply with the paternalism of black clergy such as Alexander Crummell and Henry McNeil Turner. In 1887 Blyden, a scholar and churchman from St. Thomas, Virgin Islands, published a treatise entitled *Christianity, Islam and the Negro Race*.[21] This collection of essays described his years of travel in Africa and the Levant on behalf of the American Colonization Society, which sought to spread Christianity by converting and then repatriating slaves to Africa. Assessing what he learned about religion and society in West Africa, Blyden enumerated the advantages for Islam over Christianity. He wrote that Africans converted to Islam "at home and in a state of independence of the teachers who brought it to them," whereas, Christianity "came to the Negro as a slave or at least as a subject race in a foreign land."[22] He saw Islam as a truly multicultural religion where racial distinctions were less important than among other revealed religions. The Quran and Arabic pedagogy had promoted literacy, travel, and elements of classical philosophy and science while its laws protected African Muslims from the ravages of alcohol and embarrassing instances of self-deprecating behavior in the presence of either Arab or European colonizers. Blyden noted that Muslims did not enslave each other and that a slave became free once he converted to Islam.

Blyden's intellect exerted a strong influence on the burgeoning racial consciousness of Marcus Garvey and W. E. B. Du Bois. When Blyden died in Sierra Leone, both Christians and Muslims conducted separate funeral rites for him. Although his life and work have become important symbols of Pan-Africanism, lingering questions about his personal attitudes and relationship to Islam still persist. Blyden himself equivocated, particularly in his remark that African Muslims should be logically predisposed for conversion to Christianity. From a critical perspective, it must be noted that his travel was sponsored by the Methodist Church as part of its overall missionary strategy. For a missionary to advocate anything so contrary to Christian conversion as Islam would have amounted to professional dereliction. In this regard, his idea of a separate destiny for Americans of African descent was an officially sanctioned form of political nationalism, designed to promote emigration and conversion. Over the years, most commentators have focused on his role in building Pan-Africanism to the exclusion of any serious discussion about his Islamic persona, instead portraying Islam as an irrational or immoral choice for persons of African descent.[23]

I refer to this tendency as the overdetermination of African-American history by the Black Church. As an implicit ideology of both church and academic scholarship, it limits intellectual expression by repressing the voice of the unchurched. Evidence of the struggle between churched and unchurched ideologies is also reflected in the history of the Prince Hall Masonic lodges where Ethiopianist and Arabist proponents clashed repeatedly. Ethiopianism had roots in the missionary experience as a quasi-biblical justification for emigration. It originated in the work of Martin Delany and came to rest in Marcus Garvey's familiar scenario of a pure African nation. Though radical in style, it belonged to the Black Church and constituted a theology of redemption.[24] Arabism, on the other hand, was a representation of Islam constructed out of fragmentary knowledge. Like other folk traditions and vestigial religious beliefs, it was discordant to the ears of churchmen.[25]

THE BLACK WORKING MAN'S LODGE   From the post-Reconstruction era until the 1920s, important developments in black social life occurred in the fraternal lodge, epitomizing a new type of class solidarity. The lodge responded to the economic needs of salaried workers by offering insurance protection for families, businesses, and properties. In the midst of segregated cities and towns, it functioned as a de facto black chamber of commerce, enabling the nascent black bourgeoisie to maintain professional contacts beyond the scrutiny of white competitors. It was also a cosmopolitan meeting place for generations of African-American men, who could exchange cultural knowledge, technical skills, and even political beliefs in the relative freedom of secret societies. The red fez was the collective symbol of the various lodges, irrespective of regional charters, particular rituals, names, and totems.

As alternatives to prayer rituals, the fraternal lodges clearly threatened the African-American church's monopoly of social and civic life. Describing the proliferation of fraternal lodges, one observer wrote that no other phase of African-American civic life had developed more rapidly than that which centered on the secret society. This growth alienated the clergy, who turned against the lodges despite traditional links to the great AME preachers such as Absalom Jones and Richard Allen, who were its principal boosters prior to Emancipation. Their conservative successors viewed the lodge instead as direct competition and inveighed against it as "evil because of its interference with the work of the church."[26]

The earliest successful lodge was the Ancient Order of Workmen (1869), which evolved from a burial society into an all-purpose insurance company. Its main function was to guarantee the emerging black proletariat a financial safety net. Generally, benevolent associations responded to the ambitions of black workers interested in accumulating capital in the face of financially discriminatory practices such as redlining and actuarial fraud. Economic survival made such institutions necessary after the failure of Reconstruction and the rise of Jim Crow trade unions that openly discriminated against black workers. In reviewing the charter of the Industrial Mutual Relief Association in 1902, one writer praised its desire to "intellectually, morally, financially, and religiously elevate the race . . . by building industries and home and by establishing banks and pharmacies." Similar organizations included the Order of the Lone Star Race Pride, the Mystic Temple of Light and Knowledge, and the Trade and Literary College, "dedicated to uplifting the race by furnishing insurance, working compensation, financial relief for disaster victims, a military department [!] under the management of a Major General, a Juvenile Department in preparation for entry to 'Mystic Temple of Light and Knowledge' and a business department."[27]

Besides support for black workers, such organizations preserved the ritual structure and symbols of the unchurched culture. It is practically impossible, therefore, to dismiss as mere ephemera the "pomp and splendor, colorful regalia, resounding titles and camaraderie, [and] heightened sense of importance from shared secrets, lodge meetings and ritual parades" that elicited the disdain of many black middle-class critics. The most prominent of these symbols, the red fez, furnished a symbolic connection to the free African laborers of the Atlantic world, seafarers, and the aristocratic Muslim lineages of West Africa. Accordingly, the benevolent society emerged as a vital communal institution mediating the sacred rites of life passage of New World Africans.

Given this record, it is curious that chroniclers have accorded so little attention to fraternal orders and secret societies in African-American life. Those who paid attention saw in them the African-American's "most effective mode of organization" and believed the mystical orders necessary to the kinds of social and economic development called for by reformers like Booker T. Washington.[28] Washington himself understood the lodge as a valuable institution in the struggle to overcome the legacy of slavery. Its fraternal networks intersected the various religious denominations in a way that helped African Americans overcome the limitations of a community divided by religious doctrine. Lodges were the basis of a rudimentary civic consciousness where education, professionalism, and the accumulation of both social and economic capital could become secular priorities unfettered by the concerns of a self-perpetuating ecclesiastical hierarchy. Finally, it was through the lodge that members could avoid the sentimentality and authoritarianism inherent in the church and get down to the business of deciding their own their economic and political affairs.

Despite other quarrels, both Washington and W. E. B. Du Bois agreed on the practical contribution of the lodge "to the intellectual and material development of the Negro race."[29] Washington admired its capacity to serve simultaneously as bank and classroom to promote savings and learning among those who would not otherwise have been able or disposed to learn. Du Bois stated that they represented the "saving, banking spirit among Negroes and are "the germs of commercial enterprise of a purer type." Both viewed the lodge as a means to an end but eschewed its ritual content as something of an embarrassment that was grudgingly acceptable for the sake of positive economic results. They deplored the "extravagance and waste in expenditure on outlay for regalia and tinsel," suggesting that they regarded the lodge as a necessary evil.

For example, the Mystic Temple featured "ritual and ceremony ranging from simple form to the most elaborate details carried to the ridiculous extent, regalia, including hats and caps, robes, collars, badges, buttons, tassels, spears and swords, with gavels at the desk, these features are easily the most popular ones."[30] Nearly sixty years after this description, another sociologist reaffirmed the lodge's durability, asserting that "the imposing rituals and colorful regalia of the lodges, combined with the opportunity for social intercourse that they provided, helped restore a sense of community participation to what was becoming an increasingly atomized society."[31]

By the turn of the century, thousands of fraternal lodges existed throughout the country. The most important African-American lodges established before the Great Migration were the Prince Hall Masons, Odd Fellows, Elks, True Reformers, United Brethren, Knights of Pythias, Mysterious Ten and Good

Samaritans, and the Grand United Order of True Reformers, founded in 1881 by Rev. W. W. Brown in Richmond, Virginia. If the lodge challenged the structural primacy of the church, it also threatened to blur class distinctions such as those existing between the urban proletariat and the rural farmers because fraternal associations fostered encounters between migrants from the South and the "old Negro elite," enabling business contacts, the diffusion of skills, and financial strategies. Unlike churches, lodges leveled the social playing field and increased the chances for improving status.[32] Nonetheless, they seemed to achieve this advantage at the cost of reinforcing racial separation from the white working classes. Was this just another consequence of white racism? Or were there other factors that made the lodge a more durable alternative to the labor union?

Superficially, black lodges resembled white lodges as the kind of deeply embedded voluntary associations that anchored nineteenth-century civil society in small towns and counties. They could not be mistaken for modern labor organizations or even trade unions. Their members were identified with neither a particular trade nor an economic class. They assembled freely and tended to represent themselves as practitioners of shared ideals. Lodges were part and parcel of the social landscape. The very nature of their similarity to the Rotarian fraternities of European-American society made them more of a curiosity than a threat to the white ruling class.

At another level, the lodge revived elements of the African secret society. Similar to the way that fongs, tongs, and triads have perpetuated the clan among Chinese immigrants, the lodge represented a viable social space for African Americans. Secured by ritual performance and monthly dues for the upkeep of meeting halls, marching bands, uniforms, cemeteries, and so on, it became a self-governed place of refuge from racial and economic oppression.

In the period preceding the First World War, when most of the U.S. population still lived in rural areas, blacks and whites joined fraternal lodges in equal percentages. After the war, however, rapid urban migration enabled financial entrepreneurs to compete for the insurance dollar by indemnifying hundreds of thousands of policyholders to a single insurance company. Modern competition meant better coverage for lower premiums. Mutual aid societies were small local networks by comparison. Their actuarial tables became a debt burden as the lodges paid an increasing number of benefits to their aging members. Since their finances were not subject to any controls and practically no external oversight, the opportunity for corruption was also great, leading to many defaults and bankruptcies. Due to urbanization, the new century saw a decline in the structural relevance of fraternal lodges for the white working class, who opted for new forms of social security championed by the labor union movement. For black lodges, whose members were unable to obtain modern insurance coverage and excluded from unions, on the other hand, urbanization furthered opportunities to represent the interests of workers and rural migrants.

THE MOORISH LODGE

In 1925, as Garvey paced up and down his newly occupied cell in Atlanta, a small Negro wearing a flaming red fez similar to those worn by Turks appeared in empty lots and on street corners of Chicago's South Side to proclaim a startling new doctrine. He was Noble Drew Ali (born Timothy Drew in North Carolina), Prophet of Islam and founder of the Moorish-American Science Temple.

Islam as an alternative to church-based worship emerged as part of the store-front religious movements of the Great Migration during period 1919–34 when three heterodox sects rose to prominence in urban America. The Moorish Science Temple, the Ahmadiyya Movement in Islam, and the Lost-Found Nation of Islam shared common themes in the struggle for equality, a focus on cultural history, and an attachment to land as a sign of power.[33] Those who joined were also influenced by the secular nationalism of Marcus Garvey's Universal Negro Improvement Association, which also addressed the church's failure to address problems facing black migrants. The northern denominations often resembled exclusive social clubs where income, residence, and clothing showed worthiness before God. Some did not always welcome their sisters and brothers from the South with open arms, while others called for the migrants to "citify" themselves, a nearly impossible task considering the rigid status systems of the church. Except for a few southern parishes whose congregations migrated en masse, newcomers generally gravitated to inexpensive storefronts in search of relief from the dissociative urban environment. Wealthier denominations, principally the Methodists, did not adjust their structure to accommodate the migrants until thirty years later when, following the lead of populist and grassroots southern congregations, they finally joined the struggle for civil rights.

Storefront religious movements consequently became sanctuaries for radical thought and protonationalist ideas. As these movements began to respond to human needs for protection, employment, food, money and shelter, the material foundations of an incipient black nationalism solidified. Reformers and proselytizers of this period openly promoted Islam as an alternative to Christian ethics and a way to reestablish a spiritual discourse with the world of nonwhite peoples outside the United States. During this time the elementary principles of Islamic education, lifestyle, and worship were established. Thereafter they would cement Islam firmly to African-American tradition.

Noble Drew Ali first organized his Moorish Science Temple in Newark in 1913 and then recreated it in Chicago in 1919. In his amalgamation of Islam, Christianity, and Eastern religion, he drew on the unchurched folk beliefs of slavery in which Old and New Testament prophets could be fused into a singular and powerful symbol of resistance to oppression. The text of the identity cards distributed to the Moors reveals a conscious attempt at religious syncretism:

This is your Nationality and Identification Card for the Moorish Science Temple of America, and Birthrights for the Moorish Americans, etc., we honor all the Divine Prophets, Jesus, Mohammed, Buddha, and Confucius. May the blessings of the God of our Father Allah, be upon you that carry this card. I do hereby declare that you are a Moslem under the Divine Laws of the Holy Koran of Mecca, Love Truth Peace Freedom and Justice. "I AM A CITIZEN OF THE U.S.A."

In addition to their identity cards, members of the Moorish Science Temple attached Arabic suffixes to their names, *El* or *Bey*. They wore red fezzes and practiced abstinence from "unclean" foods, cosmetics, and "theatrical, licentious entertainment." Among the symbols introduced into their literature and rituals were the Jewish "Star of David," the Islamic crescent and star, and the Masonic compass. Membership in the Moorish Science Temple was divided into a two-clan moiety system. Half the members identified with the "Bey" clan, the other half with the "El" clan, affixing these titles to their family names. During their very secret meetings, the Els wore a green fez, the Beys a red fez. The phrase "Islam!" or "Peace!" was extended as a verbal greeting between fellow members, along with the accompanying gesture of two raised fingers and right hand across the chest, customarily associated with a Masonic greeting.

Although it is difficult to know the extent of Noble Drew Ali's familiarity with the Holy Quran, he understood the rudiments of Muslim practice, which were evident in an emphasis on the separation of men and women in the temple, observance of the Sabbath on Friday, and daily prayers recited while standing with one's face to the East. Food taboos prohibited the consumption of not just pork but all meat. Intoxicants were strictly forbidden. Beards were prescribed for men. "We believe in the principles of [orthodox Islamic] teachings in so far as they can be adopted to American life," he wrote. Instead of authentic Muslim scripture he introduced a pamphlet, entitled "Holy Koran," that drew on passages from the Holy Quran, the Bible, Garvey's sayings, anecdotes of Jesus, and his own ideas[34] along with ideas liberally plagiarized from Levi Dowling's theosophical tract *The Aquarian Gospels*. In conformity with the fraternal orders, he threw Masonic belts and aprons along with dervish-like accessories into a fashion repertoire that already included silk robes, pantaloons, turbans, and kifiyeh, reminiscent of early-nineteenth-century attempts to commemorate the African-Islamic heritage of some slaves.[35] Moorish belief compared "The Prophet" Noble Drew Ali to Jesus, Muhammad, Buddha, Zoroaster, and Confucius. He claimed to embody their collective spirits.

The main thrust of Noble Drew Ali's teachings was the promotion of an incipient nationalist ideology that identified African Americans as "fallen sons and daughters of the Asiatic Nation of North America." His mythology connected African Americans to the legacy of ancient Moabites and Canaanites and a historical lineage descending from Morocco and Egypt, respectively.[36]

Through identification of these lineages, Noble Drew Ali taught that the blacks, or "Asiatics," in America symbolized humankind writ large and represented the universal message of peace inherent in all religions. Guided by such knowledge, the "Asiatics" would be able to succeed in ending their economic slavery to the white race. Christianity was for the whites and Islam for "Asiatics," that is, all nonwhites. He declared:

> We, as a clean and pure nation descended from the inhabitants of Africa, do not desire to amalgamate or marry into the families of the pale skin nations of Europe. Neither serve the gods of their religion, because our forefathers are the true and divine founders of the first religious creed, for the redemption of mankind on earth. Therefore we are returning the Church and Christianity back to the European Nations, as it was prepared by the forefathers for their earthly salvation. While we, the Moorish Americans are returning to Islam, which was founded by our forefathers for our earthly and divine salvation.

Describing himself as the avatar of all Eastern creeds and cultures in America, Noble Drew Ali built the Moorish Divine National Movement, which promised civic freedom and religious redemption. Moreover, he claimed that "the time is coming when everyone must speak his native tongue and wear his own clothes."

In 1918 an Arab immigrant appeared in Newark and professed orthodox Islam among African Americans. His efforts interfered with Noble Drew Ali's work, and a conflict resulted in the breakup of his first temple. Noble Drew Ali subsequently pulled up stakes in Newark and headed to Chicago, where he resuscitated the Moorish Divine National Movement in 1919. The emphasis for the new organization focused on the purely symbolic implications of the African American's lineage to the "Asiatic" religion of Islam.

In Chicago Noble Drew Ali became a more overt "race man," styling his political appeal on a program similar to Marcus Garvey's Universal Negro Improvement Association. Although the Moors eschewed Garvey's "back to Africa" ideology, Noble Drew Ali's general approach to religion closely paralleled Garvey's in its desire to embrace the ritual of "black" culture as a vehicle for African-American political unity. The UNIA reflected a plurality of religious viewpoints, including Judaism, Islam and Eastern Orthodoxy. Similarly, the Moorish Science Temple associated itself with Islam but admitted the prophets and avatars of other world religions.

"I've got the Europeans and the Asiatics, the silver and the gold; I got the world in a jug and the stopper in my hand," proclaimed Noble Drew Ali. His followers circulated rumors of an apocryphal summit meeting with President Woodrow Wilson at the White House where he pledged to "wake up his people with love." Responding to criticism of his heterodoxy from orthodox Muslims, Noble Drew Ali charged grandiosely that the Eastern Muslims had lost their way and needed Moorish-Americans to guide them toward the truth. While border-ing on heresy, this retort anticipated many clashes that plagued the Moorish movement as contact grew among African Americans, foreign missionaries, and Muslim immigrants.

Noble Drew Ali's "Holy Koran" assigned an uncustomary centrality to the life of Jesus, introducing the idea of God-as-Allah only in passing. The movement, also incorporated a vaguely Eastern material culture featuring occult, as opposed to Islamic, symbols and an organizational structure reminiscent of popular fraternal orders like the Masons and Shriners. He united Oriental symbolism with ideological militancy within the social space of the African-American fraternal lodge. While these factors did little to clarify or promote Islamic orthodoxy, they appealed to the masses who flocked to the movement in considerable numbers from 1919 to 1929, when temples cropped up throughout the Midwest, the North-east, the Mid-Atlantic, and even in the South.

Keeping pace with the workingman's lodge program for economic develop-ment and drawing from the rich pharmacopeia of Afro-American folk medi-cines, the Moors manufactured and sold "various nostrums and charms" such as Moorish Mineral and Healing Oil, Moorish Antiseptic Bath Compound, and Moorish Herb Tea for Human Ailments. These products were made by the Moor-ish Manufacturing Corporation. According to one old-timer, "people in the Moorish Science Temple sure knew their herbs. They learned from their people in the South. Before that it came from the old country with some of the slaves they brought here."[37]

Closely associated with "root work" were occult sciences, magic, and nu-merology. Moors preached numerology as part of their religion, gaining popu-larity hand-in-hand with illegal lotteries that were a constant source of hope to the chronically poor and unemployed. This enhanced the Moorish Sci-ence Temple's resonance with the polyvalent spirituality found in lodge rituals and dressed in the symbols of the unchurched culture. More generally, Noble Drew Ali's career as a seer illustrated the potential power of cultural resuscitation.

Catechisms along with the red fez were also characteristic of lodge organi-zations. Noble Drew Ali's "Koran Questions for Moorish Americans" resembled the catechisms and codes that need to be memorized in Freemasonry to progress through many levels of exalted membership. This system was duplicated by Noble Drew Ali, who established an "Adept Chamber" for the Moorish Science Temple, whose members resided in the "3rd Heaven" and alone were allowed to utter the name of the "First Physical Man." Later on this catechism served as a template for the "Lessons" of Master Fard Muhammad, founder of Detroit's Na-tion of Islam. In structure and content, these recitations are identifiable as ele-ments of Masonic ritual and medieval hermeticism, with deeper roots in Neopla-tonism and Sufism.

Unlike Garvey's overtly nationalist UNIA, from which he went to great pains to distinguish his own movement, Noble Drew Ali's Moorish Science Temple was a spiritually complex New Age movement, astonishingly predisposed to syncretisms, including elements of Native American culture (Drew claimed Cherokee ancestry);[38] suffragist politics; entrepreneurial economics (the Moorish Manufacturing Corp.); and an affirmative philosophy anchoring the rights of minority Americans in the Fourteenth and Fifteenth "Reconstruction" amendments to the U.S. Constitution.

Typical of those who strayed too far from mainstream beliefs and rituals, the Moors acquired a notorious reputation as outlaws and gangsters. Wearing the fez in public set them apart from other black lodges whose members sported their apparel only in private meetings and national conventions. This was a sign of cultural-nationalist militancy, and it made them the targets of police surveillance and harassment in many cities. When questioned about their appearance, some members responded aggressively by flashing their Moorish identity cards. Such incidents were apparently serious enough to occasion admonitions from Noble Drew Ali, who seemed often on the verge of losing control over his widely dispersed movement. Although reportedly married to two women simultaneously, he published an edict in the Moorish newsletter proclaiming that Moors had no civil authority over weddings and funerals. He demanded deference to local government authorities in these matters, confounding many of his followers, who believed themselves truly independent after imbibing the Moorish eschatology.

By the late 1920s, the Moors' dissonant perceptions of social reality led to trouble with the law. An examination of newspapers shows an epidemic-like proliferation of "conversions" not unlike those that had accompanied Prince Ibrahima's national tour one hundred years previously when African Americans suddenly recovered their lost Muslim names. Even more striking is the resemblance of these circumstances to the simultaneous occurrence of crisis cults elsewhere in the colonial world.[39] Crisis cults may be said to occur in contested spaces, large and small, where the forces of social disintegration threaten traditionally accepted patterns of symbolic interaction. As responses to sustained or even punctual stress, the crisis cult is characterized by a resistance to the prevailing order fostered by an attraction to ideal types and utopian schemes. As a way to offset individual and social stress, the dynamic features of such movements involve beliefs and rituals that are simultaneously innovative and synthetic yet also evocative of archaic values of a religious or political nature. In other words, the crisis cult blends the familiar and the alien in an attempt to replace a failed concept of space by another that the "true believer" holds to be universal and all-encompassing. The crisis cult may appear to be a "revolutionary" solution to class, ethnic, gender, or generational oppression; alternatively it may erupt in waves of mass religious enthusiasm and artistic expression. It often combines all these features. In any case, from mass uprisings and local rebellions to prophetic upheavals, the significant anthropological feature is the ability of the movement's adherents to consolidate and expand the application of their new cognitive and symbolic patterns over a particular historical epoch and spatial enterprise.

Moors were enchanted by tangible symbols, including their temples (lodges, really), a well-defined aesthetic style, catechistic ritual, and a nationwide business based on monthly dues, rent, and the manufacture and sale of homeopathic commodities. Seeing themselves as divinely endowed by a prophetic righteousness, many became socially rebellious. As substantial as it was, however, this movement could not possibly alter the reality of depression-bound urban America with its sad legacy of racial oppression. The lodge served the black workingman's interests in a very limited way. In terms of a politically effective class institution, it was a chimerical substitute for modern labor unions and ultimately an anachronistic exercise in self-delusion. In its devotion to fetishes and its inability to grasp history beyond the immediacy of a personal rebellion, the Moorish movement consecrated the ghosts of the old, doomed slave rebellions. Its ritual performances were meant for the secret lodge hall yet somehow were released onto the public stage—confrontational yet inscrutable and quite dangerous to all involved. One of many outbreaks followed a confrontation with police in Toledo over the disposition of the body of one Joshua Bey, a local Moorish leader. After a coroner pronounced Bey dead, the victim of an apparent heart attack, his followers prayed for his resurrection. "Thousands of curious persons swarmed through the little house that is the cult's temple taking a glimpse of the bier of the leader, [while] devotees have resisted other efforts to determine whether the man was dead or in a state of suspended animation brought about by religious fervor."[40] This episode accords with the hysteria surrounding "voodoo cults" and ritual slaughters reported among African Americas in Detroit during the same years.[41]

In Chicago with a membership close to ten thousand, the Moorish Science Temple attracted the attention of the renowned philanthropist Julius Rosenwald, through the person of his former valet, Claude Greene.[42] "Sheik" Claude Greene acquired a high rank in the movement and eventually challenged Noble Drew Ali for operational control of the enterprise. In 1929, following an argument, Greene turned up dead. Noble Drew Ali was charged with his murder and imprisoned despite his claim to be innocent. Shortly after being released on bail, he disappeared and was eventually presumed deceased. The Moorish Science Temple continued in a more decentralized form afterward. Each temple acknowledged the "prophethood" of Noble Drew Ali, although practices and beliefs diverged widely. Some followers believe that since he was a true prophet, Noble Drew Ali could never die, and they continue until the present to speak of his reincarnation.

FREE MOORISH–AMERICANS   In the period leading up to and during World War II, the Moors remained without a cohesive national leadership. In many inner-city ghettos, they were subsequently overshadowed by the incipient Nation of Islam. The latter borrowed so much ideology and ritual from the Moors that one cannot help but conclude that the two organizations all but merged, at least in some cities. (There were even persistent yet undocumented rumors that Elijah Muhammad had been a Moor.)[43] Elsewhere, some followers of Noble Drew Ali underwent a more formal conversion to Islam, becoming "praying Moors" under the aegis of Ahmadiyya Movement missionaries from India. One former Moor, Professor Muhammad Ezaldeen of Newark, New Jersey, returned from a journey to Egypt and started an orthodox Islamic group called the Adenu Allahe Universal Arabic Association, which quickly expanded to Philadelphia, Pittsburgh, and Buffalo. In other cities where the organization still survives, Moors retreated underground, calling themselves Free Moorish-Americans. The only place where they maintained a higher profile was in the federal prison system, where some were serving time for draft dodging and income tax evasion.

These two activities were fully consistent with their views and continue as a distinctive practice to the present. In December 1997 federal prosecutors arrested one hundred municipal employees in New York City on charges of income tax evasion. Many had received tax kits distributed by the Moorish Nation with detailed instructions on how to claim multiple exemptions based on claims of national sovereignty. This plot involved a formal declaration of allegiance to the Free Moorish Zodiac Constitution to claim immunity from U.S. tax laws. Moorish Nation members cited the notorious *Dred Scott* Supreme Court decision of 1857, which denied citizenship to black slaves and their descendants, and other historical records to support their contention "that the United States represents only white people."[44]

The author of the "Zodiac Constitution," C. Mosely Bey of Cleveland, Ohio, emerged in the early 1950s as an active pamphleteer among several regional leaders of the Moorish Science Temple. A self-styled "Free Moorish-American and Master Mason, 3rd, 33rd, and 360-degrees, Ph.D. and LL.D.," C. M. Bey also wrote several terse, lengthy tracts based on his "research" in the Yucatan, hypothesizing a genealogical connection between Native Americans and people of African descent.[45] Bey became the target of FBI probes during the Korean War, when three young followers—Count Don Shaw, William Spearman, and Robert Marcus—were convicted of draft evasion and sentenced to five years in a federal penitentiary. Bey tried to attend the proceedings but was barred from the courtroom because he would not remove his fez. According to the FBI reports at the time, members of Bey's "Moorish Constitution Cultural-National Club" forswore allegiance to the American Constitution, for which the "Zodiac Constitution" was substituted. Among the rights inhering to members was freedom from military conscription and federal income tax laws.

Bey proclaimed, "I am not interested in religion and the 'GOD' no one has ever seen. I am interested only in the solving of my economic problem and helping others to solve their problems in the most reasonable and intelligent manner. I am only interested in self and humanity because each individual depends upon one another for existence. I am not a religious hypocrite." His interpretation of Moorish science contained no reference to Islam, but his deep immersion in astrology and his fez were unmistakable tropes of unchurched culture. Bey also borrowed the myth of the Ishmaelites from American literary canon.[46] The Ishmaelites embodied the Moorish-American ideal of freedom, for they were descendants of Native American and African miscegenation who, according to Bey, roamed at will throughout North America before the Civil War.

In the context of racial politics, Bey was alluding to the "triracial isolate" bands who survived autonomously well into the twentieth century in the inaccessible swamps, intercoastal islands, mountains, and pine barrens of the United States east of the Mississippi.[47] This mythology concurs with claims that Noble Dew Ali came originally from an area in the Smokey Mountains in or near the North Carolina Cherokee reservation. It also hints at the existence of guerilla or maroon encampments as part of a durable though forgotten characteristic of American history. That such communities existed in the interstices of society and that their inhabitants were regarded as degenerates and outlaws by churchgoing citizens is a generally acknowledged field of inquiry known as "fugitive history." As frontiersmen and outlaws, they have become part of the national imagination, popularized in literature and folk music.[48] Only the Moors have sanctified them, however. Their literature identified several Moorish-American rural settlements, including one in Virginia where eighty people dwelled on two hundred acres of land. Naturally, the men wore fezzes, the children turbans. The circle-seven symbol hung over doors and windows of the twenty-five homes, described as "the only Moorish land in the South."[49]

The individual who carried the ideal of self-governing rural communities to its earliest and most complete expression was Muhammad Ezaldeen, a Pennsylvania native and early member of the Moorish Temple in Newark, New Jersey. When Noble Drew Ali moved to Chicago, Ezaldeen continued his work among Ali's East Coast followers from New England to the Carolinas. Ezaladeen was also a teacher and elementary school principal with a master's degree in English that earned him the title "Professor." His interest in Egypt and early Afrocentric ideas became useful in 1929 when crisis disrupted the Moorish Science Temple. Disengaging himself from the struggle between Noble Drew Ali and Sheik Claude Greene, he departed for Egypt, where he reportedly spent several years learning Arabic and studying Islam while working as a tour guide at the Pyramids.

When he returned to the United States in the late 1930s, Ezaldeen discovered that the Moorish Science Temple had been supplanted by a new and more militant sect called the Lost-Found Nation of Islam. But the Nation of Islam eschewed orthodox Islamic ritual and even Arab Muslims. Its leaders had proclaimed themselves divine—Fard Muhammad as god-in-person and Elijah Poole Muhammad as his messenger—signaling the advent of a clearly blasphemous doctrine.

Ezaldeen, on the other hand, no longer saw Islam as a storefront cult and resolved to apply his overseas experience to the goal of ennobling the links between Arab-Islamic culture and African Americans. As it evolved into the organization known as Adenu Allahe Universal Arabic Association, he promoted this kinship by reference to the "Hamitic line," in reference to the biblical figure

Ham, son of Noah, who bore a dark complexion and kinky hair. This was but one of several variations of Moorish mythology that linked African Americans to the ancient Moabites or Arabs and led through them to direct kinship with the Prophet Muhammad. As a common and longstanding practice in Africa, this motif, also known as "Sherifism," was an instrument of Islamization during the eighth century whereby the chiefs linked themselves "by whatever sort of acrobatics" to the family tree of Muhammad, "often retroactively adjusting local history" in the process.[50]

Professor Ezaldeen attempted to rally other followers of Noble Drew Ali to his movement, described as the ingathering of descendants of the Arabic-speaking Moors, both free blacks and slaves, who were now scattered across the land, living as unredeemed Negroes. The Adenu Allahe Universal Arabic Association's pedagogy included instruction in Arabic, and Quranic studies and the promulgation of the doctrine of *hijra,* or the physical migration of Muslims away from the infidels. In the context of the United States of America, Professor Ezaldeen believed in the formation of self-sufficient rural communities whose political and religious autonomy was constitutionally guaranteed.

In 1938 Ezaldeen led his followers in Buffalo to incorporate the community of Jabul Arabiyya in West Valley, New York. Another AAUAA "unit" soon migrated to a rural area of New Jersey outside Philadelphia (now called Ezaldeen Village). Other prominent "units" of the AAUAA were located in Youngstown, Ohio; Rochester, New York; Philadelphia; Jacksonville, Florida; and Detroit. The goal of each unit was to follow precedent by purchasing rural acreage to create an autonomous Muslim community living under the sharia.

Ezaldeen's principal collaborator, Sheik Nasir Ahmad, was a mercurial personality who invested his energy in several different organizations: the former Walter Smith Bey was originally a Christian preacher who had joined the Moorish Science Temple of Islam. By the mid-1920s he had pledged *bayat* to the Ahmadiyya Movement and had become Sheik Nasir Ahmad in Pittsburgh, where he assembled other Moors and some new converts to form the First Muslim Mosque. In a schism between two Ahmadiyya sects, the Qadianis and the Lahoris, Ahmad favored the latter temporarily until joining Professor Muhammad Ezaldeen in the AAUAA in Newark and Philadelphia. After World War II, he was affiliated with the Academy of Islam, at 303 125th Street in Harlem, where bebop jazz musicians first encountered Islam.[51]

2

The Diplomacy
of Missionaries and Sheiks

AHMADIYYA MOSQUES   Contemporaneous with the rise of Noble Drew Ali's Moorish Science Temple was the imported Ahmadiyya Movement in Islam. It was founded in 1888 by Mirza Ghulam Ahmad, an Indian Muslim claiming to be the "Promised Messiah" and "redeemer" of the Islamic faith predicted by the Holy Quran. Ahmad used his familiarity with Christian missions to the Indian subcontinent to introduce modern evangelical methods into Islamic *dawa*. Having decided to prove his divine mission by becoming the harbinger of Islam in the West, he opened a missionary training center in Qadian, India, that became the anchor for a vigorous worldwide movement. The first American office opened in Chicago in 1919.[1]

The Ahmadiyya Movement was (and remains) untypically modern in its focus on religious and cultural pluralism as a means rather than an obstacle to overcoming unbelief. This is evident in Ahmad's defiance of a tradition that frowns on translating the Quran—said to be the precise words spoken in Arabic by Allah and delivered to the Prophet Muhammad by the Archangel Gabriel. Accordingly, a popular English edition of the Quran that reached the United States in the twentieth century was the translation written by an Ahmadiyya named Maulana Muhammad Ali.[2]

Perhaps more striking was Ahmad's theology, laced with Hindu undercurrents and a special obsession with the New Testament gospel. In his narration of holy prophets, Ahmad claimed to be the Muslim *mahdi*, comparable to the Judeo-Christian messiah, and also the tenth incarnation of the Hindu god Vishnu.[3] He promoted the apocryphal story of Jesus, teaching that he survived the crucifixion and eventually journeyed to Asia where he continued preaching until the age of 136. This hagiography appealed to many unchurched African Americans in its criticism of the Bible as a forgery and its refutation of the myth of resurrection. It also served as powerful bait for potential converts because it related Islam more or less directly to Christianity and served as a conceptual bridge from the familiar to the unknown.[4]

Aside from these doctrines, Ahmadiyyas worshiped like other Muslims by following the Five Pillars of obedience. Nonetheless, since 1956 they have been condemned by the rest of the Muslim world as heretics, banned from Mecca, and subject to assassinations and frequent though unpublicized pogroms.[5]

Hoping to reap a conversion bonanza among black Americans, the first Ahmadiyya missionary, Mufti Muhammad Saddiq, addressed meetings of Marcus Garvey's UNIA to convey a message of sympathy for the plight of downtrodden Americans. He promised redemption through the worship of Islam and subsequently reported hundreds of conversions.[6] A 1921 edition of the mission's newsletter shows several extraordinary photos of early American converts, with women wearing homespun veils and men beaming proudly above captions citing their newly acquired Muslim names. The Ahmadiyya Movement remains active today, claiming several thousand African Americans among their followers. Ahmadiyya historians explain, furthermore, that their original mandate as foreign missionaries derived from an agreement that permitted American Protestants to work in India.

While Saddiq's mission was not directed exclusively toward converting black Americans to Islam, he demonstrated particular sensitivity to their problems and voiced the nefarious parallel between the Indian victims of British colonial rule and the descendants of black slaves in North America. His writings in the mission's Chicago-based publication, *Muslim Sunrise*, from 1921 to 1924 summarized Ghulam Ahmad's original diatribes against Christianity missionaries in India in the late nineteenth century. Furthermore, he identified the Western missionary enterprise as a cover for the enslavement of indigenous peoples.[7]

Saddiq delegated authority to a circle of indigenous sympathizers on whom he bestowed the title "sheik," meaning "honorable man" or "scholar." He made them responsible for organizing local mosques, collecting dues, and maintaining contact with the head office in Chicago. He supplied them with reams of printed bayat (pledge) forms to register the new converts. The forms were sent first to Chicago for tabulation, mainly to ensure regular collection of dues, then forwarded to the office of the khalifa (leader) at Ahmadiyya headquarters in India. By relying on local contacts and enabling the "sheiks" to draw on personal experience and folklore to construct an appealing counternarrative ("Change your name and you won't be a Negro anymore!"), Saddiq encouraged religious syncretism and the amalgamation of folk beliefs with corresponding elements of Ahmadiyya doctrine.[8]

From a ritual-religious standpoint, however, the chief missionary remained the only real expert entirely capable of reading and interpreting the Quran. The "sheiks" propagated their own fragmentary, hodgepodge knowledge of Islam, often leaving the converts to fend for themselves once it was time to leave town.

A small but determined minority of unchurched African Americans were candidates for any kind of an organized movement that spoke directly to their alienation from the Christianity. Previously expressed through the agency of fraternal orders and voluntary associations like the Masons and the Moorish Science Temple of Islam, this resentment found a new and powerful outlet in the Ahmadiyya Movement.[9] The Ahmadiyya missionaries capitalized on these "protonationalist" movements by deconstructing church doctrine. Saddiq's most successful recruiting occurred in the lodge hall, which furnished an alternative public space, external to the church, where one might see an Ahmadiyya missionary, a Masonic gathering, UNIA rallies, or Moorish rituals on subsequent nights!

Since obedience to the Five Pillars of Islam is the cornerstone of Ahmadiyya rites, their followers were the first African Americans to learn and practice salat (Muslim prayer). Their creed spread throughout the Midwestern states, including Michigan, Ohio, Pennsylvania, and Missouri. Typical of their early converts was Wali Abdul Akram (born Walter Gregg in Bryan, Texas) who took his *shahada* in St. Louis in 1925 after being approached by another black convert, Sheik Ahmad Din (born Paul Nathaniel Johnson), who exhorted him to "get back your language and your religion, and you won't be a Negro anymore." The young Walter Gregg had recently completed his studies at Prairie View, a land grant college in the Tuskeegee tradition. During his years of study, he had acquired bits and pieces of esoteric knowledge from the Masons and a relativistic approach when it came to spiritual matters. Many of the other early converts were infatuated by the Oriental regalia and mystical symbolism of fraternal orders. "There were lots of blind alleys, secret passage ways and code words on the way to establishing Islam in America," he reported.[10]

His appreciation of Sheik Din's message attracted him to study the Quran. He spent considerable time absorbing knowledge of Islamic practices and followed the Ahmadiyya circuit throughout the Midwest, traveling from mission to mission. In Cincinnati he learned Arabic under the guidance of another early convert and then tried to start his own Islamic evangelical movement. "Everywhere I went, I ran a gamut. I wanted others to follow the same faith. I even spoke to Noble Drew Ali when he was in the hoosegow. He wasn't interested in Islam though. He wanted to be the leader of all black people like Marcus Garvey. In my opinion he was interested only in money and power."[11]

Before returning to India in 1922, Saddiq had ordained at least a dozen indigenous "sheiks" who, in his opinion, were doing their utmost to promote Ahmadiyya doctrine. Their efforts had spread throughout a network of approximately sixteen missions in cities stretching from the Mississippi to the Atlantic. Besides Sheik Ahmad Din, Sheik Ashiq Ahmad and their protégé Wali Akram, one must include Sheik Nasir Ahmad and Sheik Saeed Akmal of Pittsburgh, Sheik Ahmad Omar of Braddock, Pennsylvania, Abdullah Malik of Columbus, Ahmad Rasool of Dayton, and Shareef Ali of Cincinnati. The largest contingents were in Cleveland and Pittsburgh, each with approximately three hundred converts.

Beyond the simple appeal to the American Negro that he or she rediscover a lost identity and ancestry, each sheik embellished Islamic religious doctrine with a personal flair ([H]islam in the vernacular). Books and other materials necessary for a standardized Islamic education were either lacking or too expensive for general dissemination. Dialogue and oral transmission substituted as the only alternative as each sheik increased his Islamic knowledge either through solitary study or local contacts.

The grassroots approach to Islam become increasingly autonomous during the stewardship of Maulavi Muhammad Din, Saddiq's replacement as chief missionary in Chicago from 1922 to 1925.[12] Converts were separated from any genuine source of Quranic exegesis. Their reliance on local knowledge led to conditions that were less than ideal for the organizational superstructure of the Ahmadiyya Movement. Ahmadiyya leadership remained weak thereafter and seemed unable to coordinate the many African Americans who were attracted to the notion of Islam. Following Mulavi Muhammad Din's departure and the appearance of a new chief missionary, Dr. Muhammad Yusef Khan, the issue of local autonomy in Cleveland developed into open confrontation.

Proclaiming himself the "headman" of the Ahmadiyya Movement in America, Khan arrived in Chicago on 1 April 1934, thus marking a decisive turning point for the Ahmadiyya mission to America. He immediately tried to reassert control over the local sheiks, who represented many different beliefs, often at variance with official doctrine. Such anarchy ran contradictory to Ahmadiyya creed of total subservience to the khalifa, and Khan targeted individuals he suspected of divided loyalties. First on his list was Sheik Nasir Ahmad, whom he denounced for alleged ties to the Moorish Science Temple, which he characterized as "worthless" and "un-Islamic." Rather than seeing the Moors and the Garveyites as links to a larger American audience, Dr. Khan challenged their influence. He vehemently opposed Freemasonry and insisted that membership in the Ahmadiyya Movement excluded other sectarian affiliations. While the idea of plural membership might have seemed blasphemous to any religious missionary, it should be remembered that anything approaching "normative" Islamic practice and belief in the United States still did not exist, so that the thirst for an alternative to the Church might be quenched at more than one well. In such conditions, Ahmadiyya missionaries and even amateur Orientalists often fit the bill.

Dr. Khan's status as the chief Ahmadiyya missionary in America remained unclear however. He billed himself as "Sufi M. Yusuf Khan of India, Educator, Psychologist, Metaphysician, Divine Medium . . . an authority of Sufi philosophy and the Eastern subjects" and once told a newspaper reporter that he had originally come to the United States to study chemistry at the University of Chicago in 1921.[13] Khan tailored his religious appeal to different audiences. He directed Sufi practices at white audiences and Ahmadiyya Islam at his predecessors's African-American converts. His many titles, business cards, and eclectic attire, replete with a flared turban and loose-fitting burnous-style shirt, suggested a Gantryesque infatuation with itinerant evangelism. When the Islamic movement showed its potential for growth among African Americans, it is likely that Khan came to view storefront religion literally as a business, as was evident particularly in his demands for tribute from the fledgling Muslim community.

Khan maintained at least two addresses, one in Pittsburgh and another in Cleveland. With his frequent visits also to Cincinnati, it is unclear whether he spent any time at all at the "mother mosque" in Chicago. From his Cleveland residence, he advertised lectures and correspondence courses in "metaphysical science" and Sufism for a fee of twenty-five dollars. His teachings referred to the philosophy of al-Ghazali but concentrated on attaining a meditative, Sufi-like state without "needless theory." That this approach ignored the Quran or even Ahmadiyya doctrine suggests Orientalist themes that were especially tailored for crossover appeal to white Americans. Khan's dawa pamphlets also came to reflect the local entrepreneurial techniques, resembling classic American self-help literature: "[Islam] will tone down your nervous excitement . . . improve temperament . . . [and] teach you how to have the thrill of influencing and controlling people in your personal relations."[14]

Hand in hand with Khan's offers for spiritual conversion came a knack for transforming piety into cash. He sold prayers twice each month for twenty-five cents apiece and imposed an additional surcharge of thirty-five cents every four months for membership in the mosque. He also imported turbans and fezzes, regalia, and magical charms for sale to his followers. Another valued substance the Indian missionary offered for sale was "dust from a Prophet's tomb" (which one he did not say). Apparently Khan's business was impressive enough to warrant a trip back to India in the summer of 1934. To pay for it he requested a contribution of two dollars from each of his followers explaining that he would make pilgrimage (*hajj*) and attend international meetings as the representative of American Muslims. Just before his departure he recruited another young Indian, Chaudhri Mohammed Ashraf, and introduced him as a temporary replacement, explaining that he had been dispatched from the movement's Punjabi headquarters, although no official documentation to this effect ever surfaced. Khan selected local deputies in each city, often bypassing the original "sheiks." These appointments were notarized in signed affidavits, however, and stamped with the official seal of the Ahmadiyya Movement in Islam. Finally, Khan introduced his understudy as "Professor Ashraf" and alluded to a vague political program to be revealed in "due course."

Ignorant of Arabic, Ashraf tried to teach his students Urdu. He further upset them with references to a "coming war and the need for pledges to help him by spying on America." This was anathema to the poor but law-abiding citizens of Cleveland's East Side and provoked a rebellion. Ashraf was chased from the community, then Yusuf Kahn's possessions were seized and auctioned to repay the Muslims for the hardships they had endured on his behalf.

As spokesperson for indigenous converts, Wali Akram redressed their grievances in writing to the Ahmadiyya khalifa at his headquarters in India, who responded by dispatching another missionary to Chicago. Upon his arrival, Sufi Bengalee promised that things would be different but soon demanded the payment of back dues. The converts refused, and ultimately he was unable to reestablish loyalty to the movement. In the absence of genuine missionaries, Akram and the others set off on an independent path toward institutionalizing their Islamic beliefs. Akram wrote and published pamphlets on instructional Arabic, Quranic exegesis, and Islamic history. As leader of the First Cleveland Mosque he pursued contacts with Muslim converts throughout the region and stitched together an affiliation that included congregations in Youngstown, Columbus, Dayton, and Pittsburgh.

BLACK ORIENTALISM   In retrospect, the Ahmadiyya Movement was an unsustainable creed for African-American converts, who had barely accomplished their own transition to Islam. It betrayed its followers' aspirations to Islam as a universal creed by thrusting them into a world of sectarian controversy without providing firm anchorage in Quranic pedagogy. By following the Ahmadiyya missionaries, the African-American convert immediately joined another persecuted minority. Ghulam Ahmad's messianism represented a localized response to the complex issues of modern colonialism and cultural domination, but converts in the United States had no real stake in his promise to redeem Muslims half a world away. It was ultimately an incompatible match between two sets of religious discontents lacking a shared history.

At the center of the old empire in London, meanwhile, a movement defined by the African diaspora arose almost simultaneously. It was composed of young African intellectuals who espoused antiimperialism while searching for powerful symbols capable of mobilizing the masses in their homelands. One Duse Mohamed was the son of a Mamluk military commander killed while fighting

British colonial forces in Egypt. In London he had become a successful actor and toured with two famous ensembles across Europe, the Americas, and the Near East, including Turkey, where he was decorated by Sultan Abdul Hamid in 1892. He took this honor quite seriously, appending the title Bey to his name and abruptly quitting the theater. Upon his return to London, Duse Mohamed turned to historical research and political activity. His passionate treatise on modern Egyptian history was published in 1911 when he also attended the First Universal Races Congress held at the University of London. This experience inspired him to create a journal that he named the *African Times and Orient Review*. Its aim was the promotion of solidarity among nonwhites worldwide. Emanating from London, the publication contained correspondence and news reports with a focus on national liberation movements "in the four quarters of the earth" (Masonic terminology). Written mainly in English, the *African Times and Orient Review* also contained a section in Arabic. Among its many international contributors was Booker T. Washington.

Duse Mohamed is now remembered by Pan-Africanists as mentor to Marcus Garvey, who worked at the *African Times and Orient Review* in 1913. Some of the formative concepts that Garvey injected into the UNIA and his *Negro World* journal came from Duse Mohamed and the London Pan-Africanist circle. The *African Times and Orient Review* was a radical magazine that found its way across the seas through a network of black seafarers and stevedores. It created an unprecedented international forum for debating the theory and praxis of anticolonialism. A truly innovative and broadly capable intellectual, Duse Mohamed also played a strategic role in several African liberation movements, abolitionism, and organizations for the defense of national and cultural minorities. He agitated forcefully for Egypt's independence from Britain and also lobbied for the introduction of modern educational methods in Africa. He founded the Anglo-Ottoman Society and challenged Europeans to accept an Islamically based universalism as an extension of the Enlightenment ideals into the colonial world.

In this regard, Duse Mohamed could certainly be recognized, along with Jamal al-Din al-Afghani and Mohamed Abdu, as an influential modernizer of Islam. His concept of Islam as an alternative to Western imperialism was an attempt to synthesize national and cultural issues with global trends. Like his contemporary, the Italian revolutionary Antonio Gramsci, he conceived the role of religion as potential mediator between competing and therefore dangerous extremes.

His personal religious interests extended to mysticism, evident in his second marriage to an American devotee of the Rosicrucian Order (an eighteen-degree Mason of the "red cross"). Duse Mohamed understood and used Islamic dawa as a universalist code. He brought his crusade to the United States and in 1926 founded the Universal Islamic Society in Detroit. Although little is known about this phase of his life, evidence of his ideology certainly appears in Noble Drew Ali's Moorish Science Temple, Professor Ezaldeen's AAUAA, Fard Muhammad's

Temple of Islam, and Professor Paul Nathaniel Johnson's Ethiopian Temple of Islam.[15] Moreover, his grasp of the importance of cultural and national contingencies in the anticolonial struggle and his recognition that "not all nationalists were Muslims nor were all Muslims nationalists" anticipated Malcolm X's efforts to answer African-American political aspirations with two separate organizations, the Organization of Afro-American Unity and Muslim Mosques Inc. His ideas found an enthusiastic audience in particular among unchurched lodge members, the red fez milieu. For those who had little or no experience with Islam or its symbols, the Pan-Islamic, Pan-African ideal nonetheless lured them with its cosmopolitanism. It included the Arabic language, an Orientalist aesthetic, a creed of universal brotherhood, and a philosophy of human rights. This last element was as an alternate route to modernity because Duse Mohamed, like al-Afghani and Abdu, saw the future in terms of a modern Islamic reformation.

Face to face with the forces of nineteenth-century industrial progress, the old Ottoman Empire, by contrast, drew on religion-based ideology to mobilize mass opposition to modernization and Western hegemony. One such ideology was Pan-Islam, which fueled the Khilafat agitation in British India (1920–21) by demanding the preservation of the Turkish sultan as caliph of all the faithful, the maintenance of the Ottoman Empire in its 1914 borders, and of Muslim control over the Holy Places of Islam.

Labeled Pan-Islam, this ideology meant to defend the political and territorial interests of the crumbling Ottoman realm. Sultan Abdul Hamid II devoted considerable money and personnel to further Pan-Islamic strategies, dispatching emissaries to spread its propaganda to the far reaches of the world. This was a highly organized effort.

> In most cases their missions were personal and clandestine, employing special codes for telegrams and letters. Messengers under the guise of religious preachers and expounders of the Koran were sent to all quarters of the globe proclaiming the pious feelings of the Khalifa, and exhorting the true believers to persevere in their faith and to unite in a common bond in defense of Islam. Those seemingly unofficial missions were from time to time answered by delegations from Bukhara and Afghanistan and by learned Mohammedans from India. There was a constant stream of emissaries to and from Istanbul, bearing the pan-Islamic message. Many were sheiks, some of whom were associated with fraternities, others ulema and men of religion. More rarely, they comprised notables, traders, and businessmen. Their activity was dedicated and intensive. At various times, one reads or hears of their having visited southern Russia, Iran, Afghanistan, Central Asia, India, China, the Malay Archipelago, the British Indies, and particularly Java, Japan and the Philippines where Abdul Hamid was said to have used his influence over the Muslims, in 1898, to persuade them not to fight U.S. troops.[16]

Enter the renowned white American convert to Islam, "Muhammad" Alexander Russell Webb, who founded a movement called Islamic Propaganda in America in 1893. Born in Hudson, New York, Webb published and edited small-town newspapers owned by his father in Unionville and St. Joseph, Missouri. In 1872 he converted to Islam.[17] In 1887 President Grover Cleveland appointed him U.S. consul general to the Philippines. Little has been revealed about Webb's life prior to government service. He was a journalist turned a diplomat who perhaps engaged in espionage. It is difficult to understand his early interest in Islam or know about the individuals who may have influenced him. In any study of Islam in America, he is a key figure, nonetheless, because of his links to the Muslim world.

While posted to Manila, Webb met a wealthy merchant named Hajji Abdullah Arab of Medina in Arabia. Hajji Abdullah had founded a missionary society in Bombay and spent time in Calcutta and then Singapore before arriving in the Philippines in 1892. Webb complained to him about the hypocrisy of Christian practices and apparently expressed his desire to propagate Islam in the United States. This inspired Abdullah to commit one-third of an extensive personal fortune to dawa projects in North America.

Endowed by Hajji Abdullah's philanthropic support, the Yankee Muslim left Manila on a westward odyssey through the Islamic world. He visited Bombay, Cairo and Istanbul, where he apparently quit the foreign service before returning to the United States the following year. His dawa reached a large audience in Chicago when he spoke on behalf of the Islamic umma at the Parliament of Religions, which was organized in conjunction with the 1893 World Columbian Exposition.[18] Eventually moving to New York City, he founded the Oriental Publishing Company and a bookstore, which catered to the cosmopolitan citizens of Manhattan's midtown import-export business. The bookstore included a lecture room, prayer hall, and library. Webb issued a statement of his Islamic principles and plans.

The American Islamic Propaganda is to be purely educational, although Mohammedan missionaries will come here and preach in various parts of the country when their services are required.

The first step in this great work will be the establishment of a weekly journal devoted to the elucidation of Islamic doctrines and laws, and the discussion of matters bearing thereon, as well as to record news items of interest to Musulmans in all parts of the world. It is expected that this journal will be the means of creating and encouraging direct intercourse between the Mohammedan world and the more intelligent men of our country.[19]

The Ahmadiyyas have suggested that Webb met Ghulam Ahmad during his stay in India and that he corresponded with him later. While his own plans presage the Ahmadiyya missionary effort in the United States, Webb never publicly mentioned the "promised Messiah" of Qadian and probably did not subscribe to the Ahmadiyya eschatology because it appears nowhere in his published work. According to Wali Akram, an Islamic missionary school already existed in St. Louis prior to the Ahmadiyya arrival, implying Webb's prior influence through his Missouri-based family business.

In New York Webb gained a reputation as a mystic. He emphasized neither prayer nor Islamic pedagogy as the exclusive path to an appreciation for the aesthetic, moral, and productive values of Islam and its civilization. Webb's Islam was a form of gnosis common to bohemians and intoxicated poets or those simply intoxicated by poetry. His appearance bordered on the eccentric. He sported robes and a red fez. Whatever arrived in the latest parcel from the East he would wear or sell. Orientalis, as he called the bookstore, soon became a focal point for the transmission of mystical thought in turn-of-the-century America. It was a magnet for theosophists and iconoclasts of all persuasions, whose talk and ritual diverged significantly from the orthodox Islamic worship popular today. Theosophy flourished there in the writings of Blavatsky, Alistair Crowley, and Levi Dowling, whose work, as previously noted, served as a template for Noble Drew Ali's "Holy Koran."[20] It is not unlikely that some visiting holy men introduced Sufism into this milieu. The bookstore survived Webb as a resource for Orientalist and occultist bibliophiles until the 1980s, when it became known as Weiser's. One can resist only with great difficulty the urge to explore the mystery of Webb's sectarian affiliations and the cultural milieu in which he circulated.[21]

Another relevant question pertains to his career as a member of the Foreign Service. Can we infer from his professional career that Webb was associated with the circle of "Arabists" who formed a tight clan within the U.S. diplomatic corps? This term refers to the early influence of romantic and Orientalist themes in the foreign service culture, exemplified by Washington Irving, who wrote *The Life of Mahomet* and *The Alhambra* while posted to Spain as the American consul. Is it simply coincidence that the romantic infatuations of U.S. diplomats closely resembled that of "Britons such as Sir Richard Francis Burton, Charles Doughty, T. E. Lawrence, Harry 'Abdullah' Philby, Wilfred Thesiger and Gertrude Bell, who went native in the Arabian desert and around whom hovers a gust of fantasy?"[22] Another Briton, Sir Francis Cartwright, was a practicing Sufi and Freemason, part of an apparent trend within the British foreign service where Freemasonry was employed to facilitate relations between the Orient and Occident.[23]

It is likely that Webb associated with John Porter Brown, the American chargé d'affaires in Istanbul. Brown too was a convinced practitioner of Freemasonry as form of international diplomacy. He was likewise a renowned interpreter and Sufi who believed that Sufism and Freemasonry had common origins in pagan cults, hermetic philosophy, and medieval alchemy.[24]

One should consider that in the nineteenth century committed Muslims strived to protect the cultural heritage of the Caliphate without completely for-

saking the idea of industrial modernization. This sort of accommodation occurred, for example, in Ottoman Turkey as an alliance between the partisans of
Pan-Islam and politically inclined nationalists. When the nationalists finally de-
posed Abdul Hamid II in 1909, they eliminated the sultanate but not Pan-
Islamic ideology, which continued to serve their vision of a reinvigorated modern empire. The Committee for Union and Progress commonly known as "the
Young Turks," was itself a modern political movement whose leaders believed
that Pan-Islam and Pan-Turkism could coexist and even nourish one another.
This entailed a divorce between Pan-Islamic propaganda and Quranic teachings, engendering a nominally Muslim ideology that promoted the will of the
modern Turkish state to backward peasants in the Ottoman world. Simply put,
they envisioned an Islamic analog to the Protestant Reformation.

During this period of Ottoman history, mysticism and politics were inseparable. The CUP itself was a mystical cult and counted many dervishes among
its members. In characterizing the interrelated activities of Freemasons, car-
bonaris, the CUP, and mystical secret societies, one author refers to the Sufi lodge
as an "occult antechamber of power" and vehicle for the diffusion of revolutionary ideas throughout the Mediterranean world—in Italy, where the carbonari
figured prominently in the Risorgiomento; in Egypt, where Sufism played an important role in anticolonialist politics; and in Turkey.[25]

In taking account of Islam in North America, the paths of Duse Mohamed
and Webb, whether they crossed or not, demonstrate the preponderantly secular
(as opposed to liturgical or even theological) undercurrents that flowed through
the Pan-Islamic movement. One problem with contemporary thinking about
Islam is that often such nuances succumb to an overwhelmingly popular conception of Islam as a reactionary ideology opposed to modernity. This was not
necessarily the case earlier in the century, although secularists and modernizers
have always had to struggle against the "scripturalist" interpretations of all
powerful religions.

For example, the nineteenth-century Muslim reformer al-Afghani faced a
similar dilemma in Egypt when pleading for an Islamic modernism that promoted industrialization without sacrificing the transnational character of the
Islamic umma. In the present age of increasing stridency, characterized by Islamist revolutions and the radical *fatwa*, one can easily lose sight of the liberal
religious tendencies within Islam and its enlightened theology.

LOST-FOUNDS IN THE WILDERNESS   Coinciding with the influence of
Pan-Islamic dawa work in the United States, a new era dawned in 1930s Detroit.
It saw a fusion of all the previous mystical and nationalist trends in the leadership of Master Fard Muhammad and his disciple, the Honorable Elijah Muhammad. As the Allah Temple of Islam first and then the Lost-Found Nation of
Islam, the Nation of Islam (NOI) emerged as the foremost national-separatist
movement for African Americans. Elijah Muhammad's appeal was so great that

the movement grew to influence blacks in practically every major city. According to one chronicler, "only the split between Malcolm X and the Honorable Elijah Muhammad in 1964 and the assassination of Malcolm X on February 21, 1965, prevented the Muslim movement from making serious inroads in the ranks of organized Christianity."[26]

Fard (Farad) Muhammad and Elijah Muhammad created a religion that resembled Islam only to the extent of its taboo against alcohol and pork. At times they described their mission as a two-stage process. The first phase was to purify the "so-called Negro" of his false ideas and bad habits, making him ready for the final phase of accepting true Islam. This meant the *din*, or core beliefs as practiced throughout the rest of the Muslim world, the umma. The long transitional period saw the deification of Fard, lasting four decades until the death of Elijah Muhammad in 1976.

From a normative Muslim point of view, this developmental scheme seemed anything but preparatory to genuine conversion. Wali Akram, Muhammad Ezaldeen, and others viewed the NOI creed as blasphemy because it placed Fard, a human being, on the same plane as Allah. For them the NOI was Islamic in name only, an analysis that has been confirmed by scholars over the past thirty-five years whose research indicates a theology nourished by a combination of popular mysticism and authoritarian control, lacking an essential connection to Arab-Islamic pedagogy and the Quran.[27]

While substantially correct, this assessment nevertheless fails to place the NOI within the larger context of the real history of orthodox Islamic movements. One reason for this failure has been the absence of critical perspective. Usually a system of ritual and belief that challenges the spiritual dominance of the Black Church will be dismissed or confined to obscurity. This is because of the continuing reluctance of historians and sociologists to dispute the overall representation of African-American religious space as confined largely to the Christian paradigm. To protect this monopoly, the Black Church polices certain boundaries, including the one an individual must cross in order to become Muslim. By placing a disproportionate emphasis on the NOI and its cast of characters, scholarship past and present has succeeded, therefore, in protecting the Black Church from any serious critique. A more or less permanent shadow follows Muslim orthodoxy and evacuates much of its theological and social influence by conflating its image with that of the NOI. Although there can be no doubt about the Nation of Islam's influence on the development of Islam in the United States, it can no longer be considered a central issue in light of the subsequent propagation of Islamic dawa.

Owing to a military-like discipline and the entrepreneurial spirit, the NOI achieved a modicum of material success. In its heyday from the early to mid-1960s, it attracted between seventy-five thousand and one hundred thousand followers.[28] Its conservative ideology of upward social mobility appealed to some middle-class African Americans, but its real popularity remained with the lower classes, who were attracted by the fire-and-brimstone prophecy of an apocalyptic end to the wicked white race, meaning final redemption for those who were victimized by slavery, lynching, and a brutal exploitation of their labor. Salvation in the guise of separation from white America became a sustaining myth for the downtrodden. Indicative of its heritage in the lodge, the NOI encouraged its members to practice a Bookerite fortitude in becoming independent merchants and businessmen. The assets accumulated through several of these businesses created enormous personal wealth for the NOI's leader but also gave concrete form to the practice of black capitalism, a conservative economic policy later promoted by the Nixon administration. Local ministers bought and sold property on behalf of their nation. They erected temples and community centers there and planted the foundations of wealth to give concrete meaning to Elijah Muhammad's doctrine and to satisfy the unfulfilled goals of his nationalist predecessor Marcus Garvey.

This ideology played to the apprehensions of a dislocated black population, fearful of racial segregation, economic exploitation, and Cold War repression. More than a simple catechism, its doctrine offered a blunt choice: "The so-called American Negroes (my people) are now in a time when they must decide on life or death. The world we have known is on its way out, and it wishes to carry you and me with it. But, it will not; this is the right path—believe in Allah and come follow me."[29]

The program offered by the NOI to its followers cannot be defined as an exclusively spiritual endeavor. Rather it was an unfettered development of the lodge, a secret society unchained, bursting into the street with the political beat of separatist-nationalism during the period corresponding to the Civil Rights Movement and its dream of racial integration.[30]

THE UNITING ISLAMIC SOCIETY OF AMERICA   When the Great Depression wrought economic helplessness throughout the industrial Midwest, Wali Akram outlined a pedagogy called the "Muslim Ten Year Plan," aiming to wean people from welfare rolls and foster the development of educational and practical skills. He envisioned a solution to poverty by promulgating Islam as a moral culture that would restructure urban social relations to provide an exit from the cycle of missed educational opportunity and crime. In its kinship to the lodge the scheme was not unlike the NOI's self-help programs, but the resemblance was only superficial. Members paid dues of fifty cents to a dollar per month into a banking fund that they used to purchase educational and vocational materials, with some cash held in reserve to pay for emergencies. Akram corresponded with the land-grant bureau at the Department of the Interior, submitting detailed plans to begin a rural agricultural venture that he hoped would sustain the urban communities with its profits and farm produce. The Muslim Ten Year Plan enlisted membership among former Ahmadiyya convert communities in the Ohio Valley region.

In 1938 Wali Akram contacted Sheik Nasir Ahmad who was then in Philadelphia working with Muhammad Ezaldeen's AAUAA. Knowing that the AAUAA was expanding from Newark and Philadelphia to Rochester, Syracuse, and Jacksonville, Akram solicited its participation in a unified national organization. To that end he also contacted representatives of several other Muslim groups whose agenda focused on Arabic pedagogy.[31]

Thereafter, Akram maintained regular correspondence with over a dozen of these geographically scattered Islamic groups. He became a one-man clearinghouse for information about Muslims and would-be converts scattered throughout the country. Whereas fledgling communities or even individuals were confused by competing sects, Akram concluded that unity was the only strategy possible to guide them safely toward Islamic orthodoxy. He began to work toward that goal in earnest when he heard rumors that the "Islamic Center of America" was trying to abrogate the charters of both the First Cleveland Mosque and the AAUAA. Fearing that their movement would be subordinated to the interests of foreigners, Akram later recalled, "that's when we said that there has to be some unity here."[32]

The first meeting of the Uniting Islamic Society of America convened at Philadelphia in 1943. Handbills announced:

> The First All Moslem and Arab Convention, August 18, 1943. This meeting will consist of four organizations for Al-Islam, namely, the Muslim Ten Year Plan, Moslems of America, the Academy of Islam and the Adenu Allahe Universal Arabic Association. It is held for the purpose of all uniting together as one great organization working in accord with the teaching of Al Qur'an.

The AAUAA hosted this event, which featured Professor Ezaldeen as the prayer leader and Sheik Nasir Ahmad, who delivered the opening sermon, as master of ceremonies. Wali Akram sermonized on the second day, and Sheik Omar Ali of Harlem's Academy of Islam at the third session. In the course of the fourth day, the conferees toured a farm in nearby New Jersey called Ezaldeen Village, which was the AAUAA project for a self-sufficient Muslim community. A young Adenu Allahe sheik, Yusuf Hameed, gave the final day's first *khutbah*, followed by Professor Ezaldeen's message of adjournment.

This gathering confirmed Wali Akram's growing reputation as a dynamic Muslim preacher. His vision of an expanding Islamic movement and his Ten Year Plan were received enthusiastically by the delegates, who overwhelmingly elected him to the presidency of the organization and charged him with the task of preparing a national charter for the following year. This was a gesture of respect toward Akram, who was only forty years old and had lived twenty of those years as a Muslim. "Brother Akram won our greatest respect and brotherly feeling for [his] seniority and ability in the Islamic way of life," wrote Sheik Omar Ali from Harlem a month later. Another member of the Academy of Islam observed, "Personally you have captivated my admiration. . . . You are indeed an interesting book to study."[33] Professor Ezaldeen also sent warm greetings and congratulations to his colleague at the First Cleveland Mosque, adding that he eagerly awaited the draft charter.

Back in Cleveland, Akram wasted little time drafting a national constitution. As a preliminary to its ratification he also suggested that all members of the UISA's General Executive Council sign bayat forms recommitting themselves to the faith. Simultaneously, he would ask them to pledge discretion in respect to the organization's internal politics, a curious demand for secrecy that seemed uncharacteristic of the gregarious Clevelander.

What were his motives behind this demand for secrecy? Perhaps he feared external forces such as the government, Elijah Muhammad's Nation of Islam, or the Ahmadiyyas. Any one of them might have wished to sabotage a nationwide Islamic organization based on orthodoxy. The federal government had a long record of harassing the Moorish Science Temple and the Nation of Islam because of their opposition to military conscription and, in certain instances, taxes. In Cleveland, C. M. Bey was under surveillance by the FBI also for counseling draft evasion. Anyone openly identified with foreign cultures or an unfamiliar religion might also be suspected of harboring un-American sympathies.

At this stage, when even some Muslim converts made little or no distinction between the nationalist sects and orthodox Muslims, how could the government be expected to understand the difference? What would prevent them from disrupting efforts at unity among the true believers? In addition, the Nation of Islam was aggressively pursuing economic policies similar to the Ten Year Plan. Yet the NOI doctrine was so un-Islamic that Akram was brought to tears reading Elijah Muhammad's prayer book. The characterization of white people as "devils" often extended to even African Americans who cast aspersions on the Nation of Islam. Finally, the Ahmadiyya missionaries and their loyal followers threatened unity too because of the lingering bitterness between them and the groups who turned orthodox; the rump Ahmadiyya congregation in Cleveland had labeled Akram a "traitor to Islam." Sectarian divisions already plagued the fledgling movement, with some organizations permanently alienated one from another and unafraid either to express their antagonisms or denounce their adversaries publicly.

Patriotism was another motive for Akram. The United States had entered World War II, and sedition was punishable by extreme measures. It created an atmosphere of unrestrained hysteria that invited race-baiting and other forms of vicious stereotyping. Black nationalist groups in America were being persecuted for their pacifism, their open refusal to participate in plans for war, and even for collaborating with the enemy.[34] To counteract these negative stereotypes, at least one group acknowledged the presence of Muslims serving in the U.S. armed forces and actively lobbied for equal representation in the military chaplaincy.[35]

The fledgling Uniting Islamic Society of America thus faced an awesome set of political and doctrinal obstacles to its goal of unifying orthodox Muslims. An uneasy national consciousness about race, slavery, and potential rebellion was fueling government suspicions whenever African-American organizations convened publicly. To codify the UISA's identity as Islamic but not "Black Muslim" and simultaneously affirm its loyalty to the government was probably the only way to avoid political harassment. If the leadership were pragmatic, then the UISA could enjoy freedom of worship unencumbered by external prejudice. If, on the other hand, too many people insisted on carrying their Muslim identity into the realm of politics, there would be hell to pay and the only beneficiaries would be the nationalists and other extremists.

In retrospect, it appears that Akram overreached his authority by attempting to extract a pledge of secrecy from his Muslim colleagues. His document was criticized as an untenable compromise. It demanded an awkward pledge to obey the laws of Islam with an adjacent clause proclaiming obedience to the secular laws of the United States. This ingredient would become a tremendous obstacle to Muslim unity in America in the ensuing years. It was characteristic of the more general dilemma faced by all Muslims living in the West and an especially delicate problem for those with minority status like Americans of African descent.[36] Never one to shy away from controversy, Wali Akram directly engaged this controversy between Islam and the modern nation-state. He recognized the legitimacy of constitutional states if freedom of worship was guaranteed. For religious-minded crusaders, however, his ideas represented an abrogation of orthodox doctrine of hijra because of his apparent willingness to accept the status quo.

If Wali Akram wanted to exclude potential interference in UISA affairs, why did he not simply name the hostile forces instead of reissuing a highly controversial clause of the Ahmadiyya pledge?[37] This blunder compromised Akram's reputation because it lent credence to those who contended that he had never really broken away from the Ahmadiyya creed.

Some participants in the UISA, notably Professor Ezaldeen, objected vociferously. Although he and Akram maintained a lasting public friendship, they were fierce competitors in private because each man saw himself as leader of Muslims in America. During the late 1930s and early 1940s, the AAUAA rivaled the Muslim Ten Year Plan in terms of national stature. The Ten Year Plan was strong in the Ohio River Valley, whereas Adenu Allahe was popular in the mid-Atlantic region, with chapters as far west as Buffalo, New York. Doctrinally, both stressed a program of Arabic and Quranic studies with passing references African cultural history. Their approaches diverged on the thorny issues of modernism and assimilation. Akram believed in a modern religious movement specifically attuned to the prevailing national economy. For that matter, the Ten Year Plan was really open to anyone who wanted to join regardless of his or her faith, the goal being simply one of economic advancement.

By contrast, Ezaldeen envisioned an Islamic hijra with autonomous rural communities, governed by the Islamic sharia, sovereignly incorporated, and economically self-sufficient so as to preclude any and all secular authority. "The laws of this government (U.S.A.) are not by al-Quran, and for this reason, a true believer cannot obey them," he told Akram in refusing to sign the pledge. Akram's use of the terms *Islam* and *Quran* were not accurate enough to reinforce the distinction between true believers and the "cults" that projected themselves as Islamic. As a mark of his piety, Professor Ezaldeen insisted upon employing the formal terms *al-Islam* and *al-Quran* because "it has always been characteristic of the enemy to destroy the divine language in order to weaken the morale of the Prophetic followers."[38]

Trying to assuage his rival and preserve unity, Akram quickly amended the draft. But this simply postponed the political dilemma for the nascent movement. It was un-Islamic, he argued, to dispute secular authority unless there was direct interference with worship. Ezaldeen had been wrong to reject secular law. Further defending his position, Akram quoted the Quran, "O you who believe! Obey Allah and His apostle and those placed in authority among you." Furthermore, he cautioned his colleagues to beware of unnecessary provocations, writing that

> we cannot expect to progress and have peace unless we obey the laws of the government under which we live. We will find, in the future, if the Muslims are taught to disrecognize [sic] the laws of the government it will not only impede our progress but will jeopardize the rights of all Muslims and spell *doom* to our organization. To this end, these objections are strictly un-Islamic and have no foundation inside Islamic jurisprudence.[39]

Akram thought that Nasir Ahmad could influence the outcome of this dispute and reminded him that the UISA was his own brainchild. Recalling their common experiences and their common struggle against the foreign missionaries, he sought an understanding about how to achieve unity among several thousand converts each holding sharply divergent ideas of Islam. The best way for the Muslims to consolidate their gains was to ignore any political or social issues that did not conflict overtly with Islamic religious doctrine. Akram would not be the last Muslim in America to argue the subtle contradiction between the central tenets of Islam (din) and the inherent risks of immersing oneself in the worldwide community (umma) with its diverse cultural influences.[40]

News of the Professor Ezaldeen's abstemious rejection traveled widely, leading to division and impasse that would go unresolved until a second convention could be held and the matter debated publicly. Sheik Nasir suggested that the spirit of cooperation and compromise would be best served on neutral territory at his own mosque in Pittsburgh. For the rest of the year Akram tended to business in Cleveland and spent considerable energy communicating his position to the other parties in the controversy. Outwardly, his relations with Ezaldeen remained cordial. They exchanged correspondence on noncontroversial topics, but Akram remained aware that he was under attack simply for having accepted the UISA presidency. In a letter to the leader of the West Valley community, Taleeb Sayeed, he averred that his decision to accept the post was not "an act of personal aggrandizement . . . but produced out of zeal, love and sincerity of our Faith."[41]

The August 1944 meeting of the UISA opened by welcoming delegates from several new groups into the fold.[42] To keep the peace, Akram referred the constitution to a subcommittee, burying the controversy so that he could still enthrall the convention with images of the growing American Muslim community. As a fiery speaker whose sermons emphasized the role of salat and Quran in the practical arts of civilization, Akram was praised as the most prominent exponent of the movement—"Hero of the Era," waxed one delegate by way of congratulating him on being reelected to a second term as UISA leader.

The most significant accomplishment of this meeting was the successful motion to enfranchise American Muslim women. Sadyka Abdaraz and Zainab Uthman, both delegates from the Muslim League Islamic Brotherhood in St. Louis, won appointment to the constitutional subcommittee, marking a historic first for female participation in American Islamic affairs. This did not come without a struggle that pitted traditionalists versus modernists on the issue women's rights.

Akram had a year to reflect on this new alignment of forces and to poll various individuals and groups about what directions might be expected from the UISA. Did they want a staid, doctrinaire movement or one that was progressive and optimistic? Personally, he subscribed to a broad politics of inclusion as the best way to promote Islam. In addition, his sentiments on feminist issues were obviously conditioned by his love and respect for his wife, Kareema, who had proved her own extraordinary faith, courage, and energy at the First Cleveland Mosque. Their marriage and life together as Muslims symbolized a capacity for faith and devotion that was equal between the sexes. Whatever was good for the First Cleveland Mosque would benefit the larger movement.

Yet the ascendancy of women further alienated the traditionalists, even though Akram went to great pains to ensure that they did not leave Pittsburgh empty-handed. He appointed Professor Ezaldeen "Spiritual Adviser" and nominated other Adenu Allahe members to the serve as vice-president (Yusuf Hameed) and treasurer (Saeed Akmal). Sheik Nasir Ahmad became "National Organizer." Confidence in the movement's independence was further manifest in Akram's willingness to appoint a liaison officer to maintain relations with foreign-born Muslims. Sheik Khalil al-Rawaf, an Indian immigrant who operated a trading concern in midtown Manhattan and sometimes conducted classes at Harlem's Academy of Islam was named to this post. Despite the intractable conflicts over doctrine, the UISA appeared to be thriving. Once the convention adjourned, Wali Akram rushed home to print UISA stationery in his workshop.

Victory on the women's issue promoted closer relations among some groups in the UISA such as those between Cleveland and Pittsburgh, who shared much in common. Women who achieved prominence in their respective mosques now began talking among themselves. They targeted Christian women in their communities for dawa efforts through domestic networks such as sewing circles where they featured Muslim fashions. Rashida Khitab al-Deen, the secretary of Pittsburgh's First Muslim Mosque, had established a reputation as a creative designer of Muslim attire. In Cleveland, Sister Kareema Akram collaborated with other Muslim women to expand the activities of the national Laj-Nah (Women's Society) by featuring her designs at annual Muslim fashion shows.[43] Such forms of cooperation reinforced the idea that the underlying strength of successful Islamic propagation in the United States was based on firm alliances among women converts. During this period and afterward such alliances constituted a challenge to patriarchal attitudes that relegated women to second-class status in Islam.

From the traditionalist perspective, however, tabling the discussion concerning the pledge of loyalty deepened their concerns about Islam as a source of patriarchal authority. It led to serious disputes in mosques where men chafed over the prospect of sharing power with women.[44] Eventually Akram came to realize that the UISA was doomed indeed. Disagreements about assimilation and women's rights represented not simply personality issues but genuine conflicts over interpretation of the Quran and the prophetic traditions. The two UISA conventions aimed at national unity among individuals who had little familiarity with Islam yet a seemingly limitless capacity to faithfully reproduce all the controversies that resonated throughout the umma.

In part, this was a function of the Americans' status as converts. Many new Muslims adopted a tabula rasa approach and absorbed whatever teachings came their way. They had little recourse to any deliberative religious authority or even an objective selection of exegetical literature. Competing influences ranged from the diverse opinions of immigrant Muslims to American-style evangelists who supposedly had all the answers. In the first case, the immigrants themselves were in the agonizing throes of assimilation. Much of the counsel they gave to their American brethren reflected Old World views that were being repudiated by their own children, indeed views they might ignore completely themselves when it came to personal or family business. By contrast, the popular grassroots culture of Islam implied Quranic interpretation layered with several generations of American religiosity, going back as far as the lectern-pounding exhortations of the First Great Awakening.

While many of these battles concerned style or aesthetics, other issues threatened to divide the nascent movement. The rights of women in Islam, for example, were debated throughout the Muslim world. Questions about the appropriate Islamic response to modern social change lay at the heart of religious controversies in Turkey, Egypt, the Indian subcontinent, and elsewhere. Since Islam was often synonymous with national identity in those countries, there were abundant resources, scores of learned individuals, and countless popular

traditions that informed and nourished these disputes. The Americans were isolated and uninformed by such resources, essentially going it alone at a great remove from the principal centers of Islamic scholarship and propaganda.

News of dissent came from several outposts, prompting Akram to abandon
plans for a conference in 1945. The president of Detroit's AAUAA, Karma Jee
Karachi, had rebelled against Professor Ezaldeen; rumors from Philadelphia suggested increasing factionalism inside the AAUAA, while in Pittsburgh, the membership complained that an Imam Jalajel "just wants to mess up everything."
From Columbus, A. I. Malik wrote that his Wa-Hid Al-Samad Society was under
pressure by unnamed sources to back out of the UISA, but he would "continue to
cooperate with any tangible and constructive program."[45] Akram replied with a
statement of mutual support and then lashed out bitterly at those he perceived
to be the cause-wreckers. "Many of our Muslim organizations claimed they
wanted to cooperate with us until the time of action came, then they backed
up."[46]

Akram implacably opposed separatist politics and believed furthermore that
the dissension within the Adenu Allahe movement was occurring as a result of
the first two UISA conventions, where their delegates had been exposed to his
strongly modernist ideas for the first time. His goal was to rally Muslims as a
practical force for community development rather than retreat into scripturalism or nationalist fantasies. He had examined the possibilities of self-sufficient
farming ventures at West Valley and Ezaldeen Village and concluded that scripturalism meant sacrificing many desirable benefits of modern society. More seriously, it isolated converts from their non-Muslim kin, producing a kind of institutional alienation that hindered further dawa. Had they become Muslims
simply to declare themselves morally superior like the Nation of Islam? Or to distinguish themselves as an exotic elite within the minority, like the Moors?

Professor Muhammad Ezaldeen, however, resisted calls for modernization
and clashed with those who disputed his authority. This led to further divisions
when Professor Yahya Ashraf and Brother Yusuf Hameed broke with Philadelphia's "unit" to form a new organization called the Adenu Islami United Arabic
Association. In voicing his dissatisfaction with Ezaldeen, Yahya Ashraf decried
the fledgling personality cult of the AAUAA and its secretive ways.[47] In Detroit,
Karachi's breakaway group called themselves the Arab American Business Association. At West Valley, New York, the Muslim pioneers, known to the local
population as the "black Arabs," were fighting with Adenu Allahe members in
Philadelphia.

As president of the UISA, Wali Akram did not want a public confrontation
with Muhammad Ezaldeen. He thought to let the dust settle rather than give the
impression that he intended to stir up more problems inside the AAUAA. Although postponing the 1945 convention amounted to a tacit admission of defeat, Akram felt relieved. Privately he dismissed Ezaldeen's brand of dawa as not
only dangerous politically but also reminiscent of subservience to the foreign
missionaries.[48]

The third and last meeting of the UISA convened in Cleveland beginning August 30, 1946. It was a subdued affair with representation from only five organizations.[49] Professor Ezaldeen did not personally attend, nor did any representative from the Academy of Islam in Harlem. Sheik Nasir and Wali Akram opened the conference with a summary of the efforts to unify Muslims in America, mentioning that the lack of internal cooperation had theretofore stymied progress. They put forward a suggestion to reorganize the association, adding that changing its name might contribute to a fresh start. The delegates included Sisters Khaleel from Pittsburgh and Habeebah Rasaq of Cleveland. Kareema Akram also assumed a prominent role in the second day's proceedings with a speech about unity.

Much of this final meeting focused on finances and the way money was being spent locally to buy buildings for mosques and Arabic schools. Brother Saeed Akmal, one of the UISA stalwarts, reiterated the call for Islamic propagation in the West and emphasized the importance of making mosques permanent fixtures on the American landscape. As a solution to the huge problems of disunity, he argued, that Akram's Mekkabian Press should become part of the national organization as a way of distributing normative literature about Islam. Without a concerted effort to diffuse more knowledge of Islamic civilization and history, the American Islamic movement was destined to splinter through both ignorance and individualism. Rasool Akmal, Saeed's son, explained that unless the men and women of the next generation maintained a high level of participation, the movement would never succeed.

The last convention was only a pyrrhic victory for Akram and the reformers, who were henceforth powerless to stop the project from disintegrating. When the assembly took up the idea of changing the organization's name, all the simmering passions erupted into a debilitating fight. Was it a civil rights organization? A synod? Was it concerned primarily with reproducing Arab-Islamic culture? Or was it more appropriate to seek an authentic Afro-Islamic identity? And in this connection should foreign assistance be encouraged or curtailed?

Akram was reelected president by unanimous acclamation, and the next conference was planned for Philadelphia in 1947. Unfortunately the dream of indigenous Muslim unity had metamorphosed into an ordeal of competing visions and warring personalities. The Uniting Islamic Society of America had failed. Yusuf Hameed offered a trenchant post mortem in comparing the three-year experiment to the chaotic ecumenicism that had originally alienated many of the same converts from the Black Church.

3

Be–bop to

Brotherhood and Beyond

THE EMERGENCE OF REVIVALISM In the decades following the end of World War II, new orthodox sects arose to address the changing social order. Inspired by ideas blown overseas by the winds of change, the Dar ul-Islam (DAR), the Mosque of Islamic Brotherhood (MIB), and the Islamic Party of North America (IPNA) embraced the religious and political thought of Islamic revivalism. Their origins can be traced to militant Islamic movements in Egypt and Pakistan, the *Ikwan al-Muslimum* and *Jamaat-e-Islami,* respectively. Only one of this new generation of American leaders was born in the United States; the others hailed from the Caribbean and knew something about Islam through Pan-Africanist politics but immigrated to the states mainly for secular reasons. Two had participated in the Uniting Islamic Society of America in its efforts to establish the Islamic din and had participated in its dissolution because of conflicts about autonomy and identity. Their turn to Islam as a creed reveals much about the psychology of modern conversion.

Surprisingly, one common thread was popular music. The rise of orthodox Islam during the postwar era paralleled the development of modern jazz, a trend recognized by the poet Langston Hughes, who wrote a four-line verse entitled "Be-Bop Boys" in 1951: "Imploring Mecca / to achieve / six discs / with Decca."[1] Musically, be-bop expressed strong influences of musical idioms originating in Africa via the Caribbean islands, whose many artists and intellectuals flocked to the United States. Both Talib Dawud of the Muslim Brotherhood USA (an Ahmadiyya affiliate) and Sheik Daoud Faisal of Brooklyn's State Street Mosque emigrated from the Caribbean to pursue musical careers, while Yusef Muzaffaruddin Hamid, a native of Dominica, began the Islamic Party in Washington, D.C. Only Sheik K. Ahmad Tawfiq, founder of Harlem's Mosque of Islamic Brotherhood, was born in the United States, and he too spent several years abroad studying at Cairo's al-Azhar University.

Talib Dawud was an eighteen-year old Antiguan named Alfonso Nelson Rainey when he arrived in New York with "the clothes on his back and a trunk full of books." He entered the Julliard School of Music in New York in the early 1940s to study brass instruments while supporting himself with work in the renowned Barrymore household. Early in his musical career he called himself "Barrymore" Rainey and played with the Duke Ellington and Louis Armstrong orchestras. His most important musical association, however, came with the Dizzy Gillespie big bands on the eve of the "be-bop revolution."

Gillespie was the first band leader to reject the studied and increasingly commercial "swing" style that saw black musicians taking a back seat as accompanists to white crooners like Frank Sinatra. Along with the innovative saxophonist Charles "Yardbird" Parker and the trumpeter Miles Davis, Gillespie led a blues revival by incorporating West Indian rhythms into traditional big band ensemble music. Between 1946 and 1948 several prominent Caribbean musicians joined him, including Rainey, already known as Talib Dawud, and Chano Pozo, an Afro-Cuban conga player whose 6/8 rhythm became the standard signature of true "bop."[2]

For the next decade, Gillespie's big band was a training ground for many of the great names in modern jazz, including Milt Jackson, Ray Brown, Howard Johnson, and John Coltrane. Curiously, it also proved to be fertile soil for Islamic dawa. In Philadelphia, Rainey met Sheik Nasir Ahmad. He soon converted to Islam, taking the name Talib Dawud. The band's young tenor saxophonist, Bill Evans, followed him, taking the name Yusef Lateef, as did Lyn Hope, who became Hajj Rashid after making pilgrimage to Mecca in 1958. The drummer, Kenny Clarke, changed his name to Liaqat Ali Salaam, and Oliver Mesheux became Mustafa Dalil.

In his autobiography, Gillespie voiced ambivalence about Islamic conversion among his fellow musicians. He mentioned spiritual motives but minimized considerations of piety and commitment in favor of musical esthetics and practical working conditions. Alluding to the checkered history of African-American minstrelsy, he viewed conversion as a kind of social role-playing necessary to the life of a traveling musician.

> "Man, if you join the Muslim faith, you ain't colored no more, you'll be white," they'd say. "You get a new name and you don't have to be a nigger no more." . . . They had no idea of black consciousness; all they were trying to do was escape the stigma of being "colored." When these cats found out that Idrees Sulieman, who joined the Muslim faith about that time, could go into these white restaurants and bring out sandwiches to the other guys because he wasn't "colored"—and he looked like the inside of the chimney—they started enrolling in droves.

> Musicians started having it printed on their union cards where it said "race", "W" for white. Kenny Clarke has one and he showed it to me. He said, "See, nigger, I ain't no spook; I'm white, 'W.'" . . . Another cat . . . went into this restaurant, and they said they didn't serve colored in there. So he said, "I don't blame you. But I don't have to go under the rule of colored because my name is Mustafa Dalil."[3]

For similar reasons Gillespie himself once contemplated Islamic conversion but hesitated for fear of jeopardizing his career in the recording business because it was filled with Jewish talent agents, impresarios, and recording executives. He withdrew from a formal declaration of faith completely when the press alleged that he had indeed become Muslim and published a picture of him making salat in *Life Magazine* to prove it. Yet he was not an ardent defender of Christianity. The church had forsaken him and his people through its persistent racial segregation, whereas Islam made room for all races, he maintained.

Within Gilliespie's ambivalence one discerns a positive dynamic between religious, social, and aesthetic matters. Although he preferred to work the system both ways, he respected his uncompromising Muslim colleagues for two important reasons. First, they were advancing their professional interests in ways never before contemplated by earlier generations of musicians. In contractual disputes they refused the traditional forms of manipulation. They not only defied racial segregation but aggressively protected their copyrights as recording artists and opposed discriminatory pay scales. Second, he admired their self-conscious pursuit of African-American history that contributed enormously to the innovative quality of their music.

For example, the rediscovery of African and Afro-Cuban rhythms reenergized the jazz idiom by expanding its boundaries to encompass the entire African diaspora. This was an esthetic breakthrough of immense proportions, for it allowed jazz musicians to play beyond, over, above, and around the syncopated structure of the blues and church-based gospel tunes. "Charlie Parker and I found the connections between Afro-Cuban and African music and discovered the identity of our music with theirs. We had a ball discovering our identity," waxed Gillespie enthusiastically.

> Within the society, we did the same thing we did with the music. First we learned the proper way and then we improvised on that. It seemed the natural thing to do because the style or mode of life among black folks went the same way as the direction of the music. Yes, sometimes the music comes first and the lifestyle reflects the music because music is some very strong stuff, though life in itself is bigger. The music proclaimed our identity; it made every statement we truly wanted to make.[4]

By the time be-bop yielded to "cool" and "free" styles of improvisational jazz in the 1950s and 1960s, many of Gillespie's original players were already in the vanguard of newer experiments to obliterate all national and cultural boundaries in music. Islamic conversion recapitulated this esthetic revolution in terms of social identity and spiritual belief. The musicians were exercising a freedom to explore the world and their own souls.[5]

Despite Gillespie's iconoclasm, many converts understood their new religion as a serious spiritual and intellectual quest, learning Arabic to study the Quran, attending Friday prayers, and observing the dietary laws, including the Ramadan fast. Some, like Talib Dawud, quit playing music altogether to study Islam full-time. His first wife, Sayida Faisal, was a young Ahmadiyya from Cleveland. Her father belonged to the faction of converts who had remained with the Ahmadiyyas after Wali Akram founded the First Cleveland Mosque. She stood out as one of the most desirable young women in the movement. Talib himself was a rising star who had eagerly absorbed the teachings of Islam. The Ahmadiyya matchmakers suggested Sayida as a good partner, and he went to Cleveland, where they soon married. Several years later in New York he took a second wife, the jazz singer Dakota Staton, who was not Muslim. He managed her promising career while simultaneously working with Sayida to spread the faith. But this polygamous arrangement soon collapsed when Sayida returned to Cleveland with their children. Talib later divorced both women and moved to London, where the Ahamdiyyas had relocated their headquarters after 1956.

In more general terms, the years 1948 to 1952 were seminal for the development of an international Islamic awakening. The Egyptian revolution and the creation of Israel, followed by war and then the Suez Crisis, produced a surge in Arab nationalism with strident calls for Muslim unity. During this time, Abdel Nasser's stature grew from that of an Egyptian strongman to a champion of Pan-Arab solidarity and then "first among equals" among the nonaligned Third World statesmen. In the United States, black nationalists closely followed the links of this movement to the anticolonial struggles of emerging African nations. They were similarly influenced by Western-educated Africans like Kwame Nkrumah, Leopold Senghor, Sekou Touré, and Jomo Kenyatta, who promoted different versions of Pan-African ideology. Negritude, for example, reflected Pan-Arab and Pan-Islamic tendencies already present in the writings of their predecessors, Edward Wilmot Blyden and Duse Mohamed. Encouraged by the spirit of Non-Alignment, a new generation enthusiastically endorsed decolonization and simultaneously embraced the idea of an impending golden age for Africa.

Settling in Philadelphia, Talib Dawud befriended an Egyptian emigré named Mahmoud Alwan, an exponent of the militant Ikwan al-Muslimun.[6] Alwan explained the idea of Sayid Qutb, Ikwan's chief theoretician, that true social revolution depended on an Islamic religious awakening. Dawud also met the African-American anthropologist J. A. Rogers, whose book *Nature Knows No Color-Line* (1952) laid bare the hypocrisy of racial segregation. By 1957 the three men had combined forces to found the Islamic and African Institute, where Alwan taught Arabic, Rogers African history, and Talib Dawud Islam. The institute organized parades in Philadelphia and New York for visiting African dignitaries like Kwame Nkrumah and Sekou Touré on their frequent trips to the United Nations. It also collected money, clothing, and medicine to send to the Algerian guerrillas in their struggle against the French.

One young man who studied at the institute and became Muslim was Muhammad Salahuddin. In an interview he recalled how the teachings struck an emotional chord.

> My mother died when I was two years old. I spent four or five years in Bainbridge [an orphanage]. When I was finally released, my people were strangers to me. My father and grandfather were alcoholics. I was searching for a family and searching for a god [and] finally discovered Islam when I was eighteen. My grandmother was a Moorish-American. She had participated in the Ethiopian movement and the Black Jewish movement which were both centered around the UNIA of Marcus Garvey.[7]

Talib Dawud affiliated his Philadelphia mosque with Harlem's International Muslim Brotherhood, which was run by Imam Abdul Raheem and the ubiquitous Sheik Nasir Ahmad. He coordinated with other mosques in Boston, Providence, and Washington, D.C. , but conflict ensued when the Muslim Brotherhood tried moving west to Detroit, a stronghold of Elijah Muhammad's Nation of Islam. The Moors were also hostile to the fledgling Sunni movement because it interfered with their recruiting efforts by introducing the Holy Quran to replace Noble Drew Ali's complicated mythology. From a generational standpoint, there was further antagonism between worldly hipsters, attracted to Sunni Islam as a fathomless watershed for countercultural values, and the working poor or unemployed who turned their salvation (and wages) over to the Nation of Islam in exchange for a minimal, ascetic personality cult. Talib Dawud published broadsides against the heresy and overt racialism of Elijah Muhammad and Noble Drew Ali. He claimed that the true path to salvation for the American Muslim led toward international solidarity, not racial exclusivity. Elijah Muhammad counterattacked by claiming that Talib Dawud had sold out to the "pale Arab."

The Muslim engagement in Philadelphia produced immediate conse-quences. The notoriously antiblack police department viewed their activities with more than passive suspicion and considered the Muslim Brotherhood to be a subversive organization warranting constant surveillance, if not harassment and repression. In 1958 they went into action after the movement began to cele-brate Lyn Hope's recent hajj to Mecca by intensifying dawa in a series of public events with door-to-door pamphleteering and a poster campaign in downtown Philadelphia.

Sulaiman al-Hadi, then a young man who had joined the brotherhood while in prison, recalled being chased out of town "ducking the dog and dodging the gun" because the cops—led by the notoriously anti-Muslim police chief, Frank Rizzo—were trying to kill him. Muslims, al-Hadi asserted, were perse-cuted just for wearing the red fez because it threatened insurrection. At first, al-Hadi was arrested and paraded through the community in the sidecar of a po-lice motorcycle. At the police station he was charged with "disturbing the peace and creating a public spectacle." He alleged that around the same time the po-lice killed another Muslim named Nuriddin just for making salat in the street. "They attacked him and went to take his Quran. There was a fight and two cops shot each other but Nuriddin got killed in the process. That was in 1958. It hap-pened at Twenty-first and Diamond. Funny thing however. Within a month both of those cops were killed, one in an accident on the New Jersey Turnpike, the other in a fight with his wife. Allah u-akbar!"[8]

Both Sulaiman al-Hadi and Muhammad Salahuddin found the atmosphere more tolerant in New York, where myriad sources of Islamic knowledge existed among the diverse immigrant communities and several African-American scholars.

> We got the idea that all the knowledge about Islam was in New York. So I
> moved here and began to study seriously. I never wanted to go overseas
> and I am not in Islam because of my color. A lot of people are, but not me.
> I converted because I know my Creator made all men and the only reason
> men are separated is because of the tongues of their parents. What hurts
> is when you see the children suffer from those divisions.[9]

Al-Hadi settled on Manhattan's Lower East Side on Norfolk Street, where he found other young men who were studying uptown at the Academy of Islam with Sheik Daoud Ahmed Faisal, a Trinidadian immigrant. Eventually they fol-lowed Sheik Daoud across the Brooklyn Bridge to a mosque on State Street near Arabtown along Atlantic Avenue. By 1962 Sheik Daoud's Islamic Mission to America had become Brooklyn's first bona fide mosque. It served the indigenous converts from the Lower East Side and the adjacent Arab immigrant community. What is known factually about Sheik Daoud Faisal cannot be separated from the legend surrounding his celebrated reputation. By one account, he arrived to the United States in 1929 hoping for an audition as a symphony violinist. Consistent with his claim of a Moroccan birthright, it appears that he associated with the Moorish Science Temple, although he held a Trinidadian passport. The title "sheik" also points to a prior affiliation with the Ahmadiyyas, although there was no trace of heterodoxy in his strictly orthodox Sunnism. Others have alleged an association with Professor Ezaldeen's AAUAA. His wife, Sayeda Khadija, came from Barbados. "Mother" Khadija is still remembered with great affection as the first woman of African descent to have a profound influence on the growth of Islam in New York. Her efforts resulted in a permanent network of Muslim women, mostly African-American converts, who spread dawa to their sisters in the poor neighborhoods of East New York and Bedford-Stuyvesant.

Sheik Daoud himself was deeply influenced by the grand history of Islamic civilization. He envisioned a spiritual reawakening spreading from the Middle East into the Western hemisphere and hoped to realize it by forging ties between American Muslims from all over the umma. He also saw himself as the individual best able to negotiate the difficult relationship between indigenous converts and recent Muslim immigrants. The UISA had failed, he believed, because of the lingering influence of the Ahmadiyya Movement. From the perspective of Islamic civilization, the Ahmadiyyas were to him an irrelevant sect whose beliefs bordered on blasphemy. Their organization was further divided by internal power struggles undermining its legitimacy. As sincere as their dawa efforts might have been, they could never provide the kind of leadership necessary in America. There was a need for solid connections to orthodoxy such as the venerable authority that issued from Middle Eastern Islamic institutions like Cairo's al-Azhar University and the Holy City of Mecca. The most accessible route to this legitimacy ran through the United Nations, where dozens of sympathetic delegates might be persuaded to assist the objectives and goal of his mission.

Deriving his logic as much from Franz Fanon's anticolonialism as the literature of Islamic revivalism, Sheik Daoud argued that African Americans needed more than spiritual commitment according to the liberal model of religious plurality. They needed to totally transform themselves—their language, dress, customs, and even their daily interactions—in a ritual of purification that would cement them to the real foundations of the worldwide Islamic revival that was occurring across the Atlantic. Inherent in his theology was Sheik Daoud's rejection of any symptoms of the "duality" that W. E. B. Du Bois had attributed to the life of African-Americans.

Apprehensive that others would distort his message, Sheik Daoud traveled indefatigably from city to city promoting his dawa in a pamphlet entitled "Al-Islam: The Religion of Humanity." He tailored its message for those who had grown up in the Black Church, assuring them that Islam was the authentic religion of the prophet Abraham and all his descendants. Historically speaking, therefore, it was the "oldest" monotheism. He attacked both Judaism and Christianity, the former as a cultural practice associated with idol worship, the latter as a social philosophy based on a false interpretation of Jesus as the son of God and the Holy Trinity. He preached the familiar sermon exhorting Black Americans to reject their fabricated, spiritless identities as Negroes by returning to their original religion and learning the sacred language of Arabic. They would never be accepted socially in the Christian society of "the self-styled superior man," he told them, because it was established to suppress, oppress and enslave them. "You are Muslims, not Negroes. There are no such people or nationality called Negroes. Your nationality is the country of your birth. Return and worship the one true God, in Islam, it will free you from the companionship of the devil, from sin and enslavement."[10]

Described by his followers as an overexcitable orator, Sheik Daoud was nonetheless a skilled diplomat and courageous spokesman for Islam. Years before Malcolm X suggested taking African-American problems to the floor or the U.N. General Assembly, Sheik Daoud successfully lobbied Arab delegates there to grant observer status to his Islamic Mission. In a statement presented at the U.N. General Assembly in October 1960, he proposed that the United Nations would realize its ideals only when "its entire activities [were] guided by the Laws and the Command of the Almighty God in Islam." Significantly, he campaigned against "godless" communism, asserting that Islamically guided economic and social policies would be preferable alternatives to socialism for the poor and oppressed black masses. His opposition to the influence of socialists and communists in the Civil Rights movement was vociferous. To him their doctrines were merely another form of slavery. Islam had its own political system and its own economic system. During the centuries that Islam prevailed in Europe, it provided solid economic and social foundations for a flourishing culture.

It is impossible to ignore the significance of Daoud's anticommunist remarks in the ultra conservative political atmosphere of the early 1960s. He rejected any hint of political subversion and cautioned his followers to avoid complications with the government and police. He exhorted them to obey the civil codes of the United States, especially in matters of marriage and name changes. He systematically recorded the vital statistics of his American-born converts and registered them at Brooklyn's Borough Hall.[11]

Daoud took a paternal interest in every convert. One of those individuals was Akbar Muhammad, Elijah's youngest son, who had renounced Nation of Islam teachings while studying at al-Azhar University in Cairo. When the elder Muhammad abruptly cut his son's monthly stipend, leaving him feeling rejected and miserable, Sheik Daoud, who was traveling in Egypt, paid him a personal visit. "He encouraged me and told me to keep going on the right path," recalled Akbar, with evident filial respect.[12]

Talib Dawud and Sheik Daoud were key figures for the early Islamic revival in America. The Muslim Brotherhood USA and the Islamic Mission to America viewed the anticolonial struggles in North Africa and the Middle East as modern examples of jihad that indicated the reawakening of Islam as a global force. It seemed a third way for the emerging nations of the Third World, equidistant from the godless ideologies of capitalism and communism. Their visions likewise encapsulated knowledge of those who had served in the armed forces or who had met North Africans and African Muslims. Others knew something of the religion by its nominal relationship to the Moors and Black Muslim movements, but generally their connection to Quranic scripture and the vast internationalist scope of Islam was nonexistent. Given these circumstances, the improbable construction of a revivalist Islamic movement, small though it was, owes much to these two men's personalities, particularly their abilities to construct a narrative whose central theme reflected the history of Islamic civilization as opposed to an exclusively African-American perspective.

Islamic revivalism was also a grassroots reaction to an era of political turmoil. It prospered by filling an ethnic vacuum for the African American. Conveyed through be-bop as a hieratic style adopted by a "brotherhood" of musicians committed to the modern art of improvisation, revivalism mapped out a possible itinerary for the exploration of one's tonal and rhythmic horizons through the contemplation of *tauhid*—the universal spirit of a rising humanity in the Third World. As a countercultural idiom, Islam symbolized more generally the revival of an Orientalism whose competing paradigms included the Buddhist and Hindu ideals that would nourish American politics and culture as the zeitgeist of the 1960s. As foundations of this vision, the Quran and conversion required literacy and a certain understanding of the modern historical dilemma. Unlike the nationalist catechisms of the Black Muslims and Moors, here was a new global context for the African American.

Responding to the challenge of orthodox revivalists, Elijah Muhammad promoted Malcolm X as national spokesman for the Nation of Islam. A young and persuasive orator, Malcolm X employed bravado and rhetorical pugilism to help bridge the gap between older Garveyite nationalists and the postwar generation of young black men who were excluded from the rising prosperity of white America. At a time when white policemen were unleashing water cannons and attack dogs on black Civil Rights marchers in the South, Malcolm's tough speeches about the manly way to fight racist brutality seemed more relevant than references to Islam and the Quran. By contrast, the anticolonial struggles championed by orthodox Muslims—the guerilla war against the French in Algeria, for example—were attractive topics for a more restricted community of African expatriates and Pan-Africanist cognoscenti. In the context of militant civil disobedience, even Martin Luther King Jr. was cautious about stressing the connections between his philosophy of nonviolence and that of Mahatma Ghandi in India. All eyes were focused on Little Rock, Selma, Birmingham, and Ole Miss.

FROM BROOKLYN HEIGHTS TO BED-STUY *Dar al-Islam* literally means "house of peace" and signifies the geographical division of the world into two competing spaces, one governed by Quranic holy law, sharia, the other immersed in the darkness of unbelief or the "house of war" (dar al-harb). The emergence of an indigenous organization dedicated to this idea was a dramatic moment in American religious history. The rise of the Dar ul-Islam (DAR) with three other regional groups—the Islamic Revivalist Movement (IRM), the Muslim Islamic Brotherhood (MIB), and the Islamic Party (IPNA)—paralleled sociopolitical changes affecting unchurched African Americans and new developments in the Arab Muslim world. It was thus an expression of the dire and sometimes desperate economic conditions of ghetto America merging with the nationalist aspirations of the Arab world.

The revivalist odyssey began with social conflict at Brooklyn's Islamic Mission to America. If Arab-Americans appreciated Sheik Daoud Faisal's dawa efforts, they were even more grateful for his initiative in purchasing and renovating the fashionable townhouse on State Street that became their first permanent mosque in a respectable New York neighborhood. This was positive and could only enhance their quest for assimilation into a tolerant society. But the sight of a visibly marginal band of African Americans fumbling through their prayers troubled the immigrants and seemed to accentuate the chasm between blacks and whites in their newly adopted land. The converts' enthusiasm was no compensation for the difficulties such an alliance might provoke. As the initial religious enthusiasm gradually evaporated, State Street's fraternal atmosphere degenerated into two thinly disguised factions, the new Americans (Arab Muslim immigrants) and the new Muslims (African-American converts).

Sensing trouble and acknowledging his own limitations as a teacher, Sheik Daoud hired a Quran teacher in 1960 and assigned him the task of instructing the new Muslims in proper adab (etiquette) to bridge this risky cultural gulf with new Americans. Hafis Mahbub was a missionary affiliated to the Tabligh Jamaat, yet another Pakistani revivalist sect.[13] With deep knowledge of the Quran and Hadith, a humble manner, and a very dark complexion, he quickly attracted a circle of dedicated young men around him, including Rijab Mahmud, Yahya Abdul Karim, Sulaiman al-Hadi, Muhammad Salahuddin, Hajj Muhammad, and Sheik Ismail Rahman. Hafis Mahbub became a cool and articulate foil for Sheik Daoud. Mahbub led the Americans in fajr prayer every morning and taught them Arabic directly from the Quran, patiently dispensing its wisdom. Just attending prayer at the mosque, even daily, fulfilled only a small part of the true believer's obligations. Islam, he explained, was distinct from the Western idea of church religion, for it was a complete way of life. The struggle to achieve personal transformation (jihad al-akhbar) was synonymous with the struggle for total social reform. The Prophet Muhammad led his followers into exile in Medina (hijra) for precisely this reason: to establish a community that lived according to divine law. Under Allah's guidance the small but devout Muslims gained strength, subdued their enemies, forged new alliances, and eventually grew to a position of wealth and power over their former oppressors in Mecca. This was only the prelude to the dissemination of the Holy Quran throughout the world and the development of multiple centers of Islamic culture, furthering learning for the general enlightenment of humanity in the name of Allah. Within three years Hafis Mahbub had convinced his students to emulate the Prophet's hijra by establishing their own community in Brooklyn.

Led by Rijab Mahmud and Yahya Abdul Karim, the African Americans quit State Street for the nearby neighborhood of Brownsville, Brooklyn where they founded Yasin Mosque. Relying on Hafis Mahbub's scriptural counsel, they set out to build an urban community governed under the sharia. The Dar ul-Islam, or DAR, as they often called it, was an experiment conducted under exceedingly difficult conditions. Over the following decade, the small group migrated from one storefront to another in Brooklyn's poorest, most ravaged neighborhoods. Hostile street gangs viewed the turbanned Muslims warily as opponents in a turf battle. Churchgoing neighbors were astonished at their disciplined, military style and exotic clothes. Kids referred to them as "baldies" for their close-cropped heads, usually concealed by turbans. The DAR saw themselves as holy warriors. "It became a dynamic of life and death over our religious beliefs to secure our turf," asserted Sheik Sulaiman al-Hadi.

When a new Muslim was hacked to death by gangsters in 1965, a *jenaza* was performed over his unwashed body, showing his status as a *mujahid*, or militant martyr whose soul was destined for paradise. Afterward, word spread among Brooklyn's youth gangs that the Muslims were formidable enemies, emboldened and not frightened by death. Yasin Mosque moved to 777 Saratoga Avenue, where a *suffa* (dormitory) was established to accommodate homeless young men. Adab became a serious practice as the small community amplified the daily call to prayer (*adan*) to demarcate an acoustic space representing dar al-Islam. Visually, their unusual garb symbolized a conscious rejection of non-Muslim society while serving as a casual way to expose strangers to Islamic ideas.

Women donned head-coverings (*kemar*) and sometimes veiled their faces completely (*hijab*) in their enthusiasm to emulate Islamic culture by demonstrating the stark contrast to Western gender stereotypes. Some men initiated polygamous domestic arrangements. Although the implications were not always clear, plural marriage distinguished Muslims from other religious subcultures. A few small businesses were undertaken, but the movement's finances rested mainly on the family economy, dependent in turn on wages and welfare subsidies. After much hesitation, the DAR initiated a prison dawa program, partly to assist the burgeoning conversion movement inside the state penitentiary systems and partly to take advantage of a state prison bureau eager to purchase a religious alternative to dangerous political unrest. A self-defense army was organized and recruits were trained in the martial arts at the mosque and in firearms proficiency at a legal firing range in New Jersey. The DAR actively cultivated a reputation as urban *mujahideen*.

Members of the DAR now took advantage of their contacts at State Street, who were now more comfortable dealing with their new Muslim brothers at a distance. Dawa teams accompanied Sheik Daoud around the country with the goal of reproducing the Brooklyn hijra elsewhere. They concentrated on other

mosques where Muslim immigrants had attracted a few African-American converts to orthodox Islam. This strategy also helped to avoid direct conflict with the
Nation of Islam since the dawa teams targeted primarily those individuals who
already understood the difference between Islam and the Nation of Islam. They
succeeded by gradually incorporating other loosely organized orthodox Muslims
into a national organization. Important affiliates arose in Boston, Philadelphia,
Columbus, Cleveland, Washington, Durham, Raleigh, Columbia, Atlanta, Dallas, San Antonio, Sacramento, San Diego, and Los Angeles. The objective was to
consolidate a devout core of worshipers in various locales, anchor them to the
national organization based in Brooklyn, and expand at the grassroots level
through intimate community and family contacts.[14]

But the DAR was stymied in Harlem, for many years a stronghold of the
NOI's Temple No. 7 and the scene of Malcolm X's martyrdom. Harlem had witnessed several iconoclastic attempts to establish Islamic orthodoxy, including
the Academy of Islam. Until the Mosque of Islamic Brotherhood was formed by
Sheik Tawfiq, nothing seemed to approximate the sense of community and per-
manence embodied by the Dar ul-Islam. Tawfiq was a pioneering giant, whose
light shone brilliantly though briefly. A Floridian of mixed African and Native
American ancestry, Tawfiq was an educated and highly accomplished individual: a deep sea diver, distance swimmer, yachtsman, mountain climber, classical musician, and vocalist who made his own record of Quranic recitations. He
originally studied Islam at New York's Islamic Center at Seventy-second Street
and Riverside Drive before joining Muslim Mosques Inc., serving as its secretary
until he received a scholarship to study at Al-Azhar University in Cairo. While
studying Arabic there, Tawfiq became interested in the Ikwan al-Muslimun. It
was rumored that the government expelled him for subversive activities in 1967,
and he returned to the United States with English translations of Sayed Qutb's
work, believing it strategic to Malcolm X's vision of cooperation between African Americans and the Muslim umma.

Acknowledging the universal character of "true" Islam, Tawfiq deployed
sufficient "nationalist" rhetoric to appeal to a larger African-American audience. In so doing he made it clear that the Civil Rights movement in the United
States occasioned a moral challenge to all Muslims.

> My dear brothers and sisters in Islam, I am sure that you are familiar with
> the tradition which states that "the Muslims are like one body and like the
> human body, whenever any part is in pain, the whole body is in pain."
> Surely, Black people in North America are Muslims (though in the main
> unconscious of their Islamic heritage) who are in very great pain. Are
> you also in great pain? If not, then you should be.[15]

He founded the Mosque of Islamic Brotherhood, upon return from Egypt
in 1967. Its name was far from coincidental and was a measure of the inspira-

tion he drew from the Egyptian Ikwan. Tawfiq worked to develop an Islamic community around his mosque on East 113th Street. In 1971 he began publishing a newsletter, the *Western Sunrise*. He opened a health food store, a tea room, an Islamic Academy for Boys, a literacy program for adults, and Boy Scouts and Girl Scouts for Muslim children. In 1976 he set up the "Living Islamic Community" program with a housing development based on the city's sweat equity program for restoring blighted residential housing. He always urged the Muslim brothers to get involved politically, to run for the school boards and speak out at community board meetings. He developed Drug-Free Programs and Dawa Programs. The MIB had a prison program that influenced inmates at the sprawling Rikers Island complex in Queens. As the social architect of a community of approximately one hundred families at MIB, twenty percent of them Latinos, Tawfiq succeeded in attracting a few doctors, lawyers, and other well-educated middle-class people. One of his two wives, Sister Halima Tawfiq-Touré, a linguistics scholar, involved the mosque in a literacy (English) campaign. The Islamic dawa movement in North America suffered a terrible blow when the articulate and charismatic Sheik Tawfiq died in 1988 following a long illness.

Upon the heels of Tawfiq's revivalism came Yusuf Muzzafaruddin Hamid from the Caribbean island of Dominica. He had traveled extensively in the Muslim world from 1965 to 1969, visiting Turkey, Palestine, and Pakistan, where he observed revivalist Islam in action. In Lahore he met with Abul A'la Mawdudi, founder of the Jamaat-e-Islami.

"Islam, for us, was the divine answer to suffering peoples' problems," Hamid concluded, noting that upon his return to the United States in 1970 he set himself the goal of "contacting and organizing many brothers and sisters who were prepared to shoulder the responsibility of a fuller commitment to Islamic work—not merely coming to the mosque for prayer, but the organizing of dawa programs and institution of internal discipline where life beyond the mosque could be accounted for."[16] According to what he had learned from Mawdudi, the idea of personal accountability was strategic for transforming the experience of religious awakening from a purely spiritual-individualistic dimension to a mass movement for social change.

In Washington, D.C., the IPNA made inroads into the black middle class when Hamid convinced university students to search for new formulas after the demise of the Black Power movement. Some questioned the Civil Rights model of activism and were attracted by Islamic dawa that emanated not only from the nongovernmental organizations (NGOs) but also from various foreign embassies. In January 1971, Hamid founded the Community Mosque of Washington (Masjid al-Umma) based on spiritual devotion and communal living. The movement combined communal living with the spirit of hijra, the final goal being the establishment of an Islamic state or caliphate somewhere in North America.[17] A regime of Islamic instruction and propagation was punctuated by salaried labor as the young recruits manned a fleet of taxicabs twenty-four hours a day.

Like the DAR, the IPNA expanded its network beyond Washington to relatives, friends, and Muslims in other cities. In basing the local community around collective resources, Hamid and his followers could dispense quickly with financial problems to concentrate on building a national movement. Washington became a nexus for affiliates in Akron, Pittsburgh, Chicago, and New York. Different from the Dar ul-Islam, however, the Islamic Party hastened to become a national and international concern before even consolidating its community positions. Hamid called for action and immediate unity among the various indigenous groups. During an all-Muslim conference in Philadelphia in 1972 he promoted himself as the leader of this effort. Veering away from representations of power in racial and nationalistic terms, Hamid declared that the objectives of unity should be "purely ideological" (in favor of Islam). Sounding like Fanon, too, he warned against Arabism as a false doctrine of authenticity that was incapable of remedying the problems of social oppression. There was no genuine Islamic state anywhere in the world, he argued, implying that "our national leadership must never put itself in a position to compromise with, praise, or front for un-Islamic regimes or contemporary governments. . . . Such compromising positions will only work to our detriment. The national leadership must have no ties whatever with the political leadership of such regimes."[18]

Given his close association with the twin pillars of revivalism—the Jamaat and Ikwan, both dissident movements—Hamid generated an enthusiastic response from many youthful delegates. In one copy of his document, an anonymous hand wrote: "This is a proposal that Muzzafaruddin took to the conference. I wasn't there, but those I talked to said it blew everyone away! He did his homework." This refers no doubt to Hamid's erudite command of the Hadith, which he gleaned for supporting quotations in the best style of Maulana Mawdudi.

But the conference did not end harmoniously. Delegates from the DAR and MIB were reluctant to cede leadership of the movement to Hamid, whom they regarded suspiciously as a dangerous rival. The DAR was already riven by paranoia following a 1967 attack by FBI agents pursuing a draft resister. Hamid also had directly antagonized Sheik Tawfiq by charging that he secretly harbored sympathies for the Nation of Islam.

The inability of these small movements to manage crisis proved stronger than their Islamic fervor and was responsible for their ultimate demise. Their similarities notwithstanding, the three groups could not transcend the dissociative forces at the heart of ghetto society. Despite a common vision, they lacked an essential historical perspective of the past efforts of their predecessors and the causes of their failures. Revivalism was a singularly powerful attraction yet too weak to overcome a tendency toward dominant personalities and other causes of factionalism. Hamid proved less than skillful in the art of political negotiation. He attacked those who rejected his perspective (reasoned though it may have been, according to Islamic jurisprudence) by questioning their beliefs and linking them to the Black Muslim heresy. After studying Sheik Tawfiq's publication *The Western Sunrise*, he concluded that it was generally nationalist in tone. He criticized its references to "Cushite" mythology, suggesting that they resembled the racialist formulations of the Nation of Islam. Furthermore, he insinuated that Tawfiq was too soft on the NOI, and for good measure he leveled the same charge against Mohamed Ra'uf, the Egyptian rector of the Washington, D.C., Islamic Center. Realizing that Ra'uf helped American Muslims obtain hajj visas from the Saudi embassy, Hamid portrayed his cordial but cool relations with Elijah Muhammad as anathema to all good Muslims and demanded his removal from the center. As shown by the following denunciation, compromise was impossible.

> We believe that the [Islamic] Party has done right in the sight of Allah by coming out forthrightly against the hypocrite Elijah Poole, may the curse of Allah be upon him and may he have a violent death. From 1935 to 1955, Poole's jive organization was nothing until Allah decreed that Malcolm should join it and work for it. Malcolm built Poole's organization, and—in Malcolm's own words—the only result of this was that Elijah Poole became insanely jealous of him. . . . The Party has nothing to fear from Elijah Poole and any of his *mushrik* goons or hit men.[19]

For the moment, DAR and the MIB stood together against Hamid's invectives. Unity under his guidance was out of the question. It was not simply a matter of piety or ideological acumen but really an issue concerning who might legitimately claim to wear the red fez symbolic of uncontested leadership among African-American Muslims.

Imam Antar 'Abd-al Khabir of Masjid Talib, the Atlanta affiliate of the DAR, responded with a scathing attack on Hamid, calling him "arrogant" and taking him to task for disrespect toward both Sheik Tawfiq and Dr. Ra'uf. In a devastating blow to Hamid's national stature, 'Abd-al Khabir's statement circulated widely. He charged that the Islamic Party had used the Philadelphia conference as a ploy to "bully" the DAR into relinquishing its de facto leadership position and further complained that Hamid and the IPNA sought to dominate the DAR that was the larger organization, demographically speaking.

Except for the looming presence of the NOI and the FBI's vendetta for the DAR, these arguments were matters of perception more than facts. What bothered most people was the attack on their sense of authenticity and their profession of *taqwa* (faith). The suddenly volatile rhetoric meant that it was only a matter of time before real violence would erupt.

This happened in 1974. In the wake of Hamid's failure to consolidate his power, the two other revivalist personalities, Imam Yahya Abdul Karim (DAR) and Sheik Tawfiq (MIB), planned a meeting to resolve a series of conflicts involving their respective organizations. The two men were friendly and intended to publicly settle a few misunderstandings with a view toward hammering out a treaty for a greater New York *majlis* (assembly). One particular bone of contention involved a satellite mosque that MIB was rumored to have sanctioned in Brooklyn. This unwelcome competition had led some in the DAR to repeat the IPNA's claims that Tawfiq was soft on Elijah Muhammad. Amidst this dispute, Tawfiq went to Brooklyn with an entourage that included several initiates. When voices were raised between the two imams inside the prayer hall, two men in the MIB detail drew guns and opened fire, killing two members of the DAR. After they were subdued and arrested, members at Yasin characterized it as an assassination plot against Imam Yahya. Mediation efforts ceased abruptly while the two sides continued to trade charges. The most serious allegations alleged that the MIB gunmen were infiltrators loyal to Elijah Muhammad, thus reinforcing the idea the MIB and the NOI were somehow allied.

Although unproven, the charges inflamed passions on all sides because the NOI was committed to intimidation and violence against orthodox Muslims. In some cities like Chicago, orthodox Muslims constantly feared infiltration and disruption by the Nation of Islam. In Philadelphia and Washington, on the other hand, there was intense pressure to confront the "enemy."

In Cleveland, however, there was a greater degree of mutual tolerance, fostered by Akram's age, his experience, and his stubborn refusal to fear anyone. This set the tone of the city's Islamic diversity among Moors, Ahmadiyyas, orthodox Sunni, Nation of Islam, and the immigrant community. The Islamic Revivalist Movement (IRM) centered in Masjid Mu'minim not far from the First Cleveland Mosque was the strongest link in Dar ul-Islam's entire national network. Under Imam Mutawif Abdul Shaheed, the IRM became a dominant force throughout Ohio. According to Shaheed, its national dawa program surpassed all others by converting four thousand individuals in a single year. The IRM pioneered orthodoxy in the Ohio state penitentiaries and also initiated a drug abuse awareness and detoxification program. They even rented interstate highway billboards to advertise Islam. Devout, reverent, and soft-spoken, Imam Mutawif gained his reputation as a conciliator who never wavered in his respect for Sheik Tawfiq, despite the troubles in New York. To describe the IRM as a mainstay of revivalist idealism embodying the spirit of Dar ul-Islam would not be inaccurate. In the overheated climates of New York, Philadelphia, and Chicago, territorial imperatives and personal loyalties often made Islamic revivalists look like highly ideological street gangs. While the Nation of Islam contributed to the intercommunal problems, Elijah Muhammad was hardly a singular force when it came to the question of transforming spiritual fervor into physical aggression. The FBI was also profiling African-American Muslims, as were other individuals working on behalf of foreign Muslim consulates. In retrospect, revivalists compromised themselves by excessive posturing and an unwillingness to investigate the history of their unchurched brothers and sisters. By responding to provocation after provocation, their leaders soon exhausted the benevolence initially generated by the movement. There were plenty of converts but also new problems engendered either by confusion or abuse of Islamic ideals. One stunning example was the mismanagement of polygamous marriage laws. Another was the failure to stabilize housing and labor according to an Islamic work ethic.

There was a dramatic reprieve for revivalism after Elijah Muhammad's death in 1976 when it became apparent that his son, Warith Deen, a confirmed orthodox Muslim himself, would take over the Nation. With approximately one hundred thousand members, it was the largest reservoir of unchurched African Americans. In terms of ritual, they retained only a vague idea of the Quran, the Hadith, and the Five Pillars of Islamic practice. Some old-timers knew nothing at all because they had been indoctrinated as mere cogs in the organization— working stiffs who paid their dues and kept themselves morally upright, apolitical, and unquestionably receptive to the greater will of "the Nation." If there were people familiar with the Holy Quran, they constituted a small elite who never abandoned their love for Malcolm X while remaining inside the NOI for personal reasons. There were a few, like Imam Siraj Wahaj of Masjid at-Taqwa in Brooklyn, who were close to revivalists and proclaimed their orthodoxy soon after the startling news of Elijah Muhammad's death.

The revivalists were instrumental in the great transformation of Black Muslims to orthodoxy. Despite their lingering hatred for Elijah Muhammad and his heretical doctrines, they patiently instructed many former Nation of Islam adepts in the *sunna*. Yet there were two reasons why they were unable to bring their dawa ideals to fruition. First, although he had pledged to lead his flock toward orthodoxy, Imam Warith Muhammad had no immediate plans to release them from the organizational scaffolding of the NOI, renamed the World Community of Muslims in the West and then the American Muslim Mission.[20] Second, the revivalists were overwhelmed at the prospect of so many new Muslims and sometimes unprepared to forgive the heresies committed under the leadership of Elijah Muhammad. In the face of the impossible task of deprogramming thousands of individuals who believed in the divinity of Master Fard and conflated the Prophet Muhammad with Elijah Muhammad, there were too few capable leaders and their resources were too thin to accomplish this job without help.

Assistance came from the well-endowed transnational groups whose capacity for mass dawa had grown steadily since the rise of OPEC in 1973. In its role as the guardian of the holy shrines of Islam, Saudi diplomacy always had a part in granting visas for hajj to Mecca. With adequate funds to match growing interest in Islam, this authority expanded to encompass jurisdictional fiat over the lunar cycle of Muslim holidays, particularly Ramadan. Through the Muslim Students Association (MSA) and then the Islamic Society of North America (ISNA) and the Islamic Circle of North America (ICNA), the Rabita al-Alam al-Islami (Saudi-sponsored World Muslim League) sought to institutionalize its authority and legitimacy over all American Muslims. They sponsored activities such as summer camps for children, imam training institutes, Islamic literature booklists, a centralized speakers bureau, and, most important, cash grants and building funds.

Following the Islamic Revolution in 1979, the Iranian government also made a play for sympathizers by emphasizing its commitment to Islamic independence. A report authored by one Muhammad Sa'id openly assessed the potential for dawa in North America. It criticized both the Nation of Islam and the orthodox Sunni Muslims, whose "insincerity" and adherence to Arab chauvinism had "temporarily derailed" the revivalist movement. Sa'id characterized "American Zionists"—Jews—as the worst enemies of Islam but not without attacking the Saudi influence over local African-American imams through the "trinitarian relationship" of the Rabita, MSA, and CIA. He implied an outright conspiracy to depoliticize the movement by playing on the personal vanities of indigenous imams, causing destructive rivalries among a group of individuals who had not yet overcome a predominantly Christian and apolitical view of religion. His indictment of "the senseless oppression forced upon our sisters in Islam" was an even more scathing comment about the erroneous directions pursued by Americans.[21]

While acknowledging the achievements of the revivalists during the 1960s and 1970s, Sa'id wrote that this momentum was interrupted by the intercommunal violence at Masjid Yasin, the Hanafi slaughter in Washington, and "the disgrace of the Islamic Party" caused by crimes of moral turpitude. He further accused Y. M. Hamid of squandering a three-million-dollar gift from Libya. The report concluded by calling for the Iranian mullahs to create and export more dawa literature to counter the false principles of Islam depicted in literature from Egypt and Pakistan. The report was Arabophobic in the extreme yet accurate with respect to historical facts, particularly its characterization of revivalism as a spent force by 1974. The only subsequent influence of Iranian revolutionaries on American Muslims was the assassination in Washington of an associate of the discredited regime of Shahpour Bakhtiar by an American Muslim who fled afterwards to Teheran, where he still resides.[22]

THE SPECTER OF ISLAMISM   The final blow to revivalism was the rise of al-Fuqra, a Sufi-mystical movement led by the Pakistani Sheik Syed Gilani. Beginning with his arrival at the Islamic Center in New Jersey in 1978, Gilani attracted a curious handful of indigenous Muslims who came Thursday evenings to participate in *zikhr* ceremonies. For those traumatized by years of street violence and paranoia, Sufism offered a more sedate, contemplative religious experience. It was also a welcome respite from what had become a dilemma about Islamic authenticity. As their attraction grew into infatuation, revivalists began secretly to pledge bayat to Sheik Gilani.

Some orthodox Muslims at Masjid Yasin viewed Sufism not as a passing infatuation but part of an elaborate plot to brainwash their colleagues and destroy the Dar ul-Islam. Sheik Sulaiman al-Hadi and a handful of the Yasin stalwarts alleged that Gilani was a Pakistani intelligence operative assigned to destroy their movement. They had little tolerance for the esoteric zikhr, the Sufi practice of rhythmic chanting ("supplementary" practices, as Muslim jurists call them euphemistically). As Gilani began finding many enthusiasts wherever he preached, he therefore also provoked resistance and bitterness.

Across the country, seekers of a mystical communion left the fold one by one and then in larger groups until the orthodox congregations disintegrated from New York to California. Even the DAR's leaders, Yahya Abdul Karim and Rijab Mahmud, followed Sheik Gilani. Following a series of confrontations over their detour toward Sufism, both men quit the Dar ul-Islam to follow al-Fuqra, and subsequently Yasin Mosque splintered into two smaller orthodox mosques, Masjid Mu'minim moving to Atlantic Avenue and Masjid Ikwa to Eastern Parkway in Brooklyn. Similar divisions plagued the DAR elsewhere. Those who rejected Sufism started new mosques aiming to preserve the spirit of revivalism in fact if not in the name of the Dar ul-Islam. Prominent among the orthodox refugees surviving the Sufi upheaval were Imam Daud Abdul Malik's Universal Islamic Brotherhood in Cleveland, Imam Jamil al-Amin's West End Community in Atlanta, and Muhammad Abdullah's Ta'if Tul Islam, a street ministry in South-Central Los Angeles.

One important reason for the DAR's resiliency was its penitentiary missions, which remained somewhat isolated from the Sufi epiphenomenon. Men coming from prison into the reformed DAR communities benefited from an environment that promoted, indeed necessitated, religious asceticism. Imams adopted the policy of extending bayat to men who were still incarcerated as a way of measuring their strength and keeping their congregations intact. On the outside, bayat functioned in much the same way to consolidate a geographically scattered group of believers into a community of believers. Subsequently, the imams who held these bayat chains organized themselves into a federation of North American Muslims. This system was supported by ISNA and Rabita, thus constituting a new attempt to realize the old dream of Muslim unity.

As for charges that Sheik Gilani deliberately subverted the DAR as part of a conspiracy to destroy the mass potential of revivalist Islam, there is some pertinent information. It concerns the activities of Y. M. Hamid just prior to the dissolution of the Islamic Party of North America. In late 1976, in the midst of the turbulence of intercommunal politics and the death of Elijah Muhammad, Hamid decided abruptly to relocate his party headquarters from Washington to Atlanta. The move, he said, reflected the growth of the party's national and international reputation and his desire not to be held back by preoccupation with local affairs.[23] Never explaining what this meant, Hamid took fourteen Muslim families with him to Conley, Georgia, in July 1977. Simultaneously he established branches of the Islamic Party in several Caribbean nations, including Trinidad, Guyana, Grenada, Dominica, and the Virgin Islands. Later that year, he journeyed back to Lahore, Pakistan, for meetings with Mawdudi and other officials of the Jamaat-e-Islami and Tabligh Jamaat groups. In November they founded the International Islamic Education Institute with Pakistani Supreme Court justice Bardurazman Kaikus as chairman and "Branch Amir" Sheik Syed Gilani as secretary general. The institute's charter proclaimed:

> Due to a great interest in Islam in the Western countries and the Americas in particular, our efforts are particularly designed to help the spread of Islam there. . . . As this institute is established by the untiring efforts of Yusuf Muzafarruddin Hamid, Chairman of the Islamic Party of North America, so it will extend special cooperation for preaching in North America.[24]

Upon his return to the United States, Hamid dissolved the IPNA and went into virtual seclusion. Although Sheik Gilani arrived in early 1978 and resided among the immigrant Muslims in Jersey City, al-Fuqra was not organized until 1980. According to Sheik Sulaiman al-Hadi, it was the Tabligh Jamaat who covered Gilani's activities during this time, providing him with contacts and introductions to various communities around the nation. After news of the Soviet invasion of Afghanistan in 1979, he started to talk to people about jihad, playing on their sincerity as good Muslims. He suggested that Allah had inspired him to come to the United States to help organize support for the Afghan jihad against the communists. "So they were souped up by the teaching that they were doing their Islamic duty to fight the *kufr* in a foreign war."[25]

By tying his mission to jihad, a sacred concept, Gilani conferred upon himself the authority to substitute the wars in Afghanistan, Lebanon, Israel/Palestine, and Bosnia for the economic and social issues previously central to the American conversion movement. As a tendency to subordinate local issues to the geopolitical strategies of a few sponsoring states, the internationalist Muslim perspective gained such prominence during the period of this study that a majority of persons interviewed asserted that jihad was an issue of singular importance, even surpassing the fight to end apartheid in South Africa.

Although many followed Gilani into Sufism, only a few African-American Muslims enlisted to fight in Afghanistan as mujahideen. One of them, Abdullah Rasheed Abdullah, used his training as a hospital technician to become a field medic under the command of Gulbuddin Hekmatyar's Hezbi Islami (Islamic Party). In 1993 he was gravely wounded when he stepped on a land mine during a raid on the Soviet army. He received emergency treatment in the field, then stopped in Kuwait before returning to the United States for reconstructive surgery when his condition stabilized.

While recuperating in the same Brooklyn hospital where he once worked, Rasheed professed a desire to return to jihad as soon as possible. He recalled that both his parents had belonged to the Moorish Science Temple, predisposing him to Islam as an adult. An indefatigable good samaritan who dispensed free medical advice to his uninsured neighbors in Bedford-Stuyvesant, the bearded and serene Rasheed contrasted sharply with the image of a fiery holy warrior. He never again reached Afghanistan but instead became embroiled in a plan to secure military-grade explosives for a secret munitions dump in rural Pennsylvania. Believing, inexplicably, that he was party to a training mission for CIA-sponsored mujahideen operations in Bosnia, Rasheed fell into the terrorist plot to attack the World Trade Center and other sites in New York. He was arrested, tried, convicted, and sentenced to life in prison in 1995. There was only one other American-born Muslim among his seven codefendants, indicating at best a precarious link between the actual crimes and indigenous al-Fuqra Muslims. Rasheed's career is an apt demonstration of the dilemma facing any indigenous Muslim convert who confuses radical politics with religious ardor.[26]

The police characterize al-Fuqra as a "violent . . . extremist sect" organized in a terrorist cell structure and committed to jihad against its perceived enemies, usually other minorities or other Muslims with whom they disagree. While conceding that members practice a sort of Sufi-mysticism combined with radical Islam, the same authorities have linked al-Fuqra members to a succession of villains, including a Pakistani intelligence official, and crimes, including the bombings of Shiʿite mosques, Hindu temples, and businesses; a 1991 plot to smuggle explosives and weapons into the United States from Canada, and the 1990 assassination of Imam Rashad Abdel Khalifa in Tucson, Arizona.[27]

Al-Fuqra communities are located in New York, Washington, Los Angeles, Tennessee, and Toronto. Two are rural educational centers or retreats known as the Quranic Open University. Some view the practice of Gilani's *Quranic Psychiatry* as a variant of al-Ghazali's Neoplatonism, a modern Islamic therapy for the psychologically distressed.[28] They call attention to parallels with Western psychotherapy in the relationship between a patient and his or her *murshid,* whose job is to reconstruct a healthy personality. Others see this bayat as a form of intense personal dependency and a prescription for mind control, making it easy for overzealous law enforcement agents and journalists alike to paint reclusive al-Fuqra Muslims as terrorists.

Despite such charges, those interviewed for this research eschewed violence and had dropped out of the DAR in favor of the peaceful life of contemplative Sufis. After many years of bitterness, Sufis and revivalists have begun a healing process and occasionally join together at ʿid picnics.

The themes of fundamentalist violence and Sufism thus remain difficult to reconcile at first glance. This explains the confusion surrounding Sheik Gilani's legacy. Older revivalists like Sheik Sulaiman al-Hadi, now dead, were convinced of his affiliation to the intelligence community and its nefarious effects on the DAR. If Y. M. Hamid did play a conscious role in undermining Islamic revivalism by establishing an organizational base for Sheik Gilani, then it would be a tremendous irony, because his Islamic Party was founded on the principle of nonintervention and a desire to develop an autonomous Muslim space in the Western hemisphere. Before its dissolution, the IPNA had sponsored a speech by Sheik Hassan al-Turabi, the leader of Sudan's National Islamic Front. Al-Turabi cautioned his American listeners against proceeding too quickly under the tute-lage of foreigners.

Yet the sudden success of al-Fuqra indicated a continuing vulnerability to the influence of foreign missionaries. The DAR began as an insular community, spun off from Sheik Daoud Faisal's State Street Mosque in a frenzy of idealist passion. Recalling the rise of al-Fuqra, some have commented on Sheik Gilani's charisma, suggesting that his possession of "superior" knowledge seriously un-dermined the principle of Islamic unity among converts who were loaded with faith but sorely lacking in background and perspective. The Sufi way repre-sented a detour from revival to gnosis. Its New Age appeal lay outside the dar al-Islam in a zone straddling the real and the spiritual where the believer commu-nicates with saints and angels instead of other humans; where all mysteries are revealed; and where death is simply another place. Furthermore, mystical ideas and esoteric practices are transmitted orally, as is not the case in normative Islam, which is usually acquired through a program of rigorous study of written literature.

An apparent jihad surpassing any of the alleged al-Fuqra actions in its bru-tality was a failed coup d'etat engineered by Imam Abu-Bakr in Port-of-Spain, Trinidad. On 28 July 1990 he led one hundred followers of his Jamaat al-Mus-limeen in a coordinated military assault on vital targets. They seized the govern-ment and communication headquarters and seriously wounded the nation's prime minister in the process of taking forty-one hostages. For a week Abu Bakr demanded the government's total capitulation while Port-of-Spain "became en-gulfed in widespread looting, plundering, and the burning of buildings. When the army sought to curb the violence, at least fifteen looters were killed."

As the result of mediation, Imam Abu Bakr and his rebels surrendered peacefully and were summarily incarcerated. Order was restored, and soon af-terward an American Muslim, Louis Haneef, was arrested in southern Florida for supplying the weapons used in the coup. The prime minister, A. N. R. Robin-son, revealed that Haneef's arms-smuggling activities had been under surveil-lance by U.S. intelligence services for at least a year and called on Washington to take responsibility for its alleged role in the uprising. Two years later, astonished Trinidadians watched Imam Abu Bakr and his rebels walk free when the Privy Council (Trinidad's supreme court) compelled the government to honor the ne-gotiated amnesty that had been a key point leading to their surrender. The court even awarded seven hundred thousand dollars in damages to the Jamaat al-Muslimeem as compensation for the destruction of their commune at Mucurapo Center.

Abu Bakr was a former Trinidadian police officer who converted to Islam in Toronto in the 1960s. Returning home, he joined the Jamaat al-Muslimeem and succeeded in fusing radical Islamist ideology to militant black nationalism, itself a fixture of the nation's dissident politics. On the one hand, there can be no doubt that Abu Bakr's uprising attracted a degree of popular support, especially among impoverished Trinidadians. He alleged governmental corruption, espe-

cially collusion with the international narcotics cartels, and this outrage resonated positively with many citizens who were already irate about the shameless
squandering of the country's petroleum resources. Though the Jamaatis were
mostly black Trinidadians, Imam Abu Bakr also attracted some East Indian
youths to the cause of Islamism and social justice.

On the other hand, Trinidad's Muslims are mostly of Pakistani descent, and
it is improbable that more than two hundred sympathized with his radical ideology. Abu Bakr fantasized that his actions would trigger a sustained uprising
leading to the first Islamic republic in the Caribbean. He imagined the Jamaat al-
Muslimeem as a revolutionary Islamic vanguard and dreamed of reforming the
whole island according to the sharia, establishing forever an Islamic bridgehead
in the Western Hemisphere. It was rumored that he received financial backing
from Libya and perhaps Iran for this wild endeavor that was intended to create
an Islamic "Cuba" at the doorstep of "satanic" America.

The Jamaat al-Muslimeem was an offshoot of the Islamic Missionaries Guild
and was also affiliated to the United Islamic Organization; all three stemmed from
the overseas revivalism that was so influential in the United States. But it was a
more moderate organization, the Anjuman Sunnat Al Jamaat Association
(ASJA), that spoke for most of Trinidad's Muslims when it protested the government's acquiescence to the takeover of state land—Mucurapo Center—in the
name of all Trinidad's Muslims by the Islamic Missionaries Guild who ceded it in
turn to the Jamaat al-Muslimeem. The government responded by attempting to
retake Mucurapo Center, which Abu Bakr had already converted into a ten-acre
patch of the dar al-Islam. This was the catalyst for his bloody coup.[29]

The jihadist drama in Trinidad instructs the general history of Islam in
America in several important ways. First, it demonstrates the frequent irrele-
vance of facts in the thinking of Islamist militants. The Jamaat al-Muslimeem
were not only a minority among the nation's Muslims but indeed represented an
even smaller minority among Afro-Trinidadians, most of whom profess Christianity. The notion of retributive justice painted by the Holy Quran differs radically from that image as interpreted through the lens of Islamic revolutionary
ideology. The Jamaat al-Muslimeem believed in a mystical power that would ig-
nite a mass uprising. Like a crisis cult, they saw no alternative to violence; they
were about to be delivered by Allah, and time was of the essence.

Second, the essential kernel of Islamic revivalism is hijra, a critical notion
that translates belief into divinely sanctioned action. Hijra commands the believer to live and pray within the dar al-Islam, to insulate oneself and community from the infidels' power to contravene or compromise any of the laws dictated by the Holy Quran. It anticipates a divided universe and thus sanctions
divorce between Muslim time and space on the one hand and the dar al-harb on
the other. Prayer regulates the believer's daily routine; he or she observes the
lunar calendar and refers all historical time to a date given for the Prophet's exile
in Medina—year I. In all facets of their lives, Muslims must seek an optimum
position vis-à-vis non-Muslims. If one does not live in a Muslim country, then

one is obliged to remedy that situation. For an individual, this can mean emigration to a place where Islam predominates—an Arab country, for example. It could also mean the construction of autonomous Muslim communities within a larger secular nation.

The latter interpretation of hijra has been one of the models followed by African-American Muslims. In rural settlements and urban enclaves, it suggests the type of coexistence possible in a tolerant, liberal society. When this concept begets a circling-of-wagons mentality, as in Trinidad, it will give rise inevitably to a strategy of violence—Islamism—that is altogether distinct from revivalism. When revivalism calls attention to the narrative of the Holy Quran and the prophetic traditions, it rests in harmony with a politics of survival and growth. It reaffirms a literate, reasoned view of history that is based on scripture but capable nonetheless of mediation and compromise. In denying narrative absolutely, Islamism provokes rupture with all forms of social and historical consciousness. Moreover, it becomes a system of esthetics based on symbols, not literacy—similar in many respects to radical Zionism and the totalitarian ideologies of the nineteenth-century witch's brew of nationalism, mysticism, and pseudoscience championed by Johann Fichte, J. B. Von Herder, and Count Arthur de Gobineau.

On the heels of episodic violence swirling around their movement, true revivalists began to see the handwriting on the wall and sought to distance themselves from the mounting influence of Islamism abroad. The compilation and reassessment of their history, of which this study is only a small part, was a significant step in this direction, a kind of glasnost on the part of indigenous Muslims. It is the modern way to integrate oneself into the body politic. As the experiment continues, an increasing number of African-American Muslims are also turning to Islamic scholarship in the expectation that their perspectives and ideas will contribute to "opening the gates of ijtihad," the passage to an Islamic renaissance.

The current generation of orthodox Muslims have adopted a greater transparency, separating themselves from murky trouble spots and dark agitators whenever necessary. In the case of Brooklyn's Masjid at-Taqwa, this means clearly telegraphing their respect for civil order by cooperating with police on the mean streets of ghetto America. Muslims have entered public service, public education, and public safety in force in Detroit, Newark, and Los Angeles. They continue to work with the criminal justice system in almost every state in the areas of remedial education, public health awareness, substance abuse prevention, and general rehabilitation. In all these efforts they have drawn closer to the liberal ideal of multicultural pluralism. They view themselves as entrepreneurs in the marketplace and therefore concentrate on acquiring professional skills and interpersonal networks for economic success. Having explored various degrees of commitment to their religion—from Ahamdiyya to orthodoxy to Sufism and jihad by way of revivalism—they have come full circle and now seek to assimilate.

THE WORLD OF ISLAM IN AMERICA   One final irony of this heterogeneity concerns the recent wave of Muslim immigrants from sub-Saharan Africa. As principal subjects of a long millennium of Islamic religious conversion, they are some of the Muslims whose ancestors traded slaves and sometimes were taken themselves as slaves to the New World. Their immigration to the United States opens an intriguing series of paradoxes that the Western imagination can only characterize as the return of the repressed. The children of good (or evil) ancestors disembark voluntarily in the New World seeking fortunes that are possible in a real historical sense, at least partially, because of the old slave mode of production. Impoverished Africans with better education than what is available in the dangerous ghetto high schools compete with African Americans for entry-level jobs and college scholarship opportunities. African traders look for a fast buck selling cheap copies of fashionable apparel to ghetto youngsters. They affect local dialect when they whisper: "Check this out, brother! Special price for you, sister!" The oversized sweatshirts and nylon windbreakers on their tables have brand names like "Karl Kani" or "Tommy Hilfiger" but also "Mecca." Some of the same African merchants who are busy hawking fashions plus fake Swiss watches, designer sunglasses, and baseball hats turn up at Harlem's Masjid Malcolm Shabazz for *jum'a* or 'id clad in robes and crowned with a red fez.

After deducting whatever sums are necessary for their subsistence, most of these merchants return their profits to Africa, where they are collected by the sheiks of the Muridiyya and the Tijaniyya orders. These are large, transnational Sufi brotherhoods that practice a syncretic Islam resulting from centuries of intermittent contact between Black Africa and Arab Islam. Their saints lie in tombs that have become objects of pilgrimage and worship, a practice that is regarded with suspicion and derision by many orthodox Muslims. Some women can achieve high status and personal independence. The sheiks command political power on a national scale in Senegal, Gambia, Nigeria, Mali, and Mauritania. Yet they also maintain educational, commercial, and political networks with Arab-Muslim orthodoxy.

In good times the Sufi orders have controlled local cash economies, for instance groundnut crops harvested by thousands of young initiates to the order. During hard times, such as the recent West African currency devaluations, more followers are deployed to work as traders and salaried labor in the industrialized nations. Their presence in the United States has stirred great interest in Africanized Islam, resulting in numerous cultural and social exchanges. Young American Muslims, some barely teenagers, travel to Senegal and the Sudan to learn Arabic and memorize the Holy Quran. Marriage between the African and American followers of the sheiks, indeed marriage to the exalted sheiks themselves, have produced strategic kin alliances and a material structure for future growth of the community. There are presently thousands of adepts in these orders, enough to warrant annual tours by the sheiks, who travel in relative luxury across the United States.

One of the important leaders of the Tijaniyya is Sheik Hassan Cissé, who holds diplomas from Cambridge University and the Sorbonne. During one trip to New York, he set up headquarters in a suite of rooms at the Hyatt Hotel next to Grand Central Station. The entire tenth-floor corridor was littered with shoes as Americans and Africans alike sought an audience with him in view of solving a personal crisis or even creating new opportunities for trade and employment. Sheik Hassan is said to possess *wird*, a mystical power that visits the earth through only one sufi master per generation. According to tradition, the sheik's fez does not just symbolize this power but is the receptacle and material agency for its transmission from heaven down to earth.

In the fourteen centuries since the Prophet Muhammad lived, Islam has radiated from its center of origin on the Arabian peninsula to Africa, Asia Minor, Europe, and further into Asia by various means, including military conquest, political, commercial and cultural hegemony. African Americans have sought out and devised a unique path to this religion. Moreover, they have appropriated the teachings of the Quran and borrowed many aspects of Muslim culture from around the world. For many African Americans, questions of faith are often rephrased in terms of allegiance to various struggles being conducted on behalf of Islam.

Important to this process was the crossfertilization of ideas between immigrant Muslim and African-American university students. The Muslim Students Association began as an association of foreign students who sought to establish prayer halls or mosques on campus in the early 1970s. This established a basis for dialogue with African-American students who were committed to or familiar with Islam. Many issues and concerns were shared through conferences and publications such as the journal *al-Ittihad* and the magazine *Horizons*. This bond continued to grow through university connections and rapidly dispersed into professional and community circles. Soon the MSA grew into the Islamic Society of North America, established as an umbrella organization sponsoring annual conventions, summer workshops, children's camps, travel, media and informational services, and professional organizations. ISNA has a huge campus near Indianapolis, and its charter envisions the construction of an Islamic university.

Gleaming new Islamic centers have sprouted also across the American landscape in Los Angeles, Chicago, Toledo, Washington, and Atlanta. This book is written in the shadow of the Islamic Center of New York City, which straddles the line between Manhattan's Yorkville and El Barrio in East Harlem. Its copper dome and towering minaret, which broadcasts the adan on Fridays, are within sight of Mt. Sinai Hospital, the largest and most renowned institution in the area. A large school is under construction next to the prayer hall in a neighborhood whose half-mile radius encompasses nearly all the elite public and private academies of the city. Jum'a attracts a cross-section of the city's Muslim community, including United Nations diplomats, Bangladeshi cabbies, Senegalese street merchants, and African-American professionals. A tremendous convocation swelled the grounds and surrounding streets with worshipers during the jenaza for Sister Betty Shabazz, Malcolm X's widow.

Wherever large immigrant communities reside, there is usually an Islamic center funded partially through local contributions but mainly by organizations such as the Muslim World League. Based in Saudi Arabia, the Muslim World League is dedicated to promoting the Wahabite sectarian claim over the holy sites at Mecca and Medina. There are many controversial aspects to the work of this organization in the United States.[30] Over the years, instances of discrimination against African Americans have been alleged. Cultural chauvinism and misrecognition are other complaints directed toward immigrant Muslims. Moreover, there is deep concern about the Islamic propriety of Muslims investing in expensive mosques while ignoring the needs of their destitute brothers and sisters living in urban slums.

There are other examples of ongoing debate concerning the sexual division of labor, gender roles, and ideas about marriage. Among the most controversial topics is the practice of polygyny. While the Quran sanctions plural marriage only under very specific circumstances, some new Muslims have used this as an excuse to reinforce previously held attitudes about plural marriage. Women object to these practices in private or together in groups, but in public they are often constrained to justify polygyny with references to the Prophet Muhammad, who had many wives.

There is, however, one emphatic passion that is shared by most African Americans who have made their pilgrimage to Mecca: the rapture felt by communing with the multitude of humanity who circle the holy ka'ba. This often becomes the central experience in their lives and produces a contagious effect at home. In this encounter, African-American Muslims experience directly the heterogeneous ways of Islam, and the Islamic world comes to know itself as part of the American experience.

II

Conversion Sagas

4

"From the Cotton Fields
of the South to the Sands of Arabia"

AUNT WILLIE deftly slipped her fingernail into the envelope and removed a handwritten letter from Walter up north. It came with a newspaper clipping and a small brochure. Standing at the mailbox in the parching July heat of East Texas, she stared at his news photo, her sweat moistening the page. The picture showed his face framed by a turban. A thick beard accentuated his cheekbones. His eyes and mouth bore a striking resemblance to Clarence Robert Gregg, her deceased cousin and childhood friend. The caption above the portrait read "Allah's Servant;" the name below was "Wali Akram." The headline began: "Imam of Moslems Has 10-Year Plan." With an urgent sense of pride she read that Walter was now the teacher and "chief promulgator" of a community of 120 "Negro Moslems" in Cleveland with more followers in Cincinnati, Pittsburgh, and Dayton. He was teaching them to read the holy book of their religion, the Quran. Thirty people were "more or less fluent" already. They could recite prayers and greet each other with "the traditional salutation of the desert," As-salaam-u-alaikum (Peace Be Unto You). Walter, the article continued, had dedicated himself to Islam and predicted that its followers would lift themselves from poverty through Islam. "Our people are among the lowest of the low," he told the *Cleveland Plain Dealer* in the summer of 1937.

> They sorely need the grace of Allah, the Beneficent, the Compassionate. Many of our people live in the worst quarters, poverty-stricken and friendless. But it is their own fault. The Koran says, "Allah does not change the condition of a people unless they themselves change their conditions." Our God is one who will inspire industry and prosperity and fortitude. I myself would not want a religion that did nothing for you RIGHT HERE AND NOW.[1]

To Aunt Willie and her boys, Noel and Cyrus, who plowed, planted, hoed, and picked cotton, Cousin Walter had always been a symbol of industry and ingenuity. He combined down-home fortitude with a wayfaring spirit and was always willing to work for his supper and a bed to sleep in. In Texas he worked first as a blacksmith, then as a prospector, and finally on the railroad. That job carried him north to Missouri, Indiana, and then Ohio. There in Cleveland, he answered his calling after a decade of incessant roaming. "All that traveling," he once commented, "I had to become a hobo before I could become a Muslim."

Aunt Willie and Walter's father, Clarence Gregg, were the grandchildren of Sarah, who was a slave to the Scottish Gregg clan that settled in Burleson County, Texas, in the early nineteenth century. Clarence's father was a child of African, Native American, and Scottish heritage. When Grandma Sarah was set free, she left the Gregg clan and married a Mexican named Cevina. She gave him four daughters, who inherited their father's fair complexion. Everyone in the county called Cevina "the Mexican." Three of his beautiful daughters married the Oldham brothers, sons of Captain Oldham, a white landowner and veteran of the Mexican War. Thus Grandma Sarah was the matriarch of two lineages, the Greggs and the Oldhams. Black, brown, and white cousins shared the estate equally. After the Civil War, the redistributed plots of farmland formed a checkerboard, multiracial neighborhood.

Sarah's oldest son, Simon, inherited a farm and the estate's biggest house. He butchered for a living and operated a little bar in a shack on his property. His sons tended the cotton. Their wives churned butter, canned preserves, and sold their produce across the county. All the Greggs resided along the same country road, paid homage to the same ancestors, and relied on each other's sense of reciprocity. Immensely popular, Simon had the respect and love of the entire family. Everyone knew that the white Greggs were wild about their Uncle Simon. Until his death Simon managed the entire estate and refused to sell even the smallest parcel until everyone in the family agreed. He taught his children to stick to the land and never give it up. The Greggs were an example of the solid yeomanry that Booker T. Washington envisioned as the backbone of African-American people. An affection for reading and learning permeated Simon and then Clarence's household. The Greggs were all raised as Baptists, with a Bible prominent in each home. They also read Washington's book *Up from Slavery* and were among the first families in the county to subscribe to W. E. B. Du Bois's magazine, the *Crisis*. A more practical monthly, *Popular Mechanics*, fascinated Clarence Jr. and Walter, however. Always given to experimentation in the workshop, the two brothers tinkered ceaselessly with various inventions in their forge. Eventually, they patented a machine gun (for which they received only fifty dollars) and a double-locking window sash. They supplied corrugated metal washboards and ax handles to the whole county and claimed to make the best baseball bats in Texas.

When Clarence died in 1911, the Gregg legacy faltered. Clarence's widow Leah was left with seven boys from nine months to fifteen years old. Soon afterward, Grandpa Simon also died, leaving the family without a strong, experienced leader. Responsibility for running their father's forge fell to Clarence Jr. and Walter, aged fifteen and nine, respectively. Both boys were intelligent, skillful, and energetic craftsmen. By servicing practically all the mechanical needs of the surrounding farmers, they soon established reputations as the best blacksmiths in the area.

When the revenues from this business proved insufficient, an Oldham cousin secured work for them on Santa Fe Railroad. Within a few years they were regularly contracting for repairs to the Santa Fe tracks, cars, and locomotives.

Leah had already decided to send one of her sons to college. She scraped together seventy-five dollars for tuition, enabling Walter to attend Prairie View State College beginning in 1917. He was the first Gregg to enter college. An original "land grant" institution, Prairie View now served as the black counterpart to Texas A & M, offering training in the industrial arts. Its principal, E. J. Blackshear, was an ardent Bookerite who featured a vocational curriculum that was strictly remedial and boring from Walter's perspective.

What really attracted his attention, though, was the Prince Hall Lodge in nearby Brenham, Texas, because it introduced him to the kinds of esoteric history absent from Prairie View. The lodge was the only fraternity open to southern black students, who found within it a source of new intellectual vistas. In a personal way, it made them aware of the existence of "a world of ideas with which they had no previous familiarity and constituted a major cultural intrusion into rural life."[2]

In 1919 Walter could no longer resist the mad hunt for oil in Texas. He left Prairie View and headed for Mexia, where he signed on as a "roughneck" with Deroloc Oil, a legendary group of African Americans who pioneered drilling in East Texas. Prospectors had fanned out across the state looking for salt domes or any fissiparous rock as likely drilling sites. The most enterprising prospectors hired local surveyors with knowledge of the region's topology and used their expertise to attract investors for expensive drilling ventures. The men of Deroloc (*colored* spelled backward) possessed exceptional knowledge of the local terrain and knew almost instinctively where to look for oil. They had memorized every inch of soil and landmark where they played as boys. Participating in the exciting oil boom was the realization of a world beyond the cotton fields. These black oil men were a new breed, full of promise, serious and poised, stylishly dressed and urbane. Walter and several companions showed up at the Gregg homestead in Bryan one day, making a lasting impression on his young brother Bert who recalled "They came to see us at home in a big automobile. We'd never seen those types of industrial black men like that before, especially in a big car. Walter was with them."[3]

After several months of being paid in "royalty rights" by Deroloc, Walter began to realize that the East Texas oil business was not his idea of stable employment. Without doubt there was an oil bonanza somewhere beneath the ground, but even if striking it was imminent, what kind of payoff could he expect? By the time equipment could be shuttled into place and drilling commenced, the titles to potential sites would change hands several times. Fast-talking entrepreneurs could become rich in this way even if the site finally tested dry. They were the sole beneficiaries, not the knowledgeable and honest worker. Walter decided to leave his "roughneck" colleagues and headed for Houston, where he plied his mechanical skills working for the railroad. Within a few months, he had invented the prototype for a new railroad car coupler that was patented there under his middle name as the "Reice coupler." After extensive testing and a few modifications, this device became the standard coupler until the coming of diesel locomotives after World War II. In return for his rights to the patent, Walter received a month's worth of wages, a desultory sum by any standards. Yet it was enough money for him to continue his northward trek.

Memories of the bloody Houston massacre of 1917 and rioting and lynching in Waco were still fresh in the minds of Texans. As Walter hoboed along the Santa Fe line, he heard more about the violent and often merciless persecution of black people. Nowhere in his previous experience had he experienced the kind of racism that now haunted the country. In cities like Houston and Waco as well as in the smaller towns along his route, Walter's skills were in demand. Usually he had no trouble finding a job and a place to sleep. But in the wake of the brutal pogroms in East St. Louis and Houston, Jim Crow laws now severely curtailed the public mobility of African Americans. Even small townsfolk were less congenial to a Texas journeyman, fearing perhaps that any stranger might bring bounty hunters and sudden tragedy to the household. The railroad mud flats near town were crossroads for itinerants searching for a warm campfire. After nightfall they became dangerous places where lynch mobs sometimes preyed. Privately, however, fraternal lodge membership worked like an underground passport to furnish opportunity, company, and a safe haven in the troubled sea of vagabondage. One could obtain information about jobs, rooms, or something to eat. The lodge even afforded some protection from harassment and arrest.[4] Walter also relished the conversations, which ranged from political discussions to arcane discourse about Freemasonry and the occult.

From Houston he wandered to St. Louis, Missouri, where in 1921 he found work as a janitor at Principia College, a segregated white school. Hundreds of migrants referred to St. Louis as "the most northern city in the South and the most southern city in the North." The living conditions were not much different from those in the North. St. Louis lay on the trunk line from Houston north through Dallas–Fort Worth and then Oklahoma City. Many Chicago-bound migrants found St. Louis big enough and urban enough to plant their roots. For others it served as a way station where one could learn about wages, apartment living, and boisterous urban culture. But it was not an especially accommodating world because the cold and crowded ghettos reserved for migrant Negroes were hard reminders of slavery.

Arriving in a city like St. Louis, migrants sometimes abandoned their rural Baptist or Methodist religious traditions altogether. Big churches alienated newcomers, whose rural mannerisms and dress contrasted poorly with the citified black elite. Generally, the rural and urban churches were distinct not so much because they celebrated different rites or beliefs but really because they occupied different social and physical spaces. The small country chapel was closer to the "praise house" tradition, compared to the urban church with its cathedral architecture, upwardly mobile parishioners, and ecclesiastical hierarchy. Frequently, a church's success was measured by its real estate values and the contents of the Sunday collection box. Membership in a particular congregation was a typical indicator of social status. Elites attended Congregationalist and Episcopal or sometimes Catholic churches. If these churches were filled, a newcomer would need family connections or money to join. The urban church concentrated on expansion. Its class consciousness reflected roots in the mulatto elite of cities like Detroit, Chicago, Cleveland, and Pittsburgh. Darker migrants from the South stood less chance of being accepted into the flock and often felt unwelcome.

Emerging as they did from a traditional folk culture where the church helped resolve their domestic problems and contractual disputes, the migrants needed the benefits of similar institutions when they reached the city. They needed the matchmakers, marriage counselors, baby sitters, midwives, and herbalists and the practical services they had used in the rural congregations.

Although "some were overcome at first by the pageantry of the large churches . . . after a short experience with the city church" many experienced loneliness and failed to find status and appreciation. Preachers neither recognized their faces nor remembered their names. No one seemed concerned by a parishioner's absence, although sickness or death might be the cause. Domestic abuse, money problems, and alcoholism seemed trifling by comparison to the ecumenical affairs of the large denominations. "People crushes me a lot of time but I don't say anything I just go off and cry—just see how some people step on your feet, and crush you," said one migrant in describing northern church society.[5]

Of necessity, the migrants gathered on street corners to exchange news from home or simply gossip about the neighbors. Most of the news circulating from the South was bad. Drought occurred with increasing frequency so that many families had to leverage their farms to the land banks to cover mounting debts. The fortunes of cotton declined accordingly. Self-sufficiency became harder. The least crisis taxed the voluntary associations, insurance companies, sick funds, and burial societies beyond their modest capacities. Northern financiers continued to recruit workers for their burgeoning factories, draining the region of its skilled black laborers, inventors, and entrepreneurs. A multitude swelled forth from rural counties northward, then crashed hard into the pavement of urban poverty. This human spectacle was uproarious, sometimes enthusiastic yet equally oppressive and alienating. For some, modernization meant a cheerful acceptance of the new, while others simply longed for the comforts and familiarity of the past. Success was precarious, and tragedy struck randomly. The Great Migration was a "striking contrast in levels of civilization and economic well-being baffling any attempt to discover order and direction."[6]

In the tumult of St. Louis, Missouri, Walter Gregg's life changed forever when he met a slight, dark-skinned man who was attired impeccably in a starched collar, a striped bow tie, and a thick wool suit. A turban swathed his head. From a street corner soapbox, he stared directly into Walter's eyes. "Come change your name, get back your original language and religion, and you won't be a nigger anymore!"

This appealed to Walter's sense of invention and his taste for the occult. The curious young Texan moved closer. He listened intently and eyeballed the man himself. He heard arcane references to Africa, Asia, Mayan temples, Egyptian pyramids, Masonic lodges, and the House of al-Islam. The stranger described a world peopled by the ancient prophets, biblical pariahs, the prophet Muhammad and his Ethiopian companion, Bilal. He embellished his speech with an indistinguishable foreign accent, addressing each spectator as "Mr. Ham," referring to Noah's son, the alleged progenitor of the "burnished, accursed race." The sidewalk preacher castigated his audience for praying to Jesus, whom he characterized as "a man of sorrow." The rest of the world worships heroes, he declared. "Why do you bear the cross alone and let the world go free? Are those your children whom I see hanging on those trees? Maybe your god is asleep!"[7]

The recitation of biblical characters and exotic places mesmerized Walter. It stirred his passion for knowledge as none of the teachers at Prairie View ever had. The turbaned man was openly discussing "the Negro question," as Walter himself had done often, only in different terms. Why the sorrow and shame? Walter pressed closer, rubbing shoulders with the sidewalk onlookers.

The little man paused and turned his palms toward the sky. Closing his eyes, he took a deep breath and then exhaled a benediction in Arabic. "As Salaam Alaikum Wa Rahmatullahe Wa Barakathahu, Peace Be Upon You and the

Mercy of Allah and His Blessings!" Then he began to extemporize, making it apparent that he too was once a Negro until discovering his "African-Arab blood." Sheik Ahmad Din was his name, the title *sheik* meaning "man of great learning." He claimed to be the first man ever appointed as a Muslim sheik on American soil. In a few short years of work in St. Louis, he, Ahmad Din, born Paul Nathaniel Johnson, had already converted two hundred people to Islam and established four self-supporting missions.

Walter joined the small entourage following the sheik. As the group strolled along, they introduced themselves. Brother Hakim was Congolese and had studied for the ministry at Tuskeegee for five years. Upon hearing the sheik's oratory, he became disillusioned with Christianity and converted to Islam. Brother Omar owned a store called the Lamasery Shop where he sold imported religious garments, prayer rugs, roots, herbs, incense, and charms. Reaching a dilapidated apartment building, they entered through a side door and mounted a narrow stairway to the second floor. Once inside the small apartment, Omar invited Walter to remove his shoes before joining them on the carpeted floor.

Walter had entered a small community of men who despised the poisonous stereotypes that incited lynch mobs and race riots. Habituated to mud flats and tenements, they sought a better life with warmth and shelter for their children. Their women were stooped from cleaning too many floors, exhausted at the end of the day, and unable to fulfill their own domestic chores. Their conversation had been casual to this point, but the tone changed dramatically when talk turned to the Prophet Muhammad and his legendary accomplishments. The familiar refrains of suffering, piety, and martyrdom evaporated. Walter also began to feel liberated from the weighty, "churched" sorrow that characterized much of his own religious background. In the next few hours these men would familiarize him with the Islamic rituals of ablution and prayer. They would explain the motions of bodily prostration in Muslim prayer, how each *rak'at* symbolized submission to Allah and would absolve the worshiper of his or her sins. They would enumerate the Five Pillars of the Muslim faith: prayer, fasting, pilgrimage, alms, and recitation of the Holy Quran.

At half-past one o'clock, Brother Saddiq Din rose to his feet. Holding his hands parallel at the level of his ears, he began the adan, the traditional call to prayer. Sheik Ahmad Din reminded his congregation about Bilal, the "coal black" Ethiopian whose loyalty and enchanting voice endeared him to Muslims throughout the world. He was as the Prophet Muhammad's first *muezzin*, whose sacred duty it was to assemble the faithful. "Come to prayer! Come to success!" he chanted in Arabic. The brothers marched Walter to the cold water sink in the hallway and instructed him in performance of ritual ablutions. Hands, face, ears, nose, mouth, head, and feet, "Purify yourself before Allah," they indicated solemnly. Inside Sheik Din's little room that served as a mosque, a solitary prayer rug faced the eastern corner of the building. Seven men spread their own rugs behind the sheik, forming a single row from wall to wall. Behind them Osman and Omar introduced Walter into a second phalanx of five other men and gently guided him to his knees. As he glanced around the room, he noticed behind him a curtain separating the women, who had apparently entered from another door.

Walter was embarking on a pilgrimage that would transport him far beyond the trunk routes and whistle stops from Houston to St. Louis. The sheik invited Walter to accept Allah and his Messenger, the Prophet Muhammad. Practically convinced, Walter hesitated and begged leave to think it over.

A week later in the evening he came back. This time the sheik placed a Quran in his hands and showed him the first sura, al-Fatihah. Practicing late into the night, he studied the seven Arabic verses, trying to imitate the sheik's intonations. As dawn broke, he finally recited the lines perfectly. Physically weary from this night-long marathon yet spiritually invigorated, Walter took his kalima shahada before the entire group at next Friday prayers. "La ilaha ill Allah Muhammad-ar Rasool Allah" ("No God is there except one God, Muhammad is God's Prophet"), Wala Karam recited. His new name meant "Friend of Honor" and was soon Arabicized to Wali Akram.

Following the sheik's instructions, Wali Akram signed bayat to the Ahmadiyya Movement in Islam. By taking this pledge, he acknowledged the controversial beliefs that distinguish Ahmadiyya as a heterodox form of Islam. For this time and place, this particular creed was the sole source of Islamic knowledge available.

A year later Wali married Kareema, the former Hannah Dudley of Savannah, Georgia, a young woman whom he met at the prayer hall. Following the sheik's instructions, they registered for a civil marriage at City Hall and then celebrated a traditional Islamic ceremony (*nikka*), over which he officiated. Soon afterward, the young newlyweds opened a grocery store in St. Louis. Later in the same year, Wali's mother Leah left Texas with her three youngest sons and headed for St. Louis.

A drought and a terrible boll weevil invasion the previous summer had finally broken the Burleson County farmers. With the cotton crop totally ruined, East Texas now swarmed with wildcatters looking for oil in everyone's backyard. Surmising that the time was right, Leah sold her remaining property to the land bank and left to join her son in Missouri. Another reason for her sudden departure was her distress upon hearing that Walter had discarded his family name. Upon arriving in St. Louis, she made a show of adapting to his religious conversion but still called him Walter. She reasserted her Christian faith by joining the Scruggs Memorial Colored Methodist Episcopal Church and insisted that her remaining sons accompany her to services every Sunday.

When the Greggs arrived in St. Louis, Leah found an apartment for herself and the younger boys. With accommodations tight, however, Bert moved in with his older brother and sister-in-law. Wali went to work on Bert almost immediately. He brought him to the daily prayers and began teaching him the Arabic greeting. Sixteen-year-old Bert was impressed by the exotic appearance of the converts and fascinated by their very different names. Sheik Ahmad Din invited him to convert, additionally offering his matchmaking services for several marriageable young women in the fledgling Muslim community. Yet Bert viewed the Muslims as a social circle only, and although he wanted to leave his mother's orbit, the prospect of her reaction to a second Gregg brother changing his name proved to be an insurmountable deterrent. Despite Walter's most persuasive efforts, Bert preferred the cosmopolitan life at the Booker T. Theater where Josephine Baker was the marquee performer. He stayed in high school and eventually went on to become a prominent Methodist minister.

Wali continued studying the Quran, often leaving Kareema alone in the store while he read and prayed. Often he rose at 4 AM to make dawn prayer. Rather than returning to bed like many Muslims, he continued studying until dawn while Kareema brewed his morning coffee. Then he went to work stocking the shelves while Kareema did the books. After greeting the first customers of the day, Wali then left for the mosque around 10:30 AM. He would linger with Sheik Din and other men on the carpet after prayer. He devoured their discussions about religion, international affairs, and the racial problems in America. These talks usually ended with a collective resolve to use "the light of the East" to soften the heart of America. The elementary social lesson of the Quran was more than just marginally relevant to anyone who yearned for social and economic justice. It was probably the only hope for reforming the system. It said, "Allah will not change the condition of a people until they change themselves."

Within two years Wali Akram became the sheik's most accomplished student. His energetic devotion to Islam was rare in comparison with the way some other men came and went according to their mood. He became a trusted assistant to the sheik and helped him maintain a reputation as the most successful American missionary in the Ahmadiyya Movement. They purchased a small printing press and incorporated the Sheik Ahmad Publishing Company to printed handbills announcing the arrival of a new religion that would rescue the "Negro" from the doldrums.

But Wali Akram soon outgrew Sheik Ahmad Din's limited ability to fulfill his thirst for more knowledge in Islam. The next important Islamic influence in his life was Sheik Ashiq Ahmad, who seemed to know different things about Arabic and the Quran. He was another Ahmadiyya convert who traveled between Cincinnati and Dayton ministering to several dozen converts. During a visit to St. Louis he complained about the lack of dedicated, knowledgeable missionaries and invited Akram to join him in Ohio.

Reflecting on this offer, Wali Akram consulted Kareema and Sheik Ahmad Din, who agreed that it would be better to follow Ashiq Ahmad. They formulated an itinerary billed as a "crusade to spread Islam." They wrote letters and printed flyers, which they sent north from St. Louis to Terre Haute, Cincinnati, Dayton, Columbus, Akron, and Cleveland. They announced dates and scheduled meetings to coincide with their arrival.

Before leaving St. Louis, Wali compiled a list of prominent Garveyites and received a letter of introduction from the chief Ahmadiyya missionary in

Chicago, who entertained warm relations with the UNIA. The Garveyites were useful allies since they were firmly established in many cities and practiced religious tolerance in the name of racial unity. They maintained a quiet, working relationship with the Ahmadiyyas and sometimes rented their meeting halls to the missionaries for a nominal fee.

In October 1925 Wali Akram and Kareema departed St. Louis, leaving behind not only their family and friends but also a stable business. Yet they refused to look on their actions as a sacrifice. Spreading their new faith had now become a divinely guided mission. For the next two years, Wali and Kareema "ran the gamut," talking Islam to migrants with backgrounds similar to their own who had been enticed north by the myth of prosperity only to wind up jobless in cramped slums, losing hope rapidly in the face of segregation and escalating racism.

Akram became a serious and effective orator on the road. He adopted Sheik Ahmad Din's opening pitch but relinquished his phony accent. He sported a red fez and grew a full beard, which accentuated his high cheekbones and prominent forehead. His eyes were liquid and deep-set. Before speaking, he appeared lost in contemplation, then he steeled himself momentarily. Catching an onlooker's eye, he would proclaim:

> As Salaam Alaikum! Peace Be Unto You, Brothers and Sisters! Bisimillah ar Rahman ar Rahim! Blessed Be Our Lord, Allah, the Compassionate, the Merciful! Listen here! There is no such thing as a Negro race. Black people live all over the world but they are not branded as Negroes. Get back your religion and your original names. Your natural language is Arabic! Get back your religion, the religion of Islam, and stop being a Negro! Allah-u-Akbar! God is Great! Prayers are organized like clockwork in Islam. Five per day. Every day. Would you like to see? Follow me back to the prayer hall!

He never appealed for money publicly, although he clearly explained to those who signed the Ahmadiyya pledge that they were subject to a monthly tithe of fifty cents.

ORIGINS OF THE FIRST CLEVELAND MOSQUE   They spent three months studying the Quran in Dayton with Ashiq Ahmad. According to family lore, Akram committed a large part of the scriptures to memory in the tradition of a Muslim hafis. Working with Kareema and the Sheikh Ahmad, he systematically crossreferenced both testaments of the Bible with the Holy Quran. He studied volumes of Ahmadiyya literature. He diligently read copies of their annual English publication, *Review of Religions*, and absorbed the numerous tracts written by Ghulam Ahmad himself. Many of these booklets recounted Ghulam Ahmad's debates with Christian missionaries in India and often focused on the story of

Jesus, which had obsessed Ghulam Ahmad. According this interpretation, Jesus was indeed a prophet, but he neither died on the cross nor was resurrected. An end to such a divine mission would have been tantamount to disgrace, according to Ghulam Ahmad.

The apocryphal life of Jesus in India, dying at the age of 136, proved a useful tool for proselytizing. Ahmadiyya missionaries circulated endless diatribes against Christianity and struggled for converts one by one. Mufti Muhammad Saddiq set the tone with a relentless attack. He claimed that Christian profiteers ran the slave trade. They made blacks forget the religion and language of their forefathers, Islam and Arabic. Christianity was unable to bring real brotherhood to the nations. "So now, leave it alone. And join Islam, the real faith of Universal Brotherhood which at once does away with all distinctions of race, color and creed."

In 1927, Wali and Kareema arrived in Cleveland where they rented an apartment on Woodland Avenue in the East Fifties, a neighborhood that was in rapid decline as Cleveland's blacks moved from their original homes downtown to apartments vacated by upwardly mobile Italians and Jews. Although racial segregation came to Cleveland later than Chicago or St. Louis, Cleveland's black ghetto was fully consolidated by 1920. Skilled and semiskilled southern blacks began arriving en masse during the Great Migration when jobs and housing were plentiful. After the war, however, residential segregation forced the next wave of migrants into deteriorating apartments and neighborhoods. Often they lacked normal public services like gas, electricity, and even water. On the one hand, this dynamic pushed members of the vestigial mulatto class into proximity with the southern newcomers, sparking tensions here and there. On the other hand, class and caste differences were becoming less significant. Jim Crow laws applied to all persons of color, although those with very light skin could still pass.

Amalgamating southern folk religion with spiritual holiness traditions, the storefront cults were an opportunity to cultivate a taste for Islam. Akram spent most days along Central Avenue between East Fortieth and East Fifty-fifth, collaring passersby to "learn the religion of your ancestors, Islam!" Some days, he could convince a few men to follow him to the makeshift prayer hall in the UNIA hall, the same house where John D. Rockefeller had been born on Euclid Avenue. Satisfied after a few months of mission work and expecting even greater developments, Wali Akram wrote letters to his Ahmadiyya colleagues reporting his gains and asking for their help.

He met a Muslim convert named Abdul Shakur, who was black but claimed Yemenite ancestry. He recounted a story about the difficult time he had changing his name legally. Shakur's daughter, Hameeda, recalled that her father "got his name advertised in the legal news column of the paper. That was the start. Then other Muslims went down to try to get their name changed because some of them knew about their ancestors too."[8]

Shakur introduced Akram into a circle of loosely affiliated Muslims who gathered socially at Mustafa's Delicatessen at 5211 Woodland Avenue. This small Islamic community included Turkish and Syrian Muslim immigrants who conducted their Friday prayers in the privacy of their homes. As the Association of the Islamic Union of Cleveland, they had banded together in 1918 to foster solidarity. Accustomed to the curiosity of African-American converts, they invited Akram to join their group for prayers. This was his first exposure to Sunni orthodoxy Islam.

Another sympathetic neighbor on Cleveland's East Side included James Shurney, a follower of Prophet Cherry's Church of God. Born in Georgia, he had arrived in 1896 in Cleveland where he became involved with the Hebrew-Israelite tradition. Shurney called himself a rabbi, spoke some Yiddish, and tried to raise his children according to Jewish law. He and Akram developed a lasting friendship and honored each other's religions with reciprocal observances and celebrations. Islamic and Jewish holidays were occasions for scriptural readings and discussions in each other's homes. Shurney's young son, Judah, learned the Old Testament from his father and the Quran next door where he played with the Akram children. Eventually he chose Islam.

Sinking roots into Cleveland's East Side, Akram continued to promote the Ahmadiyya teachings and worked hard to gain new converts. As membership grew to about 150 families, he sought advice from another sheik, Nasir Ahmad, who was one of the principal founders of the First Pittsburgh mosque. In 1932 Akram persuaded him to move to Cleveland where he was immediately elected to become the first imam of Cleveland's Ahmadiyyas.

Akram's participation in the founding of Cleveland's Ahmadiyya Mosque began inauspiciously. As a dedicated believer in Ahmadiyya doctrines, he supported the missionary model set in motion by Mufti Mohammed Saddiq, the movement's first emissary to the United States. As a member of the second generation of indigenous "sheiks," Akram rapidly earned a reputation as a valued deputy to the "mother" mission in Chicago. But the emphasis on the central authority of a supreme religious leader, who resided in India and barely understood the local conditions, eventually disrupted Akram's relationship to the missionaries and undermined his belief in the Ahmadiyya creed. His resentment of foreign meddling led directly to the creation of the First Cleveland Mosque as an autonomous place of Muslim worship, the first truly independent Sunni community in the country. Central to this development was the growing realization that Ahmadiyya practices were incompatible with indigenous interests.

Breaking with the missionaries would not be easy because of their strong attachment to the indigenous community. Muhammad Yusuf Khan, the Ahmadiyya missionary who replaced Mohammed Saddiq, heard about Akram's growing congregation and promptly relocated from Chicago to Cleveland. Once there he persuaded the Muslim converts to purchase an automobile for him, pay his rent, and underwrite frequent trips "in the cause of Islam."

"The community bought him a big, black Chrysler with yellow wheels," recalled Wali's son Rasool nearly sixty years later. With a shudder of childhood horror, he mentioned that "I was in the tree one day and that car came and ran over my tricycle." Pausing a moment, he reflected, "The Ahmadiyya missionaries all came here poor but not to make money as such. They just didn't realize what a money tree America was until they got here, and you see, the dark Americans worshiped them."[9]

Preparing a visit to India, Khan transferred the title of his car to another Indian, "Professor" Ashraf, a stranger he designated to lead the indigenous Muslims in his absence. As soon as Khan departed, Ashraf recalled the Ahmadiyya identification cards, asking each member to pay an additional thirty-five cents for a new Ahmadiyya stamp and official gold seal. Prodded by Akram to justify this expense, Ashraf announced publicly that the Ahmadiyyas needed Americans to furnish them with intelligence information because "a big war" was coming. They needed to be photographed and fingerprinted and to have their names legalized, all for a whopping fee of fifteen dollars each. Already suspicious of the professor's motives, Akram smelled real mischief when he proposed to teach Urdu instead of Arabic. Yet, despite Akram's misgivings, the others grudgingly submitted to this chicanery and handed over almost seven hundred dollars to Ashraf. To their dismay, he promptly left town and returned to India.

Ignoring the havoc created in the wake of his own departure, Khan angered the community further in a letter several months later. "As soon as I receive my passage from you, I shall come back," he wrote. When no answer came, he sent Wali Akram another letter, asking presumptuously, "Where is the money for my return trip? I am ready to come in January, therefore please hurry up and arrange for my fare."[10]

This hectoring was more than Akram was willing to tolerate. He called for a meeting at the mosque, where a consensus arose to seize the property left behind by Ashraf and Khan. Seething with indignation, Akram fired off letters of complaint to the Ahmadiyya khalifa, Mahmud Ahmad, and his foreign secretary, the former missionary to America, Mufti Muhammad Saddiq. "It is with deepest of regret," he wrote,

> that I am compelled to reply . . . concerning Dr. M. Y. Khan. . . . I have great respect for him, and I love him, but according to the teachings of the Holy Quran, his conduct for the past few years has been all but commendable. I acknowledge that there have been hundreds of converts to Islam by Dr. Khan in Illinois, Indiana, Michigan, Missouri, Pennsylvania and Ohio, U.S.A., but owing to the Misinformation of the propagation of Islam by him, the numbers have waned to practically nothing. During this time some of the people went hungry and were evicted from their houses and suffered many other losses."[11]

The khalifa responded by dispatching "Sufi" M. R. Bengalee to Chicago. The new missionary arrived in Chicago in late 1934 with money on his mind also. He immediately contacted all the Ahmadiyya communities about their unpaid dues, the *Sunrise* subscription fees, and his own travel expenses. All this needed to be collected at once, he admonished, adding flippantly, "If you send it in small sums, I may spend it."[12]

In contrast with Khan, however, Sufi Bengalee proved more serious about religious practice. He explained the proper ritual for celebrating the major 'id festival marking the end of Ramadan and also furnished detailed instructions for ritual ablution (wudzu), what clothes to wear, and how and when to pray. He explained both the similarity and the pronounced difference between normal Friday prayers and the 'id prayer following Ramadan (there being no call to prayer for the latter). Once the prayers were finished, then everyone should exchange gifts and feast merrily. The issue of money cropped up again in his interpretation of zakat, which is traditionally collected and distributed prior to the 'id festival. "The money could be distributed among the poor Moslems of your local community or it could be collected and sent to Qadian [India] for distribution," he added without any sense of irony about the economic plight of his subjects. On another occasion he had insisted that they send expensive cablegrams to confirm that they had dutifully celebrated the *maulid al-nabi* (birthday of the Prophet Muhammad). His tutelage resembled the practices of missionaries during the apex of colonialism. He demanded weekly reports on the activities of the converts and chastised them for seizing Khan's property.[13]

Wali Akram quietly resisted Bengalee's initiatives. He didn't wish to admit publicly what he confided at home to Kareema. He believed that the Ahmadiyya missionaries were exploiting their American converts by taking what little money they had in the name of Islam and giving them back a desultory religious education whose elements frequently contradicted the teachings of the Quran itself. Affiliation with the movement had become intolerable when even local decisions were subject to official approval. There was a relationship of artificial dependency that undermined many converts' self-confidence and caused many to turn a deaf ear to the Message. Of those who remained, many believed that only someone "from the East" could authenticate their new faith. Worried about the consequences of a public denunciation of the missionary, Akram simply refused to send money to Chicago, arguing instead that Islam approved of distributing charity directly to needy members of the community. He further decided to structure his own religious curriculum by printing Arabic grammar workbooks supplied by Cleveland's immigrant Muslims. Fearing that Dr. Khan might return to join forces with Bengalee in suppressing the community's autonomy, he preemptively denounced Khan's seditious behavior to federal immigration authorities. "There is no doubt," he petitioned, "a true Muslim prays to God for guidance, but at the same time Islam teaches one that he must obey the laws of the government where he resides."[14]

The missionaries' scandalous activities forced Akram to consider the political consequences of Islamic conversion, especially their implications for issues of African-American citizenship. Since the Constitution guarantees freedom and privacy of religion to all citizens, one might expect Muslim converts to enjoy complete protection. But history showed that the actual rights of African Americans differ from their legal status as citizens. Therefore, to avow Islam, especially as an alternative to the semiofficial religion of Christianity, was a very public action likely to expose the convert to intense public scrutiny, the arena of religious belief being a kind of litmus test for good citizenship. On the one hand, "dark Americans" needed to walk a straight and narrow path to protect their citizenship, meaning that eccentricities manifest in the religious dimension of their lives could be provocative. A Muslim, on the other hand, conceives his or her identity primarily in terms of the umma or brotherhood of believers. This perspective demands a believer's unconditional allegiance to Islamic tradition, its culture and concomitant political interests. Loyalty to a non-Islamic nation or state might be regarded as secondary at best. As an astute observer of history and current affairs, Akram feared that for an African American to outwardly profess Islam was analogous to joining the Communist Party because it immediately raised suspicions about one's allegiance to the flag. Changing one's name to conform with Arabic names from the Quran, although an appropriate measure of sincerity to Islam, was all the more provocative if it done legally in a court of law.

In theory, the Ahmadiyya Movement offered a partial solution to this dilemma by pledging followers to remain loyal citizens of their native governments, Muslim or not. This meant not opposing the rule of any legitimate government that promoted freedom of worship.[15] As far as its application to colonial India was concerned, this benefited the Ahmadiyyas who certainly needed protection from Hindus, Christians, and even the British. In the United States, however, communal religious identity was limited to three general categories—Catholic, Protestant, and Jew. To integrate Islam into this formula was a different matter from the way various evangelical and millenarian movements were rationalized and often absorbed into an all-purpose Christianity.[16]

While promulgating loyalty to the secular nation-state, the Ahmadiyyas also demanded bayat to their khalifa, who resided in India. How then could the struggle for equal rights square with nominal submission to the whims of foreigners who considered themselves above or beyond the same set of laws? Akram inferred that submitting to Ahmadiyya authority meant stepping beyond even the kind of political separatism advocated by Marcus Garvey. It forced his Muslims into an uncomfortable position. As a minority battling for equal rights, how could they afford to be perceived as willing to forfeit their citizenship to the representatives of a foreign organization?

The schism between the converts and the missionaries had widened into a gulf by the latter half of 1936, when Sufi Bengalee demanded more money for travel to India. He pressured Ahmadiyya stalwarts in Pittsburgh and Chicago while urging the Clevelanders to pay their arrears. The whole structure of Ahmadiyya authority was based on this material sign of loyalty. Any breach of unity was tantamount to blasphemy against Allah, he warned.

Rumors now began to circulate about the missionaries' racial hypocrisy.

Sufi Bengalee, it was alleged, did little to change the Jim Crow system of double standards. It became known that he organized Sufi rites for white people but kept African Americans segregated in their mosque. Those who questioned his practices were told that black people weren't ready for Sufism, an affront that prompted one antimissionary partisan to retort, "I'd rather be a friend of the white man than be a friend of yours. . . . You have nothing to offer me, not even the Arabic language because all you know is Urdu. You don't even know Arabic, just enough Arabic to read the Quran and that's it!"[17]

At jum'a prayer one day in 1936, Akram declared independence from the Ahmadiyya Movement in Islam. In dramatic fashion, he reported a dream where he saw "the truth being trampled upon." Citing passages from the Quran that oblige Muslims to elect leaders from their own ranks, he declared that Cleveland needed a local leader "from amongst ourselves."[18] When word of this revolt leaked back to Chicago and eventually to Ahmadiyya headquarters in India, Akram was accused of violating "the sacred laws of Islam," although it really meant Ahmadiyya doctrine. "A local Imam," warned the khalifa's aide, "is not elected by the people but he is appointed by the khalifa of the time."[19]

Bengalee tried to quell this insurrection by isolating Wali Akram. He rushed to Cleveland and found him at the mosque giving Arabic lessons. The congregation gave him an icy reception and ridiculed his outrageous demands for money. They bitterly recalled Dr. Khan's perfidy and asserted their right to collect and redistribute the poor-rate (zakat) locally. Shaken by his hostile reception, Bengalee shouted that the mosque was incorporated by Ahmadiyyas and ordered those who were not loyal Ahmadiyyas to leave. According to one eyewitness, "practically the whole place stood up and left."[20]

All but a small rump faction remained in the mosque. Sufi Bengalee appointed a new imam and reminded them of the obligation to send their tithe to the "mother" mosque in Chicago. This time he set the amount at two dollars per month with a promise that the money would be used to finance the dispatch of "one hundred new missionaries for the United States." He ordered his followers to find space for their new mosque and to remove the electric sign with its red-lettered "Ahmadiyya Mosque" from over the door at 5311 Woodland Avenue. Then he left town quickly, vowing that he did not want to remain where the Moslems [sic] engaged in behavior insulting to him and his wife. Actually he intended to evict Akram and the other rebels from the Woodland Avenue mosque, but with tempers at fever pitch, he thought it better to wait until he was safely out of town. When Abu Salaam, the new imam, and his faction were unable to come up with the rent to secure a new mosque, they threatened to have Akram arrested if he tried to use the Ahmadiyya trademark anywhere else in town. "Those were heartfelt, sad days," recalled Abdul Shakur's daughter. "So many of my close friends were told not to associate with me, but my parents told them that once you said the kalima shahada, you were always sisters and brothers in Islam."[21]

The split was pregnant with implications about the role that the indigenous leadership might play next in reaction to interference by foreign missionaries. Soon afterward a similar rebellion erupted in Pittsburgh, where Nasir Ahmad and Saeed Akmal broke with the Ahmadiyyas. Exasperated by the incessant goading of the peripatetic Indian missionaries, they incorporated the First Muslim Mosque and the nearby Braddock Mosque. They supported the First Cleveland Mosque and defended Akram against charges of embezzlement, calling him "one of the few sincere Muslim leaders left in America."22 Saleem Abdul Wahab of the First Muslim Mosque invited Akram to join a general effort to unite all African-American Muslims. Akmal hinted at an alternative tactic to counter Bengalee and suggested that Akram attend a confidential meeting on this issue in Braddock, Pennsylvania. "You will note," wrote Akmal, "that our organization is Ahmadiyya but of the Lahore section, and we have acting as our missionary, an American born Moslem."23

But Akram already knew about the Lahoris, who seemed keenly aware of the problems between indigenous converts and the khalifa's missionaries from Qadian. The message from Lahore seemed uncomplicated and direct in its appeal: Unite among yourselves, oppose the "Qadianis," as the Ahmadiyyas were known, and do not let other Americans sign their bayat forms. They just spend your money for their own gratification in what amounts to a form of larceny in religious garb. Sufi Bengalee was maligned as the khalifa's "viceregent for the U.S.A." and a "slave master."24

Fearing any new foreign ties, however, Akram turned against the Ahmadiyya doctrine altogether. He asserted that Ahmadiyya insistence on the divinity of their founder was at odds with traditional Islamic doctrine. Muhammad was Allah's last messenger and the final prophet. The Ahmadiyya Movement bordered on disbelief and should be shunned by true Muslims.

Technically speaking, the only subordination in Islam meant *submission to the will of Allah* without tolerance for those who interfere. Accordingly, Akram did not respond to either the Lahoris or to Saeed Akmal's entreaties but resolved instead to stop thinking of the First Cleveland Mosque as a mission attached to any movement other than the singular one undertaken by the Prophet Muhammad in Medina. It meant establishing salat in a permanent space and providing Cleveland's Muslims with a stable environment in which they might continue to learn the Quran and practice the Five Pillars. It meant salvaging the converts who had become upset or confused by the missionaries and their unorthodox teachings. On a personal level, it required genuine leadership to demonstrate the tangible benefits of practicing Islam. Having lost his taste for subordination, Akram so became one of the first indigenous converts to break definitively with outsiders. "The immigrant Muslims left their robes at Ellis Island, and we dark Americans followed behind and put them on," he observed later. "I hated to see them pandering to all the foreign Muslims waiting to take over the movement."

The dissidents rented a new space at 7605 Woodland Avenue and called it the First Cleveland Mosque. Regular Friday prayers were conducted each week with Sunday school lessons in "Beginner's Prayer," "Intermediate Prayer," and

"Quranic History." This pedagogy reflected the basic elements of Islamic practice such as interpretation of the Quran (tafsir) and proselytization (dawa) Arabic language, as well as the obligatory aspects of ritual purification (wudzu) and prayer (farz). When not busy running the family grocery store or tending to their children, Kareema Akram assisted him in mosque affairs. Both husband and wife had attained enough proficiency in Arabic to teach it along with Quranic recitation. Since Islamic etiquette meant respecting a modest separation between the sexes, Kareema conducted classes right in her kitchen, where women might bring their babies and young children.

Akram applied his technical knowledge to the service of Islamic dawa. He salvaged an old printing press and began publishing new workbooks, prayer guides, religious histories, organizational pamphlets, and other texts. One of his dawa pamphlets announced: "Abolish Negro-ism! Nationality worries disappear! Learn the Arabic language, the language of your ancestors, which is in daily used by more than one third of the world's population."

In four-column, eight-point type he explained the relevance of Arabic to the scriptural, cultural and historical heritage of dark Americans. In another handbill he listed seven reasons "why you should learn the Arabic language," concluding that

> the obstacles confronting dark Americans are not their complexion . . .
> but within themselves. There is a lack of understanding of philosophy
> and civilization. The dark American is hypnotized with European philoso-
> phy and psychology and has forgotten all about himself. When one is hyp-
> notized his mentality becomes subjected to the hypnotist and everything
> he does is for the one who has the power to hypnotize.[25]

Akram redoubled his efforts to recruit students from all over Cleveland's burgeoning eastside ghetto. Patrolling the main avenues from Woodland to Euclid along a decaying stretch from East Fifty-fifth to East 105th Street, Akram would listen compassionately to the details of every personal or family tragedy. He brought people home to Kareema; there their spiritual issues and religious beliefs could be serenely explored. Visitors got coffee, something to eat, and a sympathetic ear while children darted around the house and raised havoc. When the noise level and confusion surpassed Kareema's capacity for traffic management and his own threshold of tolerance, Wali's temper would erupt and he would chase them out of sight.

A displaced laborer or down-and-out stranger could easily sense in this typical American household the simple comforts and family shenanigans that were missing from his own restless life. Sayeeda Dillard came to Islam and the First Cleveland Mosque after years of turmoil and confusion about her own social and religious identity. Born and educated in Jamaica, she disdained the Anglican Church for its hypocritical racial policies. Her maternal grandmother was a white Jewish woman who bequeathed to her a fair complexion that would have allowed her to "pass" at any time in her life. Once, when she was still a girl, she wanted to convert to Roman Catholicism, but her mother angrily forbid it. She escaped by immigrating to the United States yet felt lost and confused by similar racial and religious hypocrisy. Eventually she found her way to Kareema Akram's kitchen and soon took her kalima shahada. She spent long mornings with Sister Kareema. "Those were the quiet hours in the Akram home," she recalled.

> The children were in school or helping at the store. The imam was either working or busy with something at the mosque. I was very grateful for the love and warmth I found there. They took me in when I was confused. The imam and Kareema especially were always ready to help. Whenever my family sent me that delicious Blue Mountain coffee from home, I gave it to Kareema because I knew she loved coffee.

Akram usually avoided polarizing discussions around racial matters. He preferred to steer discussions toward higher spiritual considerations. Cautioning against resentment or self-remorse, he regaled his guests with idealistic descriptions of Islamic civilization where justice accorded with the laws of the Holy Quran. No Western society, he argued, could claim to adhere so closely to the scriptures in administering justice and ensuring material sustenance, if not total equality. In Islam there was equality of all humankind before Allah. Some could be more powerful, more prolific, or wealthier; a woman more beautiful or talented; but all were humbled by the Prophet Muhammad, who was the most extraordinary human ever to walk the planet. His divinely guided life, recounted to all Muslims in the Traditions, served as an inspiration to follow for life. Brotherhood and unity were indeed possible under Islam. Gone were the apocryphal Ahmadiyya stories about Jesus and Ghulam Ahmad, the so-called promised messiah. Akram expounded only the Holy Quran now. It was not simply one among many existing or possible scriptures but the definitive and modern sequel to all previous religious traditions, written or oral. "The Final Testament," as some referred to it, was neither a religious symbol of despair like the martyrdom of Jesus nor a political chimera like Marcus Garvey's UNIA. A Muslim need not be resigned to the fatalism that chained many Christians to poverty. He could achieve prosperity and salvation in the here and now.

Under Imam Wali Akram the First Cleveland Mosque emphasized orthodox Islamic principles as the best route to achieve peace of mind and material stability of his congregation. Promoting social and economic responsibility through discipline and the exercise of authority, he wrote,

> the imam of the mosque is in charge of everyone, chairman of chairmen. He is a father of the people, and the imam's wife is the mother of the people. The Mosque is a family, and the imam is at the head of that family. He must at all times hear complaints of his children, be able to advise them,

aid them, and give them courage in times of darkness, and strengthen them in the time of weakness, he must share their joys and sorrows. This, and much more is the responsibility of the imam. He has no personal interests to serve. There is only one obligation upon him and that is the deliverance of the Message of Islam.[26]

To ensure the economic goals of the mosque, the imam was also the chief administrator who "should be inspired and possess in a limited form the spirit and power of the Holy Prophet, to reestablish Islam wherever possible in its true and original form, and therefore, he must be followed by a line of successors just in the form and spirit of the early Muslims."[27]

Accordingly, nearly everyone in the congregation assumed responsibility for running some committee or program. The offices were given Arabic names and linked to the ideal of democratic committees (al-majlis). Many positions and titles were redundant, but total participation was a way to maintain interest in the mosque and build character. Community service work supported any project that coincided with Islamic ideals, although it was to be tempered by a constant spiritualizing of the mosque in order to avoid secularizing tendencies. Partly Bookerite pedagogue and partly Garveyite militant, Akram cemented the First Cleveland Mosque to a modern evangelical foundation. Inventor that he was, he never hesitated once when it came to recruiting methods as long they might be effective in promoting Islam. He even devoured literature from the Watchtower Society, whose methods were highly successful among ghetto dwellers.

Incorporating the mosque as a physical and social entity was a matter of skill and experience dependent entirely on faith. But finances were beyond Akram's resourcefulness. Burdened like their neighbors by interminable periods of unemployment, the Akram family made ends meet and then stretched them further. As more people joined the mosque, Wali Akram expanded the family grocery store. He butchered livestock according to Islamic ritual to provide *halal* products to the growing Muslim community but could never concentrate exclusively on business. A troubled neighbor might stop by or a worshiper might linger after prayer. Akram would study, then brainstorm and write a pamphlet or answer his mail, which was beginning to come from interested Muslims all over the country. The family business survived, thanks to Kareema and the older children. As soon as Mahmud and Rasool were old enough, they began to help out at the store or in one of the mosque youth committees. The other children saw their father infrequently, unless it was at the mosque.

Back in his workshop Wali Akram pursued new inventions. He registered at least two dozen patents and solicited the nearby automobile and heavy manufacturing industries with devices and ideas. "I had an idea to manufacture economical housing materials for the downtrodden people. I thought that the government would contribute, but they didn't care. The manufacturers will defeat a colored man with a patent unless he has someone powerful behind him," he observed. Periodically disheartened by these setbacks, he returned to Islam and the business of running a mosque. He made rubber printing blocks by hand for the first Islamic calendar published in the United States. At one point he even tried to fashion an Arabic typewriter. He shuttled from the workbench to a small, closetlike study to study the Quran or type pamphlets and sermons. Next he might set type for his Arabic lessons or his catechism of "African and Islamic History." Kareema brewed hot coffee by the gallon to keep him going. He never spent a day unproductively.

Other stalwart Muslims at First Cleveland were Fazl Kareem, Abdu Salaam (who eventually quit the Ahmadiyyas), Muhammad Ali, Abdul Malik, Saleem Yahya, Ghams Raziz, Abdul Majeed, and Abdul Hafeez. Some were on welfare. Their sons were being drafted into the army as the country prepared for war. Their hardships had a way of making the mosque a trial of will, a crisis that was explicit in Wali Akram's assertion of a link between religion, the mosque, and finances. If Islam was the Message, then its physical manifestation in the mosque signified new creative potential. "The whole question [of money] is up for review in every relationship of life. How should men make their money?" he asked. "What is the basic purpose of money in our social order? How do men lose their money? What is the social result of periods of prosperity and periods of depression? What relationship is there between giving and the general prosperity of the people?"

Islamic prayer (salat) remained the pivotal doctrine of the First Cleveland Mosque, reinforcing its difference from all other contemporary faiths. As ritual practice, it signified a radical departure from the wooden pews and the holy altar of Catholic and Protestant churches by eliminating all furniture. It silenced the ubiquitous organs, choirs, and "shouts" and replaced the seemingly chaotic swirl of fancy clothes and outstretched, swaying hands with modest attire and a rigorous program of obligatory exercises, known as *farz*.

Akram explained the distinction between salat and iqamah, the former being an act of supplication, the latter signifying the consistency and discipline with which that act is performed, corresponding roughly to the difference between form and process. "Hence it is not the mere observance of the form [salat] that is required but the keeping up of it in a right state [iqamah], i.e., being true to the spirit of it."[28] In light of his position as an indigenous leader ministering to other converts, it is significant that he also taught that an intellectual understanding of wudzu and salat was less important than actually practicing the rite.

Even if you don't know what you are doing, you are receiving blessings for carrying out the farz. Awareness of the positions brings about an understanding. The five compulsory prayers wipe out the sins. And this is especially important in the middle of the day at the height of human activity, which explains why Allah commands particular attention to the middle prayer.

Inasmuch as the First Cleveland Mosque went further in conforming to orthodox Islamic practice than any group of organized Muslim converts at the time, it symbolized the insertion of a handful of Americans into the worldwide body of Muslim worshipers (umma). Prayer at the First Cleveland Mosque was redolent with a sense of power in its guise as spatial and temporal recapitulation of Islamic geography and history. The little mosque was a fledgling outpost of the dar al-Islam, duplicating the familiar rows of worshipers genuflecting and pressing their heads onto a soft carpet.

"We are probably the only masjid in North America that's never missed a jum'a prayer in over fifty years. There's always been someone there. If one can't do it, someone else does it. But it goes on," said Ethmet Hussain, a second-generation Cleveland Muslim. He also defends Wali Akram's struggle to liberate the converts from the missionaries' grip.

> Many times our black brothers and sisters here in America felt that a black man could not teach them Islam. That he had to be from Pakistan or India or the Sudan, anywhere but America. And this self-hate was taught to black people, a very broad doubtfulness about their ability to do things. El-Hajj Wali Akram overcame this. He learned to read and write Arabic. He learned how to interpret and teach the Quran. Many of our brethren would come down and follow him in prayer, sit there and have dinner with the brother, but then get up and go out, and follow the first Indian that would come to town . . . And you know he fought a long, hard battle to keep our mission there at First Cleveland open. And he taught me that there is no foreign Muslim that would ever, ever come to the First Cleveland Mosque and go through our schools, and partake of our programs, and have jum'a prayer with us, that would stand up there and say, "this ain't Islam." Our people that have been taught at the First Cleveland Mosque can go worldwide anywhere, make salat and partake of any Muslim activity, and people know that they have a good well-founded background in Islam.[29]

THE MUSLIM TEN YEAR PLAN   In 1935 Wali Akram dreamed that his people were marooned in the midst of a terrible flood. A large flashlight played on certain faces. There was no food or drink, but the government was handing out money. There was a bridge to escape this catastrophe. It represented Islam and induced him to create the Muslim Ten Year Plan as proof of his belief that the principal obstacle to economic success was the absence of faith, something remedied by the Quran, which also contained a viable economic plan. Akram's dream was that of a social contract intended to break the bonds of economic dependency just as the American Muslims had broken their dependency on foreign missionaries.

Rather than encouraging their followers to worship independently, the missionaries had fostered alienation and feelings of inferiority. They claimed that the Americans did not know enough Islam and threatened that Allah would be angry if they did not perform their rituals properly. But when it came to learning Arabic and the Quran, the Ahmadiyyas proved inadequate to the task. They left their converts with little to show save "broken hearts" for all the domestic problems that conversion and name changing had created. "They [converts] found no difference between Islam and Christianity other than the name," jeopardizing the reputation of Islam without offering some tangible demonstration of material progress, which was the only way the Muslims could find redemption in their rejection of Christianity. The Muslim Ten Year Plan attempted to rectify these errors by promoting the spirit of change among those who had traded their dependency on Christianity for a heterodox version of Islam that left them feeling equally inferior.

The plan was a logical outcome of the desire to overcome collective fear of the unknown and untried. Religion, as opposed to politics, summoned the impossible into existence. Much importance was attached to practicing Islamic rituals and vocalizing the Quran—something the embarrassed converts had dared not attempt under the scrutiny of foreign Muslims. As they assembled themselves at the First Cleveland Mosque, studied their lessons, and prayed, the idea of cooperative buying arose, as well as sharing one another's homes. "These were experiences which had been read but never before demonstrated," Akram observed.

After several meetings, three key members of the mosque—Fazl Kareem, Abdullah Hikmat, and Moreed Kamal subscribed to the idea. They drafted a charter that would provide the Muslim community with an educational program, a burial fund, and a benevolent fund for the sick and infirm. "Our plan is to present the true doctrine of Islam to our fellow man and secure for its members the sole necessities of life here as well as in the Hereafter." It contained the seeds of a progressive social movement as a reflection of the social forces that would fuel Civil Rights through the prism of Islam. The Holy Quran promised this kind of general advancement to those who follow its words. It even contained a written guarantee: "Whenever We cause a thing to be abrogated or forgotten, We send something like it or better."

Many "storefront" religious sects already operated as quasi-financial institutions, collecting and redistributing money and services to the inner-city poor. Sometimes disgruntled members alleged fraud and embezzlement, and during the Great Depression, especially, these activities were regarded as potentially subversive and members risked surveillance and harassment by local police and the FBI.[30] In such an unpropitious climate, the Muslim community became fearful when Akram was summoned to depose his mosque's records at City Hall in 1935.[31] It reminded some of Professor Ashraf's intimations of foreign espionage and the government's grim perception of "Black Muslim" activities. Such incidents led to serious questions about the double minority status of African-

American Muslims. Although some self-help institutions were traditionally run like lodges or secret societies with layers of oaths and codes pertaining to membership and secrecy, this was not possible in Islam, where secrecy is forbidden.[32] As a leader trying to protect his flock, Wali Akram had to think about the terms that would shield his plan from outside interference.

He reflected on this problem with a maturing sense of history and the sober realization that membership in the worldwide Muslim umma was no guarantee of support if trouble should arise. Their reality was that of a handful of obscure American converts, who until recently had been involved with the heretical beliefs of the Ahmadiyya sect, themselves pariahs in the Islamic world. Beyond a tiny circle of Muslim cognoscenti, their existence was practically unknown. Now, tough immigration laws were making it difficult for any foreigners to proselytize in America. Soviet communism cast a long shadow on any unconventional black organizations in the United States, even though Islam was completely antithetical to communism. Making a virtue of necessity, Akram inserted an apolitical pledge into the identification card and passbook issued to every member of the plan.[33] He declared that "we do not minimize the importance of political struggles, but as a body we keep aloof from them, so that we may be able to concentrate all our attention on the great religious object we have in view."[34]

He tirelessly promoted the Plan in Cleveland. Elsewhere he tried to revive the old network of indigenous sheiks. Voicing forgiveness and reconciliation toward those who had supported the missionaries, he analyzed what went wrong on the human level rather than disdaining their misleading doctrines. "They did their very best in instructing [us] as to the teaching of Islam. But they were unaware of the conditions that had existed before their arrival in America, as well as the conditions of those who had accepted Islam under their supervision." Once they left the scene, the movement struggled because "the Muslims were left alone to try to uphold and carry on in Islam as best they knew how."

It was not an any easy problem to fix because "most of the literature was in Arabic, of which no one could translate, and the most important of this literature was the Quran." Akram saw himself being chosen by his peers to develop the Plan because they trusted him and because he was a very proficient craftsman with an honest reputation of delivering what was asked of him. Consequently "the insignificant group" of Muslims in Cleveland "appointed one from among [themselves] whom they thought best fitted to try to carry on the work according to his ability."

To advertise this new Muslim enterprise, the old printing press clanked incessantly. Pamphlets challenged new recruits to honor Quranic principles and thereby lift themselves out of poverty. In dealing with individuals who feared Islam because of its supposed alien or seditious connotations, Akram confidently explained that there was nothing in "this Book of Allah's words" that could create trouble in their lives.

We have not revealed this Book so that you may get into any sort of harm, material or spiritual; but, on the other hand, it is sent as a guidance to those who fear the path of ruin and destruction and seek the right path. It is the word of Him Who created the earth as well as the high heavens. (Quran 20:3-7)

Some proselytizers might berate potential followers for being too timid. Akram, on the other hand, emphasized the divine control of everyday life. No one could get into trouble by following Allah; their words would remain pure because their language (Arabic) was blessed. He stopped short of making any claim for the Plan itself as divine revelation, however.

Ethmet Hussain, whose father was a charter member of the Plan, is now a tall, handsome man in his sixties. He dresses conservatively but wears a red fez at the mosque. He lives in a tidy ranch house located in suburban Bedford Heights, Ohio, where he has worked for many years at the Ford plant. His wife is a decorated officer on the Cleveland police force who conducts community relations and antinarcotics programs in her spare time. Although she is not Muslim, their children are being educated in Arabic and the Quran. Ethmet has older children from a previous marriage who were also raised Muslim. He fought in Vietnam. A lifelong member of the Muslim Ten Year Plan, he described how it worked and what it taught him, but he turned somewhat melancholy in acknowledging that ultimately the Plan had failed to achieve its goals. He emphatically denied that its demise had anything to do with Wali Akram's ideas or management. The people, he asserts, simply did not heed the imam's teachings.

The Muslim Ten Year Plan was a good viable plan to help those who had been disenfranchised and did not have economic strength. It was a way that we could form a commune and buy wholesale and bulk, and sell these items back to ourselves, and realize the profit in our community. But we're talking about people that were five years away from the plantation. Many of them came from Alabama, Georgia, Oklahoma, places like that, and they never ever participated in any group activity involving money other than donating to the Church. And these people were against it. And "Negroism" came in. They argued, they bickered. Some just couldn't stay the course and they left.

The idea of the Muslim Ten Year Plan, as well as the teachings of Wali Akram [was] to empower people to move out into the world, to branch out and to make money, and to provide comfortable lives for themselves and their family, and give their offspring a good education.

I was a member of the Ten Year Plan in 1964 when I was twenty-four years old. I encouraged other Muslim brothers to join. But they had no outlook for the future. I have done quite well for myself. I live in a very nice area. My wife and I, we have a nice amount of money that we have saved. We take nice vacations. We go to Florida once a year and California once a year and Arizona once a year. And we travel. She has a new automobile. I have a new automobile. And it's done through economic power. Brother Akram instilled this in me. You can believe that.

I was taught to conduct business by brother Akram. He gave me a lot of guidance. My mother and father were divorced, and my stepdad and I didn't communicate too well. . . . I did a lot of things on my own, but whenever I wanted good sound advice on something I would go and sit with "Dad" and I'd talk to him. He was never ever too busy for anyone. Islam was always first. He would say, "Well, did you pray on it?"

"Well, I tried that."

"Well, try it again, and then come back and talk to me, okay." And sometimes he would say, "Well, let's go make salat." We would say a prayer then and then he would enter into consultation and talk with you. And he would always try to give you more than one point of view or more than one way to look at a problem. So for that I love him. I will always love him. I will always have a place in my heart for him because to me he filled the void that I had in my life at that point in time.[35]

PILGRIMAGE TO MECCA   In 1957 Wali Akram became one of the first African Americans awarded a visa for pilgrimage to Mecca. During the trip he traveled extensively in Europe and the Middle East, experiences that are recorded in an autobiographical manuscript entitled "From the Cotton Fields of the South to the Sandy Deserts of Arabia." Working as an inventor, Akram was successful, technically speaking, having twenty-seven electrical and mechanical patents to his name. He had invented a coupler that was standardized on boxcars throughout America, but as an African American he was never given credit or a share in the profits that followed. Akram and his wife Kareema raised a large family of twelve children, sixty grandchildren, and more than seventy-five great-grandchildren, all of whom were educated in the Muslim tradition. An inventor by profession, so by confession he built a framework for Islam in America.

A fragment from the 1958 diary of El-Hajj Wali Akram reads:

From the cotton fields of the south to the sandy deserts of Arabia—last year I had the opportunity to travel by rail, bus, camel, donkey and rickshaw through Europe, Turkey, Syria, Saudia Arabia—where I made pilgrimage to Mecca, Egypt, the Sudan, Pakistan, Afghanistan and India canvassing and observing the people in these countries and remembering the conditions and misunderstandings that prevail in America: discrimination, segregation, prejudice and envy. The task ahead requires honest dedication and direction.

The failure to achieve unity among Muslims in America left a scar and a certain bitterness in Wali Akram's heart. He retreated to his duties at the mosque and managing the Ten Year Plan. Postwar Cleveland remained an important industrial center and continued to attract diverse waves of migrants from the southern states and abroad, including potential converts who sometimes attended prayers at the First Cleveland Mosque. Wali and Kareema Akram acquired reputations as progenitors of an extended Muslim family that included their own children, the oldest of whom were now entering adulthood, and an adoptive family of many colors and nationalities. Children from broken homes grew up in the Akram household and learned Arabic alongside their own children—Rasool or Mahmud, Khadija or Mubarka. A few married into the family; others drifted away, only to return in times of crisis. Letters arrived from all over the country and around the world, their words and emotions recalling the warmth and love found with the Akrams "like an oasis in the desert." Remarkable to many travelers was the simplicity and dedication of the First Cleveland Mosque. Word of the pious and indefatigable imam who had devoted his life to the cause of dawa in America became a small part of the Muslim oral tradition known as "travelers' tales."[36]

Ironically, Imam Wali Akram's pilgrimage came about as a result of his growing renown among immigrant Muslims. Immigration from the Middle East and the Indian subcontinent increased in the decades after the war, when the majority of foreign Muslims took advantage of new quotas to seek work in the United States. Generally, the immigrants had no idea that their religion was being practiced here and formed their own associations.[37] Members of another Pakistani missionary society called the Tabligh Jamaat traveled to the United States in the late 1950s.[38] With his reputation as the leader of the indigenous revolt against the despised Ahmadiyyas and the general recognition of his religious sincerity, Imam Wali Akram became an excellent candidate for the Tabligh Jamaat. When he agreed to participate, the movement immediately sponsored his pilgrimage. Saudi immigration officials at Mecca told Akram that he was only the second native-born American to be officially admitted to the Holy City.

The repercussions of his pilgrimage were felt back in Cleveland, where a curious relationship developed between the Muslim students attending the public schools and their mostly Christian teachers and peers. The stigma of skin color receded quietly into the background. Often the teachers were so preoccupied with the novelty of Muslims in their classes that they ended up treating the children deferentially. Khadija, one of the Akram daughters, said, "Until I was twenty-one, I didn't even realize that I was being treated differently than other black children in the school. I was Khadija and had all the privileges accorded to white kids." In the turmoil of court-ordered desegregation, religious conversion could have a profoundly beneficial effect. "[O]ne day it didn't matter anymore," she observed. "We were raised without color. Our religion is our freedom."[39]

Like her four sisters and six brothers, Khadija excelled in class and eventually became a public school teacher herself. Many third-generation Muslims in Cleveland learned Arabic from her at the mosque. While her life has not been easy as a self-supporting single parent, she exudes a sense of joy and serenity. Her role, inherited from her mother, is that of stabilizing the community of Muslim women. Women have as much say in community affairs as the men and often take precedence as the organizers of civic programs, excursions for the children, and outreach to the community at large. Khadija's son Abbas was the first Akram to graduate from a four-year college; he is now a high school English teacher as well as the varsity football and basketball coach for at a large Cleveland high school. In 1988 he succeeded his grandfather as the imam of the First Cleveland Mosque.

In its sixty-year tradition, Khadija describes the First Cleveland Mosque as open to all who come with the same respect they would have for a church or synagogue. There is no political agenda, and even in respect to the practice of Islam, she deemphasizes the arcane issues of etiquette regarding women's fashions that may often surface in other mosques. Echoing her father, she declares that Muslim prayer is the essence. She also perpetuates her mother's legendary hospitality, which prevails likewise in the homes of many other members of the mosque.

There is a genuine sense of freedom from the albatross of race when Khadija comments,

> We don't refer to ourselves as African Americans. We refer to ourselves as Muslims. This has been the downfall of all of those people not knowing who you were or where you're from. But the Quran comes to show us that we are Muslims, born in America. I know who I am and I have no complexes about it. We don't feel anything negative about our identity. We can go anywhere and feel equal.[40]

Imam Abbas reinforced his mother and grandfather's sentiments in a powerful sermon delivered to almost five hundred Muslims who gathered for 'id prayers in April 1990. "Islam is not blackism! Islam is not Africanism. Islam is not Negroism. Get that through your heads! Islam is not nationalism: O, Muslims, we are not to be called Black or African or American or Canadian. No prefixes, no hyphens, no suffixes. Just Muslims!"

In Cleveland one does not discuss the history of Islam in America by mentioning Wali Akram and Elijah Muhammad in the same sentence. "Wali Akram tried to let people see the beauty of Islam," explained Abbas. "Elijah Poole tried to kill it! They [the Black Muslims] are just waking up now. If I am a Muslim I cannot be a nationalist. That doesn't have anything to do with it at all. The Quran says, 'O, Man! I have not placed two hearts in you.'"[41]

Wali Akram died at the age of ninety-three in August 1994. His funeral attracted over a thousand mourners from Cleveland's Muslim and African-American community. Waiting for the service to begin inside the sweltering

Martin Luther King Jr. Auditorium, two of the very few representatives of the large immigrant Muslim community across town spoke of their enduring admiration and affection for Wali Akram. He was the only "true American Muslim," according to one. "When I moved here to work as an engineer in 1956, I looked in the phone book for mosques. I found Muhammad's Temple and went down there thinking I could make salat but it turned out to be Elijah Muhammad's people. They didn't like Arabs and wouldn't even let me in. Afterwards someone told me about the First Cleveland Mosque."

In many conversations Wali Akram always emphasized the universality of Islam as opposed to nationalist or racialist doctrines. He conceived his acceptance of Islam as a transition from specific to universal identity. Once he abandoned "negro-ness" he never looked back, preferring, whenever necessary, to use the term "dark Americans" instead of "Afro-" or "African American." This was an act of religious faith that allowed him maximum freedom, carrying him indeed from the East Texas cotton fields into a spiritual world centered in the Arabian desert.

El-Hajj Wali Akram in his study, Cleveland, 1990

Imam Abbas embraces El-Hajj Akram

El-Hajj Wali Akram, eighty-seventh birthday, Cleveland, 1989

'Id al-fitr 1990, First Cleveland Mosque (top)

Recreation, First Cleveland Mosque (bottom)

El-Hajj Wali Akram, 1992

Imam Daud Abdul Malik (top)

Betrothed teenagers, Cleveland, 1992 (bottom)

Sister Hassinah Rance (top)

Third grade, The Islamic School of the Oasis (bottom)

Learning the Five Pillars of Islam (top)

Students attend jum'a prayer at Masjid ul-Haqq, Cleveland 1992 (bottom)

West Valley, New York, 1992 (top)

West Valley pioneer, Sheik Daoud Ghani (bottom)

Sister Fareeda Saadek, West Valley, N.Y., 1992

Haaneyfan Rafeek at home, West Valley, N. Y. (top)

Original signpost (circa 1939) at West Valley (bottom)

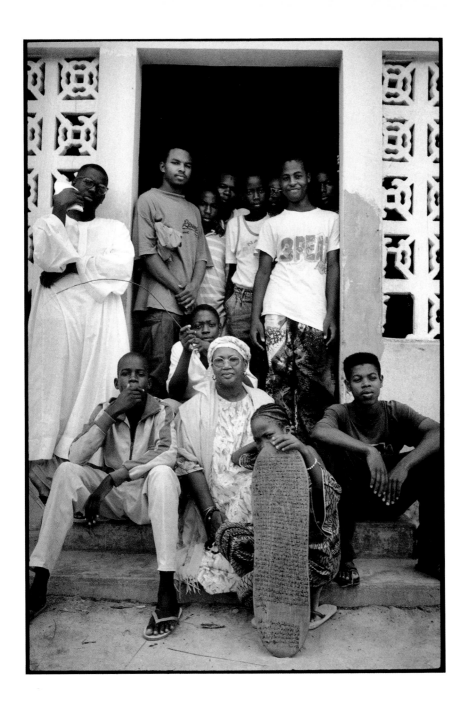

The American suffa, Medina Kaolack, West Africa, 1991

Entrance to orthodox mosque at Green Haven Correctional Facility

Sankore's Imam Salahuddin, Stormville, N.Y., 1988

Greeting visitors to prison 'id al-adha celebration Wende, N.Y., 1989

Friday prayers at Masjid Sankore, Stormville, N.Y., 1988

The family album, Queens, 1991 (top)

Public health outreacy, Coney Island, NY (bottom)

Teaching Islam, Brooklyn, 1987 (top)

Muslim women, Penta Hotel, New York City, 1989 (bottom)

Al Borhaaneeyah Tariqa, Brooklyn Sufi lodge

Zikhr chanting at Sufi lodge, Brooklyn, 1990

Sheik Sulaiman al-Hadi, 1988

5

West Valley

CAROLINA TO BUFFALO   From Springville we crossed the Cattaraugus River to New York Route 240 and headed south toward West Valley. The landscape was hilly and unattractive because the trees had not kept pace with an unscheduled spring heat. They were barren and could not hide the rocky, uneven surface of the ground. A steady downpour soon turned the unpaved road into a mudwash. On the right a little handmade sign nailed to a tree read in English and Arabic: "Jabul Arabiyya, Muslim Community, Governed By Sharia."

Nothing stirred except raindrops dripping from the branches of the trees overhead. Further up on the same side of the road we saw a white shotgun-style building set back from the road with a sign, "Masjid Ezaldeen." The front and side doors of the mosque were locked. Around back a dilapidated picnic table supported another sign leaning against mosque's rear wall. This decaying slab of plywood was perhaps the original sign. It had the same inscriptions but also noted the settlement's population at fifty-seven and date of incorporation in 1938.

Mohammedan Village Byproduct Of Depression: Worshippers Of Allah Carve Out Community On Hillsides Of Cattaraugus County, read the headline from a Sunday feature article in the *Buffalo Courier-Express* of 2 June 1946. The text said: "Instead of selecting desert sands as a site for their village, a group of Mohammedans is carving out a community in the wooded, windy hillsides of Cattaraugus County. With the steeples of New England-type churches in sight, they bow . . . in prayer to Allah five times daily."

Less than a hundred yards away, the hill inclined steeply. On either side were old handmade shacks of wooden planks and tar paper roofed in galvanized metal. The boarded windows showed that the first two were uninhabited. To the right another house stood in the corner lot. At the hilltop were several more abandoned houses. They were uniformly set back ten yards from the road to accommodate drainage ditches running along both the north and south sides. There was ample space around each dwelling, each set on a quarter-acre plot with wide-open fields in back and a driveway in the front. There were a few chicken coops and utility sheds. Secondary or tertiary woods encroached on the fields from beyond. The entire scene was nearly colorless. It seemed like a ghost town. Toward the center of the village, a few houses were painted. One was particularly well kept, with two cars in the driveway. Next door was a white house with a big suburban picture window and an opened garage door. Flowers grew at the edge of the lawn just above the ditch. In the adjacent lot a large mobile home was anchored to a cinderblock foundation.

At ten o'clock in the morning, the hamlet seemed quiet. The rain slackened as we slowly rolled another quarter mile down the slope to West Valley. On the right a small sign read "Ghani," and a Buick Skylark was parked in the driveway close to a small garage. There was a free-standing hammock and chaise longue beneath a large oak whose blossoms had responded to the unseasonable heat. The yard was a patchwork of grass and mud. A short man appeared and then disappeared. Engaged in a tug-of-war with his goat, he tried to restrain the animal as it lunged toward some chickens who were busy pecking their breakfast on the ground. He wore a weather-beaten leather jacket and a woolen kufi on his head. Squinting at the visitors with the resistant goat in tow, he said, "Happy to see you! I didn't know if you was coming or not." He flashed a broad smile now while the goat continued its struggle and then ran in a circle, wrapping Ghani's legs in the leash.

David Duffy was born in 1903 in Columbia, South Carolina. His sharecropper parents were devout Baptists. They prayed often in his house, "not just on Sunday." He attended school only to the fifth grade but learned to read the Bible and eventually became a church deacon at fourteen. When asked to reflect on the influence that led to his conversion to Islam, he begins with a story told by his maternal grandmother, Rollie.

At the end of the Civil War when Rollie was a young girl, the Union army conquered Richland County. Victorious soldiers immediately set about dispossessing the slave-owners from their property.

Then the Yankee told all the niggers, "Now you all go out there and walk yourselves off some land. You know, show them. You go walk it off, and drive your stakes down there, and come back and tell us how many acres you got, and we are going to give you a deed for that. And that's your land. And when we leave here we are going to leave the federal government right here in this old house. And if any of these people bother you about that land, you come in, we'll kill them!

Rollie inherited that fifty-two acres of land and some cotton money which belonged to black folks anyway. She had no education, but she had land. She was a root doctor and got all of her medicine right out of the woods. Went out there with a shovel and hoe and dig it up and make you tea and pretty soon you'd be better. A lot of white people used her. They wouldn't even get the doctor. They would say, "Go get Aunt Rollie." She was the midwife too. She had all the babies—all the whites around the neighborhood used my grandmother. She wouldn't take no pay. You know why? Because of her land and that money.

During World War I, the U.S. army repossessed Rollie's land, claiming eminent domain for the construction of an artillery range at Camp Jackson. The family ended up as sharecroppers, indentured once again to the white man. "You ain't got nowhere to live but on his land. You can't go to another white man for help."

Young David, her grandson, hardly participated in childhood games and sports. His mother voiced her trepidations about the boy's future, remarking to Rollie, " 'Mama, you know one thing? I'm worried about Bubba. He don't act like other kids. I watch him play. And other kids be playing and jumping up and down, but he don't do it, he watch. He just watch. I believe there is something wrong with his head.'

"Don't you worry about that boy. God makes people like he wants. He going to be different from a lot of others. That's all there is to it. I can't tell you what he going to do though," prophesied Rollie.

David resisted the authority of his peers. His young companions used to sneak off into the woods to drink liquor, and he followed them because he wanted friends. When his turn came to take a swig, however, he would put the bottle to his lips and block the opening with his tongue.

I said to myself, Now how am I going to be with them if I don't drink that junk? We'd be sitting in the rain in the woods. When you hand me the bottle, then I said to myself, "Block it with your tongue!" So I made like

that and blocked it. That was my first time to drink, you see. I blocked it!
And I said, "Okay man, you next." Now what I got to do now? As long as I
with them I got to play drunk. Jesus Christ, I get tired playing drunk. So I
just come out and told them finally, "I ain't gonna drink it." So I didn't
have no more friends then.

At the age of fourteen he daydreamed about owning land.

I could read the bible pretty da'garn good. And I read in the Bible, "And
God created Eve and Adam in the garden of Eden." Not here on earth but
in Paradise, according to the Bible. And I read this, many times. And then
I see the preacher. He didn't say a word about that! In my way of thinking, that was very important but as long as I was in Sunday school he
didn't ever mention it. His main subjects were be a good person, pray, and
pay your dues in church and when you die you will go to heaven.
     Around my birthday, I thought to myself, if everything is in the
earth, why don't we buy a little piece of the earth? And at least we could
get food, beans, peas, potatoes, sheep. Everything you need is there. Well,
why do you let someone else buy it all up and then set you on it, and you
have got to come to be a slave just for a little piece of bread? Get some and
make your own.

David spoke to three fellow deacons about pooling their resources to buy some
property, a few acres of land where they might build homes when they got married. "You help me build my house, then I will help you build your business. Three
of them—they were deacons too. And gee whiz, I had to run! They wanted to
whoop me. They got mad at me. See. So then I just shut up. So then I just went on
in the church, getting a little older, a little older, and I'm still thinking about this."
     The vision lay fallow until he reached marrying age and began to contemplate
how to provide for a family without becoming indentured to the white planters. He
joined the Masons, thinking that he might encounter some open-minded individuals, but was rebuked again when he suggested a collective land ownership scheme.
Considering what the future held for him, he started to resent his parents.

I looked at dad and mom, and I said to myself, "Gee, you're dumb! You
slave yourself, raising that cotton for the white man. You get half and he
get half. Then you have got to eat out of his store all the summer on
credit, and you have got to pay for half of the fertilizer. Then you go to
pay your bill and you come up, you wind up a hundred dollars in debt for
the next year. You never pay out!"
     "I never mentioned that to mom and dad. It was a feeling that grew
inside me. Eventually Allah fixed it that I leave the South. He run me from
the South here. I guess He said, "Well you go there, you find what you're
looking for!"

He took a childhood friend in marriage and they became a part of the Great Migration. "I was driving a truck there. I was making pretty good money, but I told the wife, let's take it all. So we came to Buffalo in 1929. Basically looking for work. To go in the steel mill, because I had a brother up there already, you know, and he told me about how much money he make and this, and that, so I said I will try."

After finding work at the Republic Steel factory in Buffalo, New York, David and Lallie Duffy settled down in an apartment in the city's black ghetto. Lallie gave birth to a son whom they named Roger. They were lucky to have work and a comfortable apartment in the midst of the Great Depression. "When the depression hit Buffalo . . . it was like a wildfire. People dying in the street, dying in storefronts, women and men, white and black. I seen them starved to death."

A year after their arrival, one of Duffy's coworkers invited him to attend a class given by a man called Sheik Suphan.[1] He joined the sheik's classes, but soon many of the students became frustrated at the sheik's lack of knowledge. After six months of study all they had learned was the Arabic alphabet.

One brother complained, "Hey, see we have been doing the alphabet all this long time. Say, when are we going to get some books?"

He said, "I have given you all I know."

"What!!?? Just the alphabet!"

"Yeah, that's all I know. Okay."

Another student piped up. He knew about a man in Pennsylvania with greater knowledge of Islam.

He said, "We ain't got to bother with him [Sheik Suphan]. See, I know a fellow down in Pennsylvania, he is a master of English and he's a master of Arabic. And he'll do it. If you want, I'll go get him." So everybody [said], "Yeah, go get it."

Now this guy is on welfare. He ain't got a dime. So the next time we had the school, we didn't see him. He'd gone. About two or three days later, here he come walking in there with Muhammad Ezaldeen, and we asked, "How did you get down in there? Where have you been?" He answered, "Ask Muhammad Ezaldeen."

So I asked him, "How did he get you up here?" He said, "None of your business!" I said, "What is the matter with you guys?" It was more than just me, you know. Remember, this guy ain't got nothing. So we finally got onto how he got down there, and how he got up there. This guy hoboed down there on the freight and then hoboed with the professor back to Buffalo. And we told them, "You're crazy! What if you guys got killed hoboing on the freight?" So now we got Muhammad Ezaldeen. He got right up there. He left the alphabet . . . on the board, and then he went to writing words under there, in English, and he put the Arab word right under there in Arabic, and we moved on. Oh, we moved on!

Ezaldeen agreed to stay when the class pooled their resources to rent an apartment for him and his wife in Buffalo. Only Ghani and four or five other men had steady factory jobs. Most of the others were on relief. Together they managed to rent a storefront that served as their Arabic and Islamic academy, called the Adenu Allahe Universal Arabic Association (AAUAA).

Ezaldeen knew of the Ahmadiyya missionaries' work and worried about their growing influence. One of his first lessons in Buffalo was to explain the difference between al-Islam and the other pseudo-Islamic sects that were active. He warned the members that the Ahmadiyya Movement and their schools were no different from the Christian church. He told them about other organizations going around setting up Muslim schools in Missouri and other places. "But I'm going to tell you all now, them brothers, they're trying to set up the schools. Which they are supposed to do. But what they looking for, is like the Church, like the preacher. The money come, you give it to the preacher and goodbye money. So now I'm telling you, they are not interested in your well-being, they are not interested in your advancing. All they are interested in is you paying dues and that's it."

Ezaldeen lectured on many subjects and taught three nights a week for five years from 1930 to 1935. Drawing from his studies in Cairo, he taught Arabic, Quran, Hadith, tafsir—"the whole works." Membership grew to about 140 people. "He taught us all by himself," said Ghani. He exhorted his fellow African Americans to abandon the Christian names assigned by their forefathers' slave masters long ago. Going even further, he taught that their material and spiritual salvation lay in reclaiming their original "African-Arabic" culture, as he called it. This encompassed the Arabic language, Arab customs, and the religion of al-Islam. Their names were symbolic of the rediscovery of their roots.

He was teaching us though for about a year, you know, and he gave me a name out of my ancestors [to replace] my slave name. I didn't know all this, but he told me. But it seemed funny. He asked me my name. I told him David Duffy, that's my name. That's the name my dad give me. Then he dropped it on me, you know, and he said, "Look, that's not your name."

I said, "It's not?"

He said, "No." He take time, and he really laid it on us straight. "That there name is supposed to be McDuffy. That's an Irish name. And I can tell you how you come by this Irish name. That's a slave name. I want to give you your real name and your real religion that your forefathers had before slavery. The Irish, the Jewish, the Polish, the Spanish, they come here from their countries, but they still got their own religion, and got their own forefathers' way of life. But we do not. So where we're going now, we are going up and we pick up from the beginning of slavery and get right back and serve Allah and we gonna pray five times a day, and they going to love each other, and they are going to teach each other al-Islam religion. If you go for it."

So after he got through talking to me, I said, "I'm for it."

He said, "Your name is no more David Duffy. Your name is Daoud Ghani, that's what your name is. You can have it changed if you haven't got any debts or bills." He give me a little card.

Now at this point, I felt a little funny. I didn't tell the wife even. I had quite a few people come around in my lifetime, shooting a whole lot of bull. So I said, this is one guy, me and him going to jail, that's what I'm going to get. I am supposed to go to work next morning but I went downtown instead. I said to myself, I'm going to put this guy in jail, and I am going to get a reward. I'm tired of people shooting the bull on me. So I went to the old Post Office in Buffalo and walked up to the window and asked the woman to talk to one of the FBI agents. She told me to go down the hall to the second window and wait until someone opens it. Sure enough, a guy walked over to me. He looked to be about in his thirties or something. I had the little card with my Muslim name. I said, "Look, I am under the impression. . . . but you know who I am, don't you?" He said, "Oh yeah. I know who you are. Right away. Yeah, I sure do. American Negro." I said, "Well that's what I'm here for. A brother of mine told me I'm not American Negro. He told me I'm American-Hamitic. He told me that in the Constitution of the United States, if a Negro was born in America, raised in America, and be able to lift himself out of the predicament [in] which they live, they let him go. That is what this guy told me."

I said, "My negro name is David Duffy but now I done went and this brother changed it, gave me Daoud Ghani. Is it legal for me to do this?"

He read it back like that and he smiled. He said, "That guy is real good. I can show you in the Constitution right now, if you want to look. That's what it says. The guy who did this for you, he knows what he's doing. So good luck."

I said thanks. See, I thought he was just shooting the bull. But this is true. So then I went everywhere I'd been, like paying for cars, furniture, I just went and told the people, "See here, I'd like to record my religious name on my bill." They didn't challenge me.

But then I went to the steel mill, Republic Steel, with the same thing. "Hey, my name is changed now. I'd like you to record my Muslim name on my record, here in the steel mill."

"Oh no, I can't do that. Give me about two or three hours and I'm going to go upstairs and talk with the management."

So I went into work. After awhile the foreman said they want you upstairs. I went upstairs to the manager, he looked at the card and asked me why I wanted it on my record.

I said, "To tell you the truth, it ain't any of your business why I want it on there. That's my name, and I am just asking you to put it on."

He said, "We can't do that."

I said, "Well, I'll go down and see a lawyer."

Then he said, "You have got to give me time to get the company lawyer from Pennsylvania."

About a week later they called me upstairs again—me, my superintendent, and, his secretary—and we go upstairs. Now the management—the man was up there with his secretary, and there were three women and three men. And the company lawyer is sitting there too. I told him, "I just went back and picked up the custom and tradition of my forefathers before Emancipation. That called for me to get a name out of my ancestors."

So then the lawyer said, "Well, the company ain't gonna do that. We ain't gonna do it."

I said, "Okay, you just want to make me spend some money now, I'm gonna get me a lawyer. I'm going to have it done." And all the time I'm speaking, they be writing, all them secretaries.

I went out and I got me a lawyer in Buffalo. I explained what I want done and what Republic Steel refused. He said, "They didn't refuse that!"

I said, "They sure did."

He said, "Well just leave it to me. Give me fifty bucks and you will get a letter to your house. You ain't got to go nowhere." And I live in Cattaragus County, and the County seat is Little Valley. I went home [and] one day there was an envelope and when I opened it up, my name was Daoud Ghani and so forth. So that's the way I got it in Republic Steel.

When my parents heard that I'd become Muslim, they was very nice about it. My dad was the first one who spoke. He said, "Bubba, do you know one thing? I'm really glad you do that. Even if I wanted to do it, I couldn't. If I had pulled a trick like that in those days, they would shoot me." That's what he told me. He said, "I'm proud of you." I explained to them what I really had in view, like getting a few people together to buy land and raise our own food and meat. That's what was in my mind even when I was fourteen. So my mom said, "That's all right for that, see, but the religion, see, you are going to get in trouble." I told her, "I am staying right there on the land where I can work and I get this for myself. Or else I'll go to hell." And she smiled, though. She couldn't see really, but she smiled.

HIJRA   Ezaldeen emphasized the Islamic concept of hijra as the key to genuine religious and political autonomy. This would safeguard the new Muslims' reclamation of their African (or Hamitic) identities. By banding together in "units" (communes) they could purchase property and incorporate themselves as a religious institution. The self-sufficient community would be governed by sharia law. The process of retreating from the world of the infidel to consolidate a community of observant Muslims was called hijra, first undertaken by the Prophet Muhammad in the year 622 C.E.

Ezaldeen's explanation of hijra resonated loudly with Ghani. Finally, there was someone who understood his heart's burning desire to own land. The professor knew how to transform this dream into reality. "That's when I said, Goodbye Christianity!"

> After I went to Muhammad Ezaldeen for about a year, he said, "I will teach you gentlemen how to help each other and how to put your money together and buy land."!
>
> When he said that, I hollered! Wow! It struck me. Ooo! I hollered. My wife hit me in the belly and said, "Shut up!" I was waiting on that for years and years and years and years. Afterward he asked me why I hollered. I said, "Muhammad Ezaldeen, that is what I was trying to do since I was fourteen."
>
> He said, "Well, you are the guy."

Coached by Professor Ezaldeen, the Muslim converts scoured the region in search of suitable acreage. According to Ghani, they went "around and around," but the most they found was a five-acre parcel. "Not enough" they were told when they reported back to the professor. "You keep going, go again," they were told. Finally after combing the area for several weeks they discovered a three-hundred-acre tract in the hills between Springville and West Valley.

"I have to give him credit, he really knew what he was doing," says Ghani of Jabul Arabiyya's mentor. "So Ezaldeen said, 'Okay, that will be enough for a start because you brothers who are working have got to buy it. Those other sisters and brothers on welfare can't buy no land. They can't hardly live.'"

The next day they found the real estate agency in Springville and learned that the land was in foreclosure and the price was equivalent to the total back taxes owed to Cattaraugus County.

> So we got together and shook hands and we were sure, you know. Because all of us got a few dollars in the bank.[2] We got good credit. We can't fail. We went back to Springville and met with the real estate agent. She wanted so much down for the whole three-hundred-and-some acres. The next day I stayed home from work, and some of them guys was working nights. We lined up down near the bank. Get my money. I got mine and you've got yours. When we went to school that night . . . one of the brothers said to Muhammad Ezaldeen, "Professor, we got the money." He said, "Well, don't tell me, I ain't got no land, go to Springville!" So we come right there and paid down on it, and so someone started building

right away. I didn't, but some of them did. We could just depend on each other.

After closing the deal, the core members moved onto the hilltop property and set about constructing their family dwellings. They named their settlement Jabul Arabiyya (Mountain of Arabic-Speaking People). Ezaldeen instructed them to keep quiet about their plans lest their white neighbors resist an all-black rural settlement. "Get as many acres of land together as possible because once you buy a place and the neighbors get on to what you're after, they are going buy right up under you and you won't be able to expand," he told them. "If it's sure you are going to pay for the land, then you don't have to wait until it's all paid for to build on it. If you have a few brothers to buy the place, you can start building on it after you pay the first payment."

We really learned how to work together. So it went on like that from then on until we paid for it. The sisters, the ones on welfare, they'd pay fifty cents, seventy-five cents, a dollar, two dollars, anything. They got family, so we didn't pay it no mind. We just put ours there. Make sure we put it there. Hey, because we was making, well at that time, at that time I was making fifty-five dollars every two weeks. That was back in the thirty's. And I know people who were working back in that time, the kind of work they were doing, when we could get it. You couldn't get no work, see. And them that was working, what did they do, getting about five dollars a week? The tips, something like tips. So the people on welfare come up with a dollar every now and then. That's all they could do. See. The sisters that had no husbands, they got someone to build them a house. Sister Sherman had a house right up there. She ain't had no husband, but she got a guy come out there and build a house for her. That's nice. But we had a time doing it.

Some of Ghani's coworkers at the steel mill ridiculed him for driving sixty miles a day to his job when he might have continued living in a comfortable five-room apartment in the city. "Oh boy! I can't tell you certain things they called me, but they did tell me, 'You're crazy! You crazy to go and drive thirty miles back and forth. Working in all that snow and ice and you have got a five-room flat up there on Peckham Street.' Paying about what it was at that time, about thirty dollars a month. They said, 'You crazy!'

"I said, 'Okay, if I'm crazy, I'm going to stay crazy.'"

As Ezaldeen predicted, problems developed with white people in the surrounding communities. At one point Jabul Arabiyya was spared from a violent attack by the intervention of a white army veteran who claimed that a black soldier had saved his life during the war. In another incident, young rednecks burned a cross at the settlement but were quickly apprehended by the community militia and then turned over to the New York State Police. Today people in the neighboring towns of Springville and West Valley refer more benignly to "the black Arabs" on the hill.

Ezaldeen also instructed them to build stores and develop businesses. Realizing that the settlement needed a stable cadre of wage-earners in order to grow, they tried to attract members of the black middle class to Jabul Arabiyya.

Before we even bought the place, I discussed it with an undertaker in Buffalo. Me and him were good friends. He was a very nice guy, Undertaker Walker. The city give him that job to go down and pick up dead people. They paid him only ten dollars a body. He picked them up in doorways, anywhere you can find them, women and men, white and black. And if someone don't claim them, the undertaker would just put them away and come out to a great big old farm out there and throw them in the fire. So I went straight to him, because I figured he could do us a lot of good. Me, him, and his wife sit down in this front room, and I said, "Mr. Walker, I am here to ask you and your wife to join the Muslim school. Come to our school and learn how to speak Arabic, learn about al-Quran." You know what he told me? He said, "Duffy, I tell you, the reason I won't join that, because there are not enough of you will support my business."

Ghani made a similar overture to his wife's doctor, who also refused, saying that there were not enough Muslims to sustain his business and he would fear losing his Christian patients if he converted. "I quit asking. The only ones we got were the poor that's on welfare, or some poor people that ain't working. And there were a few of us working in mills and things, and we talked to our friends and buddies and so forth. 'Man, don't you say nothing to me. I'm working. They think I'm coming down there and giving that man [Muhammad Ezaldeen] my money? You are crazy!'"

Ghani worked the night shift at Republic Steel. He would pull into Jabul Arabiyya around dawn, drink some coffee, and get busy working on his house. Even the boards were harvested from the timber-rich woods and cut at the local sawmill. "This was all beautiful farm land. They was growing corn there when we bought the place. The woods are back up there," he pointed across the street and north to the hill, "nothing but forest, back up that way. We built the houses with our own hands, about four before we stopped.

"So we figure we would stop building the houses and start on the mosque because Muhammad Ezaldeen told us, 'First thing, build your house, second, build a mosque, third, you put up a store, and the fourth thing, you build a jail.' So we got our houses, and we got the mosque, but never got around to the store or the jail yet.

"Muhammad Ezaldeen told us when we bought the place, 'This is your country. Nobody rules this but you. When you get settled, you go down to the county seat and you pick out the brother that you want to be policeman in your country, and they are going to give it to you.'"

Maintaining the colony's financial integrity was a difficult task. Since the West Valley "unit" belonged to the AAUAA, they had to pay dues to the national organization. "We were supposed to send so much money to New Jersey. Like we'd pay maybe fifty cents here or there like dues. So we did that for a while. But after we bought the land, we needed every nickel that we could get to maintain it. So we stopped. I guess they got angry when the money stopped coming in."

The community struggled financially and most people had to live on livestock, mainly chickens, and small gardens. Whatever cash they had disappeared quickly. A dispute soon arose about the location of AAUAA's national headquarters, some claiming West Valley and others New Jersey. In 1938 Ezaldeen and his followers in Buffalo incorporated the community of Jabul Arabiyya in West Valley, New York, as part of the AAUAA national charter.[3] After the founding of Jabul Arabiyya, Ezaldeen then returned to his home at 45 Prince Street in Newark with his wife, Set.[4]

They stayed out there awhile, maybe four or five months. In a little shack, a little shanty. But they preferred to go back to New Jersey.

About a year later, Muhammad Ezaldeen tells us that we're supposed to pay New Jersey, that New Jersey is the headquarters. And he told us, each member should send out an amount of money to New Jersey, I think it is each month. It wasn't too much, you know. One dollar. And we did that for awhile, okay. Now our school was going so well, and we got pretty near 150 students, and New Jersey ain't got but a few. This was among us now. We didn't cater to Muhammad Ezaldeen. We told him, "Now look, we give you all respect, but the way we see it, you tell us to build a home on this land. You build your home. When you build your home, then you build a mosque. And when you build your mosque, then you put up a store. And when you put up your store, then you build a jail. Now how in the world are we going to do all of that and send our money to New Jersey where they ain't doing nothing, and can't do nothing?" They in the city, what can they do? If they go to buy one piece of property, it cost them thousands and thousands of dollars, so we just decide we are going to let New Jersey do her own thing.

Jabul Arabiyya severed relations with the other AAUAA units, yet the problems continued as the original pioneers either died or retired from their factory jobs, leaving the community little in the way of cash income. Some families broke up. Many children moved away. The community lurched from one crisis to the next, always punctuated by nine-month winters. Tax problems arose because the county did not recognize the settlement's religious exemption as the state and federal government did. As a result of unpaid back taxes the community risked foreclosure.[5]

Over the years other Muslims proposed solutions, but Ghani dismissed such offers. For example, a group of immigrant Muslims wanted to invest in a farm to produce halal dairy and meat products. In exchange they wanted to take advantage of the community's autonomy to bring immigrants into the country from Canada.

> A couple of guys come here. Muslims. We talked for a good while, and then I asked him how he was going to go about it, and he told me, "There are lots of Muslims in foreign countries who want to come to the United States. But somehow the United States won't deliver them visas. But now this is your country, and it's a Muslim country. If you let us build houses, for them, you could sign the papers for them to come here in your country."

Ghani called a special meeting and explained to the residents of Jabul Arabiyya that if many immigrants came eventually the original settlers would become a minority and lose everything. "All my sisters and brothers thanked me very much how I handled it. So that was that. And they never tried to get back in touch. I ain't never called them, and they ain't never come back. So you see, that's what we are up against."

More recently an African-American lawyer from Buffalo suggested constructing a halfway house for recent parolees. As president of the community and sole surviving pioneer, Ghani rejected this too.

> This lawyer said that the community wouldn't be threatened by bankruptcy again. He told us he was Muslim too. He told us he could get the place tax-exempt if the organization would let him bring these juvenile delinquent kids out here. Now all these kids done did some kind of crime. So right away, before he could get the word out of his mouth, I said, "No! That's one of the reasons we buy our place as far out from the big cities as we possibly could—to get away from this kind of carrying on. Now we are going to sit here and let them haul them out by the truckload and keep them here?"

Despite rejecting that plan, he accepted the recommendation of Dawoud Adeyola (the current imam) of a few parolees who proved to be observant Muslims. However, Ghani remained skeptical of the idea of populating the colony with ex-convicts and fearful of their influence.

> The imam [Adeyola] works in the prison system. He said , "I've got two brothers, pretty nice guys, they didn't do nothing bad. And he said, [he] would [take them] out if I had trouble.

And so one parolee called that house over there and told that sister to ask me to be over there because I'm the president. I met with him and explained how we'd work it. He is very nice, very nice. He's working, and he married Badija. I don't want to see all my efforts go down the drain. The imam warned him, "If you don't want to listen to brother Ghani, you're gone." So them two brothers who came out on parole, they're very nice. Trying to work. So I guess that's why Allah is keeping me here."

Finally, there are tales of attempted armed takeovers by militant black Muslims in the 1970s, and rumors that Farrakhan's Nation of Islam once tried to purchase the community by paying the back taxes. "He knew about our tax problems in the mid-1980s and tried to buy the place out from under us. He came here with his lawyers and tried to pull the carpet out from under our feet. He thought we were just country bumpkins. We've been here for almost sixty-odd years, we're still here, and people like him still fear us."

Another Muslim imam formulated plans to populate West Valley, demonstrating Jabul Arabiyya's value not only as a legally chartered Muslim village but also as the symbol of the oldest continuously populated community of *muhajirun* in America. Ghani feared for the future nonetheless.

It really worries me. I just wonder about it. Now these brothers that were with me, there was four, we went and did it. What worries me today, all them brothers are dead. [New] people are coming so slow. We sacrificed to get this paid for. So it worries me that when I die, or maybe even before I die, we might lose this place. I will tell you the truth, it is worrying me. Because we went through quite a bit. And then like the new brothers coming in, I was so glad to see them. Of course they can't do no more than what they can do. But at least, [if] I drop dead, at least, I [can say] "Well, we have got two brothers to come." But the way it looks to me, and if it don't pick up a little bit, we're going to lose this place, and that will kill me.

Ghani died in 1995. Stewardship of the community was then shared between Shabburn Abdul-Naji, grandson of another pioneer, and Dawoud Adeyola. Muslims from this area seek to cultivate Jabul Arabiyya's symbolism yet understandably remain defensive about making it too visible for outsiders.

There were two centers for social life at Jabul Arabiyya. One was Masjid Ezaldeen, where the men linger after prayers; the other was Sister Saadek's kitchen, a gathering-place for the women who prepare and serve communal meals there. We participated in gatherings at both places and tried to understand the basis for Ghani's apprehensions about the future of the settlement whose population had dwindled to less than twenty adults.

Fareeda and Hafeez Saadek built the biggest and the best house back in the thirties because they expected Professor Ezaldeen and his wife to stay with them.

Fareeda and Sister Set Ezaldeen became very good friends in Buffalo and remained close despite the professor's decision to move back to Newark after the founding of the community. When we visited, the ranch-style house was still well maintained. It had fresh paint job, white with red trim, and the lawn was landscaped, with flowers planted in the front and along the driveway. Between the garage and the entrance to the house is a large open-air breezeway that serves as a kind of antechamber for the house. Above an old wicker couch is a posterboard that says, "Please Take A Seat, I'm in Prayer."

The house is spacious with a large kitchen and adjacent dining room connected to a hallway. Off this space runs another hallway with two or three bedrooms and the bathroom. The other side opens into a large carpeted living room that is often used for prayers. Both the dining and living rooms have big picture windows that look west onto Bigelow Road, giving a panorama of the homes across the street and the fields rolling out behind them. Once filled with truck gardens and pastures, they are now fallow. The woods have grown to about five or six feet in height. The mosque lies nestled beyond these trees off to the north.

During our visit, Sister Saadek had just recovered from a bad cold, but Ghani invited us to her home for lunch. Several women were in the kitchen fixing a meal. Sister Saadek sat in a rocking chair next to the woodstove and dozed occasionally. Badija, who lives next door in a house trailer and had been caring for her elderly neighbor during her illness, oversaw the preparations. Two young women in their late teens or early twenties were visiting from Buffalo, their heads covered in kemar. They helped with the meal and talked with Badija. Both of them belonged to the AAUAA mosque in Buffalo. One girl was a recent convert to Islam and betrothed to a man with another wife already. She anticipated moving to West Valley but seemed to have no idea about how she intended to support herself and her family. Ghani had commuted back and forth to Buffalo for forty years in the wind, rain, heat, and snow and blizzards. Was this girl's husband prepared for the same life?

Badija herself migrated to Jabul Arabiyya from Harlem, where she had belonged to the Mosque of Islamic Brotherhood on 113th Street. She had eight children and came to Jabul Arabiyya around 1983 to escape the corruption and violence of New York City. Most of her children who accompanied her drifted back into the city after they grew up, but she has stayed on even after suffering two heart attacks. Recently she married a younger man who is on parole from state prison, Ali, who seemed very enthusiastic about trying to make a new life for himself on Jabul Arabiyya. He worked hard to create a pleasant environment and even planted the flowers that lined Bigelow Road between their home and Ghani's.

Undaunted by the brutal winters and arduous travails of a pioneer life on Jabul Arabiyya, Badija exuded warmth and a hospitable demeanor. She seemed not only happy in her resolve to stick it out but also comfortable with taking over Sister Saadek's responsibilities. In Ali she had found a reliable man. A skilled electrician, he was constantly hustling work in the small valley towns below.

Imam Dawoud Adeyola arrived the next morning from Buffalo to help the other men clear a field for spring planting. They busted sod all day. Each man worked until the combination of fatigue, hunger, and heat made him stop. Lacking organization or any real plan, this was their work philosophy: Pick up a tool and help out. The innumerable rocks and small boulders on the half-acre plot made for endless and apparently futile labor. Had they selected the wrong garden site? Out of earshot Ghani observed that there was nothing wrong with the land. The problem was their ignorance of farming methods. The men had plowed the ground too deeply, removing the topsoil altogether instead of simply turning it over. Ghani confided that he noticed this mistake earlier but didn't want to meddle. "They've got to learn for themselves," he observed solemnly.

This gardening experience indicated that after fifty years there existed no practical guidelines to assist new migrants to Jabul Arabiyya. Professor Ezal-deen's little book for the community dealt exclusively with religious and civil matters by the rule of sharia. This anarchic division of labor was echoed in a conversation between Ali and his friend Bilal, who complained about the lack of any community system. Evidently this was at the root of Ghani's trepidations for the future. In fact, the newest members of the community seemed unprepared to sustain anything more than a kind of exurban residential arrangement, dependent on either wages or welfare This was exemplified by Umar ibn Shabazz Abdul-Azziz, a muhajid from Beverly Hills, California. One Friday he delivered a very esoteric khutbah at the mosque, talking about the difference between Islamic knowledge and "infidel" knowledge. Ali and Bilal confessed afterward that they could not understand one word of what he said. When Imam Dawoud showed up he scolded Umar for his unwillingness to put the values of labor and participation above his idealistic and decidedly subjective version of Islam.

THE SECOND GENERATION   Most of the offspring of the original muha-jirun departed Jabul Arabiyya long ago. Shabburn and Haaneyfan are two who remained despite all odds. They provided the only commentary on growing up at Jabul Arabiyya. Shabburn serves as the muezzin at Masjid Ezaldeen and spends most of his free time there. The grandson of the pioneer Sheik Ibn Abdul-Naji, he is craggy with a round face and inviting smile. He usually appears at the mosque wearing an oversized *jellaba* to fit his ample frame. Shabburn was born and raised at Jabul Arabiyya. He traveled as part of the Tabligh Jamaat for five years and refers to it as "Islam out of a suitcase." Some of the Tabligh Jamaat, he claims, are like born-again Christians. "When they came to West Valley, they said that they wanted to stay. They listened to Sheik Ghani and left after five minutes," he said. "The AAUAA was the strongest representative in the world for the interests of African-American Muslims. It has always been in the vanguard as far as they were concerned." Shabburn is the community's unofficial spokesman, although he defers to the nonresident leadership of Imam Adeyola. According to him, the settlement's problems derive from a contradiction between Professor Ezaldeen's intention to "bring Islam to the people who were way down" and the fact that although Islam has been relatively successful among the underclass, not many of them are prepared to "test themselves against the kinds of hardships we experience."

Haaneyfan Rafeek lives next door to Ghani's house in a dilapidated shack about twenty-five meters up a slope. The remains of an old barn sprawl flat on the ground in back of the house. He waved one day as we were sitting in Ghani's yard. Hesitant at first, he slowly walked over and crouched on the ground, listening respectfully to Ghani's stories. When Ghani left a while later to take care of some chores in town, Haaneyfan invited us over to his place. Empty beer cans littered the yard. Entering his house through the back door was like passing through a time tunnel into the pioneer era of Jabul Arabiyya. The old house had not changed since its construction in 1938. An ancient gas stove was rusting, the only water in the kitchen sink was from a leak in the ceiling above, and the cupboards appeared to have been empty for years. A potbellied stove supplied heat in the winter; oil lamps provided light. A half-dozen notebooks lay unevenly on a rough hewn kitchen table. Haaneyfan described them as notes for an autobiography. He writes in solitude on a nearby hilltop. Emphasizing that he reads not only the Quran but all the revealed scriptures of the world, he says that the notes contain his meditations on all religions.

Haaneyfan's parents were also pioneers, and he was born at Jabul Arabiyya. His voice was that of a rebellious dissident who grew up isolated and confused. He resented the Islamic sharia that, he claims, made growing up extremely difficult, like life in a gulag where fear is the most prevalent form of social control. But the strict Islamic rules were not the only problems. Jabul Arabiyya was constantly in crisis, from his perspective. Each problem threatened its very survival and made it impossible for the adults to minimize what was a devastating instability for their children. Many children reacted by leaving the community forever.

There were terrible domestic conflicts. Families broke apart, one parent often taking the children away. The hilltop settlement was beset also by problems originating in the outside Muslim community that brought a new kind of fear and even violence. Haaneyfan described an incident in which Islamic fundamentalists armed with guns and swords determined to make their hijra at Jabul Arabiyya with or without the cooperation of the original settlers. "They tried to impose their theory of life. A group of them would come out and eventually they would try to take over. You'd see one and pretty soon there would be four or five, and then there would be a bunch of them, and they'd have guns in their homes and there was a time that it was pretty bad. And they moved into these houses here."

The militants tried to assume both religious and secular power, saying,

"Allah sent me here to do this, or to do that, and I'm just going to tell you what you're supposed to do, and if you don't do it, that's between you and Allah."

It started happening when I was pretty young. I came home from the service when my mother died in 1975. My brother, Ahmed, warned me that it had become so dangerous out here that if he walked to visit somebody, he would actually carry his gun. He said, "They got some bad Muslims out here."

Abdullah [Ashraf] was president during the seventies when some of the militants moved in.

I saw them hide their guns in the mosque and reported it to Ashraf. When he confronted them, they swore up and down they didn't have any guns. He called a state trooper, who threatened to search the place. They went to the closet and they got their guns out. That will make you not want to go into a mosque when you know that they have weapons in there. Some of them had been wanted by the FBI. They were from New York. They'd come from Detroit. They'd come from Boston. It was very frightening.

Haaneyfan's parents, Abdullah and Fadela "Faye" Rafeek, were students at the original Islamic school in Buffalo in the 1930s. Abdullah Rafeek was the man who, according to Ghani, left town with no money in his pocket, hopped a freight train south, and returned a few days later with Professor Muhammad Ezaldeen. The couple had thirteen children, but life as a muhajirun did not agree with Abdullah Rafeek. He deserted his family and quit Islam soon after moving to Jabul Arabiyya. Faye was left to care for the children and provided for them by raising livestock and tending a garden.

Some women came with no husbands, just children. And the winters are nine months, you know, it's hard. So for a woman to do that, I think that's an enormous amount of courage and sacrifice. My mother raised thirteen of us. Many, many kids. And that whole field, it was all a garden. We would go out there and work that garden, and she had every kind of food you could think of in that garden. We had a barn here where my mother raised goats, chickens, geese, and ducks. She could raise about five hundred chickens. We would come home from school in the autumn and she would make us kill maybe twenty chickens a day during fall so she could freeze them for winter.

To conceive of a woman's difficult life at Jabul Arabiyya is to transpose the image of a nineteenth-century pioneer into the mid-twentieth century. In addition to raising her children, Faye was an active force in the settlement's affairs.

She was the recording secretary for the council. However, her children strayed, and as they became adults, each followed in their father's footsteps, leaving either the community or the religion, both perhaps. "They knew they had to do it. They wouldn't raise a family out here under these conditions . . . to be confined like they were confined. They wouldn't want their children growing up like they did either," reflects Haaneyfan. Faye did not oppose them. "She finally just turned the books in, more or less, and she wouldn't make us go to the mosque anymore."

They left Jabul Arabiyya because they wanted to worship as they pleased," says Haaneyfan of his siblings and other contemporaries.

They left because they wanted to marry whomever they pleased. [Ezaldeen's] bylaws stated "never shall a believer marry a nonbeliever." But these young kids here, my age, chose to marry Christians, chose to marry white. They didn't have jobs, it was hard to get a job way out here. So they go and marry whom they want and get a job and they believe in God, but they had to go make their living. They had to make their livelihood. So I encouraged them to go.

When Faye died in 1975, her children returned to the settlement for the funeral. It was the last time Haaneyfan saw his family together. Of thirteen children, only five girls and three boys, including Haaneyfan, were alive. His closest brother lives in Rochester, and they talk on the phone occasionally. Otherwise the family has disappeared from his life. "They died out pretty good," he laments while surveying the relics of his home and its yard. Haaneyfan dreams of restoring the porch and the barn, and his childhood perhaps, to the way it used to be when Faye was alive. "Living here all your life, you can remember just where everything was."

By comparison with Sheik Ghani's youthful ninety years, Haaneyfan had aged prematurely into a sad, melancholy character. Old and grey at fifty, he looked like a man in his late sixties or even seventies when we first met. He seemed starved for human contact, burdened by a life of repressed desires, and relieved, temporarily at least, to have visitors hear about his troubled, lonely life.

His religious upbringing at Jabul Arabiyya included Islamic and Arabic classes, but he claims never to have gotten further than learning to say "As Salaam-u-Alaikum." "They were trying to bring back the customs and the traditions of their forefathers" Haaneyfan observed "trying to go back, even before they came over here as slaves. Their intent was to build a nation within a nation."

Haaneyfan attended public school in West Valley, where he participated enthusiastically in the school's social life and athletics, earning the esteem and friendship of many non-Muslim classmates. Ignoring his Muslim background, they nicknamed him Tommy, which stuck throughout the years. This symbolized to him the all-American identity he so desperately sought. After high school he worked at the Fisher-Price factory and at the Borden's dairy plant nearby. He tried to live two lives. In the valley at school or at work, he was Tommy; on the hill, Haaneyfan. The older he grew, the more he realized these two personalities were irreconcilable. This confused him and eventually pushed him over the edge, driving him mad and prompting a personal rebellion against Jabul Arabiyya's rules and the established norms of sharia. "People told me, Rafeek is a French name. And I asked myself if Rafeek is a French name, and Haaneyfan is a Muslim name, and then they nicknamed me Tommy, and Tommy is a Christian name . . . I began to wonder about which one am I? Am I French? Muslim? Christian? It got pretty confusing."

To escape these dilemmas, he enlisted in the service. That proved an even worse nightmare. He was persecuted for his Muslim name. After rebelling furiously against combat training, he was court-martialed, sent to the stockade, and eventually discharged.

I was with the Eighty-Second Airborne Military Police Company. I was identified as a threat. Just the name made them watch me, made them never really actually put trust in me. And then I went there and I was speaking about God, and I really made them bitter. And they persecuted me pretty severely, too. They ended up putting me in a stockade, and they put me in the basement of the MP station like they were afraid of me, in their own way. And they put me in hand irons and put me in leg irons. They marched me to chow. You know, it was pretty cruel. For about two weeks. I guess they were trying to break my faith because I reached a point where I couldn't train to kill. I couldn't train to actually take a weapon and kill somebody. I told them to give me a job working at the chapel or as a clerk. Work with anything except the guns, but they wouldn't approve of that. And I told them my conscience didn't agree with it.

I really believed in my country. I grew up believing in America. And I really felt that to serve the country was right. But for a country to hurt you like that . . . to be put in chains because of my belief like that, I never thought people would go through such a thing. I thought those days were gone. I knew at any time it felt like they could have actually put me to death and say that it was an accident, on a training exercise. I had a lieutenant named Polk, and he actually told me that I was asking to be crucified. And nobody had ever told me such a thing like that or . . . and that instilled fear in me. You know, when somebody tells you, you are asking for that. I was young. About twenty-four. And I didn't say the things I said to try and cause a problem, you know. When you feel something strong within you, and you know that what you're speaking is the truth, you are not safe. Sometimes I wished a lot of things that I had said, I hadn't said. But if you hold things in you that's true, you're not being true to yourself, and you're not being true to people.

Upon returning from the army, he tried to participate in the civic life of the settlement, serving as the sergeant-at-arms of the village council. In light of the violent atmosphere he described, this was "one of the most dangerous positions" in the settlement. His duty was to enforce the decisions of the president, especially chasing away the many undesirables who came up to Jabul Arabiyya. "That's when I really wanted to just get away." Yet it was the only home he'd ever known. He found it more difficult than ever to abide by the rules of sharia. The elders wanted him to marry a Muslim and go to the mosque and raise his kids their way—the way their own children had already refused.

This made him defiant and determined to stay there on his own terms, although many others had already left. "What would happen," he wondered, "if one of them stood up to the entire community and said, 'I am going to become whatever I become?'" His return was an effort to assert his birthright in the land without embracing the will of the Muslim community. Not an easy job. To the general disapprobation of the community, he never attends the mosque. Instead he openly flaunts the sharia by carousing with his non-Muslim friends from West Valley.

When I saw what they were trying to do with me and to me, I just broke away, to let them know that I won't go along with it. More or less to say to them they can do what they want. But I'd go out and I'd actually get drunk just to let them know I am not identifying with anybody at the moment. And they would say things like, "He's living up there and he called himself a Muslim. I've seen him drink a case of beer the other day. I saw him with a bottle of Yukon Jack, and he was so drunk today!" I'm trying to let them know in a nice way that I'm not trying to walk this earth and be Mr. Perfect. I am trying to let them know that I will continue to search throughout my life, but I'm not going to let them confine me to a certain bunch of rules that we're going to lay down and you have got to do this. And it's not being disrespectful, it's just trying to tell the world straight out that I don't think I'm better than anyone else in the world. But God knows my heart, and I will always strive to return to him in good standard.

He professes belief in all religions. "People have said to me, you study so many Bibles you don't know which one to believe in." He has carried his spiritual independence to action by attending area churches. Once he got baptized in a local church, provoking a strong negative reaction from the Muslims, who branded him an apostate and agreed that he was possessed by Satan. "When I got baptized they went haywire. There was a time they would tell me how crazy I was and how stupid I was. And that makes you withdraw from the world, too. When people consider you mad or possessed by demons, that hurts."

Confusion and doubts about his faith, similar to those concerning his name, relate to an unstable sense of place and his ambiguous position in it. There is the valley of Christians and there is this "hill of Arabic-speakers" where he was born, and between them lies a boozy twilight in which he basks much of the time. "You know, but I hate for somebody to actually classify me as like, up here. I am close to the people in West Valley. But because I live up here, people say, he is one of them. And then the people up here say he's not one of us because he can't go to the mosque. And so you go get drunk today and I won't be one of nobody."

He views Jabul Arabiyya and its philosophy of hijra with understanding and respect but resents being made to feel different vis-à-vis the world beyond. He has many friends in West Valley and wants everyone to know he is part of the real world down there. Flaunting the sharia for Haaneyfan is a way to demonstrate his difference, exemplified when his friends drive around to take him drinking or when he attends church. "I've been to a lot of churches and I get entranced in listening to a preacher. I find you can find times to laugh, you can find times of fellowship, it's a lot of fun. I found joy out there in the Christian churches. And I know I have. But it fills them [Muslims] with bitterness when I'll go out there to one of those churches, but I won't go to the mosque. It's like a crime against God to them."

There seems to be no future for him on the hilltop and none down in the valley either. He survives on welfare and dreams of another life. "I'd like to take my guitar and go out there and entertain the world. I'd like to take my piano and go out there and entertain the world. And that's one of the goals that I want to do. I'd like to build my home and settle down and get married and have some kids because I know now if I do I can raise them up and teach them of God, and I don't have to send them into no churches, synagogue, or mosque or nothing."

He now spends his days on the hilltop reading the Bible, the Book of Mormon, and literature from the Watchtower Society. His relationship with Ghani was stormy once, then they grew closer. Ghani disapproved strongly of his rebellious ways, but he and Sister Saadek encouraged Haaneyfan to study the Bible. Perhaps they acknowledge some of the failures of Jabul Arabiyya. "I guess now they wonder, What have we done!" observes Haaneyfan dryly.

From his viewpoint many problems started with the intolerance he experienced as a form of religious persecution. It began at an early age in the form of a certain attitude: "You have your religion. We gave it to you. What more do you need!" He feels that this was deleterious not only on a personal level but for Jabul Arabiyya's society in general because it fostered an attitude of exclusivity. The more he compared the conditions of the Muslims to those of the surrounding Christians, the more it appeared to be a case of intolerance and hubris. The community was supposed to grow into a self-sufficient town with shops and services. Instead it depended on facilities and cash from the outside. It was supposed to promote a sense of communal spirituality embodied in the Islamic umma. Instead it produced an isolation that was all the more shocking in comparison to the pluralism of religions and creeds that any child might witness in the neighboring towns where everyone still worked and socialized together although there were several different churches.

Nonetheless, love remains between this abandoned child and the solitary roots of his anguished past. Sometimes, he thinks, he stays out of love for Ghani, Sister Saadek, and those now dead who all treated him like a son but certainly not out of any conscious fidelity to the ideal of an American hijra. "I know with my whole heart I love these people. People I grew up with, people who were old enough to be my father, and treated me real kind. And I stay here mainly too because of that."

At other times he questions the object of his belief, asking God why he had to stay when everyone else left. In his willingness to interrogate God he sees the point of his conflict with Muslims. He observes that the model of Abraham questioning God "as a son speaks to his father" is a way to get answers to the questions of life, whereas "Islam looks at the Quran and the Sunna, and all the answers to any question you could ever have are there."

Finally, from the perspective of a person born into an American Muslim family, a backslider who got himself baptized, he senses a kind of cruel irony perpetrated against the descendants of slaves. For him it is a self-defeating logic.

They are trying to go back and pick up the customs and the traditions of their forefathers, which means they will probably be trying to go back and worship the way they our forefathers did when they were in Africa. But even in doing that, many of them I saw that came out of the South were baptized. If you are baptized you would become a disciple of Jesus Christ. And then they came and they picked up this faith [Islam], and then after they picked it up there was an oath you had to take, and the oath was that there was is no God but Allah and Muhammad is his Apostle. Therefore, they have been disciples of Christ, and disciples of Muhammad, and it really confused me because more or less it would teach the Quran, and yet they knew the Bible. They actually would have had to know Christ at one time.

His observations concerning West Valley raise many questions about the feasibility of the plan to sustain hijra in the midst of secular America. Of Professor Ezaldeen, he recalls that when the elders began to see their children drifting away, some decided that they weren't ready to live under the "bylaws," as they called the book of sharia that Ezaldeen prepared for each of the AAUAA units.

6

The Place That

Didn't Belong in Brownsville

FEAR OF THE "BLACK NATION" In 1972 Shuaib
Abdur Raheem lived in Brooklyn. At twenty-three, he
was a practicing Sunni Muslim, having served in the
Air Force. Devotion to the strict discipline of Islam was his priority in life. He
worked as a night clerk for the Metropolitan Transit Authority. His day
began with *fajr*, morning prayer, in the minutes before sunrise, followed by
physical exercise and scriptural study with a few of his Muslim brothers. He
dreamed of making good with the van and moving company recently set up
in partnership with his close friend Dawud Rahman. Business was growing,
and they intended to purchase two more trucks.

The subway job was good but temporary. The sooner it was over, the
better. Not because of the Transit Authority or the excellent benefits offered
by the Transit Workers Union, but because of problems that had recently
developed concerning Shuaib's identity as an orthodox Muslim.

Before converting to Islam in 1969, Shuaib had learned to distinguish between orthodox Islam and the Nation of Islam, known popularly as the "Black Muslims." Orthodox Islam follows the teachings of the Holy Quran and the exemplary life of the Prophet Muhammad ibn Abdullah. The NOI indoctrinated its "brothers" into the racialist ideology of their leader, Elijah Muhammad. He preached that the black man was "God" and the white man the devil. Shuaib professed Sunni orthodoxy as a universal religion and the true unity of mankind, tauhid according to the Holy Quran. Under one supreme god, Allah, all racial distinctions are secondary. All men must submit to their Creator and work together as brothers on earth.

Malcolm X discussed these beliefs in his autobiography, published after his conversion to Sunni orthodoxy in 1964. His subsequent assassination culminated a long history of antagonism between orthodox Muslims and members of Elijah Muhammad's Nation of Islam. More than ever, they regarded each other with suspicion and fear now. Whenever members of the two faiths found themselves face-to-face there was palpable tension and the ominous threat of violence.

As a new man in the Transit Authority, Shuaib rotated job assignments frequently. He was now working in the token booth inside the 116th Street subway station in Harlem, where his presence created an uneasy situation. The Nation of Islam Temple No. 7, Malcolm's former pulpit, was just upstairs. Black Muslims sauntered by the ticket booth trying to sell him the paper *Muhammad Speaks* and mumbled insulting remarks when he refused. The subway had no uniform requirements for railroad clerks at the time, so Shuaib wore traditional Islamic garb to work—robes, khamisa, and turbans.

"Well, brother, when are you going to accept the Messenger?" a Black Muslim asked him provocatively one day.

"I already accepted the Messenger. His name is Muhammad ibn Abdullah," replied Shuaib.

"No, no, no, no! Not him, brother. Elijah!"

The man went upstairs but quickly returned in the company of a dozen comrades. They warned Shuaib not to insult Elijah Muhammad, the NOI, or its teachings and advised him to transfer to another station. They didn't want him around. Although he remained in that location, Shuaib purposely kept a very low profile and even avoided going upstairs if possible.

Four months later a Transit Authority auditor showed up to check his books. He wore a bow tie and a blue jacket with a Fruit of Islam insignia on his shirt. "Open the door. I'm from downtown," he demanded. Recognizing the insignia of the Black Muslims paramilitary organization, Shuaib refused to open the door before inspecting the man's identification and telephoning his supervisor to verify its authenticity.

After completing his audit, the man scolded Shuaib. "Brother, we know about you. Everybody knows about you. You better watch yourself! You keep saying that the Muhammad ibn Abdullah is the Messenger and that Elijah is not the Messenger, that his teachings are not Islam."

Though frightened, Shuaib remained indignant. "Listen, I believe what I believe. If somebody asks me what Islam is, I'm going to tell him the truth."

The man grew tense. "Brother, I'm just telling you to watch yourself because we are watching you," he threatened.

Toward the end of the year in late December, Shuaib's doorbell rang one Friday morning. His wife answered the door and called upstairs announcing some visitors.

Peering from his second-floor window, Shuaib was unable to identify the three men standing on the sidewalk. Suddenly one of them stepped back into the street to make himself more visible. Shuaib recognized him as the auditor from the Transit Authority. "As–salaam-alaikum, brother! Why don't you come downstairs, brother? We want to talk to you."

Opening the window, Shuaib yelled back nervously, "I don't have anything to say to you."

"Come down and tell them what you told me in the booth about the Messenger of Allah."

Shuaib guessed that the auditor had obtained his address from the Transit Authority's personnel files. The men finally left, but a few days later someone broke into his house while his wife was in bed. The intruder entered through the bedroom window before dawn while Shuaib was still at work. His wife awoke and fired a gun to chase the man away. Then she called Shuaib and reported what happened.

"She called up in hysterics, screaming," reported Shuaib.

When I came home and there was blood on the windowsill. Three days
prior I had purchased a twenty-five-caliber automatic with four bullets
from a junkie on the street. Gave it to my wife, I showed her how to use it,
and that's the only reason I believe to this day she wasn't hurt. She
reached under the mattress and pulled the pistol out and emptied it at the
window. She hit him. And there was blood on the windowsill, blood on
the fire escape. It was on the second floor. He jumped off the fire escape.
There was blood at the bottom of the steps. Blood all the way around
to the alleyway, and it ended at the curb. The intruder departed by car. We
reported it to the police. They came and took it down. They confiscated
the gun but quashed charges because I was a city employee. There was
some camaraderie between the transit authority and the police department back then. They didn't make no big thing about it, just told me to
get a license next time.

Shuaib's paranoia intensified a few weeks later. On 18 January 1973 a brutal crime occurred in Washington, D.C. where seven orthodox Muslims were murdered in cold blood in a Washington house owned by the professional basketball superstar Kareem Abdul Jabbar. Two adult women and two children were shot to death; three other children were drowned in a bathtub. They were the wives and children of Hamaas Abdul Khaalis, an orthodox Muslim and founder of the Hanafi sect. The lone survivor of the execution-style killings reported that one of the gunmen had shouted "Don't mess with Elijah!" as he fled the scene.

Khaalis had been prominent in the Nation of Islam before converting to orthodoxy in 1958. He had defected from the NOI but held onto some incriminating files from their Chicago and New York offices. According to some reports he possessed details of financial corruption along with proof of a long-rumored collusion between the NOI and George Lincoln Rockwell's American Nazi Party. Khaalis kept these files to protect himself while denouncing Elijah Muhammad as a "false prophet." He blamed Malcolm X's assassination on Elijah Muhammad and intimated that he would soon publicize the documents.

News of this horrifying crime spread quickly among orthodox Muslims in New York. This vicious act smacked of retribution against those who spoke out against Elijah Muhammad. For Shuaib, the Hanafi massacre fit the pattern of harassment in the ticket booth and the burglary at his home. Black Muslims did not make empty threats. They carried them out. Fearing an attack on Sunni Muslims, he spoke to the police, trying to explain a connection between the Washington murders and his experiences in New York. They looked at his beard and strange garb and just called him paranoid. Few outsiders understood the intense feelings simmering between Sunni orthodox Muslims and the Nation of Islam. The more Shuaib insisted, the more the cops interpreted it as a dispute between two street gangs.

Shuaib convinced himself that an assault on the Sunnis in New York was imminent. He summoned his closest Muslim friends—Dawud Rahman, Salih Ali Abdullah, and Yusuf Abdul-Mussadiq to join him in prayer and discussion about how to protect their families against a threat that others ignored. "Some of the brothers in the community had experienced similar close encounters. 'Man, listen, we've got to do something about it. These guys have started to kill women. I'm not going to have them coming to my house again.' "

They quickly decided on the need to obtain guns for self-defense. The problem was money, so on Friday, 9 January, Shuaib, Dawud, Salih, and Yusuf entered John & Al's Sports at Broadway and Melrose Street in the Bushwick section of Brooklyn, planning to steal some guns and ammunition. Intentions notwithstanding, it was an ill-conceived plan that degenerated almost immediately into a tragedy of epic proportions.

Seeing the holdup, one patron in the crowded store rushed out to alert the police. Several minutes later, police surrounded the store and positioned themselves behind the elevated subway tracks running along Broadway. Massive reinforcements soon arrived with the heavily armed tactical squad. Inside, Shuaib and the others realized that their attempt had failed. They conferred and decided that it would be best to end things peacefully by surrendering to the police. Preparing to negotiate, Shuaib stepped out the back door in the company of the store's co-owner, but they were greeted by a hail of police bullets pushing them back inside. Surrender would not be so easy. A withering barrage of gunfire lasted for more than an hour, further endangering the lives of everyone inside.

Upon seizing the store, the bandits had cut the telephone lines, making it impossible to communicate with the police directly. With a full-scale police offensive in progress, Shuaib believed that he and the others had to return fire to prevent a blitz. They saw an armored personnel carrier in front of the store and over five hundred heavily armed policemen surrounding them. From inside it seemed as if the police were massing to storm the place. Outside there was little coordination among the troops. No one had assigned positions. Nobody was really in command. The tactical squad had little experience in this type of urban warfare. In the early moments of the battle, amid thunderous shotgun blasts and ricocheting bullets, an officer was struck in the neck and died instantly. Two of his comrades in blue were also wounded.

By the time the press arrived, everyone was speculating about the identity of the holdup men. Rumors circulated that they belonged to the Black Liberation Army. They were assumed to be ruthless and, like most African-American radicals, determined to die rather than surrender. Cops and reporters traded stories. There were little fact and much hyperbole. The mood in the neighborhood grew carnivalesque when many Latino and African-American residents of the area gathered behind police barricades to cheer for those inside the store. The police were outsiders and an unwelcome presence in the community. Symbolic perhaps of the massive police intrusion into a predominantly minority neighborhood, the crowd of bystanders cheered whenever the robbers answered the police shots with gunfire of their own. Few really knew about the Muslims or why they were inside.

The police seemed to care as little for the safety of the bystanders as for that of the four robbers and ten hostages inside the building. They exercised no crowd control to clear the streets from the lines of intense and misdirected gunfire. It was a quasi-military operation, among the first of its kind in New York City. It seemed that public safety was secondary to the ends of subduing an alleged renegade group. The police believed that they were facing black radicals seeking to touch off a race war. The other Broadway, in Brooklyn, had become a Hollywood stage, and the drama was as unreal as it was out of control. A platoon of inexperienced law officers and four amateur crooks had transformed a foiled larceny into a hellish conflagration. Eager reporters and photographers fashioned it into a citywide spectacle, increasing the police department's determination not to back down. Conflict resolution teams and hostage mediators never entered the realm of possibilities.

Two days later, the people trapped in the store between the violent police phalanx outside and the four orthodox Muslims escaped unscathed by mounting a stairway to the roof of the building. They emerged with the first clear picture of the intruders and their motives. Several averred that the Muslims had never attempted to stop them from leaving the store; it was the police siege that had prevented them from leaving earlier. Nearly forty-eight hours after the bungled robbery, Shuaib and the others finally negotiated with the police for a peaceful surrender. At a news conference following the incident, the Brooklyn district attorney, Eugene Gold, announced that the Muslims would get a fair trial and an opportunity to tell their side of the story.

During the siege Shuaib had issued a written statement explaining their presence in the store. They made three critical points. The first was a confession of their faith. "We are taking firm steps in the establishment and defense of Islam. We bear witness that none is worthy of worship but Allah and Muhammad is his servant and prophet." The second comment tried to explain how the police officer died "as a result of his trigger-happy comrades who sporadically fired shots at the hostages in the store." Finally they proclaimed their "actions are an expression of our opposition to oppression. Our demand is that justice be meted out to all." This last declaration, it was later explained, referred to the tragic Hanafi massacre in Washington and those Black Muslims responsible for it.

The arraignment was a continuation in another form of the media circus that had begun in front of the sporting goods store. Heavily armed officers cordoned off access to Kings County Criminal Court, where the proceedings took place on Monday, 22 January. Helicopters swooped overhead. In front of the press and their cameras stood Robert M. McKiernan, president of the Patrolmen's Benevolent Association, demanding that the accused be sent to the electric chair. Despite the absence of capital punishment in New York at the time such public pronouncements would make it virtually impossible to select an evenhanded jury.

It was alleged that the defendants had stolen some footwear from the sporting goods store, so they were stripped of their shoes and socks and forced to enter the courtroom barefoot. Uniformed police officers packed the room. When herded before the bench, the four accused men were a vivid reminder of rebellious slaves brought to heel.

Further developments around the arraignment would decide the fate of the accused. Despite a published statement to the contrary, they were portrayed as fanatical Black Power radicals. Two leftist defense attorneys, Gerald Lefcourt and Sanford Katz, had rushed to Brooklyn during the siege in the belief that this was a politically motivated crime involving young African Americans. Lefcourt had become famous as the second chair in attorney William Kunstler's defense of the Chicago Seven. During the battle the two attorneys managed to talk with the defendants and relate their thoughts to the media.

To dispel the momentary frenzy, Katz tried to clarify the defendants' identities. His impression was that they were thoroughly dedicated Muslims. "It is a question of who shot first. I don't get the sense that these are people fighting a race war. They make it quite clear that they are not racists. That would be contrary to the teachings of [Islam]. They are concerned about poor people and eradicating injustice."

The media reflected the initial confusion about the robbers and their motives. Reflecting a general ignorance of Islam in America, the *New York Times* mistakenly identified them as "Black Muslims." A more accurate description emerged two days later on 23 January 1973, when readers read of the links between the Brooklyn robbery and the Washington murders.

The presumptive defenders of the "Williamsburg 4", as Shuaib and his codefendants were known, encountered a more serious hurdle when they asked the judge to formally assign them to the case. Citing the prisoners' indigence, he refused the motion and directed them to submit to the system where attorneys were chosen by lottery from among state-approved lawyers. Katz and Lefcourt countered in affirming the defendants' right to designate preferred counsel. Eventually they would have prevailed on this point except for another ugly problem that permanently ended their efforts.

Following arraignment, the four men conferred with fellow Muslims who offered support in frequent jailhouse visits and telephone conversations. Someone floated the idea of a defense fund and suggested appealing to immigrant Muslims. Unlike the general public, Muslims might understand the often violent relations between Sunnis and the Nation of Islam. It was a long shot, however, because support was weak even among indigenous Muslims. Some orthodox leaders wanted to avoid getting involved with the defendants. To change their minds would be difficult, especially if the defendants insisted on retaining Jewish lawyers. Shuaib and the others would have to fire the "Zionists" or else go to trial without the support of other Muslims. Someone suggested quizzing the two attorneys about their views on Israel to prove that they were the wrong people to defend a Muslim cause. So, with only a vague notion of the real potential for an all-Muslim defense fund, the four picked a fight with Katz and Lefcourt on religious grounds and summarily dismissed them.

The Muslim defense fund never materialized unfortunately, but they now had to find a new defense team quickly. Although few capable attorneys were willing to take on a high-profile case involving a dead cop, one notable exception was William Kunstler. In preliminary conversations with Shuaib, he informed him that he could take the case only if the judge would agree to postpone the trial. If the "Williamsburg 4" case could be delayed for several months, he would do it. Otherwise, they would have to find another lawyer. Fearing a political circus and yielding perhaps to outside pressure, most likely from the police union, the judge proved intransigent and refused Kunstler's request. Instead he selected as the defense lawyer a man who had just finished a stint with the prosecutor's office, virtually assuring compliance with the state's case.

After a couple of interviews with the new lawyer, who seemed singularly unresponsive, Shuaib concluded that the defendants would have to represent themselves. That meant access to law texts and codes in the prison library. Owing to the enormous publicity surrounding the case, however, they were under very restricted confinement at the Brooklyn House of Detention, where conditions severely limited their access to the prison law library. Although permitted to carry some books back to their cells, neither Shuaib nor his codefendants could make extra time for study, and after the cellblock lights went out at 10 PM, there was no reading except what could be done by the dim ambient light coming from the corridor bulbs.

Another setback was the opening of the trial when the judge decided to familiarize the jury with the crime scene by holding a court session at the actual crime scene in Brooklyn. The prisoners were taken there in shackles while newspapers and television reminded the public of the horrible death of an officer in the line of duty.

The charges included intentional murder, felony murder, assault with intent to commit murder, kidnapping, and robbery. The robbery charges stemmed from the attempt to steal guns, whereas kidnapping implied that the clerks and customers were forcibly detained inside the store against their will. Intentional murder, the final charge, implied an action calculated not just to harm or maim but to cause death. The prosecution alleged that the police officer was hit by a bullet from an assault rifle like those in the store, but the gun never materialized as evidence. In general, the ballistics information was so haphazard that nothing was ever submitted to the Grand Jury that issued the indictment and handed down the charges.

On forensic evidence, the jury heard that the dead police officer had worn a bulletproof vest to protect his chest and stomach from direct gunfire. A single bullet fragment lodged in the neck had killed him instantly. However, the officer did not fall backward, as would be expected from gunfire emanating from the store. He had keeled over horizontally instead. Crime lab evidence showed that the fatal fragment had "opened after striking something solid," possibly ricocheting off the iron pillar of the elevated subway platform. No further material proof was ever introduced as concrete evidence. The direction from which the fatal shots were fired was never firmly established.

Acting as his own attorney, Shuaib began to build an argument based on "defensive justification." He maintained that once trapped inside the store, the robbers were forced to return fire at the police to prevent them from overrunning the place and killing everyone inside.

There was eyewitness testimony to corroborate this perspective. Many people inside the store testified. On the one hand, they felt victimized by the initial robbery. On the other hand, however, they felt they had been placed in double jeopardy once the building was surrounded by a legion of undisciplined police officers. The jury saw with their own eyes the aftermath of the incident. Many rounds of ammunition had penetrated the store. Its interior and exterior walls resembled Swiss cheese, which can still be seen today. All that firing proved only one thing, the police acted recklessly.

Who shot the police? In his crossexamination Shuaib managed to show that even the police reports were contradictory as to the fatal bullet's trajectory. Three police officers, including two of those wounded, were unable to testify that they knew where the shots originated. A veteran ballistics expert testified that he discovered three different types of ammunition near the elevated-track pillar where the policeman died. He never said whether any of it matched the calibers used by the police department.

In his own defense, Shuaib suggested that the officer might have died as the result of "friendly fire." This reasoning unsettled the courtroom, but he persistently argued that the mere fact of a robbery in progress did not call for the excessive use of force that followed. Accordingly, the excessive amount of police force was unlawful and constituted a nuisance to public security. The police had transformed a public area into a free fire zone, and they alone should be held responsible for the fatality.

The judge had promised to allow the jury to deliberate Shuaib's "defensive justification" plea in deciding the different murder counts. When Shuaib's cross-examination began to substantiate this logic, however, the judge grew more fearful that the jury might hesitate to deliver convictions. With the press, police, and politicians already clamoring for maximum sentences, the judge feared any deliberation based solely on the material evidence. When it came time to charge the jury, he astonished even the prosecution by retracting his pledge to Shuaib.

Nonetheless, the jury considered the defense arguments. Twice during their deliberations they requested clarification of section 20 of the criminal code that defines the idea of conspiracy. If the defendants were guilty of plotting a robbery, were they also guilty of felony murder? Each time the issue was raised, the judge became angry. In response to other questions concerning the relative timing of the robbery and shootings, the judge insisted that if the jury found the four men guilty of the robbery, then they would have to convict them on the murder charges too. He explained that it did not make any difference whether the police officer died by stray gunfire. Finally, he screamed at them and insisted on a conviction.

A pyrrhic victory for the defense was their acquittal on the intentional murder charge. The lack of material evidence caused the jurors to realize something was wrong. Although they attempted to clarify their understanding of the law pertaining to the serious charge of felony murder, the judge allayed their concerns. The fate of the "Williamsburg 4" was sealed. The judge sentenced each man to a term of twenty-five years to life.

On 5 August 1974, Shuaib was transported from New York City to Sing Sing accompanied by police helicopters and a long motorcade up the interstate. Three days later he and all three codefendants were taken to nearby Green Haven prison, where the warden refused to accept them. They sat sweltering in the paddy wagon for nearly two hours until a compromise was worked out. They were finally taken inside but stayed at only two weeks. Next Shuaib and Dawud were sent to Clinton in Danemora, New York. Yusef and Salih went to Great Meadows in Comstock, a maximum security facility so tough that prisoners call it "Gladiator School." This arrangement lasted until September. Shuaib went next to Auburn. He spent the rest of 1974 and 1975 at Elmira until he was expelled for participating in an inmate's assembly for constitutional rights. This led him back to Auburn in early 1976. He returned to the county jail in Elmira briefly in April 1976 for a court challenge to his expulsion from the state facility, but he stayed at Auburn until May or June, when he went back to Green Haven.

Shuaib still has vivid recollections of an incident en route to Auburn in the autumn of 1974. When the Department of Corrections transferred him from Elmira, the move took place in the middle of the night. As they were traveling across the state, he signaled from the back of the van that he needed to urinate. In response to this request, the vehicle slowed to stop on a dark side road. The guards opened the doors and ordered him out of the van. Fearing that they would shoot him and claim he tried to escape, he tried to reason with them. Perhaps they could stop at a gas station along the highway. But the guards insisted and tried to drag him out of the van. "If you're going to kill me, let it be inside the van where you'll have to explain all the blood," he countered defiantly. Only when the lights of another vehicle illuminated the scene through the woods did the guards abandon their game and proceed to the highway. There was no rest stop, however. He arrived at the facility wet and humiliated. Several months later he received a visit from Benjamin Ward, commissioner of New York's Department of Corrections, who told him that he would "never see the streets again."

Between 1978 and 1982 Shuaib went from Comstock to Attica and then back to the "box" ("Secure Housing Unit"; solitary confinement) in Comstock; then to Attica again, on to the "box" at Auburn (he remembers that his mother died while he was in confinement at Auburn in 1980), and to Attica again until August 1984. Then to Wende, situated between Buffalo and Attica, for forty-five days, Elmira for two months, Comstock for six months, Downstate for four days, Attica for one week, and finally to Wende in 1985, where I met him four years later and began a series of interviews documenting his conversion to Islam.

The remainder of this chapter is Shuaib's story in his own words.

THE BALDIES   Malcolm was assassinated in February 1965 in Manhattan. This was around the same time that I had come in contact with the Five Percenters. And they attracted a lot of black youth in the community. I was about fourteen or fifteen years old then, and one of my friends had become a Five Percenter. Sammy was always into anything new, the one that experimented with everything. He was the first one to sniff airplane glue on the block, the first one who took acid, the first one to smoke reefer, the first one to drink—he was the first one to do everything. "Here, you got to try it, it's terrific, take my word for it." That's how Sammy was. He might even still be alive. He's the kind of man that has that luck. Nine lives, they say, of a cat.

I saw him in 1964 after we moved from Bedford-Stuyvesant to Canarsie. Sammy was still living in Bedford-Stuyvesant and came by the neighborhood when he heard that we were there. He had this little beanie on his head with a little tassel hanging off the back. And he was very stern and severe. He was clean. He wasn't high or anything. I said, "What's up man?" He said, "Peace. Peace." And he started running the standard line of the Five Percenters that the black man is your God, and he went on and on with this strange new philosophy. It was appealing because for Sammy to be taken in by anything there had to really be something to it.

He told me he was a Five Percenter. He explained what it was and stayed for dinner. Then my mother asked him what he was talking about. "Well, what do you think of Malcolm?"

He said, "Malcolm is our leader."

The following December, I became a Five Percenter too. It was just before Malcolm was killed in February 1965. Sammy took me up to Manhattan where I met "The Father"—Clarence 13-X Smith—the man who called himself "Allah." This was my first exposure to anything to do with Islam other than listening to Malcolm and seeing him on television.

I was attracted to Malcolm X, very much attracted to him because of my parents. I was born in Brooklyn but raised in the South, so I knew about the Klan. I had been chased by them. My uncle's funeral home was burned down by the Klan. I went to a Jim Crow school. I knew what it was to sit in the back of a bus, to be thrown out of Woolworth's, to be told "You can't sit here! You can't go there!" So all of those memories were still fresh. And much of the teachings of the Nation of Islam and the Five Percenters spoke to that. It struck a cord which just about any Afro-American could relate to. And there the humiliation of the white man having trampled on black people for so many years and slavery. I was drawn to that, and I became a Five Percenter. I remember we went into Manhattan to a few of their meetings, which they called "parliaments." All of them get together and stand around in big circles and they preach and they teach to one another and anyone else that will listen. They had those in Morningside Park in Manhattan. The Five Percenters were very much into culture, identity, and black women. We ran the pimps out of our neighborhood. We stopped women from standing on street corners. We were against drugs too. We wouldn't even allow people to sell reefer to kids. That's when the black awareness movement really began. And I got swept right up in it.

Later that year one of my friends, not a Five Percenter, invited me to his home for Thanksgiving dinner. I met his older sister there. She was dressed in this garb. Her head was covered, hijab. To me that was garb and I had never seen anything like that before. She looked so elegant and dignified and so different. I asked her was she Muslim and she said Yes. I said, "Well, I'm Muslim too." And she looked at me and said, "You're a Muslim! When did you take shahada?" And I didn't know what the word shahada meant because there was no shahadas [for Five Percenters]. You just said you was a Five Percenter and that made you a Five Percenter. We went to their classes, got notes and the lessons. She continued to ask me other questions, and apparently I didn't give her the right answers. Finally she said, "You're not a Muslim!" And I got real offended.

She says, "Well, I'm getting married this weekend. Why don't you come to the wedding? Come with my brother and my sister." Her mother refused to go to her wedding because she was against her conversion to Islam.

So I went. It was on a weekend in Brownsville [another section of Brooklyn]. Now I didn't know anything about Islam or Muslims other than what I learned from the Five Percenters and the little I knew from seeing Malcolm on television. But Sammy had told me that the Five Percenters couldn't go to certain parts of Brownsville because of the "Baldies." He said that the Baldies would chase us away from certain areas from Hopkins Avenue to East Ninety-eighth Street [and] from Newport to Pitkin Avenue. The Baldies don't like Five Percenters, they hate us. They don't want us anywhere in that area. They don't like us. I didn't understand really, except that I wasn't supposed to go in this area. Well, it just so happened the wedding was set in a place on Tapscott Street which is right in the middle of Brownsville within that area between Hopkins Avenue and East Ninety-eighth Street. So when me and my friend were walking I said, "Hey, where is this place at?"

He said, "Tapscott."

I said, "I can't go over to Tapscott!"

"Why not?"

I said, "The Baldies."

He said, "Oh man, don't worry about the Baldies. We'll go anyway."

So off we went to Tapscott Street, but we took a circuitous route, all the way around down Hegeman and come up the back way just to make sure that I wouldn't run into any Baldies. He told me to take my beanie off, and I said, "I'm not going to take my beanie off. I'm a Five Percenter man, you know, I'm God."

Anyway we got to the apartment building and we go upstairs and he knocks on the door and his sister answers the door and she's glad to see him. Oh, she just lights up because this is the only family member who came to her wedding. We went into the kitchen where she was cooking chicken with a few other sisters. I smelled the chicken. Great chicken. So she told me, "Go on in the room and just have a seat with the brothers."

I went to walk in the room from the kitchen and she says, "No, no, no! Take your shoes off."

Take my shoes off? Oh boy! Me taking my shoes off back then. Sneakers. Oh God! I was just too embarrassed to take my shoes off. I know my feet must have smelled like . . . goodness gracious, you would have to fumigate the whole place. I said to myself, "No, I can't do this." I didn't tell her that. I just said, "That's all right, I'm going back home."

She grabbed me by my arms, pulled me to the side and gave me a bar of soap and said, "Go in the bathroom. "

I said, "What are you trying to do?"

She said, "Go ahead, I know you. Go on in the bathroom and wash your feet and come on out."

So I did. I took my shoes off. I washed my socks. Put my sneakers out on the window ledge, closed the window, and came back in inside. There was a little curtain. I went through and was absolutely blown away by what I saw. It was like something out of a *National Geographic*. I had never seen a thing like this in my life at that time. The walls were white and this black stripe around it with gold letters and all these funny little paintings that have got all of this scribble on it but it looked exotic. And I seen that men were all sitting on one side in a little circle and the women were sitting across from them in another circle and they had this strange music playing in the background and all of the women wore hijab. They were laughing and giggling. There were plates of fruits and candy. They were the prettiest women I had ever seen in my life. I just fell in love. I mean I just couldn't believe it. And naturally, as a young man, I'm going to go sit with the women. I even recognized one girl from my neighborhood. I used to try to talk to her, but she ignored me all the time. When I saw her there, she looked at me and appeared shocked that we were in the same place.

As I went to step her way, one of the brothers said, "Hey, where are you going?"

I said, "I'm going over here."

He said, "No, no, no, no! Get over here!"

The guy told me to sit with the brothers. They were having a conversation. Maybe twenty to twenty-five men and about thirty or forty women—on opposite sides of this big room. So I sat down with the brothers, and most of us were sitting down in a cross-legged position. I had never sat like that before on the floor. As I sat on the floor there was a break in their conversation. One of the brothers turned to me and said, "Who are you?"

And this is exactly what I said. I said, "Peace. God. My name is Allah God Walik Supreme." Everybody heard me, including the women on the other side of the room. They all turned and stared at me with a look of disgust that I'll never forget. Even more than disgust, it was anger. They just stared. Then I remember this guy grabbing me around my collar and slamming me on the wall.

"How the hell did you get in here!? Who let you in here?" And men stood up around me and grabbed me by my arms and they grabbed me like they were going to throw me out of the apartment.

I was thinking, they're dressed like Arabs—one had a dagger in his belt— but they were Afro-Americans. But they looked like something out of *National Geographic*. I had never seen nothing like this. It was like the whole room was out of place—it didn't belong. This place didn't belong in Brownsville.

After the guy grabbed me around the neck and was dragging me out of the room and the men came out of the back and they had me by my feet they turned to one man in a corner who was sitting in the corner very quietly and they said, "What do we do?"

He said, "Just throw him out!"

The other one said, "Well, we've got to do more than that to him. He's got some nerve coming here!"

And then the leader says, "Well just get rid of him. Throw him outside. Throw him out on the street." So the men who were going to take me out went and got coats. They tucked their robes down in their pants. They put on these overcoats and they took off their turbans and every single one of them had bald heads. And I said, "Oh my God!" I screamed, "The Baldies!" I just screamed. I just knew they were going to kill me.

When I screamed, the sister came out of the kitchen and she said, "What are you doing? What are you doing!"

And he said, "He has no business in here. We don't want these people around us."

She was crying and pleaded with her husband for the brothers not to hurt me. "He doesn't know any better. He doesn't know. I invited him."

He said, "We're not going to hurt him, we are just going to throw him out, kick him in his butt and teach him a lesson."

She said, "No, no! Don't do that! Don't do that. Teach him, he doesn't know."

They were debating. They looked at the imam. That's who he was in the corner, the imam. And the imam nodded his head and they threw me on the floor, slammed me up against the wall. Three brothers sitting right in front of me, and he told me like this, "The first pillar in Islam is that you bear witness."

That's how I learned about Islam in 1965. They taught me the five pillars, the articles of faith. They were Sunni Muslims from the Dar ul-Islam movement. That's how I met them.

I was fifteen years old. They were getting ready to kick the living daylights out of me. They were the ones who kept Five Percenters and the Nation of Islam out of Brownsville. Brownsville has never been a stronghold for the Nation. That was like a desert for the Nation all those years. And I was confused. He told me about Islam. He told me about Allah, he told me about the Prophet Muhammad. I thought he was talking about Elijah. When I said, "Elijah Muhammad," he smacked me in the mouth. He said, "No! the Prophet Muhammad ibn Abdullah." That's the first time I ever heard that name before. He told me when he was born, when he had died, that he had come from Arabia. He told me about the Holy Quran. He showed me the book in the corner that was on a book stand. The Holy Quran. He told me about the five prayers a day. He told me about wudzu— purification—and I was very curious. And he told me that they wash their hands and their mouth and their nose and their face and their feet. And he told me that he washed his feet five times a day. These guys are serious, I thought. Anybody washing his feet five times a day, I figured, has got to be sick. His feet are cleaner then most people's faces, man. And I don't know but right away I just became overwhelmed by everything.

The wedding ceremony had taken place before we arrived. This was the post nuptial feast. They brought in this big platter of food. I had never seen this much food in my life—heaps of rice, chicken, and goat and lamb and a big platter full of fruits and candies and big jugs of juice, like orange juice, grape juice, and they would just pass this around. I never felt like this in my life, man. I mean this was the most beautiful thing I had ever seen in my life. And I was impressed to say the least—very much impressed. All during the feast they are talking to me. They warmed up to me. They have taken to me and I've taken to them. I fell in love with all of them immediately. They were so clean and so different. I just can't explain it. There was something beautiful about all of them that I just couldn't explain. Until this day, I can't put it into words. Their faces glowed. Their complexion was so clean and their teeth were so white and their eyes were so white and bright. They smiled and it was a smile from the heart. You very rarely saw that in many people. Very friendly. Afterwards, very friendly—very warm to me and made me feel like I belong there and they answered every question I asked.

Later on, I was really confused, very confused. They told me about the Five Percenters. They told me about Clarence 13-X. And then I asked them about Malcolm. When I mentioned Malcolm's name they all got quiet and they told me about Malcolm. And they told me that when Malcolm left the Nation he came to them and they protected him. They were his bodyguards. And when Malcolm came to them he was viewed by them as their savior, the one who would help them and give them what they were missing. They needed a personality like Malcolm. Charismatic and very outspoken, very intelligent, very well read, very articulate, and they needed someone like him, and Malcolm had set up many meetings with them and had met with them and they helped him start his Muslim Mosque Inc. up on 125th Street. They volunteered to be his bodyguards.

They loved Malcolm. And they hated all of those who killed him, and they told me about Elijah Muhammad, about his teachings of hate and racism. They also told me that in Islam there were Muslims who were white, and I couldn't believe that. From everything I had learned [previously], whites couldn't be Muslims. He told me, yes, they were, and that if I came back to classes on the following weekend I would meet one—a few of them, and he would take me to these other places where there [were] whole communities of Muslims who are white right there in the city. I couldn't believe that.

Anyway I told myself, well, I wanted to be Muslim. I thought I was Muslim when I was a Five Percenter. And since I'm not a Muslim and I thought I was, I want to be one. So, well, I want to take my shahada. So the imam was in the car. He was looking at me. He asked, "How old are you?" At that time I was fifteen. And he says, "Well, what does your mother say about it? I think you'd better talk to your mother about that."

I said my mother would never agree to this. My mother would never accept the fact that I was Muslim. It would create all kinds of problems for me. And since I was only fifteen years old, she would throw me out, and who was going to take care of me. Where was I going to stay? Who was going to look after me? And the imam asked the brothers, "Could one of you put him up if his mother put him out of the house and he wants to be a Muslim? Could any of you put him up?"

And one brother says, "Well, I don't know. . . . I have some daughters. I wouldn't want him around my daughters . . ."

That was a wise thing. . . . But the bottom line was no one was willing to put me up in their house. Then someone suggested letting me stay in the mosque.

The imam said, "No. If he stays in the mosque and his mother calls the cops and the cops come here . . . then they want to kick the door of the mosque down, and we can't have that. So he either has to stay in his own home, or if he can't stay there, then he has to stay in someone else's home. And one of you brothers will have to open up his house."

No one volunteered, so he told me, "Well here's what you do. We don't want to give you shahada right now because it would create a lot of problems. But what you do is, you continue to come back and come to the classes. This way you are going to learn more about it and make sure this is what you really want to do. This would give you time to talk to your mother and, you know, get things right with her and find out exactly how she's going to react."

I said, "Well, as soon as she finds out that you love Malcolm and that you are against the people that killed Malcolm, I think she would look at you differently."

So I went back home to my mother. She was confused, and I didn't really know how to articulate it that well. It was like being flooded with so much. In a few hours I learned an entirely different way of life. Entirely, with a new perspective and outlook on everything. And I was just overwhelmed by it and impressed.

My mother was angry with me, and she said, "You still have got that beanie on that head, don't you?"

And I said, "Mom . . ."

She said, "Take it off."

I said, "Mom, I'm not going to wear this no more. I'm going to wear a turban."

She says, "Oh, my God! Now he wants to wear a turban!" And she told me, "Well, you are still a young boy. I want you in school. I want you to stay in school. It is all right if you go over there on the weekends and go to the classes. They sound like good people, but I want to meet them myself."

And I told her that they were married and they were working and all of them were good people. They were decent people. They had children. They were clean.

One weekend I tried to go back, but they weren't there anymore. Afterwards I just sort of like lost contact with them until '69.

FACE-TO-FACE WITH FARRAKHAN   Between '65 and '67 there was a lot of gang fighting. A rival gang from across town came to our neighborhood breaking windows, and we fought them and then ran them out of the neighborhood, but we got arrested, juvenile charge you know. It was a meatball situation. But anyway as a result of that my mother said, "Listen, you are going to mess up your record and everything, so maybe you ought to go in the service." So she signed for me to go into the service and I went into the air force on 5 October

1967. I was sent to Texas for basic training and that was when I ran into racism in the military. This was around the same time that you have the [Black] Panther party coming up. You had the whole black awareness movement at its peak and the riots in Newark and Brooklyn. As a matter of fact I went in right after the riots that took place in Brownsville, downtown Brooklyn, Bedford-Stuyvesant, Manhattan, Newark, Detroit, all of that. I went in the service in that same year. I went in from Brooklyn where they had deployed the National Guard, and when I got to Texas the first thing someone asked me was, "Are you one of those niggers from New York? You are in Texas now, nigger!"

I just looked at him. I didn't say nothing. He was talking. He wanted an answer. Finally I said, "My name is not nigger." I told him what my name was, and so he was smiling and he grabbed me around my collar, pushed me up against the wall. This is at an airport before I even got to the base. He was a sergeant, and I punched him in the face. Then he called the MPs with the dogs and they cornered me in the airport and put handcuffs on me when they took me to the barracks on the base, and that's where I stayed, in the brig. Welcome to the air force!

I went through my basic training there. After six weeks they threatened to make me go through it again, but in the end they didn't. I made up for the time I was in the brig by doing a lot of extra exercises and drills and details. I did it all. I didn't want to stay there no longer then I had to in Texas. After basic, I wanted to go into air conditioning and refrigeration because I had been to an after-school training program where I [had] learned air conditioning and refrigeration. I took a bypass test and I scored very high on it, so I didn't have to go through tech school in the air force. As a matter of fact, they wanted to put me in one of their big units, the Strategic Air Command (SAC). It was a real big deal, and I had to qualify for top secret clearances. There was a delay because of the arrest I had for the gang fight; when my fingerprints came back it was still on my record. So they held me up for six more weeks until the FBI finished their investigation. But finally, I got my orders to go to a SAC base up in Massachusetts at Westover Air Force Base. It was while I was there that I had a very bad experience.

I had a big picture of Malcolm in my room—a big poster. Picture of Malcolm, and just imagine this on a SAC base, now, you know. When they found out, that caused problems. But I had a big picture of Malcolm, Huey P. Newton, Kathleen Cleaver, hanging up on the walls. I originally had a white roommate. He moved in one day—[he] looked at those pictures, and when I came back from work he was gone. He moved out of the room, and he said," This guy's crazy." I had Malcolm X's albums that I listened to, and that's when I read Malcolm's autobiography. That really, really just further solidified in my mind what I wanted to be.

A black roommate finally moved in, and he seen these pictures of Malcolm and said, "Why have you got his picture up there, man? He's a traitor."

I said, "Hold up, man. We're not going to get along. I'll tell you right now."

He called Malcolm a traitor because he was leaning toward the Nation of Islam. And every Sunday morning two guys would come in from town to pick him up and take him to the meetings in Springfield to their temple. We used to have many arguments about Islam. I was telling him that he wasn't Muslim and this wasn't right. Anyway, these guys kept pressing me every Sunday morning. I'd be sleeping but hear them saying, "What about your roommate, why doesn't he come down too?"

So they woke me up, and I said, "No, man, I don't want to go."

One guy said, "Man, you ought to take that picture down."

I said, "Listen, man, if you want to come in and talk about Malcolm and say anything derogatory about him . . . I don't want to hear it. As a matter of fact, don't say one word against him in this room. If you've got something to say, you take it out in the parking lot."

This went on and on for two months, and they kept pressing me. One Sunday they said, "Listen, Muhammad Ali and Minister Farrakhan are going to be in Springfield, and I want you to come out with us just this one time brother. You've just got to meet them."

I liked Muhammad Ali even though I didn't like his affiliations. I said, what the heck, I'll go. So I went to the temple, and they frisked me down like they do everyone—they frisk you—and I had a straight razor I used to carry with me, you know. Normally I didn't carry it but when I went to this temple I carried it because I didn't know what these guys were about. They found it when they frisked me. Boy did he put me under a lot of scrutiny there at the temple. "Why did you bring this here?"

I said, "Protection."

"Protection from who?" he was interrogating me.

I said, "Look, man, you got it. Put it in the paper bag. I'll get it when I come out." So they put it in a paper bag. I went into the meeting, and I heard Farrakhan speaking. They had some . . . Muslims that were there in the audience, and it's the first time that I heard Farrakhan.

One of the members of the audience, was an old lady; she said, "What about Malcolm? What about Minister Malcolm?"

Everybody got quiet and looked at her and stared like shooting daggers at her. Farrakhan says, "Every place I go there are always people who keep asking about this traitor." He called the man a traitor. He said, "The man is no good. The man betrayed the messenger of Allah. He's a man who spoke out against him [Elijah Muhammad], and Malcolm got just what he deserved."

That's the first time I ever heard him say that. Anyway, I was quiet. I didn't say anything. Muhammad Ali got up and told a few jokes and talked about boxing. Most of the people were there because of him. After the meeting was over Muhammad Ali was signing autographs, and he signed a little autograph for me. And he put his arm around my shoulder and he said, "When are you going to send in for your X?"

This was a process you went to with the Nation. You sign this piece of paper and it was a letter that you wrote to Elijah Muhammad saying that you want to be a Muslim and you wanted to regain your identity and that you wanted your X. Well, you would drop your last name and take on an X. And I told him, "No, I don't want to do that."

And he asked, "Why?" This is Muhammad Ali.

I said, "Well, I have my reasons."

He said, "What reasons, brother? You don't want to be part of the black nation?"

I said, "Man, I'm Muslim, but I don't want to be affiliated with you all. I want to be a Muslim but not one of you." So when I said that all of these guys, the Fruit of Islam, his bodyguards standing around, got very quiet.

Farrakhan, who had his back to me talking to somebody else, turned around and he looked at me and he said, "What did you say?"

And I told him I didn't want to be part of the Nation. He said, "No, you said something about being a Muslim."

I said, "I want to be a Muslim."

"How are you going to be a Muslim and not be with the Nation?"

I said, "There are other Muslims besides the Nation. I'm talking about being a real Muslim, an orthodox Muslim, Sunni Muslim. I don't want to be affiliated with you. I want to be the kind of Muslim that Malcolm was when he died."

When I mentioned Malcolm's name these guys grabbed me around my neck [and] put my arms behind my back and Muhammad Ali moved out of the way. He didn't stop them. Farrakhan stopped them. Farrakhan said, "No, leave him alone. We asked him a question, he gave us an answer. There's no reason for you to punish him for that. But take him in the basement and let him think about it for awhile."

They locked me up in the basement for three hours. In Springfield, Mass. In the temple. And they sent down these four or five guys, big guys from the Fruit [of Islam] standing around me and cracking their knuckles, staring at me. They said, "You know, we ought to kill you. We ought to kill you. We ought to kill you right here and now."

They brought my roommate down there with me. He said, "Man, I'm not with him. I mean, he's only my roommate."

They said, "No, you brought him with you!" So they subjected him to that too. He had to stay down in the basement with me. And about three hours later one of the other lieutenants came down and said, "Bring him upstairs."

So they brought me upstairs, and all the people had left the temple, and Farrakhan was on the top of the stairs in the vestibule, and Muhammad Ali was still standing in front, and people—all the kids in the neighborhood—were coming over and they were surrounding Muhammad Ali, and he was talking to them. And I was standing right at the front of the door, right in their vestibule area on the way out, and a guy came up to me and he stuck his hand in my face and he said, "If we ever see you again in Springfield we're going to kill you." And I never forgot that.

And we was coming down the stairs and Farrakhan told me, "Brother, did you think about it?"

I said, "Yes."

He said, "Well, what do you think now?"

I said, "I'm more determined now to take my shahada. I could never be one of you guys." And I just walked away.

The car pulled up, and they opened the door and said, "Come on, get in." And I wouldn't get in. I slammed the door back, and I walked away and went into town. I had a girl there, and I called her up and she drove me out to the base. And that was the end. I just really began seeing something about them that I didn't like more than anything else. They tried to intimidate me into becoming a Muslim. Any time you try to intimidate me that's the worst thing in the world you can do. That's what I rebelled against in the military. Don't make me do something that I particularly don't understand or I think is wrong. You have a problem.

I went back on the base, and me and my roommate we had a very cool relationship. I continued doing my work as an engineer on the base, working with the military doing what I was supposed to do. But then I became more and more politically conscious, and that's when I really had second thoughts about being in the service. I didn't want to be in the service anymore. Because that's when I became really politically aware, and more importantly, I wanted to take shahada. I knew if I took shahada they were going to kick me out. I was trying to put it off until I was discharged, but day by day, especially after I read *The Autobiography of Malcolm X* and everything else I remembered about the brothers and sisters in Brownsville and the experience I had in the basement in Springfield, I really wanted to take shahada right then and there. Between the racism I experienced in the service and a growing urge to take shahada, I was just being pulled between conflicting poles. Since I was a kid it was my lifetime ambition to be in the air force. I always wanted to do it. Because to fly has been one of my lifetime dreams. Yet I'm becoming more Islamically conscious. I am getting bits and pieces of Islam and negative experiences with the Nation and racism and discrimination I saw in the service. So I became involved with a number of Afro-Americans on the base, and we started the black soldiers' union, and they elected me as the president. And it was nothing big or radical. It was just addressing some of the issues. One of the guys on the base was a Jehovah's Witness, and they were trying to force him to pledge allegiance to the flag. He told them he couldn't do it, and they kept him in the brig, so we got together and raised money and [a] defense fund to fight for this guy. Got him a lawyer. And they told us we couldn't wear afros, so we fought for that. And he had a beard, and they wanted him to cut his beard, and every time he cut his beard his face broke out, and we got expert testimonies from doctors and stuff. So it was a real positive thing. You know, we had stopped some of the racism on the base. You know, guys being attacked on base and off base by different groups of rednecks. We used to call them rednecks. Guys from the South were attacking the guys on the base. We reported that and kept a little file system going, and we kept the base commander's desk filled with memos and letters and complaints and grievances.

KALIMA SHAHADA   By coming home to New York on the weekends, I also got involved with the black awareness movement in the city, the Panther party, Republic of New Afrika, the Black Students Union; the Steering Committee for Black Solidarity Day started in 1968. I got in the middle of the Ocean Hill–Brownsville incident.[1] My mother was involved too because my brothers and sisters were going to that school. I would go home and read things, and I would attend a lot of political rallies. I read a lot of books about Malcolm, Che Guevara, and these are the books I had with me on the base. I had a copy of Mao's Little Red Book with me. I used to keep it and read it while I was sitting in a very secret U.S. military installation. I had an assignment there, and the lieutenant came by making his rounds, and he seen this little book. He said, "What the hell is that?"

I said, "It's Mao's book. You want to read it?" I pushed it over to him, you know, and he looked at it and thumbed through it and shook his head, and that's when all hell started breaking loose. You know, they came in my room, broke open my locker, and found all of these books by the Panthers and the Republic of Africa papers and political rally posters and flyers. Things I brought back with me from the weekends, you know, and tapes and albums. They really started monitoring me in the meetings. They took my pass from me. Gave me a lot of extra assignments. I was supposed to have been promoted to sergeant. They took me off the sergeant list. They busted me down to airman basic. I had to work my way back up to airman first and then to sergeant. Then every time I went for the sergeant list, they kept knocking me down off the list.

But I became more and more politically conscious as a result of what I experienced on the base. I met a lot of B-52 bomber pilots because we used to spend a lot of time in mole holes underground. We used to service the jet bombers. And every six months practically our whole base would tactically deploy to Guam, and they would fly missions from Guam to Vietnam. Every day, daily missions. Particularly during the big bombing raids. That was done mostly by our unit—Eighth Air Force—and the bomber pilots that came back were like full colonels and majors. We spent much time playing pool with the flight crews.

You have environmental controls, comfort cooling, equipment cooling. Equipment cooling covers the whole gamut. We did liquid oxygen for missiles, this, that, and the other thing for the planes. We worked on stuff that was mind-boggling, man, and I got a lot of good experience. A lot of good exposure, and by me being with these guys and spending time with them in flight simulators and on the planes—on the ground not flying—a lot of them told me about how they felt about the war. They didn't know what they were doing. They felt bad about the bombing. And it was primarily from the experiences of officers who were white, not black, that I became more and more dissatisfied about being in the service. Even when that was something I wanted to be since I was a kid. You couple that with reading more about Vietnam, what the Viet Cong were about, and reading a lot about communism. I was never a communist. I could never be a communist because I'm a Muslim because I do believe in God very firmly. And I do understand Marx and Leninism enough to know that Islam and Marxism-Leninism don't mix. It's like fried ice cream. It don't make no sense. It just don't all add up.

But anyway I was curious. I wanted to find out about communism. So I read it, and I caught flak, and it went in the files, and that kept me from getting promoted, and plus I was the head of the Black Soldiers' Union. Eventually they gave me an ultimatum. If you stay in, we are going to eventually court-martial you. Actually I wanted to go to Vietnam, believe it or not, but they wouldn't send me because they said I was too politically conscious. I wanted to go see for myself about 'Nam—they wouldn't let me go. They let my brother go. My stepfather went, but they wouldn't let me go.

So they gave me an ultimatum, court-martial or a general discharge. They had actually started court-martial proceedings but then just gave me a general discharge. This was like a plea bargain, I guess you can say. And that's because my mother went to Congresswoman Shirley Chisolm, who went to the secretary of the air force and stopped the court-martial. She also got a lawyer for me out of Brooklyn and brought the lawyer to the base, and we fought, you know, because I wanted to stay.

But I had left my application blank where it said "religion," and I was there one day and one of the secretaries said, "You know you never did fill this out." So I put "Islam" in there. And after I put Islam in there she said, "You know you're going to have a problem because you can't be a Muslim and be in the air force." I said, "I'm a Muslim and I'm going to be in the air force and if they try to throw me out because of my religion I'm going to take them to court because it's discrimination." That's what started the threats. That was the straw that broke the camel's back. I changed my religion on my records. And I got out in July '69 and went back to Brownsville trying to find these brothers. They were gone.

The turbans, the Baldies, were gone. They weren't in Brownsville. And anyway, I was living with this girl, and I had told her that—you know, she asked me what I wanted to do. You know, she wanted to get married, but I said, "Well, I'm going to be a Muslim one day so if we are going to be married you have got to be a Muslim too. I know that."

She said, "Well, I'm not going to be putting on none of them [Muslim] clothes."

I said, "Well, we're not going to get married. Forget that."

She says, "Well, if you are really serious about Islam, I know a Muslim sister."

I said, "What kind of Muslim? Where is she?"

She said, "She lives upstairs."

I said, "Upstairs? I never saw her." Because I used to come by on the weekends, but I never came during the week.

So she went upstairs, and a few minutes later she came back down, and she said, "Go upstairs. You can't go in, but . . . she'll talk to you at the door."

I came to the door, and she said, "Your girlfriend tells me you wanted to become Muslim."

I said, "Yes, I do."

She said, "Well, I'm not really supposed to be the one to tell you about it, but when my husband comes back you can come upstairs and meet with him and then he'll introduce you to some other brothers and take you to the mosque." And then I was ecstatic, man. Because finally I could see by her demeanor and her dress that she was orthodox, she was a Sunni Muslim, and sure enough I met her husband. He took me to the mosque, which was a few blocks away, and I met the brothers there, at what was known as Sumpter Street—240 Sumpter Street—the brothers in the DAR, we used to call it the suffa, where unmarried brothers would live, and they lived together. It was an apartment house. There was absolutely no furniture. Everything was on the floor—throw pillows and sleeping bags—because the brothers would live there; and I met these brothers, and I sat down in some of the classes, and I decided to take my shahada. The brother who gave me shahada was young. He was about sixteen, and when he became Muslim, his family threw him out. And so he moved into the suffa and went to school and college and got his master's degree—everything right from the suffa. He's a parole officer out in New York City now. Very intelligent. He speaks Arabic fluently. He's the one who gave me the shahada. And that's how I came in contact with the Dar ul-Islam movement. After becoming a part of it and the community, I realized that we had moved right on the fringe of a Muslim community. My mother lived about two or three blocks over—that whole area for that ten- or fifteen-block radius, Muslim families were on every block, and they lived there.

It wasn't until after I took shahada and went to jum'a at 52 Herkirmer Place, which was the old Yasin masjid—when I went there and saw it—[that] I said, "This is where I belong. This is what I've been looking for. This is what I wanted to do." And I met some beautiful brothers and sisters. I even met my first wife there. It wasn't a very good marriage, but I credit her more than anyone [with] putting up with me during a very trying period, you know, and I was young. I was nineteen years old. Right out of the service.

I forgot to tell you about my mother, God bless her soul. She and I were so close, we were more like brother and sister. We were very close, and I said, "Mom, I'm going to take my shahada. I'm really going to become a Muslim." I told her I had met these brothers. I had been over to the place. They gave me some little pamphlets to read, little books.

And I was reading them, and she said, "Well, let me read them too."

I said, "Well, I'll tell you what. You read them first." Because my mother was a prolific reader. She loved to read, and I gave her these books to read. I said I'd come in a couple of days for them because I am going to take my shahada on a Friday after I get paid and clear up all my old debts. I was going to clean up my life and everything and straighten up.

That was a Tuesday. I returned on Thursday, and she answered the door, and she was in hijab. It blew my mind. I said, "Ma!!"

She said, "As salaam-u-alaikum."

I said, "I thought we were going to do this together."

She beat me taking shahada by one day. And we became very, close friends. I mean even closer then. She met my first wife, and then her and my first wife became very close, and we lived there for six months until I got my own place. And it was just beautiful praying together in the morning and at night.

7

"Island in a Sea of Ignorance"

"Islam allows you to look beyond the wall." —Umar Abdul Jalil

ONE OF the most compelling and popular twentieth century narrative is *The Autobiography of Malcolm X*. It tells of the religious conversion of a petty criminal nicknamed "Satan" who emerged from prison to become an eloquent orator and international political figure. For all of its literary weight and its tremendous gravitational influence on successive generations of black Americans, however, this work has never provoked a serious inquiry into the phenomenon of Islamic religious conversion in the prisons of the United States. Despite the canonization of Malcolm X and the popular traditions to which he largely contributed, there has been only silence about hundreds of similar testimonies of symbolic death and rebirth, heroism, sacrifice, and commitment to Islamic worship.

How can one explain the popularity of Islam in prison? Is it possible to identify the elements of Islamic belief and worship that respond directly to the needs of prisoners? Is there something about Islam that relates to the conditions of incarceration differently from Christian worship? How are prison mosques established and perpetuated even when inmates are transferred constantly from one correctional facility to another? What generalizations can one extrapolate from the prison experience that apply to the spread of Islam in America?

These questions pertain to those at the bottom of the social hierarchy, not just the misfits and dropouts but state prisoners: some guilty, others falsely accused or wrongly condemned to prison—all choosing to reconstruct their lives based on Islamic worship. Many of them would agree with the enthusiastic statement of a man like Imam Salahuddin A. Rashid, who, summarizing his khutbah at Green Haven prison on 11 November 1988, said, "I was happy to come to jail! I love it because Allah has chosen me to become a good person. How many guys got fifty-years-to-life and can smile and laugh every day? However long we've been in jail, adversity is a nourishment. We are physically slaves and Allah has made us winners."

One can get a reasonable indication of the popularity of Islam among African-American prisoners by looking at the statistics in New York. In 2000 the New York State Department of Corrections (DOCS) counted 11, 335 registered Muslim inmates residing in seventy different prisons, annexes, and reception centers. The number of Muslims ranged from as few as five or six in some temporary reception centers to about five hundred at Clinton and Attica, representing 17 percent and 20 percent respectively, of the total population in those prisons. These figures represented more than 16 percent of the total state prison population of over 70,342 in 2000 and 32 percent of all incarcerated African Americans. There are approximately three hundred Muslims registered among the women inmates at Bedford Hills and six different penitentiaries, including Bedford Hills (87) and Albion (112). This study excludes Muslims at the New York City municipal prison of Rikers Island, a massive facility holding over fifteen thousand prisoners, where there has been a very active dawa program for many years with participation by Muslim corrections officers themselves.[1]

Each facility presents an imposing sight: the older "max" prisons are surrounded by eighteen-foot-high brick walls punctuated by medieval guard towers; the newer "super max" prisons like Sullivan and Wende resemble concentration camps; there are long cell-blocks whose perimeters are enveloped by ribbons of razor wire unfurled in double or triple rows of shimmering coils sandwiched between walls of chain-link fence. Small scavenger animals often die trying to cross this barbed terrain, and their little carcasses are strewn about in varying states of decay. The walls and coils stake out an impermeable physical boundary. They create the geographical illusion of a Devil's Island in the midst of upstate farmland and pasture. They are not identified on any commercial road maps, and to get there the visitor needs explicit directions because there are few signs. Prison space is not officially on the map. Green Haven prison, for example, has more than five times the population of the neighboring village of

Stormville but does not have its own five-digit zip code. Sullivan Correctional Facility, located near the Catskill Mountain town of South Fallsburg, is tucked into the old borscht belt of derelict summer camps and tumbledown ghost resorts. To the informed traveler, these prisons compose the unpublicized landscape of rural New York state. They define what it means in Harlem or Bedford-Stuyvesant when someone says that a relative is living "upstate."

Prisons like Green Haven and Attica surprise the motorist when their medieval walls erupt from the rolling landscape. Adding to the element of visual shock are the expansive parking lots that abut prison walls like concrete aprons around suburban malls. Scores of cars and flatbed pickup trucks are parked in neat rows. Order is everywhere. Moving closer to the prison gates, one glimpses designated spaces for officials in the administrative hierarchy: the superintendent, his deputies, the watch commander, chaplains, and so on. The guards, civilian coordinators, teachers, program directors, maintenance staff, and others who have business inside the prison park randomly in an area that must be large enough to hold overlapping work shifts. The visitor's parking lot is set off to another side, clearly designated and, like the rest of the area, under permanent surveillance by a watchtower guard or someone behind the large window pane above the front entrance. Next to the visitor's parking area is another zone for the many vans and buses that transport wives, mothers, children, and friends from New York City to these fortresses. Driving into this parking lot creates an immediate dilemma. Unlike that of the suburban driver, one's first impulse is to park far from the gate yet not too far, lest one appear suspicious. One seeks anonymity in the parking lot as a shield against an impersonal, indomitable space. On the road you obey the traffic laws because they seem reasonable; here you see the hulking prison and feel compelled to acknowledge another set of rules because you are fearful.

The reality of this limbo is that of a compact urban entity, increasingly composed of racial and ethnic minorities, under the rule of a predominantly white, rural labor force. The prison dominates its immediate environment like a small city propped onto a country hill. It evacuates the surrounding rural ecology and substitutes a hulking, rectilinear form that has led some commentators to imagine it as simply a vast warehouse for human bodies. Inside the gates, a metallic smell is pervasive. Heavy iron doors, bars, gates, fixtures, locks, and jangling keys bring to mind the idea of a freighter on the high seas. Paint is thick and ugly, color nearly absent. Windows are dirty glass or scratched translucent plastic. A strong antiseptic odor drifts through an atmosphere charged with a fluorescent glow. Furniture at the checkpoint is dingy. Guards execute their gestures with a perfunctory glaze in their eyes. The worst factory you can imagine exudes more charm than this grotesque, vacuous space.

However sterile it appears, the prison is not an empty space but an urban machine evolved from centuries of architectural tradition and penal reforms. The buildings, cellblocks, exercise yards, workshops, chapels, offices, and fields become the fixed points of a simulated city: "A block, B block, go down to 'Times

Square.' Go to D block, E block this way, D block is straight down. All right. When I got down there again, I was in the yard, and a Muslim called to me."[2] The prisoner moves about these spaces according to a detailed schedule that dictates a nearly absolute control of his quotidian activities.

> Their whole concept of the prison system [is that] they are going to tell you when to wake up, when to go to sleep, when to shower, change, shit, eat. We're going to tell you the whole thing. We don't want you to make no decisions. We don't want nobody to run [anything] because we have hired G.E.D. morons [guards] out of the countryside. We know they can't think, but we can't have no prisoners making decisions.[3]

What is the purpose of this enterprise? Where does this punitive model come from?

Sociologists maintain that the twentieth-century prison is the evolutionary result of punitive ideals developed by eighteenth century social reformers who meant to punish criminals according to a liberal, rehabilitative ethic.[4] The goal of punishment was to transform or convert; reformers borrowed certain architectural and pedagogical models from medieval Christian monasteries and other religious practices. Organizations such as the Quaker-inspired American Prison Reform Association had an apparently unyielding belief in the salutary effects of these models, which were adapted to modern conditions and employed at places like the Walnut Street jail in Philadelphia and Auburn prison in upstate New York. The ideal prison was to be supplied with "Bibles and other books of religion [and] clergy of different obediences to be found in the town and suburbs [are to] perform services once a week and any other edifying person may have access to the prisoners at any time. Work on the prisoner's soul must be carried out as often as possible. The prison as an administrative apparatus, will at the same time be a machine for altering minds."[5]

Similar models applied in 1948 in Massachusetts, where Malcolm X was imprisoned, first at Charlestown ("built in 1805—in Napoleon's day—and . . . even styled after the Bastille"), then at Concord (where he first heard about "something called the Nation of Islam"), and finally at the Norfolk Prison Colony ("the most enlightened form of prison that I have ever heard of [where] a high percentage of the . . . inmates went in for 'intellectual' things"). He reported, "At Norfolk we could actually go into the library, with permission—walk up and down the shelves, pick books. There were hundreds of old volumes, some of them probably quite rare."[6] "The prison's superb library had been willed to the Commonwealth by State Senator Lewis Parkhurst of Winchester, who had devoted his career to penal reform. Malcolm pored through the books on Buddhism, Hinduism, Islam and Christianity."[7]

At first Malcolm seemed interested in the Jehovah's Witnesses but then decided to follow the path of his siblings into the Nation of Islam. Not only was his conversion ideal and complete but he became a model prisoner also.

For the next years, I was the nearest thing to a hermit in the Norfolk Prison Colony. I never have been more busy in my life. I still marvel at how swiftly my previous life's thinking pattern slid away from me, like snow off a roof. It is as though someone else I knew of had lived by hustling and crime. I would be startled to catch myself thinking in a remote way of my earlier self as another person. [8]

He eventually became a self-disciplined, spiritually oriented orator, just as capable of an articulate argument before the Oxford Debating Union as of a fast, smart street-corner rap. But there was something atypical about this conversion. Would Senator Parkhurst have guessed that his library might have contributed to producing a stalwart Muslim convert? A man who would end up making a pilgrimage to Mecca and die as a martyr in the name of black liberation? Would he recognize his reformist ideology in the description of another prison conversion that occurred nearly twenty-five years later?

I was in A block, and I had seen a group of orthodox Sunni Muslims praying. And at that point I was just drawn to Islam. It was like a natural conversion. Before anyone had said anything to me. I didn't know what they were doing, but I thought, whatever that group of men were doing, I was going to be a part of it. That was on either Tuesday or Wednesday. On Friday I went to the masjid.[9]

Would Senator Parkhurst understand that his reformist ideal of stringent discipline would engender an equally powerful though "alien" counterdiscipline that appealed to the sensibility of a young Los Angeles gang-banger?

Islam has changed my life tremendously. It has caused me to be disciplined to an extent I never thought possible for me. I came out of a culture that reveled in undiscipline and rebelliousness, etcetera. So to go the opposite direction was major for me. I firmly believe and see that for the 1990s and beyond, Islam will be an even more dynamic force and alternative for many prisoners, especially the confused and angry youth who are more and more receptive to the teachings of Islam and the self-esteem, discipline and respect it provides them in abundance, not to mention the knowledge.[10]

EARLY HISTORY OF MASJID SANKORE AND THE DAR PRISON COMMITTEE   Early attempts to establish Islam in federal prisons were reported in the 1930s for members of the Moorish Science Temple and the Nation of Islam who were jailed for draft evasion.[11] These "Islamic-nationalist" cults drew their adherents from an alienated segment of northern blacks who voiced open rejection of white-dominated American culture. They also regarded the Black

Church as an essentially rural institution that failed to redress increasingly complex social problems arising from the Great Migration (c. 1917) and the ghetto phenomenon.[12] In prison the "Black Muslims" and "Moors" represented cultural and religious predilections that made them a minority among black prisoners. This situation did not appear significant until the mid-1960s, when blacks and Hispanics first began to outnumber whites in state and federal prisons.

Neither the Moors nor the Nation of Islam practiced Islam in any conventional sense. Both referred to their places of worship as "temples." The Moors celebrated Friday as their Sabbath and worshiped three times daily at sunrise, noon, and sunset. When praying, they faced east and raised their hands but did not prostrate themselves.[13] Members of the Nation of Islam gathered on Sundays and prayed standing in the same manner as the Moors. When Elijah Muhammad became angry with "Arab Muslims," he ordered his followers to pray westward toward Chicago. Neither group recited the kalima shahada nor practiced the Five Pillars. Ignoring Ramadan, the 'id feasts, and the Prophet's birthday, the Nation of Islam celebrated 18 February as Founder's Day, marking the birthday of Master Fard Muhammad, the organization's mysterious creator. Sociologists have suggested that both groups incorporated many Christian elements into their beliefs to attract greater numbers of blacks to their essentially secular programs of political and economic nationalism.[14] Others have viewed the politics of the Nation of Islam, especially the rhetoric of Malcolm X, as the "antithesis of the assimilationist civil rights doctrine" of the 1960s and a rejection of the "turn the other cheek" dictum of the Black Church.[15]

Activities of proto-Islamic cults among black prisoners reached an apogee in the years following the 1965 assassination of Malcolm X, and soon several thousand inmates across the country were changing their names and declaring themselves "Muslim." Some prison administrators regarded this as a legitimate religious affiliation and valued the Muslim ethical code of hard work and sobriety as congruent with prevailing corrections philosophy of personal rehabilitation, yet few wardens or Christian chaplains were ready to sanction this form of worship, despite their awareness of the constitutional issue of religious freedom[16]

Sometime between 1962 and 1968 Sunni Muslims began to worship openly in New York state facilities. At Green Haven a community of Muslims came together under the leadership of Yusef Abdul Mu'mim. These prisoners were not yet formally organized, nor were they recognized by the administration as a legitimate religious community deserving an area designated as a mosque. In 1968 Mu'mim wrote to Imam Yahya Abdul Karim of Brooklyn's Yasin Mosque asking for outside help in ameliorating the conditions for incarcerated Sunni Muslims at Green Haven.

Imam Yahya was the extremely popular leader of the Dar ul-Islam movement, an indigenous Muslim organization that had developed among the African-American followers of Sheik Daoud Faisal. He responded by dispatching Bilal Abdul Rahman to ascertain the conditions facing Sunni Muslims at Green

Haven. Rahman reported that the Muslims at Green Haven needed assistance from their brothers outside in negotiating legitimate "ministerial" privileges with the prison's top brass. The next DAR emissary sent to Green Haven was Sheikh Ismail Abdul Rahman, who discovered that the Muslim prisoners were forced to worship in a space beneath the facility's theater. Salat groups were consequently interrupted by the clamor of inmates cheering and stomping in reaction to loud, vulgar movies. Sheikh Ismail negotiated an agreement with the warden to grant the community a permanent prison masjid located in an unused storage room. Sheikh Ismail made weekly trips to Green Haven as a volunteer to assist Muslim prisoners. His efforts were complemented by those of a Muslim Indian immigrant who worked as an engineer in a nearby IBM plant. This was the beginning of the Dar ul-Islam's Prison Committee dawa and teaching program. Green Haven's Sunni Muslims named their mosque Masjid Sankore after the African Islamic center of learning in Timbucktu, Mali.

Sankore rapidly outgrew its cramped space, eventually taking over the prison's old tailor shop. The prisoners devoted much time and effort into making the space into a genuine masjid and a place of refuge. Though modest, it contrasted favorably with the drab confines of the rest of the prison. "When you walked in there, it was another world. You didn't feel like you were in Green Haven in a maximum security prison. Officers [prison guards] never came in. It was like going into any other masjid on the outside; you felt at home," commented Sheikh Ismail. Among his other first impressions of Islam at Green Haven, he recalled that both the Sunni Muslims and the Black Muslims (NOI) practiced a cadenced march through the corridors as if to mark out their own militant counterdisciplinary culture. That was the only thing they shared however. The Nation sought and demanded their own mosque and competed fiercely with the Sunnis at Sankore for new initiates.

From 1968 to 1970 the DAR Prison Committee received correspondence from Muslims in other prisons about the conditions in which they worshiped. The letters noted the competition and hostility that Sunni Muslims often faced from members of the NOI and prompted the committee to expand its operations to other prisons around New York. Masjid Sankore was already a self-sufficient mosque with many connections to the outside world. It would set the standard for Islamic religious freedom in other prisons. Whenever they were routinely transferred to other prisons, inmates demanded the same privileges and amenities as at Green Haven. To achieve this it was always advantageous to have the DAR negotiating in a diplomatic fashion with the local warden.

The DAR Prison Committee functioned on a volunteer basis until 1972, when the State Department of Corrections began reimbursing them for expenses and educational services. The committee was active in bringing outside Muslim visitors to the prison mosques as lecturers and entertainment. They organized and presented concerts by one of their own members, Sheik Sulaiman al-Hadi, who belonged to The Last Poets, the immediate precursors of contemporary rappers, whose music represented a fusion of Islam, the prison experience, and 1960s radical politics.[17] In very direct though unpublicized way, the Prison Committee was responsible for spreading this form of popular culture long before the commercial successes of the 1980s.

By 1970 Yusuf Abdul Mu'mim was succeeded as the leader of Sankore by Jamal Pasha Blaine, who "wore a red fez and looked like a Moroccan sultan." He continued the militant tradition of what the Prison Committee called "joint-Islam" denoting the differences, exceptions, and innovations (bid'a) of intramural Islamic practices compared to the way Islam was practiced by orthodox Muslims outside. Jamal pushed for as many privileges as he could extract from the administration. Rasul Abdullah Sulaiman succeeded him as Sankore's third imam around 1972. Prior to his incarceration, Rasul was already a Muslim and a member of Malcolm X's inner circle at Muslim Mosques Inc. In prison he benefited from this association, which conferred a status previously unrivaled by any Muslim inmate. Under his stewardship, the rate of conversions soared during the years 1975 and 1976. Sankore had more converts to Islam than any other mosque in America, according to a report published by the Washington Islamic Center. Some of these converts were outside guests or even corrections personnel, who would often volunteer to work at Sankore religious events without pay.[18] This established Sankore's reputation as the "Medina" of the prison system, a place of refuge and Islamic pedagogy.

In 1975 DOCS offered to hire Muslim chaplains as direct employees of its Ministerial Services Division. This was a significant step in the legitimation of Muslim authority by the state. Imam Yahya hesitated, thinking that the Prison Committee's autonomy would be compromised, and ordered a retreat from all prison dawa activities. Sheikh Ismail resigned as the head of the Prison Committee, and in 1976 the DAR did not renew its agreement with DOCS. "When you're doing it as a volunteer, then you're practicing your religion straight up and down and not because you want a paycheck," explained Ismail's colleague Hajj Hassan A. Muhammad many years later as justification for Yahya's resistance to a professional Muslim chaplaincy.[19]

Most Sankore Muslims agreed with this policy, until the status quo for incarcerated Muslims started changing too rapidly to ignore. With Elijah Muhammad dead, his son Warith Deen moved decisively to liberate the "Black Muslims" from their allegiance to the NOI's bizarre doctrines. Specifically, he emphasized instruction in learning salat and reading the Quran, which was interpreted as deliberate thaw in relations with orthodox Muslims. This was an opportunity for mosques such as Sankore to grow quickly if the conversion of "Black Muslims" were handled properly.

Seen in this light, the Prison Committee's strategic retreat was premature, if not ill-advised, because the incarcerated Muslims lacked the resources to implement a large-scale transformation of scores of "Black Muslims." It was in fact a difficult opportunity to resist for Al-Amin Abdul Latif, who succeeded Sheik Ismail as the head of the Prison Committee. Latif signed on with DOCS, and Ismail rejoined him in 1978 when the DAR finally changed its policy. This left two chaplains from the DAR and two from the NOI under direct contract to the state to supply services and counseling to Muslim inmates. The policy of balanced hiring continued unofficially until the distinctions between Sunni Muslims and members of the former Nation of Islam began to blur. As many had surmised in advance, this change engendered monumental problems in some facilities.

A few successful mergers occurred because of this enlightened conversion to Islam, but there were also lingering antagonisms, which militated against complete unification. Because of the history of violence between the NOI and Sunnis, old rivalries did not always evaporate, and many older members of the NOI, who still regarded Elijah Muhammad as a deity, were unable to forget the beliefs that lay at the core of the separatist, nationalist movement.[20] One Sunni inmate described the conversion of a former member of the Nation.

> They had never performed salat before. But W. D. Muhammad [Warith] gave them instructions to learn from us. Just a few months previously he [the convert] was ridiculing us for prostrating to the "spook god" [an unseen deity]. He used to pray to a picture of Master Fard Muhammad that he had on the wall of his cell. And he would face toward Chicago also! It was therefore humiliating for him, but all over the state we taught them salat and Arabic. And we thought we'd come together as one community. But they put on the brakes and maintained their differences with us and continued to adhere to the cult.[21]

THE CONVERSION OF BLACK POWER MILITANTS   An important counterpoint to the development of Islam in New York prisons during this period was the more popular history of Black Power militancy, which drew inspiration from Malcolm X but also differed in significant ways from the orientation of Muslims. Political militancy among African-American and Hispanic prisoners came under intense scrutiny by prison officials and sometimes caused inadvertent complications for Muslims. For example, when Sunni communities tried to establish congregational prayer in the prison exercise yard, they met invariably with resolute opposition, to the extent that prison administrators viewed all inmate organizations as potential adversaries and prohibited gatherings of more than three individuals. However, this attitude changed abruptly after the 1971 Attica uprising, where the Muslims interceded as mediators and protected the hostage-guards throughout the siege. From that moment onward DOCS granted more privileges to Muslims than ever before. Rules varied from one prison to the next, but officials gave Muslims whatever they wanted, including the right to observe congregational salat (sometimes in the exercise yard but mostly in the mosque), Ramadan (with special halal meals), and sadaqa (which gave the intramural jamaat relative financial autonomy).

If Attica provoked a period of liberalization inside these largely uncontrollable institutions, it also stimulated intensification of the covert domestic war the FBI waged against black revolutionaries, whom they held responsible for the prison uprisings and for waves of bombings and armed attacks on government targets. In New York, at least a dozen Black Panthers or Black Liberation Army members went to prison with sentences of twenty-five-years to life. The decapitation of the entire political spectrum of the black movement, including the assassination of Malcolm X in 1965 and Martin Luther King Jr. in 1968, led to a general crisis of demoralization among urban blacks. Aided by the Islamic conversion of H. Rap Brown, the imprisoned leader of the Student Coordinating Committee,[22] an alternative began to attract numerous revolutionary figures whose apprehensions about religion were assuaged by his opinion that "Islam was not inconsistent with their revolutionary goals." Like Brown, who changed his name to Jamil Al-Amin, they applied their skills in grassroots organizing to Islamic dawa and soon began to offer the Quran to fellow inmates as a substitute for revolutionary or nationalist literature. The programs of former militants came to envision personal rebirth as a prerequisite for social transformation, a position supported by the passage "Verily, never will Allah change the condition of a people until they change it themselves with their own soul" (Quran 13:11 or 8:53).

The testimony of a member of the Black Liberation Army, sentenced to life imprisonment in 1973, reflects the tremendous effect of these words on Black Power advocates.

> I was a very determined socialist when I was placed in a jail with another black leader. He had already become Muslim, and I was confronted [by] his daily prayers. At first I could not understand why he was praying to a god who, I felt, had abandoned black people. We argued and battled, but eventually Islam helped me become more relaxed. It relieved a burden, because I had become frustrated by the failure of the political movement. And then you read the ayat in the Quran where Allah told the Prophet, "Maybe we might show you a victory in your lifetime. Maybe we won't, but you must keep striving." So then you start to see things in a broader perspective, outside of yourself as an individual. It was then that I realized that we didn't really suffer a major defeat but that we were part of an ongoing process that eventually would culminate in victory.[23]

In its historical context, the founding of Masjid Sankore appears as the defining moment in the rise of orthodox Islam in prisons throughout North America. The inmate founders working with the DAR Prison Committee succeeded in amalgamating diverse cultural and political trends into a religious movement that attracted some of the most socially alienated and emotionally demoralized prisoners. It appealed to principles espoused by Malcolm X and contemporary forms of Pan-Islam, which articulated a growing frustration with the ideological choices between capitalism and socialism in the Third World. One might venture further to suggest that the religion established at Masjid Sankore under the inspiration of the DAR represented the apotheosis of the old unchurched sentiment, which found therein critical acceptance and a suitable form for mass participation. These beliefs and practices eventually spread as far as California, where Imam Muhammad Abdullah administered dawa according to the DAR model among thousands of men in penitentiaries and youth correctional facilities. Directing his efforts primarily at the young gang-bangers languishing in a culture of poverty, violence, and narcotics, he explained that incarcerated youth are now more open than ever to the message of Islam. His comments were echoed by a former member of the notorious Crips, who wrote, "There are many young Afrikans within the prison who were previously involved with street gangs and much crime yet are attracted to and transformed by the teachings of Islam."[24]

ISLAMIC PEDAGOGY BEHIND BARS   Prison is a bizarre and violent "university" for those who reach maturity behind bars. There the brutality and corruption of the street are magnified to gargantuan proportions. Even to the extent that he complies with the rules of incarceration, the prisoner becomes entangled in a world of material desires and moral prostitution. From the lowly prisoner up to the warden, by way of the prisoners known as "big men," snitches, guards, program instructors, and bureaucrats, prison is a pathological society asserting a unique institutional order. This regime codifies various methods used to alter and perhaps destroy the inmate's physical and psychological integrity. It forces him to regiment his personal habits and behavior according to the social ecology of the prison. In preparation for his eventual release, the inmate studies a "curriculum" of ruse and discipline. He learns few of the many skills necessary to lead a law-abiding life back on the street. Even worse, the prisoner is subjected to physical brutality, psychological manipulation, and frequent homosexual rape. The prison is an administrative-bureaucratic space that marks every aspect of the inmate's existence unless he can use his minimal rights to circumscribe an autonomous zone whose perimeter cannot officially be contested.

Acting through the principle of freedom of worship, Islam meets these challenges and shows a remarkable capacity to redefine the conditions of incarceration. A new Muslim repeats the attestation of faith, the shahada, before witnesses at the mosque. His Islamic identity then means a fresh start, symbolized by the choice of a new name, modifications in his physical appearance, and an emphasis on prayer. He is linked to his Muslim brothers worldwide, as suggested by frequent representations of Mecca on the mosque's walls.

More immediately, he is linked to his fellow Muslim prisoners. Inmates like those at Masjid Sankore, thanks to communal prayer, Quranic and Arabic scholarship, and invocation of sharia, can exercise significant group control over their fellows. In contrast to the jailhouse standard of status that is measured by physical strength or a manipulative intellect, the Muslim community reassigns status on the basis of the prophetic dictum that "the strongest is he who can control himself."

Islamic pedagogy engenders an independent morality of justice, implying a separation between divine law and the canon represented by the criminal justice system. Since the community ethos remains more or less impermeable to the prison administration, the sharia helps define and reproduce an alternative social space where the inmate's behavior can be monitored and judged according to Islamic rules. Failure to comply may result in banishment from the community. The total effect is to bolster the spirit of resistance by asserting an alternative legal space inside the prison. It applies even in cases where non-Muslims "come to the mosque and file charges, [or] corrections officers bring us their problems, saying, 'Hey, I don't want to lock this guy up. Could you please talk to him?'"[25]

Historically, Christian prison reformers envisioned conversion as cloistered reflection or silent prayer. Islamic teaching, however, changes self-image and social relationships primarily through communal prayer and Quranic recitation, which establish ties of identification and action between Muslim believers and the sacred texts of the Quran and Sunna. Through religious practice, the prisoner distances himself from the outside world, conceptualized as dar al-harb, and migrates (hijra) toward the ideal of dar al-Islam, defined not by territory but by Islamic practice. The greater the capacity of the prison jamaat to establish the privilege of congregational prayer, the greater the potential effect on the Muslim. It is an impressive sight to see fifty or a hundred prisoners bowing and kneeling in prayer in the middle of a prison exercise yard or in a room isolated within a maze of corridors and cells. Since 1973, after consulting the Islamic Center of New York City, DOCS has recognized three holidays: Maulid al-Nabi (the Prophet's birthday), 'Id al-Fitr (the feast commemorating the end of the Ramadan fast), and 'Id al-Adha (the feast of the sacrifice). During the Ramadan fast, Muslims can requisition halal meat and are permitted to use the kitchen to prepare *iftar* meals. For breaking the fast, they are permitted to take some food back to their cells.

The Muslim's cell can be recognized by the absence of photographic images and the otherwise ubiquitous centerfold pin-ups of naked women. When a man becomes a shahada, he gradually learns the proper etiquette for a Muslim inmate. To reorganized personal space corresponds a changed attitude toward his body for the new Muslim. He tries to avoid pork and other non-halal foods. Some prisoners even object to the use of utensils that have touched forbidden foods. The issue of providing halal diets to Muslim prisoners in New York State has been in litigation for many years, with the state now using the excuse of budgetary constraints to refuse. The convert also becomes concerned with wudzu, here transformed into a code of personal cleanliness and grooming. In addition to their skullcaps, beards, and jellaba, the Muslims are usually well scrubbed and, as advised in their orientation booklet, often wear aromatic oils when entering the mosque. The use of personal toiletries defines the Muslim's body as different from the sweaty, disciplined body of the ordinary prisoner. Cigarette smoking is also frowned on among orthodox Muslims.

With respect to a prisoner's repressed sexual desire, the Islamic regime acquires a double significance in its strict opposition to homosexuality. On the one hand, the regime upholds Quranic injunctions and encourages the sublimation of desire into a rigorous program of study and prayer. On the other hand, and more subtly, a man's adherence to these injunctions illustrates counter disciplinary resistance to the more overt dominance hierarchies encountered in prison life. Sexual possession, domination, and submission represent forms of "hard currency" in prison. Thus by asserting the distinction between halal and haram, between what is permitted and what is forbidden, the Muslim community simultaneously follows Islamic law and negates an important defining characteristic of prison life.

The most contentious issue regarding the prisoner's body involves surveillance and personal modesty. For example, during the 1970s, the DAR Prison Committee worked with the state to arrange special times for Muslims to shower as a way to ensure privacy. Eventually, DOCS designated Thursday nights for Muslims to coordinate showers among themselves. A similar yet unresolved issue concerns the "strip search," when men are forced to strip and submit to an inspection of their body cavities. Every maximum security prisoner can expect a random "strip search" after coming into contact with outside visitors, including family and attorneys. Muslims express extreme indignation at submitting to this practice and regard it as an unjustified invasion of privacy and a violation of Islamic modesty. Indeed, the search frequently becomes a vehicle for guards to make homosexual gestures and verbal insinuations. Many prisoners refuse to undergo this procedure. They file grievances and risk being "written up," sent to "hole," or even beaten if they refuse too vehemently. Belief in Islamic standards of sexual modesty conditions this attitude and reinforces the counterdisciplinary urge to defend one's privacy. Some attempted searches have ended in violence because of a guard's vulgar gesture. Another indication of the humiliation of strip searches is the presence of female guards, which creates more embarrassing and demeaning situations loaded with potential obscenities. Finally, the act of prostrating for the prison guards symbolizes the ultimate submissive gesture, which is a sacrilegious sign for any Muslim.

Throughout the country, Muslims are becoming increasingly resistant to the prison "strip search." They claim that since their religion forbids alcohol and narcotics, there is no reason to impose this regime on them. Reports about incidents in other states show that incarcerated Muslim there are also ready to fight over this issue. Lawsuits have been filed, but so far the courts have backed up the wardens, who insist that security issues take precedence over freedom of religious expression.[26] Nonetheless, this remains a potentially explosive issue involving Muslim prisoners across the country. Islamic wudzu as a reference for personal conduct is understood seriously as a separation from the vulgar, redolent space of the urban prison. Its success lies in the possibility of enveloping the Muslim in physical signs that reinforce privacy through religious counterdiscipline.

The Muslim community generates a certain degree of physical, emotional, and even biological relief from the grinding prison discipline. This extraordinarily synthetic capacity to alter the cognitive patterns of an inmate's world may even carry over to the realm of taste (halal diet), sight (reverse-direction Arabic script, calligraphy, absence of images, geometrical motifs, etc.), and smell (aromatic oils, incense). By staking out an Islamic space and filling it with a universe of alternative sensations, names, and even a different alphabet, the prison jamaat establishes the conditions for a relative transformation of the most dreaded aspect of one's sentence, "the terror of time." No other popular inmate association has proved its capacity to redefine the prison sentence in such a long-term way, for in its most successful manifestation, fundamentalist Islam has the power to reinterpret the notion of "doing time" into the activity of "following the Sunna of the Prophet Muhammad." Prisoners spend much of their time engaged in Quranic study, conducted according to a nationwide curriculum, moving through various levels from elementary instruction in beliefs and behavior (akida and adab) to advanced scholarship in law, Quranic commentary, and theology. There is even a course in leadership training to prepare prisoners for their roles as imams in other facilities or on the street.

Materials for these classes, including cassettes, videotapes, and books, were initially donated by concerned Muslim organizations. Recently, Muslim inmates themselves have earned surprisingly large amounts of cash through their commercial monopoly of aromatic oils, incense, and personal toiletries throughout the prison system. These funds are also used for the elaborate carpentry and calligraphic painting done in their mosques and for the catering of ritual holiday feasts. They contribute to the sponsorship of intramural cultural events, which are often staged for the purpose of dawa. Sankore even published a critically acclaimed newsletter, *Al-Mujaddid* (The Reformer), which found its way to important readers throughout the Muslim world. Its news and letters sparked international concern for Sankore's inmates, prompting donations in the form of Qurans and other literature from Muslim countries and their New York–based emissaries, who sometimes traveled to Green Haven to visit Sankore. Ironically, the late Rabbi Meir Kahane, founder of the Jewish Defense League, met with Green Haven's Muslim community to thank them for the hospitality extended to a Jewish inmate who was welcomed to conduct Hebrew prayers in a corner of the mosque after being ostracized by his own synagogue.

LOOKING BEYOND THE WALL   In cases of harassment or personal assault, Muslims take an activist role by contacting attorneys, legislators, or prison watchdog committees. This is not to suggest that Muslims alone are the only inmates likely to turn to such action or that it is a principal community orientation. However, many cases over the years indicate that Islamic pedagogy nurtures a sense of heightened scrutiny and critical views when it comes to unreasonable regulations. More generally, this political formula sets Muslims apart from the rest of the population and may actually elevate the community's image within the prison hierarchy.

On another level, the accomplishments of Muslims as students and teachers in the Islamic curriculum demonstrate an increased respect for knowledge. This extends from high school equivalency programs to the college and graduate courses offered at some prisons. Such accomplishments expose the prisoner to extramural influences and contacts; they expand the range of alternative conduits to the outside world and are likely consequences of a respect for knowledge fostered by conversion. When leaders of the Attica Muslim community implemented seminars so they could decide their own curriculum, "it unleashed much creative energy. We were trying to open up lines to these brothers so they wouldn't be misinformed. The ideal was to educate them, but they began to educate themselves also."[27]

Another form of extramural experience that the Muslim community takes enormous pains to nurture is contact with families, friends, "brothers in Islam," and prospective mates. These endeavors are not always successful, mainly because finding a wife or reconstructing a badly fractured family is practically an impossible task to accomplish from behind bars. Marriage to a man doing "hard time," a sentence longer than ten years, is not an attractive proposition for a woman. Most of the men interviewed for this study had been married before incarceration and were subsequently divorced. Even the handful of men who were already Muslims before incarceration lost their Muslim wives. Muslims learn that "marriage is half the religion," so they are constantly anticipating liaisons with women.

The 'Id al-Fitr and 'Id al-Adha feasts are the best occasions for family reunions, when the community mounts a collective effort to recast the prison setting as a space suitable for intimate conversation and enjoyable recreation. Basketball courts are opened for noncompetitive family games. Weather permitting, couples can roam the prison yard in search of solitude and privacy. Communal prayers involve wives, children, and friends, creating a feeling that there is a sacred family space within the confines of the cold, heartless prison, a transformation that, by contrast, is difficult to achieve in the open visiting rooms, where non-Muslim prisoners publicly engage in sexual petting with female visitors.

DOCS finally prohibited female guests at Sankore in 1982, but this did not stop the Muslims from inventing new ways to breach the wall in search of potential wives. The following excerpt illustrates one way the intramural jamaat can play a role in matrimonial contacts.

Three brothers were having a discussion on the gallery one day. They asked me to write to this sister who asked a lot of questions about Islam. She was the girlfriend of one guy's wife, and he described her as a "heavy Muslimah" who was not currently married. She studied a lot and was looking for a pen pal. He asked if I wanted to write her, and I said, okay, but I didn't want to be aggressive, so I gave him permission to tell her my address and to write to me.

Soon afterwards I was transferred to another prison, and it was a very long time until she was able to get my new address. Then one day I got a 137-page letter! It was a sort of journal she'd kept from the time we agreed to become pen pals. So we began corresponding on a regular basis, and occasionally she would come up to visit me.

During one visit she suggested that we get married. One of her reasons was that her local imam was pressing her to marry and she wasn't particularly fond of the man whom the imam had chosen for her. She asked me first and said that my sentence was not important. She came for the 'id where a nikka was performed. Then four years later when the state finally granted lifers the right to marry, we got married civilly.[28]

Although it did not last forever, this was an exceptional case of a successful Muslim marriage behind bars. Others have not been as lucky. Another man was married through a very similar process, but his wife was unable to adapt to the rigors of being married to a prisoner. She was unprepared for the visiting room scene, the frequent collect phone calls, a disembodied voice, and the emotional deficiencies of maintaining a long-distance marriage. Her family, already dismayed at her conversion to Islam, turned up the pressure when she married a man serving a life sentence. After only a couple of weeks of marriage, she began to refuse phone calls and would not return letters. The prisoner agonized over the proper adab to handle this situation. Finally his wife admitted her confusion over the whole affair and obtained a divorce.

A third marriage ended in divorce after the prisoner's wife fell in love with the paroled inmate whom her husband had appointed to be her wali. The incarcerated husband miscalculated by appointing his young Muslim protégé on the inside to be the guardian of his wife and children in an outside world from which he had been absent for more than a decade. The unchaperoned relationship with her wali generated uncontrollable passions, given the circumstances of a young female convert living on welfare. Since the children were still very young, a bitter divorce meant that the father would not see his children. Threats and counterthreats were exchanged by mail and collect phone calls. The woman refused to bring her children for a visit, declaring that they expressed no desire to see their father and furthermore that they were now happily adjusting to their "new" abu. When they wanted to visit, she would bring them to the prison in the company of her new husband.

There was little recourse for the imprisoned party to fight for access to his children without engaging a long and costly legal battle. After recovering from his initial rage, he sought consultation from a Brooklyn imam who agreed to mediate. All the parties eventually met in the prison visiting room and worked out an agreement whereby the woman agreed to bring her children for regular visits while her new husband, the former wali, waited in the car.

Marriage across the wall is difficult at best. It requires the intervention or involvement of other parties, which adds an element of unreality. Women thinking about marrying a prisoner, especially someone who might be paroled in the future, need as much information as possible concerning his past. This has given rise to another role for the prison wali as an insider who can tell the woman more than she learns in letters, visits, and phone conversations with her prospective mate. The job is controversial, to say the least. One man who served as wali in more than ten prospective marriages testified that he now refuses to vouch for any of his fellow inmates in their matrimonial quests. "Brothers in here act differently than outside, and you can never know them," he admits, after reviewing several failures and personal recriminations from imams on the outside.[29]

Intramural leaders may also be faced with problems of illness and death in the families of fellow Muslim prisoners. For example, a man received a letter from home explaining that his father was dying. The prisoner was in solitary confinement, however, and thus unable to even make a telephone call home. To arrange a "deathbed" visit to his father, the inmate's imam interceded with the prison chaplain.

The skills acquired in prison mosques bring out undiscovered capacities in some men. A few have even become respected community leaders in New York, Atlanta, and Detroit. This has enhanced the reputation of prison mosques as places where "pure" Islam is practiced. "We are better Muslims in here than brothers outside," is a refrain heard sometimes among Muslim prisoners.

ISLAM, PRISON, AND CULTURAL IDENTITY   The prison mosque not only is the center of religious instruction but also serves as an alternative focus of authority within the prison. Its power depends on a large membership, who legitimize the influence of their chosen leaders with respect to the larger inmate hierarchy, which encompasses representatives of powerful ethnic gangs such as the Mafia and the Chinese triads or white fascist parties such as the Aryan Brotherhood and the Ku Klux Klan. In the late 1970s, for example, Sankore's inmate imam, Rasul Abdullah Sulaiman, quickly rose to such a powerful position within the prison that he had his own telephone and traveled around the place at will, accompanied by a corps of surly bodyguards. He arranged the visits of outside Muslim dignitaries, brought families and friends of the prisoners into the masjid for prayer every Friday, and reportedly even constructed a network of small bunks inside the mosque for conjugal visits after Friday prayer.

This was the period when Sankore achieved its reputation as the most important center for Islamic dawa in North America. Before his release in 1980, Rasul married the mother of a fellow inmate, and his new stepson, Shuaib Abdur Raheem, was elected imam. This union resulted in the effective and orderly transition of power in the mosque after Rasul's release on parole. But the burly men who idolized Rasul were not "good Muslims," according to Shuaib, who described them as "some of deadliest brothers ever." Upon taking over the reigns of power from Rasul, he recalled weeding out some of these overzealous Muslims who were more committed to Rasul than to Islam.

It is possible to explore the deeper implications of Islamic pedagogy by looking at the process of Islamization as a negotiation between the prison authorities and the Muslim inmates. Here the state's logic of institutional order meets the fundamentalist doctrine of pax Islamica. The reorientation and purification of personal space are possibilities for the Muslim prisoner through a serious counterdisciplinary regime. Once he becomes Muslim, the prisoner has little choice but to follow this new set of rules, or he risks at least the disapprobation of his fellow inmates and possibly a physical lashing. Non-Muslims who have been around long enough to understand the alternative set of rules will even admonish the novice convert (mubari) if he is derelict in performance of his obligations.

"We have to deal with discipline in the ranks of the masjid," reported a life-term Sunni Muslim.

> There have been times in which brothers have received stripes [whip-pings] for stealing [or] gambling or [been] expelled from the mosque for engaging in homosexual activity. This is how we apply the sharia. When-ever these mild sanctions fail to accomplish the disciplinary regime set by the local imam, other methods can be invoked. In certain instances people have been severely beaten up or stabbed, depending upon the severity of the transgression and the threat its presents to security of the Muslim community.[30]

As enforced by the incarcerated community in general, the sharia becomes an autonomous self-correcting process administered by and for Muslims. "A Muslim's blood is sacred. We will not allow anyone to shed a Muslim's blood without retaliation. The prison population knows this and would prefer for us to handle our situation."[31] So widespread is the fierce reputation of the incarcerated Muslim that the most ruthless urban drug dealers carefully avoid harming any Muslim man, woman, or child lest they face extreme prejudice during their inevitable prison terms.

If this capacity to purify and control Islamic space is remarkable in its consistency, it is not without problems. Inmates may come to Islam merely for protection, not to find a new life. Or they may mistakenly believe that they can absolve themselves of past misdeeds and change themselves simply by changing their names and reciting the kalima shahada. They then give the outward appearance of devotion but end up returning to prison having committed the same crimes. Generally, however, low recidivism rates and success in the rehabilitation of drug and alcohol addiction win tolerance, even approval, for Muslims.[32]

The numbers of practicing Muslims remain significant, and their influence continues to rise among the transient populations who fluctuate between prison and the devastated streets of America's urban ghettos. Consequently, all African-American youths have at least some familiarity with Islam, either through a personal encounter or a fashionable item of apparel or, as is more frequently the case today, in the form of rap music poems. Islam constitutes a virtual passport whose bearer may exercise the option to depart the anomie of ghetto life for destinations mapped out by the Quran and Sunna. Nowhere is this more evident than inside the maximum security prison, where the literal interpretation of the Prophet's hijra functions as a utopian itinerary and an alternative vision of truth and justice. It insulates the prisoner from the dulling experience of incarceration and induces him to a regime of obligations that not only transform the physical relationship to his immediate personal space but also restructure time according to rituals that correspond with those of neither the prison nor American society.

In this sense, Islamic pedagogy invigorates the prison convert. The Quran becomes his instructional manual for counterdiscipline. Its study opens more than new scriptural potentials and interpretive traditions and more than simply a new grammar, phonetics, and vocabulary (Arabic): an impenetrable code whose messages elude all but the most devout. As a consequence, this counterculture is not simply a ritual of distraction but an ontological reconstruction occurring within a well-defined space, dar al-Islam, characterized by a common set of sensory values evident in smell, sight, sound, taste, and touch. New intellectual values focus on the Islamic sciences, particularly fiqh, and new ideas about geopolitics and history from an Islamic perspective.

These values have compelled many African Americans to review traditional interpretations of their ethnohistory, literature, and folklore. Through the prism of Islam, the African-American Muslim invokes a new hermeneutic of power: historically captured, enslaved, and transported to the New World, then miseducated and forced to live an inferior existence, the African American is frequently haunted by weakness even in the act of remembrance, celebration of, or reverence for his ancestors. His conversion to Islam adds new dimensions to that history, particularly as it emphasizes the presence of African Muslims and nonslave populations, evidence of resistance to Christianity.

Islam symbolizes the aggregate value of an authentic African-American culture. In the past, dance, music, fashion, narrative, and even certain forms of Christianity (e.g., Afro-Baptist) have served to mediate, if not transcend, social, racial, and economic oppression. As revealed through the experience of prison dawa, Islamic discipline has the power to effect this ontological transformation through a series of counterdisciplinary measures. In terms of social relations, Islam teaches that those who lack the power to transform their material conditions need only reflect on the ideal Quranic past to see themselves as contemporary actors in a world whose rules of social distinction are neither tangible nor fixed unless they are divine. In this way, Islam deals with social difference—even the distinction between freedom and incarceration—by collapsing the past, the present, and the future into a simultaneity of space and identity. To the extent that Islam succeeds in America's prisons, it offers a closed but definitive response to the modern dilemma of justice in an unjust world.

By instituting a strict code of behavior and by networking with other prisoners, the Sunni Muslims established a unique identity. While they are predominantly African American in membership, there are now Arabic or Urdu-speaking prisoners and, more recently, a handful of West African Muslims.

STRUGGLE OVER THE PRISON UMMA   In 1982 Sankore mosque was ransacked and partially destroyed by rampaging guards. An incident that triggered the attack occurred when a guard was physically prevented from entering the mosque. Apparently in retaliation for this act of insubordination, "they went into the masjid and sliced up the Quran and destroyed the place, writing 'Nigger' on the walls." After the initial reaction of dismay and hurt, violence ensued between Muslims and guards when "brothers went looking for the guards who were responsible and beat them up." Seven officers were assaulted during two months by Muslims who eventually were sent to the solitary confinement. "It was a tense situation, and there could have been deaths if it got out of hand."[33]

This was a turning point in the history of Masjid Sankore, and Sunni power at Green Haven diminished accordingly when the state rescinded nearly all the privileges previously bestowed on its leaders and their congregation. Allocations for supplementary food and other necessities for the mosque were denied, and Muslims were forbidden to use their existing funds for the purchase of Islamic or Arabic books. The mosque's leaders were gradually dispersed and transferred to prisons in far-flung corners of the state. The loss of educational programs meant disruption of the contact with Muslim emissaries beyond the wall and a reduction in extramural contacts, including lectures, college courses, incoming books and videotapes, and outgoing newsletters. The imam lost his personal telephone, thus breaking another stable information circuit and surrendering an important symbol of power in the prison.

Central to this conflict were two major disputes that continue to influence the development of Islam in prisons. One focuses on the DOCS policy of appointing Muslim chaplains as nonresident imams in prisons. The other involves the endless struggle to unite all prisoners who identify themselves as Muslims. Underlying both is a power struggle fed by mutual suspicion between Muslims and the administration, on the one hand, and between orthodox Sunnis and all other Islamically defined sects, on the other.

The struggle over the legitimacy of an elected imam arose in 1982 following the violent incidents at Sankore. During other prison crises the imam could mediate directly between Muslims and the administration. To a more limited extent he could also act as an intermediary in extramural affairs. As an institutionalized role, therefore, the imam symbolized the ability for Muslims to render the wall permeable, and he used that role to direct the collective energy of the Muslims toward expanding the realm of dar al-Islam both within the prison and beyond the wall. Once their power and range were restricted by the administration, however, it was imperative to find new ways in which these practices could continue. Eventually, the prisoners contracted outside Muslims to function as civilian coordinators, a designated role in the penitentiary system with status similar to the Protestant, Catholic, or Jewish chaplains serving the prison.

When the DOCS responded favorably to this initiative, the Sankore majlis met to explore the implications of bringing in civilian coordinators to assist in masjid affairs. The Sunni Muslim prisoners agreed that some form of external assistance was necessary to conduct Islamic business within the context of a new prison regime. Nonetheless, they were apprehensive about plans by DOCS and their top Muslim adviser, a paroled inmate and former member of the Nation of Islam, then the American Muslim Mission, with clear lines of allegiance (bayat) to Warith D. Muhammad in Chicago. They were adamantly opposed to relinquishing the authority to govern affairs at the mosque. As a safeguard against the civilian coordinator acting as a "Trojan horse" to usurp inmate leadership, the Sankore imam insisted on writing the job description for the prospective Muslim chaplain.

The role of the chaplain was to provide for the maintenance of the traditional conduits beyond the wall. This was consistent with the goal of resisting the worst effects of incarceration and excavating new links to the extramural world of Islam. Each point indicated a desire to preserve the mosque's integrity while helping prisoners build more humane conditions without attempting a radical redefinition of their status as a self-governing religious body. The civilian coordinator, they thought, represented a pipeline between Muslims in the facility and their anticipated needs, which eluded the authority of their elected leaders. In other words, by hiring a Muslim mediator, they were increasing the domain of their religious authority.

DOCS saw this development from an adversarial perspective. The idea that the inmates had initiated this request furnished the warden with an opportunity to change the power equation by undermining the authority of the elected imam and his majlis ashura (council). This also allowed the administration to peek inside the unknown world of the Muslim community. Since the Muslim coordinator would be under the jurisdiction of the Christian head chaplain, it was therefore likely that the chaplains and the department could begin to understand the growing popularity of Islam, enabling them to take appropriate measures to limit and control this autonomous movement.

In the ensuing years the Muslim chaplaincy grew into an established institution throughout the state prison system. "DOCS began hiring right and left," recalls Hajj Muhammad, an original member of the DAR Prison Committee. DOCS accorded the Muslim chaplains parity with the representatives of other denominations, although this was not always acceptable to the Catholic, Protestant, and Jewish chaplains. It was only after their colleagues were able to observe at close range the transformations effected by Islamic dawa on some very hard-core inmates that they began to look upon Muslim coordinators as co-equals. As state employees they received substantial salaries and the benefits usually reserved for clergymen holding master's degrees. Some of the Muslim chaplains had not even attended college; that created a situation where they were looked on as illegitimate, an attitude that seemed to affect some of the inmates too. At some prisons the inmates alleged that the chaplains hired by the state were embezzling the mosque's funds. In other instances they felt they had been deceived by the coordinator's halfhearted attempts to reverse negative decisions by the state. They were not abiding by the job description, often refusing to execute the duties they had pledged to fulfill.

Several chaplains were former members of the DAR movement or other Sunni organizations like the Mosque of Islamic Brotherhood at 113th Street in Harlem. But according to the prisoners, the majority were followers of Imam Warith Muhammad (the AMM) and were hired through the direct intervention of his representative at the Department of Corrections in Albany.

The confusion over hierarchy exploded nearly a year later, when Green Haven's superintendent decreed a ban on all former inmates from entering Sankore. This was regarded as extremely provocative because it seemed directed at several former members of the DAR who enjoyed great influence and popularity. Soon afterward, all extramural imams and Muslim dignitaries were banned from Sankore, a signal that the administration was intent on closing down the masjid or at least cutting off its access beyond the wall.

Aggravating rumors that the warden's goal was to shut Sankore and force the Muslims to merge under the imamship of the civilian chaplain was a new order concerning the call-out procedure, which allows prisoners to attend mosque functions.[34] A grievance report filed by the Sankore majlis complained that the mandatory call-out system was being used to monitor attendance at classes to establish a certain quota that would be necessary to maintain the mosque's operation in the face of increasingly stringent state budgets. Subsequently, the chaplain downgraded the imam's institutional pass from "Imam" to "Program Aide" in a further attempt to ruin his position by limiting his physical mobility in the facility. Further complaints included the warden's rejection of a petition to enlarge Sankore and the imposition of new limits on the ability to transfer funds from individual accounts to the mosque's account. Finally, the imam and the *naibu* were dispatched to other facilities in the aftermath of an incident when they opposed an "administrative visit" to the mosque by the chaplain and his supervisor from Albany. It was alleged that the administrative delegation in question was trying to estimate membership numbers at Sankore with an eye toward further limiting its privileges, forcing a merger with Masjid ut-Taubah (AMM) and imposing the rule of the chaplain as imam.

The threat implied by these moves indicated that the commissioner intended to retake the turf that had been consecrated as Muslim space over a period of fifteen years. By breaking up the majlis and exporting them to other prisons, the administration sought to destroy continuity in leadership succession and to dispel what they regarded as the myth of Sunni predominance at Green

Haven. "These chaplains are like priests and cooperate with the antagonistic role engineered by the state," was typical of the comments elicited during this period. Another Muslim prisoner observed that the Department of Corrections had the idea of the Christian model of "jailhouse religion" as applied to Islam and that this inaccurate notion was being reinforced by the presence of a former Nation of Islam minister. They charged furthermore that the head Muslim chaplain was collaborating with DOCS to depose elected imams throughout the state.

At the root of this conflict was the opinion of the head Muslim chaplain in Albany that a prisoner cannot serve as imam because, Islamically speaking, an imam cannot be of a criminal element. His logic was based on the concept that since an imam's behavior must be beyond reproach, someone who has committed a crime or shocked society should never become an imam. This remains an unresolved problem for Quranic doctrine, which holds that an imam must come from among the local community of believers.

The community remains unstable because of ongoing differences between Sunnis and members of Farrakhan's Nation of Islam, who suddenly appear ready to embark on a reconversion of Black Muslims to Islamic orthodoxy as established in 1975 by Warith D. Muhammad's followers according the pattern described earlier. Sunni Muslims whose legacy is tied to Masjid Sankore have labored frequently to promote homogenous practice but not to the extent that they will compromise their vision of dar al-Islam. In order to safeguard this vision, therefore, they have eschewed growth simply to increase their numbers and sometimes pay the price of losing space to another sect in any given prison.[35]

For all these problems, the goal has always been to create a territory that is neither "of the prison" nor "of the street" but a "world unto itself" defined by the representational space that is common to Muslims worldwide. The profundity of this spatial vision is evident in the metaphor in this chapter's title, which was used by one prisoner serving a life sentence: "In here the Muslims are an island in a sea of ignorance." Islam's attraction for prisoners lies in its power to transcend the material and often brutally inhuman conditions of prison. Although it may seem to some just another jailhouse mirage, the Muslim prisoner sees entry into that space as a miracle of rebirth and one that may even spread from the prison to the street.

8

The Many Dimensions of a

Muslim Woman

I came kicking and screaming into this religion. —Naima Saif ʿullah

CONVERSION AND MARRIAGE Naima Saif ʿullah's biography is a study in the religious conversion of a modern woman. It concerns especially the influence of her family on her emotional life and career. When we first met her in 1987, Naima, at age thirty-six had been Muslim for almost five years and had already married and divorced Islamically four times. Yet she claimed that her life as a Muslim was more carefree than before her conversion. Despite other problems, she no longer smoked crack or marijuana. Her chronic health problems had consequently disappeared. Emotionally, she became more conscious of her roles as daughter, sister, and mother. She credited her faith in Islam as the reason for this psychic stability. Worship gave her confidence and the determination to confront her problems as a strong-willed adult. Her religious worship is conducted mostly in private because she discovered that the mosque was neither a safe nor comforting domain for a single Muslim woman.

Naima is at once openly critical about certain aspects of Muslim society yet fiercely defensive about any broadsides against her new religion. Her frankness extends to her work and personal life. Soon after our initial meeting, we became friends, meeting her at holiday events such as the 'Id al-Fitr feast in Brooklyn's Prospect Park and frequently exchanging telephone calls, when sometimes we rambled on for hours from general subjects to the intimate details about her life. She welcomed us to follow her on the job, an invitation that eventually led to a newspaper story and photos about her community outreach work for the Department of Health. Naima's narrative is important to the structure of this book not only because it raises general questions about the relationship of an African-American woman to Islam but also because it reflects the very specific historical context of the independent Sunni movements of the 1980s. What does conversion offer to a single woman who is professionally successful yet personally unsatisfied? How does Islam address the overtly sexual nature of consumer society? Does it foster steadfast opposition by providing an alternative set of moral and ritual prescriptions for relations with the opposite sex? Or is it really a method of selective compromise like those of other religions, which concede individual autonomy to secular society while drawing boundaries around the family unit, staking its claim as moral protector of last resort? Does Islam succeed any better in this realm than Christianity or Judaism, where male resistance, laced with strains of a patriarchal backlash, offsets the secular achievements of women?

The response offered by revivalist movements to these dilemmas sheds further light on their historical and theological positions concerning both America and Islam. As revivalist Islam was a particular response to the nationalist politics of the 1960s, its adherents were confronted by problems similar to the ones that flustered political movements, like the Black Panther Party, where the business of confronting issues of male dominance and female subordination was all too often dismissed or relegated to fantasies of a postrevolutionary utopia. By considering Islam as a viable alternative to social revolution, African-American activists came face to face with a new dilemma. They needed to choose between studying the progressive, modernizing tendencies within Islam or accepting the inevitable implications of the second-class status ascribed to Muslim women in many parts of the world. Malcolm X himself, whose conversion to Sunni orthodoxy in 1964 might be considered an acceptable starting date for the revivalist movement, showed more than passing interest in this question when he expressed the opinion that the human values of any Muslim society had to be judged by its progress on respecting the inalienable rights of women. In his view, no nation and no religion could be exempt from this responsibility.[1] What rights were conceivable in terms of scripture and how this progress could be judged in light of economic underdevelopment and big-power hegemony were questions formulated by reformist and modernist Muslim thinkers as early as the nineteenth century. In this respect Naima Saif'ullah's encounters with the Islamic customs of purdah—the segregation of women—and polygamous marriage occasion a further discussion about these trends and the debates they spawned. Such controversies are especially evident in the works of the Moroccan sociologist Fatima Mernissi, an ardent feminist who points out the many inconsistencies in the application of Quranic scripture to Islamic society.[2] Finally, Naima's conversion can also be understood as a manifesto addressing problems of marriage and the family in a social-historical perspective.

Before converting to Islam in 1982, Denise worked at the New York City Health Department as a specialist in community health and STD outreach services. She was an attractive woman who wore fashionable miniskirts, silk stockings, and Afro-blush cosmetics and crowned her head with a waxprint tam. She was the epitome of the 1980s "fly-girl" to those who knew her. Most evenings after work she partied with a fast crowd that included businessmen, musicians, and cocaine dealers.[3] In her twenties and living on her own, Denise had close relationships with her mother, Marcie, her sister, Tanya, and her brother, Tomas. Her father, Cliff, was an army veteran who abandoned the family when she was just ten. Although he still lived nearby, she saw him infrequently. Her maternal uncle was a renowned journalist.

After her parents divorced, her mother had married a retired police officer named Barclay. Denise disliked her stepfather intensely because he had tried to molest her several times. The same thing happened to Tanya, four years younger, but neither sister ever discussed these incidents with their mother. Her brother was a puppeteer who assembled his own troupe that performed for parties and church groups. Denise was his part-time manager and was successful in booking other jobs for him around the city. Tomas had graduated from a military academy and converted to Catholicism while there. Back home he joined the local Methodist Church, mainly for the contacts it provided in the entertainment business. He was determined to become a successful performer.

With her job, part-time career as Tomas's manager, and network of friends and colleagues, Denise had many apparent opportunities to fulfill her desire for friendship, marriage, and success. Above all, she wanted to start a family. But finding a good man proved very difficult in her milieu, and she drifted into the world of drugs and casual sex to fill the void. Starting off as her preferred weekend companions, marijuana and cocaine quickly monopolized her social life, reducing all her other desires to a single, vast craving. She slid into addiction and ended up living with a drug supplier whom she did not love.

Eventually cocaine took its toll on her physical and psychological well-being. She developed severe hyperthyroidism and began to suffer acute paranoid crises that left her frightened and helpless every time she got high. Toxicomania, she thought, unable to do anything about it. She felt isolated and desperate until one day she confided her troubles to a colleague at work.

For several months, she was attracted to Omar's muscular six-foot-seven frame and his sartorial features. He resembled a young Harry Belafonte, with slightly reserved mannerisms that Denise admired because they set him apart from the leering homeboys who were constantly outdoing each other's unsuccessful and frequently clownish attempts to court her. If Omar stoked Denise's fantasies, the feeling was not obviously mutual, judging by his initial response to her advances. He just handed her a copy of Maulana Abul A'ala Mawdudi's book *Toward Understanding Islam* and explained that he had been Muslim for almost ten years. He deflected her attempted seductions by turning their conversations to spiritual matters. Soon he introduced Denise to Maryam, a Muslim woman who also worked City Hall. It was not until months later that he gradually confessed his own romantic inclinations, although he remained insistent that he was looking for something very different from the relationship she imagined. If she were serious about him, then everything would have to change. She would have to accept Islam, pray five times a day, change her wardrobe, and read the Quran.

Denise regarded such demands as extreme. While she was generally open-minded and usually tolerant of different religions, Islam was out of the question for her. She was born and bred in the church, she worshiped there regularly, she prayed almost every day. She taught Sunday school "even when I used to get high. No matter how zonked-out I was, I always used to say my prayers and learn new prayers from the Bible. So I did have that religious inclination."

But the closer she moved toward him, she realized that Omar's ultimatum meant she would have to become Muslim or eventually lose him. It was shocking and made her recoil at the idea of a religious conversion. This was asking for too much, and Denise became confused. She knew this could not be an ordinary relationship because Omar was demanding a tremendous commitment. Wasn't that exactly what she thought she had always wanted from a man? She wanted to acquiesce, yet somehow this was much different from the romantic scenario she had once imagined. "The more he pushed, the more I said, No! . . . Finally he stopped calling me and stopped being involved because he felt that I wasn't going to follow it."

The chief obstacle to conversion, she recalls, was the idea of praying to a deity who was different from the one she had known, different from the God of her childhood, her family, and her friends. What would her family think of Islam? How would her friends react if she could no longer socialize the same old way? How would her colleagues treat her when she showed up at work in Muslim garb? As much as she had tried to separate Omar from his religious beliefs, it seemed impossible. Without committing herself to Islam, she would never have him.

Denise could not decide between her passionate desire for this man and her raucous past. She felt herself going literally "out of her mind" as she tried to fathom why Omar would marry her only if she promised to convert. She strained to see beyond her own reflection in the mirror, to get a more objective, out-of-body sense of herself than she had ever before risked. Then she lost balance and fell head first through the looking-glass, not knowing what would come next, yet shattering forever her previous self-image and provoking an intense crisis, an incapacitating emotional turmoil. This experience was so upsetting that she avoided work rather than confront Omar. Would changing religions affect her personality beyond recognition? Was everything interrelated, what she liked and disliked about herself? To get beyond her drug dependency required courage and stamina. She believed she possessed these qualities, although they were often unavailable in light of all her failed opportunities. The choices all had faces resembling her friends and family. Some smiled, like Tanya, her sister, and made her feel great, while others disrupted her spirit, like Cliff or Barclay, and alienated her from her inner strengths.

> Just then I started really to believe I could change. It inspired me to break up all my crack pipes. I had a big bust-up with my boyfriend, because I flushed some cocaine down the toilet. He got very angry and couldn't understand why I did that. "Why? Why? Why?" he kept asking. I was searching for something to say to explain myself. All of a sudden I told him that I wanted to be Muslim. If he wasn't coming along then we would have to break up. Our relationship ended right there.

Denise returned to work and sought out Omar's friend Maryam, who was married to his best friend, Bilal. Maryam invited Denise to visit her at home the following weekend.

"What does it mean to 'take shahada'?" asked Denise upon arriving at Maryam's.

"Do you believe what you read?" asked Bilal, standing beside his wife. "If you walked out of here today and got hit by a car, would you want to die a Believer? . . . It's just a matter of reciting kalima shahada, the article of faith. You put your entire life in the hands of Allah and his Messenger, the Prophet Muhammad. It doesn't mean you have to change everything overnight. You just affirm your belief, and whatever changes are going to take place can come later."

"That's when I took my shahada," Denise, now called Naima, said, pointing to her kemar.

> Bilal ran to the mosque [Masjid Yasin in Brooklyn] and came back with three other brothers to witness my conversion. I didn't know them. They were older, black men, wearing robes and skullcaps, and two of them had full beards, one of them almost completely grey. They removed their shoes and entered the house. The grey beard carried big green copy of the Quran in one hand, prayer beads in the other. We went into the living room, which had practically no furniture, just a bookstand and a coffee table. It was carpeted wall-to-wall in green. The men lined up, dropped to their knees, and began reciting prayer in Arabic. Maryam and I were watching from the kitchen. After about fifteen minutes, they stopped but remained seated on

the floor. Bilal motioned for us to come in, and we sat cross-legged facing them. I remember that it was stormy that day. Big raindrops were pounding on the windowpanes. I was staring over their shoulders, thinking about my friends and other people I knew. It seemed like a movie, where people are standing on the dock waving to others who are leaning over the railing of an ocean liner that is slowly drifting away. Just like that . . . although I wasn't sure which side I was on. Then everyone raised their right index fingers into the air. I did it too. They recited the lines slowly so I could repeat after them. "La illaha Muhammad ar-rasullulah" ("There is only one god, Allah and Muhammad is His Messenger.") The older man with a grey beard suggested the name Naima. His words were very comforting and sincere, not at all insistent. He said I should try this name to see if it was comfortable. We had a short conversation afterwards on what it meant to be Muslim. That I had to study and pray regularly and come to the mosque for lessons. That I should listen to those who could instruct me in the proper manners. Maryam said she would help me. All this happened on April 10, 1982.

Afterward Naima returned home and called to tell her family of her conversation. Her mother's silence concealed what Naima knew was her certain shock at hearing this news. Although Islam seemed like a weird cult to her, Marcie acted nonchalant, as if it were just another phase in her daughter's crazy life. The next day her uncle appeared unexpectedly at her apartment. He confessed that Marcie had asked him to find out more about this change and listened to her for nearly two hours. Though skeptical about Islam too, he finally conceded that it might have some positive effects and left, promising to assuage Marcie's worst fears.

Heartened by her uncle's support, Naima purchased some fabric to make Muslim-style clothes. She carefully selected cotton brocades to make the pantaloons and ample jellaba tops that were popular Islamic women's fashion of the day. Maryam had given her some dress patterns. Now as she aligned the thick indigo-dyed cotton to the dress pattern, the numerous pinholes were comforting signs that other sisters had fashioned new lives on the same design. Then she stitched the pieces together on her sewing machine, the one possession she had managed to hold onto through her years of drug use and temporary abodes. She modeled each garment in the mirror and complemented each outfit with a matching kemar, the traditional kerchief for covering a woman's hair.

Trouble erupted almost immediately when she paid visits to her parents clad in her new outfit. Marcie's demeanor betrayed her skepticism toward Islam. She had never openly acknowledged her daughter's personal difficulties—the drugs, an unwanted pregnancy, and an abortion—and now acted as if Islam were the worst of all possible misfortunes. Her husband's behavior was insulting. Barclay muttered disapproval and showed his dim view of Islam by joking around. He bowed down and "salaamed" his wife in mock of Islamic prayer. It was Denise's real father, however, who provoked her rage. Cliff's domineering, almost violent reaction seemed totally out of proportion. They argued terribly when he first saw her dressed "in garb." He accused her of abandoning her family and the church and forbade her to wear Muslim garb in his house.

Driven to tears, Denise unleashed a torrent of emotions. Why hadn't he shown any interest in her life beforehand? Didn't he understand how empty she always felt? How she smoked cocaine and pot to hide the pain of his rejection? Had he ever cared at all, and if so, then why did he walk out? His scorn for Islam meant nothing. The garb and her Arabic name just provided new excuses for his same old disapproving attitude. Nothing in her adult life had ever stirred his interest. Now that she was trying to improve herself, he attacked her efforts as misguided and delusional. She left his house in tears, and they did not speak for an entire year.

Tanya understood her sister's torment better than other family members. Despite personal misgivings and her general ignorance about Islam, she stood firmly by Naima's decision. She thought the rest of the family was being hypocritical when they showed more distress about her religious conversion than her drug habits. Tanya refused to abandon or criticize her sister. No one had paid much attention to the effect drugs had had on her health during a period of dramatic weight loss. Since she had kept her job and wore fashionable clothes, nothing else mattered. "I was zonked out and didn't look good, but that wasn't anywhere. It just was not an issue," Naima observed. "The only person who knew and commented about it was my mother. And my sister sometimes. But she was getting high too."

For Tomas, Denise's conversion spelled disaster. "When I was freebasing and getting thin, I could still put on a skirt and drum up interest in his act. When I started wearing a kemar, he got angry, thinking it would ruin his chances of success. The troupe always came first, he insisted. Tomas wanted to pull my strings too. He acted as if I needed his permission to cut them."

One incident symbolized her family's steadfast opposition to her conversion. Soon after the fight with her father, Naima went to her Aunt Kristina's house for her cousin's "sweet sixteen" party. She wanted to lend a hand in the kitchen and watch the kids enjoy themselves. Upon seeing her in Muslim garb, however, Kristina exploded. "Go in the back. Just go into another room!" she yelled.

"What's your problem?" Naima shot back.

"You're my problem. You're embarrassing me because you look ridiculous!" Kristina shrieked.

Naima became very upset. "I just got my stuff and left," she said. Recalling the bitter moment a decade later, a tear of regret fell onto her cheek.

Despite these disappointments, Naima struggled to get clean. Meanwhile, her friends continued freebasing cocaine and smoking strong marijuana. None pursued any organized worship, yet they interpreted Naima's conversion as a personal insult and treated her like a deserter. Gloria, previously her best friend, called the others to report that Denise had "totally flipped." Too much coke, they concurred, had pushed her over the edge. They were so opposed to Islam that Gloria suggested either confronting her as a group or hiring a professional deprogrammer, like one she'd seen on Oprah, someone who specializes in rescuing the victims of religious cults. Finally, they simply abandoned Naima.

Naima hit a hard wall of silence in her family and friends. Whenever she reflected on their negative attitudes, she felt depressed and isolated. Yet she sensed that Islam was a powerful force growing inside her, helping her to turn a corner. The isolation would be temporary, she thought, as she shifted gears and tried to make meaningful choices. Her health improved immediately as certain evidence that she was on the right path. The chronic thyroid condition disappeared almost as soon as she gave up smoking cocaine. She regained her normal weight and felt much better. She had more money, too, because it did not fly out her hands into the pockets of drug dealers on payday.

Omar, Maryam, and Bilal introduced Naima into their Muslim circle at the mosque where shahadas attended classes for beginners in Islam and Arabic. The curriculum for women was based on the concept of adab, the rules of etiquette between the sexes. The mosque was a crowded place with many newcomers to Islam, including more than twenty women. Besides the educational programs, there were athletics and discussion groups geared toward social networking.

So many new Muslims in one place inevitably led to confusion and discrepancies in their understanding of Islamic worship. It was an extremely heterogeneous network that connected ex-convicts with former drug users in various stages of rehabilitation, abused women, and even formerly homeless men. African Americans had many different ideas about Islam, different reasons for converting, and various goals. In theory everyone was moving in the same general direction, but conflicts arose frequently, particularly in relations between men and women. Despite efforts by some experienced and knowledgeable leaders of the congregation to maintain proper adab, the mosque sometimes became a sexual arena where men were constantly on the prowl.

Naima recalls the discomfort of this milieu:

> [It was] like I was on display, with everyone whispering, "that's a new shahada." It's like you have this sign on you that says, "I'm Fair Game." The brothers are not really supposed to look at you as you go by, but everybody stares. At one point Bilal said, "Just come outside and get in the van!" It was scary. Every time somebody came who was new . . . all the brothers would be right there. Even brothers who were married already would be homing in on you.

At first Naima was impressed by the imam's leadership qualities and his mastery of the Quran. "He made sense. If I had paid attention to him, it would have kept me out of a lot of trouble," she lamented by way of introducing the narrative of her four failed marriages.

Since converting, Naima has been married five times. She conceived a son, Sulaiman, while in a polygamous marriage and is currently married to Omar, the Health Department colleague who originally introduced her to Islam. Between her debut as a single "sister" at the mosque and this last marriage, she also had four different wali or male guardians who were appointed by the imam to protect and counsel her in her marriage choices. She blames many of her mistakes on them, implying that they did not properly understand their roles as guarantors of social order in the African-American Muslim community.

Naima's experiences are probably atypical because most Muslim women have stable monogamous relationships. Their husbands are devoted family men who often work two or sometimes three jobs a week to provide a comfortable home and nurturing atmosphere for their wives and children. Some men are also cooperative when it comes to sharing domestic labor and seek to prove the benefits of Islam to the entire community. They support wives who work outside the home and will go to extraordinary lengths in pursuit of the family values depicted in the Quran and Traditions. The ethnographer's problem is that such families are so busy that they are seldom found at the mosque or elsewhere in the day-to-day public life of an Islamic community. When available, they are reluctant interlocutors and resentful of any attempts to discern significant differences between conjugal relations in Islam and in other religions.

Consequently, there is an imbalance in the public perception of the family among African-American Muslims. Where marital problems are manifest, they necessarily acquire an Islamic dimension in the sense that African-American converts have inherited a patriarchal legacy that appears outdated in comparison to the rights and privileges gained by Western women in the past century. The existence of plural marriage influences these perceptions with overtones of a throwback to an archaic period when male dominance went unchallenged publicly. This is terribly embarrassing to some Muslims because they feel unfairly singled out and attacked, whereas, in truth, even Jewish and Christian women have only recently emerged from a condition of complete social inferiority. Inevitably, some Muslims respond by pointing to "Negro" culture as the source of women's status while others point to Arab cultural attitudes toward women as the problem's source. Properly informed or not, these opposing positions miss the point because they circumscribe the issue of sexual relations within the realm of myth and fail to understand sexuality in Islam. This leads to confusing opinions about the attraction of many women to Islam, especially when its interests stand in the way of their liberation.

Naima's story reveals much about the travails of African Americans who seek Islam as a remedy to social anomie and personal turbulence. It is also a caution for those who expect too much from marriage, an institution characterized as fully "half one's religion" by Muslim traditionalists yet often subjected to the same illusions and social pressures as domestic life anywhere in the world. Her first three marriages serve as an example of this episodic quest for stability and love. The first one was disastrous but short-lived. Soon after her conversion in 1982, Naima met a man at the mosque and married him two months later, against the imam's advice. " 'Something is wrong with the brother,' he kept saying. But I pursued marriage anyway." She quickly discovered that her new husband was dealing drugs for a living. Sensing danger, she immediately went back to the imam, who persuaded the man to divorce her two weeks later.

The second marriage lasted longer, but there were many problems and much anguish. After months of flirting with Denise and waiting for her to convert, Omar had given up and married another woman. Now that she was Muslim herself, Naima experienced many latent emotions. While feeling better physically, she was still adrift emotionally, isolated, and now lonely after losing friends and family. The episodes with her family were especially awful, and she sought to compensate for this loss of harmony by plunging head-first into a relationship.

As New Year's Day of 1983 approached, Naima grew apprehensive and nervous. Thanksgiving at Marcie's had been difficult. The stares and whispering behind her back made her feel paranoid and unwanted. At Christmastide, she was therefore grateful when Maryam's husband, Bilal, invited her to join him at the youth home where he worked as a counselor. She accepted without hesitation and gladly helped him in preparing a dinner for the children. Afterward, they talked for most of the night. Naima reminisced about past Christmases with her family, the funny presents they used to exchange and stories about distant relatives who often turned up for the holiday feasts. Bilal shared his childhood holiday experiences too, and by the end of the night they had become friends. She was thankful for Islam, grateful not to be lonely or stoned on dope somewhere.

Naima fell in love with Bilal that evening. Although married, he made little effort to discourage her attentions, which always related to the idea of marriage and family. They saw each other frequently at Maryam's place. "She brought Bilal and I together at the house. She was the matchmaker. She made us talk to each other and then just sort of sat on the other side of the room. She'd go in and out and whatever, but her presence was there."

Soon Bilal was driving her to work everyday and sending love letters, clearly violating orthodox adab yet by Naima's standards nonetheless "respectful" of her status as a single Muslim woman. To a neutral observer, however, Bilal was stretching his sense of Islamic chivalry toward the new "sister."

Remarkably, her friendship with Maryam flourished too during this period. Naima marveled at the young woman's talent and determination. She had married Bilal at sixteen, completed her high school education, and was just entering college while raising their two children. She succeeded financially by collecting welfare and running a successful hair-braiding business out of her home. Most of the Muslim women in her circle wore their hair in tightly braided extensions or natural dreadlocks underneath their kemar, thanks to Maryam. "She was a girl who could pull money out of her hat," described Naima in praise.

One day Maryam unceremoniously suggested plural marriage. This came as a complete shock to Naima.

> I really wasn't planning on getting married. . . . I was very independent at the time. But I wanted to have a child. That was going to be difficult. So I looked at this guy, and thought, He's really nice, he's understanding, I can talk to him, he's nice looking. Maryam kept saying to me, "I really want you in my family, to be my cowife." We were very close. We

still are kind of close. I told Maryam, "I'll marry him." Then she broached the subject with him, and right away he said, "Okay." He felt flattered, I guess.

After she agreed to marry Bilal, Naima was surprised once more to learn that she was going to become not Bilal's second wife but his third! Maryam had failed to report the existence of Jameela, the first and eldest wife. And for her part, Jameela was infuriated when Bilal announced his intentions to take a third wife. "Jameela was totally against polygyny from the get-go. He had married Maryam over her objections, and she was still smarting from that marriage. There were a lot of bad feelings and nasty rumors flying around the mosque already, when all of a sudden, Bilal says, 'Hey! I'm getting married to somebody else!' "

Jameela tried to exercise her veto power as Bilal's "principal wife" by scapegoating Naima around the mosque. Maryam fought back to protect herself and Naima by mobilizing the women who were sympathetic to polygyny. They were mostly women who were themselves involved in plural marriages. Then Bilal entered the fray by provoking Jameela and openly discussing a divorce. He said that she was the troublemaker, in contrast to Maryam and Naima, both of whom accepted plural marriage and promised to build a lasting friendship based on their devotion to Islam. To put Jameela on the defensive, Bilal insinuated that by refusing to accept this marriage, she was repudiating Islam. After much bickering, threatening, whispering and conspiring, Bilal forced Jameela to acquiesce to the marriage, and in the end she agreed to attend his wedding to Naima at the mosque.

Briefly, the three women, Jameela's children, and Bilal were one big family. The nikka itself was a modest ceremony followed by a reception with fruits, dates, and sparkling cider. Though Maryam and Jameela neutralized each other's presence, it was not an especially joyous affair. Naima had reluctantly covered her face in hijab in deference to Bilal's wishes. No one from her family showed up, and only two of her non-Muslim friends came. "They were nonjudgmental. I'm sure they probably didn't understand it, but they liked Maryam, and they liked Bilal," she recalled.

After a ten-day honeymoon at Naima's apartment, Bilal was supposed to establish a routine by dividing his time and money equally among all three wives, following Islamic law.[4] This rule is strongly emphasized by Muslim scholars for its function in moderating the potential unfairness in polygyny. Elsewhere in the Islamic world, this rule can make the practice of polygyny successful, depending on the man's wealth or ability to withstand public criticism. However, in North America public assistance for single mothers often provides the enabling material context. Since the state does not legally recognize more than one spouse, the women involved in plural marriage can support their households independently by filing for AFDC (Aid to Families with Dependent Children) benefits. Coincidentally, this allows the husband to comply, albeit passively, with his quranically defined obligations of equal distribution. Severely criticized on both religious and secular grounds, this practice occurred frequently before the Welfare Reform Act of 1995, which replaced AFDC with a more rigorously supervised and limited program called TANF (Temporary Aid to Needy Families). Until then, the abuse of welfare was often heard as a strong critical refrain from those opposed to plural marriage—even among Muslims. Practically speaking, it is difficult to know with any accuracy the extent of this practice because most African-American Muslims remain monogamous. Polygyny, while rare, never fails to provoke controversy and is discussed frequently by both men and women.

During the 1970s some Muslims raised their voices against the "welfare pimp" mentality they associated with polygamous behavior. They were frank and sometimes angry in assessing the abuse of Islamic marriage customs. For example, Aunt Hameeda Mansur, a retired Cleveland schoolteacher, stated bluntly that "unless it becomes legal, you don't marry two women in the United States. That's against the law." Some Muslims, she explained, set out to ignore these rules in the name of Islam, and by so doing they compound the destructive effects of racial oppression.

> These black men in America don't be successful at a whole lot of things. "So that if I could be as successful as a husband, if I can physically attract, physically take care of more than one woman, that makes me a man." Now that's their own thoughts. That's not Islam! Then they add a little bit more to it. "I don't have to tell you whether I can take care of another wife or not. It's not your business. I'm taking care of you. So if I take on another wife you have to accept it." That's wrong!

Men who initiate polygamy are responsible for supporting their wives and children but frequently circumvent Islamic law to exploit the welfare system.

> These woman are doing this and when they get married are on welfare. If you're on welfare and get three or four hundred dollars for you and another one—third one on welfare, and then I look around and three women are married to this one man, naturally your clothes are better, you've got beautiful furniture in your house. Three checks coming in—that amount of money, the people sitting down to the table where you've got one pot you're eating from, naturally you can afford a whole lot of things. It's happening in Cleveland. I dare anybody to tell me I'm wrong. I can tell off some of these brothers. I am dying to tell them off. Polygamy here . . . is done wrong. None of it's right because it's illegal. First Cleveland Mosque doesn't. They ain't going to marry you in the first place if you are not legally married according to this law. Everything is done according to the law.[5]

Naima soon recognized that Bilal was not very good at budgeting his time. "One night here, one night there, one night there. He always got confused. I think a lot of times he didn't know where he was supposed to be," she remarked, noting also that Bilal didn't like criticism on this matter. In retrospect, Naima concluded that his strategy was to stay wherever his responsibilities were lesser and the resources (money, sex, food, and solitude) greater. Ironically perhaps, he gravitated to Jameela's residence, where the children were grown and no longer required supervision. Next was Maryam because she demanded so little attention from him. His visits to Naima were mostly for sex. Within a year their son Sulaiman was born, and then he seemed to fade away completely, paying less and less attention to Naima's burgeoning needs.

When she insisted that he live up to his conjugal duties as outlined by Islamic law, he brought some gifts. By her own account, however, Bilal was simply reshuffling his resources from one household to another. If he gave something to Naima, then it meant to her that he was taking it away from another wife. For that matter, when Naima's money and credit finally gave out, she found it impossible to wait for Bilal and decided to go directly to Maryam.

"She used to send me diapers and food. For the whole time I was on maternity leave, she used her food stamps to buy all my meat and all my formula. She helped support me . . . as opposed to him. He would come and bring the stuff to me like it's from him, but it wasn't. It was from her."

Bilal refused to help with the hospital bills, rent, and utilities, which forced her to return to work before the maternity leave expired, requiring a baby sitter. Although she needed Bilal "just once in a while . . . he was never there, emotionally or physically. And there just came a time when I said, 'Hey, I can do this bad by myself.'"

"Well, what do you want?" asked Bilal angrily one day.

Naima replied, "I want you to do right or get out!"

"Fine, I'll get out," he responded and put her "in adab," meaning a verbal repudiation and the suspension of sexual contact for three menstrual cycles, as required for divorce under sharia. In less than two years her experiment in Islamic plural marriage had become a nightmare.

During this period, Bilal feared for his reputation in the Muslim community, reasoning that if people learned he was incapable of managing three wives, his status would suffer terribly. He tried to reconcile with Naima, appearing at her apartment and trying to seduce her as a means to invalidate the divorce. But Naima wanted the divorce finalized, her house keys returned, and child support paid on time. He refused and continued his advances more aggressively.

In desperation she took her case to the mosque but found little support among the women, who remained loyal to Jameela. Once they learned that she was in adab, they grew openly hostile because of her impending status as a single woman. Even the imam seemed reluctant to interfere until Naima's strident and persistent claims commanded his attention as a threat to the integrity of his congregation. By then she had retreated to a different mosque in the same neighborhood where the sisters were known to be more accommodating to working women. Naima's new imam, who happened to know Bilal, agreed to mediate a "just settlement" between them.

Mediation was one way to keep sensitive problems out of civil court, especially disputes concerning polygamy. Naima's new imam, like the old one, practiced polygyny. Another Brooklyn imam allegedly had at least four wives. Naima's threat to "go downtown" to civil court provoked a unified response designed to shield the community from public scrutiny and possibly outside intervention by non-Muslims. Bilal attended the mediation session, claiming to be overwhelmed by his paternal responsibilities—eight children, one about to enter college. Naima retorted that his other wives actually provided him with money from welfare checks, whereas he assumed little or no financial role in any of his children's lives. If he were so strapped for cash, then how had he managed to purchase a new minivan and a brownstone house, she asked? Unless he agreed to pay her something for Sulaiman's upbringing, she reiterated her determination to seek redress in civil court.

I was pursuing this money issue with Bilal because I'd have to hunt him down every payday for money, and I really needed it then. It wasn't a matter of principle, it was a matter of need. My imam said to me, "I don't think you should go to the city or state or whatever. I think we should handle this in-house, you know."

I said, "Okay, if you can be fair."

"Well, what do you want and how much do you need?" he asked.

Bilal came and sat down and was giving a whole song and dance about all the expenses he has to pay, and this, that, and the other, and I was shooting them right down. All kinds of foolishness. Finally, the imam ruled that he had to pay me the grand fee of thirty-five dollars a week! I was really upset. He never paid it voluntarily. I still had to track him down. Finally I took him to court. I had him served and everything, but he never showed up in court, so the judge awarded me ninety dollars a week [in] child support.

They attached his paycheck, and I got four weeks worth, $360. But he quit his job with the Division for Youth Services. He quit after working there for ten years rather than give me the money. From that time on he wasn't doing anything on the books anywhere because they were monitoring his social security number. He started something illegal. I'm not sure whether it was drugs or what, but it was enough to buy a really nice brownstone. When the court finally decided to seize the house to pay me—he owed me about eighteen thousand dollars—what did he do? He let it go into foreclosure. He stopped paying the mortgage. As opposed to letting me have it. I'm telling you. He is very slick and a Mr. Charming but a bum.

Bilal contacted Naima a few months later and begged her to drop the lawsuit so he could take a new job at the Board of Education. This infuriated her because she had typed all the paperwork for his master's degree in social work, a very important qualification for the civil service promotion he was being offered. To assuage her demands, he offered her a single payment of twenty-five hundred dollars. It was a small fraction of what he owed her but the largest sum they ever discussed seriously. Naima needed the cash but wondered whether this was just a ploy to get her to drop the charges. When he refused to show her the cash, she simply turned away and vowed to pursue the full amount.

By now things became so bad that Naima even contemplated moving in with her mother, though they had never reconciled their differences about Islam. Just before taking this step, though, she met a man named Mustapha at her new mosque. He had a steady job, and her new wali vouched for him— "Naima, this is a good guy"—despite knowing that he had just been paroled from a Mexican prison after serving time for gunrunning. In her desperation all that seemed to matter was Mustapha's ability to pay some bills.

"That marriage lasted six months. I needed financial assistance, and this is how I looked at this particular brother," she admitted.

Six months was a remarkably long time, given all the wrong reasons for the marriage in the first place. They fought constantly. When Mustapha started hitting her, Naima appealed to her wali and then the imam, who convinced him to end the marriage.

Afterward Naima seemed resolved never to marry again. She decided to move to California, where Omar was now incarcerated for a felony he had committed after moving there with his first wife. Nothing prevented her from seeing him or even staying by his side. She felt a kind of resiliency, a strengthened ego and determination to get back on track. Whereas conversion had represented an escape from her drug problem, she discovered that religion alone was not the only solution. Her attempt to secure child support for Sulaiman had been as unsuccessful as her quest for a nurturing Muslim community. Unless she was married, other Muslim women saw her as a threat and treated her coldly, and when she did marry, she could neither trust the judgement of her wali nor rely on her husband's religious piety for protection and security.

Her job had complicated the task of becoming a pious Muslim woman. As an outreach fieldworker in STD awareness, she traveled throughout all five New York City boroughs distributing pamphlets about safe sex and dispensing prophylactics. Some Muslims disapproved sharply, saying that such a job was inappropriate for a Muslim. Others told her that it was more important to use the opportunity for spreading Islam instead of tips about safe sex. Islam was the real solution to AIDS, they argued. This was very discouraging for Naima, a conscientious public servant who often injected her religious zeal into her civic work.

She became serious about leaving New York for California and inquired about a leave of absence from her municipal job. She wrote to Omar, asking for his friendship and his spiritual guidance but not necessarily marriage. It did not matter that he was in prison. Leaving the city outweighed all the potential risks of unemployment and loneliness out west. She reasoned that she would be better off starting over with Omar nearby for moral support. In anticipation, Naima budgeted her expenses tightly and managed to pay off some debts; gave up her lease; sold her furniture and stereo; and temporarily moved into a duplex, sharing the rent with another woman.

After an exhausting day canvassing the city's outer boroughs from the South Bronx to Coney Island, Naima would return to her neighborhood in the evening to pick up Sulaiman at the baby sitter's house. On the way home she frequently stopped at a halal Muslim restaurant for a cheap but wholesome meal. This small extravagance allowed her more time to play with Sulaiman once they arrived home. Mustapha, husband number three, had taken her to this restaurant several times. His reputation was a looming presence there. "Good riddance! He looked mean," commented the Muslim waitress one evening, following their divorce. She seemed genuinely relieved that the marriage had ended without any real violence. "By the way," she added, "there's a good Muslim brother that you just have to meet . . ."

Despite Naima's reluctance, the waitress eventually prevailed, and several weeks later Naima agreed to give the guy "five minutes" at the restaurant. That led to a long conversation with Jaffar Muhammad one cold February night in 1987 as Sulaiman slumbered nearby in his stroller. Naima rebuffed Jaffar's suggestions of marriage. She was still planning to go to California. After several months, however, Jaffar Muhammad pressed the issue, explaining that he owned a house and worked two good jobs, earning enough to support his own three children plus Sulaiman and Naima.

Naima remained steadfastly opposed to the very thought of marriage until one night when Sulaiman swallowed a bottle of cough syrup and was rushed to the emergency room.

> He was in the ICU and I was sleeping on two chairs just outside, uncomfortably, almost sitting up. Who comes and taps me on my shoulder at six in the morning? I said to him, "Oh, I'm so surprised, Jaffar!"
>
> He said, "Well, I told them downstairs I was your husband. I just wanted to show you that I would be there for you at times like this."

Two or three weeks later they exchanged prenuptial agreements and got married. Separate provisions were written for their respective children in case one of them died. Unlike her previous Muslim fiancés, Jaffar Muhammad agreed to a civil marriage in addition to the mosque ceremony. Moreover, he even grew a beard and started wearing a robe to assuage the criticism of Naima's wali, who regarded with suspicion Jaffar's previous affiliation to the Nation of Islam.

Unaccustomed as she was to moving into a man's home, Naima felt that things were going to be different this time. Jaffar Muhammad was "sensible, stable, and nice." She and Sulaiman settled into his home with high hopes for a stable Muslim family. For the first time in many years, Naima experienced some financial relief. Jaffar Muhammad was at work most of the time and usually tired when he got home. This didn't bother her. Neither cerebral conversation nor romance figured importantly in this marriage: all they had to do was carry out the bargain. There were domestic arguments, of course, with Jaffar Muhammad sometimes threatening to take a second wife. This posturing made Naima jealous and angry, but domestic tranquility reigned for almost five years.

In 1991 Naima was hospitalized for an ailment that eventually required surgery and ten days' recuperation. Jaffar Muhammad ran the household as best he could during her long absence. Upon her return, she noticed his oldest son behaving strangely and then discovered that he had molested his younger sister. Trying to maintain her cool, Naima whisked the boy into a halfway house and then arranged counseling for the other children, Sulaiman included. Feeling betrayed by her husband's parental negligence, she renewed her correspondence with Omar, asking him for advice and seeking once more his acceptance. After so many years of reticence and hesitation, she discreetly rekindled her plans to leave for California and Omar.

Early the following year she asked Jaffar Muhammad for a divorce. She explained that it was impossible for her and Sulaiman to continue living in his household troubled, as it was, by psychological problems. Her boy had voiced confusion about what he had witnessed between his step-siblings, and to avoid further incidents she decided it would be better to part now. It would be best to split amicably especially, she added, since this marriage had no genuine basis in romance. Sulaiman's welfare was her principal concern although the old fantasies about Omar also strengthened determination to leave. This idea of creating a new life for herself in the West with him nearby had assumed a life of its own. Called marriage or not, it seemed like a relationship where she could be in charge but still have a man whom she admired.

Reluctantly, Jaffar Muhammad put her in adab, and she quietly moved to a sublet. A few months later, things fell neatly into place when the new mayor offered city workers an early retirement plan. She took a cash settlement, paid her debts, and departed for California. There she found an apartment, a car, and a new health service job similar to the one she had left in New York. She visits Omar in prison at least twice a week and maintains that moving west to be with Omar was the best thing she ever did. "I have my own bedroom for the first time. I'm sitting here looking at the mountains. I miss very few people back in New York."

Although she tried to force Bilal into acknowledging his paternal obligations to Sulaiman, Naima always felt closer to Omar and designated him as the boy's father. "He came to the hospital when Sulaiman was born," she reasoned. Naima has experienced a great source of spiritual and marital stability since moving to California where she married Omar. The geographical distance now separating her from scenes of her bitter conflicts with her family and her four failed marriages has enhanced her feelings of self-confidence.

Naima's story suggests that marriage (or courtship) and conversion to Islam are often interconnected, demonstrating the similarities between romantic love and the sensation of rebirth achieved through religious experience. It seems that Naima's platonic liaison with Omar symbolized an affective attachment to the inner tranquility and moral assurance she sought in Islam. Just as her infatuation with Omar survived the other relationships, her faith remains intact despite her failed marriages and the lack of support from community and friends. This is an example of the courage obtained through religious transformation, the awakening of an instinct that changes a convert's perception of the people and circumstances around her. In this instance, faith provides an ultimate goal as well as a means for rationalizing difficulties and sacrifices which the onlooker will never quite understand. The power of allegory and here Omas's missionary-like charisma derive from scripture which serves the convert as an unerring set of directions guiding her over rough terrain and cushioning the insults that would ordinarily lead to self-doubt and moral collapse. Finally, the release from substance dependency, a direct result of her religious conversion, unleashed in Naima an extraordinary capacity to endure abusive husbands, sexual temptation, financial ruin, and social ostracism. In this sense, her faith was a form of beatific gratitude, a visceral manifestation of the survival instinct, in other words, the embodiment of divinity.

Another example from this fieldwork shows that sexual politics and gender stereotyping are continuing problems for Muslim converts in America. Aminah Ali also converted because of her engagement to a young Muslim but soon abandoned the religion when she realized that being a Muslim wife implied a particular status that excluded her from camaraderie with her husband and his friends. Aminah was a young Puerto Rican political activist in a reputable high school during the late 1960s. She fell in love with an older man, named Muhammad, who nourished her passion for political and theological discussions. They quickly became inseparable companions, attending civil rights demonstrations and antiwar rallies together. When she began to frequent Muslim social circles in Brooklyn, she converted to Islam as a preliminary step to marrying Muhammad. Like Naima, her initial enthusiasm for Islam focused on a romantic infatuation with a spiritually oriented Muslim man. When Muhammad took Aminah as his "betrothed" into Masjid Yasin in Brooklyn, the Muslim women greeted her with suspicion. They seemed to resent her status as a single woman who was uninterested in becoming a mother. She also reports feeling self-conscious about her light complexion. If she sought the company of Muhammad and his male friends, then she provoked hostility from other women at the mosque. Aminah soon began to question her conversion. "Sometimes I felt like I was trespassing . . . that I really shouldn't have been there talking to the men. Like I was doing something wrong, that I should have been somewhere else doing something else."

For their part, Muhammad's friends pressured him to conform to certain masculine ideals and succeeded in undermining his respect for Aminah. "He felt he had to assume a certain responsibility toward me. The men play roles," Aminah charged, "and they encouraged each other to play those roles that reinforced images of patriarchy and male superiority." When someone recommended that she figure out her own role by reading a tract by Abul Aʿla Maw-dudi, she tried hard but found many of his propositions about womanhood to-tally disagreeable.[6] Meeting a young Muslim woman who was entangled with her child in a disastrous polygamous marriage, like Naima, caused Aminah to feel increasingly unsafe and even less assured of her religious convictions. Dis-traught by her fiancés transformation, Aminah finally called off the marriage and abruptly stopped going to Yasin.

In retrospect she admits, "I was more interested in the spiritual side . . . and I was never the kind of person to see these gender divisions as so inflexible and significant." Although she studied the Quran and Islamic traditions inde-pendently and continued to wear a veil, Aminah started to backslide. "I don't re-member the reason that I stopped covering my head, but that first day it felt really strange after an entire year of covering, like [I was] naked."

She continued salat for a while longer and always covered her head during prayer, but the nature of her estrangement from Muhammad sealed her disen-chantment with Islam. Against the popular assertion that polygamy is truly a vi-able solution for the dearth of marriageable men among African Americans, she contends that contemporary circumstances do not warrant the application of historical solutions that might have been appropriate in seventh-century Ara-bia. "After all," she concluded, "there aren't marauding Visigoths in Brooklyn waiting to take women as their slaves!"

For Aminah, *purdah* symbolizes a form of mental and physical bondage that is not necessary if a woman desires to practice Islam. "I've known situations where through the relationship with a particular man, a woman gets into the religion and then basically he tells her what to do and she does it. Whereas other women absorb the religion and they are really very sincere within themselves." In retrospect, Aminah clearly identifies with the latter group.

Generally, sexual attraction can be considered an important component of the charisma associated with the male leaders of religious movements. For ex-ample, the prophetic traditions abound with tales of romance between pious men and female converts. Hebrew prophets married pagan women, integrating their tribes into monotheism through kinship and ritual. Similarly, the Prophet Muhammad married several pagan and Jewish women. Thus the Quran's state-ment that marriage is "one-half the religion of Islam" suggests not only the pri-macy of family and reproduction but also a pattern of simultaneous matrimony and conversion. This has led some scholars to view the Prophet Muhammad as a liberator of women from the barbaric constraints of pre-Islamic marriage, in which they had no rights whatsoever.[7] The question of whether conversion re-inforces patriarchy exclusively is considered in the following chapter.

TRAGEDY AND DEATH IN THE COMMUNITY   On a bright mid-November Sunday in 1989 Aliyah Abdul Kareem held a fund-raising luncheon at Sheila's, a family restaurant on a tree-lined block of ornate brownstones in Fort Greene,

Brooklyn. The guests represented a diversity of Muslim New Yorkers. They attended out of concern and sympathy for a very public tragedy in their midst. It happened in a public housing project on the lonely isthmus of Far Rockaway Beach, where a Muslim sister, Aminah Abdul Salaam, had suffered a nervous breakdown, undressed her young children, and started throwing them one by one from a window in their high-rise apartment. One boy died. Another child escaped death when she bounced off her sibling's lifeless body instead of the ground. The other three children were rescued when housing police rammed their way through the heavily barricaded front door. They arrested Aminah and took her to the psychiatric prison ward at Elmhurst Hospital in Queens, while the district attorney remanded the surviving children to their maternal grandmother. When her neighbors and friends explained the events leading up to her tragedy, the police and outraged Muslims began to search for the father, Sultan Abdul Salaam. For the next few days New York's tabloid papers feasted gruesomely on this heartbreaking tragedy.[8] One ignominious fact emerging from the reports was that the Abdul Salaams were regarded as a stable working-poor family until the husband, Sultan, took a second wife, abandoning Aminah and the children in the process.

As a result of this catastrophe, the Muslim community buzzed with talk about polygamy and speculated about the person who, in the eyes of Allah, was ultimately responsible for the child's death. One highly vocal woman said that although she held Sultan personally responsible for Aminah's breakdown, she was nonetheless opposed to implicating him in the crime itself because that would put Islam on trial. "We don't want that to happen!" she added emphatically. On the other hand, a devout man who had spent many years immersed in the Quran and other sacred Arabic texts concluded that according to Islamic law the husband was indeed guilty of pushing the children out the window even though he was not in or near the apartment. For the first time, Muslims were beginning to speak openly of their own experiences with polygamy. This prompted Aliyah Abdul Kareem to become involved in this emotionally volatile situation.

Aliyah was a singularly powerful woman among American Muslims. As school teacher and union activist, she played an active role in the bitter school decentralization struggle in Ocean Hill-Brownsville. She converted to orthodox Islam in 1965 following the assassination of Malcolm X in Harlem. For more than thirty years she has occupied herself with Muslim affairs, and if there is one female voice to command attention from the men's leadership councils, then it is hers. But she is no feminist. Aliyah once proclaimed that Islamic polygamy was the great solution to the problem of single-motherhood in America but then described her own experience with polygamy as something that lasted "less than the blink of an eye." Bad for her, in other words, but okay for the many women who couldn't control their own lives. Never bashful, Aliyah is the type that can buttonhole local politicians and intimidate outsiders. These traits make her a valuable ally for the Muslim male leadership, even though they may be uncomfortable sometimes with such an outspoken woman.

Under Aliyah's direction the luncheon became an exercise of innuendo and subtext as most female speakers avoided mentioning polygamy openly, appealing instead to their Muslim sisters for a greater solidarity and better communications. Many of the comments were so evasive that a casual observer might have left with the impression that the real cause for Aminah's tragedy was her loss of faith. There was even a note of criticism of Aminah for having strayed from the religious orthodoxy by becoming involved with a mystical Sufi order, suggesting that the real deserter might well be Aminah, not Sultan.

Aminah followed the Tariqa al-Borhaaneyah Sufi order, whose sheik, Mulana Ibrahim, resides in Germany. According to certain accounts, Aminah had traveled to meet her sheik in Germany immediately before the tragedy, leading some to conclude that she returned angry and confused about her marital situation. Sufism is heavily condemned as deviant by many orthodox imams who portray foreign Sufi masters as interlopers whose practices spread confusion and backsliding among recent converts. This attitude derives largely from the perceptions of former members of the Dar ul-Islam, who blamed Sheik Gilani's al-Faqra Movement for the demise of their nationally powerful organization. Indeed Sufism has been subject not only to doctrinal criticism but intracommunal violence in the past.[9]

During the long program that followed the gourmet lunch, impassioned pleas were made to confront the real problem without so much as mentioning the words *marriage* or *polygamy*. A tearful appeal by a mother of eight children, herself a refugee from polygyny, visibly moved the audience. She complained of the abject loneliness and stressful isolation that engulfs Muslim cowives. "Outside the home, inside the home sometimes, the situation is really hell! Aminah just snapped because she couldn't take it no more. It could happen to any one of us." Her voice cracked and her knees quivered as she spoke. Steadying her elbows against the lectern, she was publicly denouncing polygamy in all but name. Most of the fifty people in attendance recognized her as the long-suffering cowife of a prominent member of the Muslim community. A palpable shock settled over the room as women glanced at each other cautiously. Finally, she referenced the tragedy in a Christian rather than Muslim allegory: "Our children are products of virgin births, metaphorically speaking."

Aliyah Abdul Kareem then intervened, laying the ultimate blame squarely on white power and pleading for the renewal of family values that had been destroyed in the "holocaust of slavery." Recreating families was the key to survival, success, and both spiritual and social redemption. This task required taqwa above all else, she explained, adding that women should not feel alienated by the apparent privilege given to men by the Quran. Men are responsible to Allah for "passing on love and the Muslim mandate." He will judge them by their treatment of women in this life. If Aminah were responsible for the act of murder, then her delinquent husband bore the ultimate guilt for his desertion of a Muslim family.

This admonition was not wasted on the women and men present who practiced polygamy. Among the several imams at the affair was Sheik Sulaiman al-Hadi, who had two wives—two families—as well as many grandchildren from a former Islamic marriage. Like some other practicing polygamists, Sulaiman led a tough, busy life divided between his job and two households. Always in transit, he was as difficult to reach as a Hollywood executive. The young children who frequently answered his phone seldom knew when their father would be at home. Also present were some of his older children, who paused to reflect on their father's weekly schedule. If one were lucky enough to catch a woman on the line, she would know if he were expected at her home or "at the other number," code for his alternate domicile. One learns quickly not to ask for this "other" number because most women resent taking messages for their cowives. They disdain such tasks as insults that reduce them to mere secretaries for their husbands' other sexual partners. For his part, Sulaiman once confessed that he was saddened and depressed that many men in his situation did not strive to honor Quranic law, which prescribes absolutely equal treatment for all wives. Acknowledging his share in the collective guilt, he sheepishly declined to give a benediction at the luncheon, although it is usually an honor to be asked.

Three weeks later, a dozen Muslims came to Aminah Abdul Salaam's arraignment in Queens Criminal Court. There were ten women and four men present in the grimy courtroom, including Dawud Surillo, a Puerto Rican Muslim and leader of Aminah's Sufi lodge in East New York. The women, also Sufis, were covered from head to ankle in complete Muslim garb, purdah. Sitting on the back benches, they peered expectantly from side to side waiting for Aminah to appear amid the constant traffic of manacled hoodlums.

"This is a much different trip than just a criminal court. I am expecting a miracle here today," whispered Dawud, an MTA bus driver. But as the morning wore on, he became truly bewildered by the serious nature of the proceedings and, to cope, resorted to describing the child's death as an act of divine will. "My heart is bleeding, but this is her destiny. All was preordained by Allah." According to his mystical interpretation, the judicial proceedings were inconsequential. Allah was the defense lawyer and also the presiding judge. Justice would be rendered, if not in Queens then in heaven.

When she appeared briefly in handcuffs, Aminah responded lethargically to the greetings and nods of her friends. She seemed heavily sedated and remained in the courtroom only long enough to hear the judge deny her bail and remand her case to the state supreme court for a ruling on her mental competence to stand trial. After eighteen months in the hospital's psychiatric ward, several hearings, and many psychological evaluations, the judge accepted an insanity plea and sentenced Aminah to the psychiatric unit at Bedford Hills, the large women's penitentiary in New York. The Muslim chaplain there, Hajj Muhammad, described her as the most heartbreaking case he had ever ministered to in his career. With limited access to her own children, Aminah remained depressed and despondent, prompting the doctors to sedate her most of the time. Having come to an understanding of Aminah's state of mind and the circumstances surrounding the case, Hajj Muhammad was particularly acrimonious about the way she had been treated by men, not only her husband but also her Muslim attorney, who had in effect abandoned her to the whims of court-appointed psychiatrists.

CONFRONTING AIDS AND EMBRACING DEATH   Aminah's personal tragedy initially stimulated discussion about Islam's rigid hierarchy of the sexes, but a disaster of much wider consequence was required to bring Muslim women together against male cupidity and polygamy. This was the AIDS epidemic, and it was Naima Saif'ullah who courageously forced everyone to pay attention.

Many women at the mosque disapproved of Naima's job as an STD outreach worker for the municipal health department. Some regarded it as un-Islamic for Naima to go around handing out contraceptives and discussing sex publicly. In their eyes it violated the adab of sexual etiquette. Naima understood these opinions not only as an extension of the sniping and backbiting she experienced as a single woman in the mosque but also as a sign that both the women and men were dangerously uninformed about sexually transmitted diseases. Despite any personal feelings, she was determined to pull their heads out of the sand and force them to confront the reality of AIDS in their own community.

Because polygamous men frequently introduced new wives from outside the religious community and practiced rotating conjugal "responsibilities," mothers and infants were especially vulnerable. Easy "repudiation" leading to rapid divorce and remarriage thereafter also produced a system of serial monogamy that resulted in patterns of sexual intercourse that were similar in all but name to those of polygamy. Having experienced the desperation of such relationships herself, Naima felt deeply enough to confront these problems as a woman of the faith. She was determined to struggle against calamity and wasted little effort trying to persuade her sisters about the Islamic propriety of her work. Instead she spoke directly to her imam and eventually convinced him to exercise authority and leadership in dealing frankly and quickly with the problem of HIV infection among Muslims.

Implementing a program of safe sex and prevention required further study and evaluation of the various Islamic customs prevalent among African-American followers. Under the imam's supervision, the mosque experimented with HIV testing of prospective marriage partners. Pamphlets and flyers were distributed containing advice about the use of condoms, deemed permissible according to the imam's own interpretation of the Traditions. This crisis meant that sisters had the right, if not the obligation, to exercise their veto power over plural marriage. "Just say, I ain't down with that polygamy thing!" the imam advised women. He even acknowledged the distorted nature of polygamy in America, explaining that while only two percent of all Muslims worldwide practice polygamy, there are more such marriages in the United States than all other Muslim countries together. Whether the figures were accurate or not, his emphatic point was the urgent need to reconsider this practice and for women to take responsibility to curtail it.

Despite the tremendous efforts of Naima and the imam, AIDS plagued the African-American Muslim community. Healthy men and women disappeared for months and then returned as infection-riddled skeletons. Some died, shaking the Muslims from the mystical fantasy that they were somehow immune, excluded or protected by their faith. Other men and women stepped forward to admit they were infected, while a few died without revealing their affliction, further straining family relations, draining mutual confidence, and diminishing the edifying aspects of the faith.

Prompted by this sudden and devastating upsurge of AIDS, Muslim women demanded action to control the epidemic. In one mosque, men who practiced high-risk polygamy and serial marriage were publicly identified and repudiated. Although poor and without communal funds, the women at many mosques raised money to sponsor informational programs, health care services, and blood screening for all newcomers. At another mosque, a suggestion to create a halal, or Islamically pure blood bank, was taken into serious consideration but then abandoned as impractical. There were intense, emotional discussions, characterized as a "feminist revolt" by several observers, culminating in an open forum on 21 April 1991—a striking instance of the power of Muslim women to set the social agenda for their community. Significantly, the forum's scope reached beyond issues of managing sexually transmitted diseases to other controversial topics of marriage and death.

Following the Friday afternoon prayers, about fifty women remained behind the curtains of the prayer hall. For all the extraordinary nature of this event—a "female takeover" as one person called it—only a few men stayed around. Most of the forty male worshipers filed out after the prayer session, leaving no more than a dozen men to hear the female speakers over a loudspeaker without seeing them.

Naima Saif'ullah began the session by reciting from the Quran and then quickly got down to business. "Preventing and slowing the epidemic in our community is a lot about truth," she began. "AIDS is a lot about secrets. Many brothers and sisters came from a very turbulent past. Some might have brought AIDS into the din. Muslims don't talk about IV drug abuse, crack addiction, and excessive promiscuity. But there is no denying that the virus is already in our communities."

She characterized the principles of silence and invisibility as the burden of womanhood. She described the wali as irresponsible Muslims when they failed to question or investigate the male suitors of the women they were supposed to protect. Marriage partners who avoided testing out of ignorance were dishonoring the Quran's emphasis on knowledge, to be disseminated in all forms for the benefit of all believers. Finally, those men and other women who mocked and berated her for the "un-Islamic" aspects of her work had better know that "everyone to whom I hand a condom out there in the streets has to be regarded as a potential Muslim. We are not talking about birth control! If you don't take precautions in the midst of an epidemic, you may be guilty of killing another believer. According to the Prophet, the consequence for that is eternal hell!"

The men's section of the prayer hall remained silent. The women and teenage girls gave rapt attention to the demystification of a previously taboo subject. Then a longtime member of the community, Sister Tahara, took the microphone and publicly confessed that she had contracted AIDS from her husband of eighteen years. Tears fell on the cheeks of many women, including her friend Naima. Tahara begged the sisters to support her and others who were infected with HIV. Confronted with the inevitable topics of death and burial, the seminar terminated with a call for more women to volunteer for the *jenaza* (funerary) committee. "When you are in the presence of someone who is dying, you see God. You get the same experience washing bodies. Teams that do the washing have a profound spiritual connection, deeper than those shared by cowives." Thus revealed in these dire circumstances was a secret too big to conceal: the discussion of Muslim death rites provoked comparisons with polygamous marriage.

9

Patriarchy Revisited

ARECURRENT motif in the declarations of faith by new Muslims is the recognition of personal tragedy brought about by sexual or familial disorder. "I lay every problem that we've had as a people to the breakdown of the family," declares Nur Ali. Amplifying this point, she continues: "The model, the first structure in society that we learn from, is the family—two individuals not related by blood, who have come together to do things they couldn't do as individuals. From there you get a village, a tribe, a nation, a world."[1]

Nur Ali might be called an advocate of "family values" in a world of ever-disintegrating conjugal and parental ties. The mission of African-American Muslims, both men and women, is often conceptualized as an attempt to overcome this social disorder and construct a new way of life based on Islamic values of marriage and sexuality. Are these values consistent with American society? Do they provide a sense of place and belonging for others? Or are they a source of confusion and even tragedy? The experiences of African-American Muslim women can help to illuminate some controversial aspects of these religious values, as I have shown in the preceding chapter. Many patriarchal customs associated with Islam are not necessarily new to the American experience, which needs to be described in an ethnohistorical perspective.

In 1989 the appearance of a book entitled *The Blackman's Guide to Understanding the Blackwoman* created bitterness and controversy for its extreme characterization of domestic disorder, which the author, Shaharazad Ali, blamed on the African-American woman. She charged that the "Blackwoman" does not understand her rightful place in the cosmic order of things, causing her to engage in aggressive, manipulative and, ultimately, injurious behavior toward her husband and family. She argues that behavior that is antithetical to motherhood and unprincipled in its other domestic obligations disrupts black society, leading to despair, drug abuse, and violence. Black people cannot therefore aspire to freedom because their morality reflects the hypocrisy and dishonesty that plague domestic life. For example, Ali labels conventional marriage a sham institution and a dungeon for the volunteered slavery of the black male, who has been brainwashed from early childhood to accept monogamy and the total surrender of his fate into the hands of women. In acquiescing to this cosmic disorder, black females willingly perpetuate a state of ignorance that leads to bitterness, nihilism, and fatalism. This is the formula for self-destruction and genocide, unfreedom and personal frustration. "No nation can rise when the natural order of the behavior of the male and female have been altered against their wishes by force."[2]

The solution, accordingly, lies in accepting the polygamous natural tendencies of the male.[3] Women ought to submit to this rule, which is the "natural truth" of his existence—his earth, his universe. Any attempts by women to constrain the exercise of male liberty should be met with justifiable violence by the man.[4] In sum, the absence of pleasure is caused by universal disorder, which will be restored only when the "Blackwoman" accepts her destiny as a secondary creature.

Ostensibly, the author does not speak in any formal religious capacity, although her book addresses issues that arise regularly in discussions with indigenous Muslims about marriage and morality. Marriage for Muslims differs from the Christian idea of "holy matrimony" in that its prime objective is neither theological nor ceremonial but reproductive and therefore sexual. Moreover, the Quran prescribes in precise detail the modes of behavior between the sexes in private and public. It defines Islamic morality as the complete basis for social justice. In this context, both men and women are natural beings whom Allah guides toward human redemption with divine rules about sexual and reproductive behavior and the orderly transmission of possessions (social and economic capital) from one generation to the next. Thus, the object of marriage and kinship in Islam is to regulate sexuality and the inheritance of property as part of

the plan for reproducing Islamic society. Accordingly, most Muslim commentators regard sexuality as a purely carnal activity that will wreak chaos and confusion (fitna) in the social body if it is not systematically controlled. To paraphrase
Abul A'la Mawdudi, a major influence on contemporary Muslims, marriage and
divorce satisfy passion within the limits of Allah's law.[5]

The contemporary Muslim feminist Fatima Mernissi contends, on the other
hand, that "[t]he fear of female self-determination is basic to the Muslim social
order and is closely linked to fear of fitna. If women are not constrained, then
men are faced with an irresistible sexual attraction that inevitably leads to fitna
and chaos by driving them to zina, illicit copulation."[6]

Mernissi distinguishes between the Quranic laws regarding polygamy and
the customs of patriarchal societies. Polygamy evolves as a way of humiliating
and oppressing a woman through its implication that she is unable to satisfy her
husband sexually. "The Muslim theory of sexuality views women as fatally attractive and the source of many delights. Any restrictions on the man's right to
such delights . . . are really an attack on the male's potential for sexual fulfill-
ment."[7] Furthermore, the conjugal unit is sexual by nature and ceases to function if the woman is unavailable to the man for any reason at all. In other words,
extramarital relations (zina) arise not because a man cannot control his sexual
impulses but only because the woman cannot properly satisfy him or because
there are women who somehow escape male control.

As far as this logic is concerned, Islam does not differ from other religions
based on the Genesis narrative. As the root of evil, the woman represents a
condition anterior to Revelation. She is an unmanageable, erotic creature. According to this interpretation, there was nothing extraordinary about Naima
Saiaf'ullah's sexual impulses or the reactions of men and married women at her
Brooklyn mosque. The only thing that changed after her conversion was the ob-
jectification of her sexuality in terms of Islamic law. It existed to be controlled by
Muslims and neutralized as an external source of fitna.

Shaharazad Ali's book sold very well and continues to circulate through
street vendors and specialty bookstores. Soon after its publication she became
an outspoken and oft-maligned guest on the television talk shows that thrive on
domestic controversy. Part of the uproar she created may be attributed to her
general description of African-American social life as disorderly, "out of sync
with the natural order of the universe." Unwittingly, perhaps, she nourished the
white racist stereotype of promiscuous welfare queens, doubtless contributing
to her notoriety. African-American women, she alleged, are unable or unwilling
to follow the principles set forth in a systemized [sic] existence."[8] Coming from a
woman herself, such statements were extremely provocative. Sometimes she
was dismissed as either a misogynist or a shill for obsolete patriarchal values.[9]
But her charges concerning the violation of moral principles and the apocalyptic consequences this has had for the black family struck a common theme,
which fueled her popularity in the media and contributed to her financial success. Morover, the spatial dispersion of the black family—its "disconnection and

scattered family ties" in the absence of a generally respected moral code—was her call to arms for African Americans to reassert their obedience to the divine laws.[10]

On this crucial point, she makes an important leap from a secular to religious perspective by belittling the usefulness of the church to solve these problems. She refers to the Black Church as one of the problems—a den of immorality, "fashion show," and "spectacle for shouting,"—giving voice to a popular Muslim critique of Christianity.[11] Her intentions are more obvious when she alludes to "natural" tendencies toward plural marriage. According to Ali, the woman engages in hypocrisy, dishonesty, and disenchantment by forcing her man to live up to European rules and expectations of marriage, particularly the "uncompromising rules of monogamy."[12] Subjected to such constant domestic pressures, men have simply acquiesced, forgetting that an alternative exists.[13]

> She has never heard of or met a Blackman who stayed with one woman for the duration of his life, yet she expects her own Blackman to be the first one to do so. She thinks she can change the nature of the Blackman through prodding, trickery and nagging. The Blackman's nature is not governed or controlled by American political or social laws. Including monogamy. He practices serial monogamy. . . . It is rare to find an adult Blackman who does not have a lengthy history of being with other women, several children and the emotional scars of those involvements.[14]

In other words, the black woman refuses to accept the black man's polygamous nature, and her refusal of this truth reinforces the power of white society to dominate blacks. She is a willing accomplice of oppression and, worse, the principal agent of a self-debasing attitude transmitted to the next generation by which young men are "brainwashed" against their nature. From slavery to the present, finally, the black woman has abandoned "the principles of civilized Black society . . . instead absorb[ing] a set of mores that helps destroy black people."[15]

The alternative, implied by Shaharazad Ali but overtly stated by many African-American Muslims, is the institution of plural marriage, known in the orthodox community by its technically correct term, *polygyny*. Plural marriage is one issue that divides African-American Muslims as much among themselves as from the rest of American society.

Few women know anything about polygyny before conversion. For some, it becomes an initiation rite and a test of faith even before they have grasped the essential definitions, institutions, and rules that apply to Muslim marriage. The full understanding that Islam includes a set of strict guidelines for the practice of plural marriage comes at great cost for many women, while others either misunderstand these laws or have no way to compel men to follow the prescribed rules.

From the anthropological perspective, marriage in America is generally a system of preferential choices leading from courtship to engagement to matrimony. What Lévi-Strauss called "the complex laws of kinship" are based on mathematical models of probability and random choice.[16] Options and popular alternatives include concubinage, common law marriage, and cohabitation. The only instances of clearly prescribed marriage rules occur within orthodox religious communities and marginal cults, small and too numerous to catalogue here but not without a cumulative effect on American society. Such rules are enforced as a condition of group membership. To ignore or transgress them invites penalties or even excommunication. Some ethnic communities, particularly recent immigrants, also exert great pressure on their children to conform to the prescribed traditions of the "old country" through arranged marriages, dowries, and other practices consistent with their cultural points of origin abroad. But these rules often dissolve in the fury of intergenerational conflicts that, for these communities, represent milestones, modern rites of passages, on the path to assimilation.

Contemporary African-American marriage does not correspond to these prescriptive models. It resembles the preferential model of white Americans within the constraints imposed by demographics of racial minority and economic class. African-American Muslims are unprepared for the prescriptive marriage systems of Arab-Muslim countries. They may favor these practices ideologically as revivals of the social forms lost during the Middle Passage or as statements of national identity but still cannot compensate for the absence of the traditional authority necessary to make such systems operate efficiently from one generation to the next. Consequently, the institution of Muslim marriage has been a source of confusion in the United States. In addtion, polygamy violates state and federal law. Its practice perpetuates the unjust stereotype of black male lawbreakers, and its misapplication sometimes results in abuses that reflect negatively on the entire Muslim-American community.

To prevent such embarrassments, some communities, such as the First Cleveland Mosque, avoided the issue assiduously. Hameeda Mansur, a lifelong member of the First Cleveland Mosque, endorsed Wali Akram's position, although she does not necessarily reject the interpretation of male sexuality found in Shaharazad Ali. "Now, you know, unless it becomes legal, you don't marry two women in the United States. That's against the law," she maintained, explaining that the ethically correct practice of polygamy according to the Quran is beyond the present condition of American Muslims.

> A man in order not to bother other women, other girls, he's allowed to have more than one wife. That's the law of Islam. The Quran says he can have two, three or four. . . . Men have more physical need. You have to be married to a black man to know that this is true. Rather than having him bother your daughter, your wife, or to be [instigating disorder] in the community, he may marry another woman . . . The first wife has to say I can't give you what I should be and I'm your wife, why don't you

take on another wife. That's her suggestion. Because she has to agree
to it before you ever put the thought out there. You understand. She
may find a second wife for you. Then it's a way of the woman keeping
control of things. And keeping her husband and seeing that he has all
that he needs. Physical needs, mental needs are important. And the
only way a man has his needs attended to is by a woman. No other
way.[17]

Mohammed Kabbaj, the Moroccan-born rector of the State Street Mosque
in Brooklyn and a longtime observer of Islam in America, is more succinct.

We have big trouble here. It is tough for Americans. They are poor and
they marry two wives and they can't even support one. Don't forget, in
Islam if you buy one penny of something to one wife, then you have to
take the second penny to the next wife. Otherwise you are in sin with
God. And the Quran says if you are afraid you cannot be equal to both of
them, then keep one. And it is not very easy to be equal. As a matter of
fact it is impossible.[18]

When it comes to secular law, he urges strict compliance. In terms of Islamic
practices, he feels that many customs sanctioned by the scriptures are being distorted. Like Hameeda Mansur, he bemoans the results—marital instability and
disrespect for women. For him, any married Muslim intending to take a second
or third wife is obliged to consult his first wife. Although she cannot stop him,
her refusal is sufficient ground for divorce.

Muzaffar Zafr, a prominent African-American member of the Ahmadiyya
Movement, explains his personal aversion to plural marriage by alluding to the
punishment that, according to tradition, awaits an irresponsible husband.

I think most of us men shy away from it because when you read the Hadith and the punishment that comes when a man didn't deal fairly with
the wives, I don't think I want to be raised up with one half of my body
torn away on the day of resurrection. And I'm not going to run the risk.
Unfortunately a lot of our brothers who practice polygamy here give a
very bad image to it. Because they are tied up in one house sometimes,
when each woman should have a house.[19]

Orthodox communities defend a literal interpretation of the scriptures
when it comes to social policy. To forbid any marriages described as "acceptable"
by the Quran, they feel, is shirk—blasphemy—because it shows a human challenge to the law commanded by Allah. Whether prescriptive or preferential,
Muslims have no right to legislate in the Creator's place. Even practices that the
Quran defines as merely "acceptable"—as opposed to "recommendable" or
"obligatory"—must not be tampered with or constrained by rules originated by

humans. What Allah has ordained has a status of Truth that surpasses human rationale. For example, Jamiel Rahman, formerly of Cleveland's Universal Islamic Brotherhood, offers premarital counseling and supervision to individuals and families who want to explore this option. It is not necessarily effective in preventing discord and confusion, but it somehow assuages collective sentiment by adumbrating the specific Islamic laws regarding plural marriage and making compliance a public responsibility. In this case, there is a good deal of damage control required when plural marriages go awry.

Having no formal institution for exercising their own leadership, some women display public solidarity with their imams by extolling the apparent virtues of plural marriage for others but not necessarily themselves. One example is Aliyah Abdul Kareem, who learned about polygamy the day after she converted to Islam in the 1960s. Her personal involvement in a polygamous relationship was limited to a "brief . . . sort of an eye-blinking experience."[20] Nonetheless, she maintains a position that plural marriage conforms to both African and Islamic tradition and sees its general application as "necessary," given the economic, social, and political realities of contemporary African-American society. Her teenage daughter, also Muslim, noted that she was "not down with the program," meaning that polygamy was unacceptable for her because there is no indigenous tradition to guide Americans in its practice according to Islamic law.

In other words, plural marriage is acceptable in theory to some women who themselves do not practice it. Hassinah Rance has been married to Imam Daud Malik of the Universal Islamic Brotherhood for over thirty years. They have traveled around the Islamic world together and are still in love. She often counsels women who are prospective or actual cowives in the community, but rather than contravene what is already a reality for many women who look up to her, Hassinah speculates about what her own reaction would be if thrust into a similar situation. "If Daud had four wives, for example, we'd all be busy all the time and we'd have two or more sisters working also! Perhaps I've been selfish about him. In time he might take other wives, but it won't bother me." It would be difficult indeed, however, to imagine a strong-willed, gregarious woman like Hassinah Rance acceding to such an arrangement.

When it comes to implementing plural marriages according to the Quran and Hadith, Islamic dawa has "image" problems in predominantly Christian North America. Though Muslims acknowledge the validity of Quranic scriptures for all time and in all places, most leaders are concerned with propagating their faith in twentieth-century America have minimized the importance of polygamy to Islam. Historically, this strategy amounts to accommodation with the dominant form of monogamy in a society where polygamy itself transgresses the definition of marriage. The general view of polygamy is that of an institution alien to American culture and generally incompatible with modern society. If Muslim men are reluctant to admit this publicly, it is also because they avoid this very controversial issue among themselves.

THE MORMON PRECEDENT   The historical and evolutionary antagonism between adherents of polygamy and monogamy is difficult to characterize. The conflict occurs infrequently and seldom as a dispute between major religious traditions. Usually it concerns conflicts between missionairies and host societies or else between parties engaged in civil lawsuits. In the United States, depictions of the life of an accused bigamist can stimulate a limited moral debate, but only until the next sex scandal takes over the front pages of big-city tabloids. Even social activists who militate for lesbian and single-parent families don't tackle polygamy sui generis except as an issue negatively affecting immigrants from the Third World. In the absence of a clearly defined social drama, this struggle occurs more often in literature which is a subjective and romanticized medium where controversy can be neatly resolved before rising to the level of serious conflict.

The exception that proves this rule is the controversy surrounding Mormon polygamy, outlawed by the U.S. Supreme Court in 1890 yet still smoldering over a hundred years later.[21] To study contemporary Muslim polygamy in the context of the Mormon experience is to comprehend American Muslims' capacity to accommodate American social mores. If the Mormon Church had to disavow polygamy in order to survive, then the same dilemma might eventually confront Muslims. Can they accommodate their religion to a minority status in a predominantly Christian nation where women actively and forcefully assert their claims to power? Will Muslims find it necessary to abandon polygamy too? Conversely, could Islam emerge as a force challenging the present rules of marriage, the bedrock of the present society?

From 1842 to 1890 the Mormon Church professed polygamy and defended its practice as a freedom of religion expression.[22] After the Mormons settled in Utah in 1847, "rumors of polygamy . . . sent many opponents into a frenzy that remained undiminished until they were forced to renounce it in 1890 under a ruling by the U.S. Supreme Court to either desist or dismantle the church." Muslim attempts at Islamic polygamy one hundred years later bear certain resemblances to accounts about the period of Mormon plural marriage. Both religions sanction polygamy as consistent with divine will. For Mormons and also Muslims, knowledge of polygamy follows closely on or accompanies religious conversion. This suggests that conversion, as a rejection of the established moral order, produces alternative social engagements. Activities such as polygamy may generate new roles for individuals and new communal identities. Finally, an important corollary to Mormon and Muslim polygamy is the need to make divorce as simple as possible. It is a way to guarantee quick resolution of the unique problems created by this form of marriage.

For Mormons, polygamy was neither hedonism nor a countercultural alternative. The Mormon project to reorganize sexual and familial relationships was built on the revelations of Joseph Smith, the Mormon prophet, who sought to distance his community from "the corrupt and debased state of the wicked external world [where] adultery, fornication, whoredom, abortion, infanticide and all manner of evils" allegedly prevailed. Monogamy, in other words, was a modern or "gentile" innovation and responsible, as such, for the disorder that the Mormon believers were fleeing. According to their doctrine, monogamy was impractical and ultimately contrary to human nature. It was to be rejected on faith, a faith promoting "medieval ideals in which religious and social life were inextricably linked, and the good of the community took precedence over individual self-interest."[23] The term "puritan polygamy" is frequently associated with Mormon polygamy to emphasize its conservative, pioneering spirit.

The Mormon reasoning for polygamy resembles that of Shaharazad Ali. In one notable example, Lawrence Foster refers to the *Peace Maker*, a famous defense of Mormon polygamy as an eloquent social justification for a new order requiring the restoration of patriarchal authority and related patterns of female and male roles. Women's "unnatural usurpation of power in the family [had] led to unruly and ungovernable children and to male desertion of their families. . . . Recognition of the personal tragedies brought about by sexual disorder and family disorganization was one of the earliest themes of the Mormon faith."[24] This recurring motif in religious conversion has a powerful effect on many individuals who have been touched deeply by domestic tragedy making them good candidates not only for spiritual transformation but also for accepting the concept of the restoration of a pyschosocial order based on patriarchal authority that derives ultimately from a prophet, whether Joseph Smith or Muhammad.

In his description of Mormon women's first experience with polygamy, Foster reports feelings of "shock, horror, disbelief, or general emotional confusion" followed by "periods of inner turmoil lasting from several days to several weeks" that are often punctuated by bouts of fasting, praying, and extreme isolation. "Those who eventually accepted plural marriage almost invariably had a compelling personal experience revealing the truth of the new standards."[25] Foster could be talking about the experiences of Muslim converts, particularly women making the transformation from a world of bilateral sexual relations to one governed by the single principle of male prerogative. As a keen observer of Mormon marriage customs, he notes the ambiguous consequences of these practices. Once the initial shock wears off, he explains, the belief and practice of plural marriage "provides a source of . . . organizational strength and a means of self-definition which was closely associated with the intense commitment of the transitional or liminal phase of development [although] in the long run . . . such unorthodox marital systems hampered the continuing growth of each group, causing internal tensions and external conflicts."[26] While polygamy initially reinforced social cohesion, its defenders' inability to legitimize this practice eventually led some members to question the wisdom of a sustained defiance of secular law. Likewise it alienated potential converts. What appeared to be an attractive strategy for expansion became instead a formula for demographic stagnation.

The importance of polygamy to a nascent religious community lies in its ability to spawn large family units, linking them closely in an ever-expanding web of interpersonal relationships. Polygamy effectively saturates the shahada in a network of believers helping to reinforce a new social identity. From an organizational perspective this increase in the number of adult worshipers, linked by affinal or consanguineal ties, opens new possibilities for geographical expansion through a network of brothers, sisters, cousins, and their children.[27]

However, the creation of such consanguineal networks through polygamy comes at the expense of young adult males who see their marriage plans obstructed when their female age mates are married off to older, wealthier men who can afford to support two or more wives. Such demographic imbalances manifest themselves in discontent and repression, representing a potential for social destabilization. The Mormon Church resolves this eventuality by conscripting all young adult men into a period of missionary service. By sending them away from home to spend part of their sexually active careers in proselytizing activities among "gentiles," the Mormon Church simultaneously exports its discontents and furthers its own potential for expansion. Pressure on elders, who are financially more able to practice polygamy, is temporarily alleviated in this way—and often permanently, for successful missionaries who recruit new female partners through conversion. In this sense the worldwide growth of Mormonism owes at least part of its success to polygamy and the institutionalization of sexual drives. One could infer that by frustrating the drive toward domestic polygamy the government helped the church expand abroad successfully.

For African-American Muslims, the problems are different. According to a noted Harvard sociologist, chronic unemployment has made young males unsuitable candidates for responsible family life, a condition to which polygamy responds as a stopgap solution to reinforce family morality and Islamic values. One prominent Muslim in Brooklyn has at least four wives and justified his marriages by alluding to the Prophet's habit of rescuing the orphaned and widowed victims of war.[28]

In such cases, a sacred logic serves the goal of mechanical solidarity. Children from polygamous marriages enter a system of parochial schools where they are segregated by sex and taught according to Islamic pedagogy at a very early age. Attendance at Friday prayers is compulsory and often forms the centerpiece of an education that emphasizes the Quran and Islamic traditions. Premarital relationships are strictly forbidden, although contact between unmarried teens of the opposite sex is hard to prevent. Adolescent social contact in Cleveland's Universal Islamic Brotherhood occurs under parental supervision, where the terms *boyfriend* and *girlfriend* are replaced by the word *betrothed*. Even at this age, children must confront polygamy in theory if not reality. Young women are often more forceful than their mothers in rejecting the prospect of a polygamous situation for themselves. This bolsters a sense that most candidates for polygamy are young women who experience conversion and plural marriage almost simultaneously. "The question is," writes Sharifa Al-Khateeb, "why do the women accept this? The answer is that most of them are newly converted Muslims and understand even less of it than their husbands."[29]

What about women who express satisfaction in polygamous marriages? Some refer to their enhanced status as women associated with powerful men. They use this status to outrank monogamous women and their less experienced and often younger cowives. Principal wives form a class that dominates secondary wives, monogamous women, and maidens, corresponding to the polygamous male elders' dominance of monogamous men, bachelors, and adolescents. The institution of a new polygamous structure could not be otherwise, because consent depends on tangible advantages for both sexes. To the notion of a conservative "puritan polygamy" there corresponds a social order that confers generational priority in both sexes just as it promotes patriarchal authority.

From the perspective of analytical kinship, a relaxation of laws governing repudiation and divorce frequently accompanies polygamy. This does not necessarily imply freedom from prescriptive marriage laws, yet it shows the importance of providing an outlet for tragic mismatches that would otherwise disrupt the social order. Marriage and kinship rules are more susceptible to sudden change than is commonly acknowledged, and major transformations are also highly dependent on historical contingencies.[30] In his comments on Islamic kinship, W. Robertson Smith attributed liberal divorce practices to an earlier transitional period in Arabia where marriage was an unstable institution at best.[31]

In the case of modern America, "there is necessarily a great difference between polygamy as accepted in a long established tradition and polygamy when newly introduced into a situation in which people have no previous experience of the practice.[32] Although in some states divorce laws are stricter than in others, what matters are the expensive processes of dividing property and determination of child custody.

Minority religious communities strive to avoid such encounters at all costs. A repudiated cowife who threatens to take her complaints "downtown" invites unwanted scrutiny from the outside. She must be assuaged and her anger restrained. Consequently, community leaders can do little but facilitate divorce, which occurs frequently. For instance, the imam may not wish to enforce penalties or negotiated payments on the husband, yet he must support a woman's option to end the marriage. This goes for both monogamous and polygamous marriage among Muslims.

This strategy recapitulates a pattern similar to the one found among Mormons in Utah, whose 1852 divorce law remains exceedingly liberal by almost any standards. It also reflects Brigham Young's 1861 sermon giving women the "primary initiative in deciding when to terminate a relationship."[33] Even the most ardent propagandist of the Mormon patriarchal restoration argued for a scriptural standard of divorce as a corollary to the institution of polygamy. It was church responsibility to enforce the split between "irrevocably alienated spouses" as a means for restoring domestic order by releasing women from captivity against their will. Order in such cases meant peace at any means, including the woman's right to repudiate her husband and his cowives.

The blurring of the distinction between social and religious order is also evident in the dissonance between polygamy as a religious ideal and its actual practice. The faithful Muslim husband must understand his obligations to treat all wives equally, a nearly impossible task, given the subjective standards against which such behavior must be measured. Again, Foster indicates similar problems for the fledgling Mormon community in Utah when he writes: "According to Mrs. Richards, even her husband's most sincere efforts to treat his wives equally led to frustration and heartache. Even with the best intentions, individuals who had been socialized to monogamous norms found the transition to new patterns of relationships in polygamy difficult."[34]

Serious problems also arise from confusion about the appropriate residency pattern for the polygamous household. In some polygamous societies, a newly married woman lives in her own house or remains in a compound with her siblings and parents (matrilocality, uxorilocality). In other societies, in contrast, the new wife shares a household with her husband or his relatives (patrilocality). Rarely, as in aristocratic polygamy in parts of Africa and Asia, cowives and their children will share the same residential space. This custom became part of the Islamic system under the Prophet Muhammad, whose wives maintained separate "apartments" inside the Muslim compound at Medina. According to the Hadith, he visited each wife according to a fixed, rotating schedule.

Some American Muslims have attempted this practice without substantial knowledge of its origins, its historical context and cultural traditions. Sister Ifetayo Muhammad of Brooklyn's African Islamic Mission says for example, that cowives should definitely live together under the same roof, pool their resources, and share domestic labor.[35] Her communalism appeals to Muslims who believe it replicates the cultural model for polygamy in Africa. Sister Muhammad portrays it as economically advantageous for poor people also, but she does not refer to the Quran or scriptural authority. Her argument is based instead on utility, and it merely reinforces an existing practice. The appeal is characteristic of the kind of dawa that confronts young women coming into the religion who have not had the time to examine its moral impact. Their ignorance can have the disastrous consequences depicted by another observer, who writes: "In American interpretations of polygamy I've often encountered a man with several wives getting along fine, only to take a closer look and see the women having sex with each other, all of them having sex together, and the children quietly confused."[36]

What happens when cowives and their children live separately depends largely on the ability of the husband to begin and maintain a regular schedule of visitations. These difficulties became manifest within the study whenever it was necessary to contact a polygamous man. If he cannot be reached at work, then one must try to call him at home. Very rarely is he going to publish his visitation schedule, especially to non-Muslim colleagues at work. Reaching a cowife on the day her husband is staying elsewhere usually provokes a frigid tone on the other end of the line. If the caller only has one home phone number, he or she may be out of luck unless the cowife reluctantly offers the "other number." Young children, we found, do not know when their abu is expected home and are sometimes unaware of the existence of a parallel family in the same city or state. Even with only two wives, men can spend much time in transit as commuters. Their permanent routine has to make allowances for family illnesses, urgent home repairs, tough homework assignments, and inevitable disciplinary problems. While cellular phones help to resolve some of these issues, they are nevertheless expensive substitutes for the man's real presence in the family. Modern city living is already a very complicated affair requiring much coordination, phone calls, and plain luck to assure that a mother, a father, and their children can sit down to an evening meal at the same time. Multiresidential polygamy profoundly raises the odds against this model of domestic success.

According to Sheikh Abdullah Hakim, who served as imam at Toronto's big, multiethnic Jami Mosque, there are three specific obstacles to successful Islamic marriage in America.[37] The first problem relates to the difficulty of trying to consecrate Islamic marriage practices in the context of a Christian, monogamous majority. Polygamy, he noted, puts an extraordinary amount of pressure on the woman. She faces negative stereotypes, often from her own family, even in cases where she might earnestly wish for success. In turn this connotes all the negative images of the harem and a lecherous hashish-smoking Svengali, in turn leading the woman to feel exploited. "How can she then look at another woman's face or her parents?" Second, he blames the concept of machismo that many African Americans carry into Islam. Alienation, not Islam, causes men to be rough, distant, and a little cruel with their women. It's the same "pimp mentality" prevalent in ghetto culture and accepted uncritically as a media stereotype. Finally, if a polygamous marriage conforms to the Quran, then there might be a chance of success, particularly in cases where biological infertility is the motivation to take a second wife. However, if it's a case of the man simply wanting a younger wife—"like getting a new car"—the faith will not support such motives, and failure is guaranteed.

Urban industrial society is constructed around monogamy in a way that makes polygamy a veritable challenge for the Muslim whose principal responsibility goes to observing the Five Pillars of the faith. Lacking "an efficient, detailed technique" for managing polygamy, each family has to develop its own culture. When variations proliferate in the absence of definite residential patterns and rules, it becomes difficult for Muslim authorities to articulate or enforce rules, especially if this confusion is exacerbated by the tacit code of secrecy about this practice.

Among Mormon polygamists, Foster observed similar contradictions.

Since the entire movement to introduce plural marriage was carried on secretly, unrecognized by law, and in direct violation of existing moral and religious standards, Mormon authorities must have found it very difficult to check variant interpretations arising within the group. There is necessarily a great difference between polygamy as accepted in a long established tradition and polygamy when newly introduced into a situation in which people have not had previous experience of the practice.[38]

Nor is there any way of enforcing new codes outside the local power base that is the Muslim community. Consequently, monogamy prevails, thanks to a different and more compelling set of utilitarian reasons. To attempt otherwise may put a man at the risk of sin and divine retribution in the next life, but in reality it causes too many complications. Despite the acknowledgement of legitimate polygamy by American Muslims, its practice is limited mainly to imams, sheiks, emirs, and other community leaders. Still, it had been claimed that the ratio of polygamy to the Muslim population is more elevated in the United States than elsewhere in the umma. While this may be an allegation circulated by leaders anxious to assert some control over a potentially dangerous situation, it may also reveal an interpretation of Islamic redemption as something very different from Christianity by its stress on the ideals of social harmony and sexual pleasure according the divine law.

Theologically, the principle of "celestial marriage" reflects a belief that divine redemption comes only after all Mormons become linked as a "family of spirit." Every Mormon male was summoned to practice polygamy to help accelerate "the eternal progression of godhood for men"[39] despite the practical complications, or even pleasure deficit, it might cause to him as an individual. The complications engendered by its legal practice are to be endured but not celebrated. Here ends the comparison with Mormon polygamy. By contrast Islam does not promote polygamy as an obligation "made in heaven" but leaves it as a terrestrial option for individuals who are truly exceptional, after the example of the Prophet Muhammad, in their capacity for lawfulness, their desire, and their passion.

Fatima Mernissi engages this point in her book *Beyond the Veil* by making the connection between Islamic sexuality, ideas about power, and identity. In her view, Islamic marriage and its psychology revolve around the question of sexual relations of dominance and subordination. "As a matter of fact," she writes, "worldly self-enhancement is so important for Islam that the meaning of spirituality itself has to be seriously reconsidered."[40]

Another assessment of the conditions and prospects for modern polygamous marriage comes from the anthropologist Philip Kilbride. His empirical study of American kinship indicates that the nuclear, monogamous family has been transformed as a result of demographic, economic, and psychological factors. For Kilbride, the underlying social principles that supported the monogamous ideal have been eroded by changes in employment opportunities for women, especially African Americans; advancement and educational opportunities for women have had a negative effect on the availability of marriageable men. This conclusion resonates with William Julius Wilson's empirical observations concerning the coefficient of marriageable inner-city males that has diminished in concert with middle-class and working-class migration to the suburbs. Accordingly, economic and social factors have tipped the demographic balance toward a surplus of women of childbearing age with limited prospects for finding marriage partners capable of sustaining successful monogamous families.

In discussing the erosion of the nuclear family ideal Kilbride also cites the rising frequency of divorce and the emergence of a new form, the "blended" family. "Primarily because of divorce," he writes, "we are moving into an extended family context, but one that has not yet been defined and been given cultural recognition and standing—namely, that of the blended family."[41] The soaring rate of divorce gives rise to a new category of relatives, especially in the realm of parenting, where responsibility and authority are often distributed among wives, ex-wives, husbands, and ex-husbands. He labels the most significant relationship in this nexus as that of "wife-in-law," depicted in terms of a cowife who often raises her own children and her step-children together in a single residential unit. Kilbride proposes institutional legitimacy for the "blended family" and refers to its reality as a form of polygamy in fact, if not in name. He refers also to concomitant trends such as hypogamy (marrying older, richer men) for reasons of material and financial stability as factors contributing not only to the divorce rate but, more important, to the morphological shift in family ideals.

Kilbride gives his view of the confusion and disorder prevalent in monogamous society in a discussion that resembles Shaharazad Ali's polemic. After presenting his evidence, with frequent allusions to African-American society, he concludes that the perception of disorder stems from a dissonance between the normative ideas about marriage and the real evidence of bonding, reproduction, and parenting in America. This evidence shows current family morphology to be clearly in contradiction to the old monogamous standard. Referring to historical and recent studies of Mormon kinship, he then establishes a body of qualitative data that would adequately describe the social dynamics of the estimated fifty thousand polygamous families in the Rocky Mountain states.[42] Although his sources are based on incomplete ethnographic research, he identifies the "minimal matrifocal household" as the prescribed form of contemporary Mormon polygamy. He emphasizes the importance of spatial continuity for institutionalizing the pattern where each cowife resides separately with her children and receives conjugal visits from her husband on a rotating schedule. The household is an independent economic unit in the sense that the costs of subsistence are born principally by the woman, although the husband participates by supplementing her income. The extended polygamous family, on the other hand, has become a highly dependent sociological unit, constituted by "female networks of cooperation concerning community activities, domestic child-care routines and work outside the home."[43] Presumably, the stability derived from this type of polygamous sharing conforms more precisely to domestic, educational, and even psychological needs and the ability to satisfy them in the modern flexible economy. Changing employment opportunities, rapid shifts in the demands for skills and technical knowledge, and even the fluctuation of real estate prices imply a need for versatility and adaptability that gives the "minimal matrifocal family" a decided advantage over the monogamous (and frequently dysfunctional) nuclear family. This is so if and only if the residential unit is embraced within a larger polygamous family web. The institutionalization of a two-tiered domestic family (the residential unit plus the polygamous extended web) empowers the woman, Kilbride argues, because as an individual she is free to maximize her skills in the job market while managing domestic life and deriving the benefits of the cooperative network of cowives. Reproduction of the religious community is secured by the constant, although flexible, circulation of domestic goods and services. The polygamous husband is not seen as external to the domestic structure since his presence is routinized according to a fixed schedule. He remains within the collective orbit of his wives, who are empowered to initiate the courtship of a "prospective new wife for the family."[44]

Kilbride correlates the principle of network maximization with the experience of the frontier Mormon community in the Rocky Mountain states. His hypothesis of Mormon polygamy as an adaptive practice debunks the ideology of "celestial marriage." He points out that "female support networks were especially evident in crisis situations such as childbirth, economic hardships, and bereavement."[45] Reconsidered in the urban context of black ghetto life, his hypothesis gives new meaning to Muslim polygamy. It also recapitulates Carol Stack's analysis of African-American extended-family networks and their capacity to guarantee survival and promote domestic values in the devastating conditions of chronic unemployment and substandard housing. The advantage seen by Kilbride for legitimate polygamy over Stack's nameless cooperative networks is more than simply the formalization of a sociological trend, because the former succeeds in diminishing the havoc caused by frequent divorce. It makes divorce unnecessary, or, as he puts it, "divorce and polygamy are in dialectical opposition to each other."[46]

Kilbride's ideas merit a close look for those concerned about contemporary Muslim polygamy, which is contested most frequently by the very women it is supposed to benefit. The initiative for divorce passes from the husband to the wife, who finds herself without any economic support and either involuntarily dependent on the munificence of a cowife (Naima's relationship to Maryam) or totally alienated (Naima's relationship to Jameela and, by extension, the sisterhood of the mosque). In terms of children's experience, Kilbride may be correct when asserting that domestic stability is superior to divorce and the chaos that accompanies domestic struggles. After all the evidence has been carefully weighed, however, he undermines his position as an advocate for polygamy by confessing that among the Mormons it "was indeed always, and remains, an ad hoc state, as can be seen when we consider housing arrangements."[47]

The Mormon examples cited by Kilbride and Foster, among the few available studies, are relevant for the African-American Muslims, "for any attempt to reinvent polygamy for whatever reason cannot proceed far without serious study of the Mormon experience."[48] In the final analysis, Kilbride bases his exegesis on mostly positive examples, which can be balanced with Foster's historical information along with Muslim ethnographic data presented herein. Kilbride's identification of the monogamous nuclear family as the cause, not the agent, of social disorder does not differ significantly from the polemics fashioned by Shaharazad Ali. Both address problems of African Americans with the implicit recognition of Islam as a propolygamy force within the black community, but neither refers directly to the Muslim experience. Why not? Does this omission reflect a reluctance to mention (apparently) negative perceptions concerning the status of women and the universal image of a male-centered polygamy?

Sensitivity about these issues is not just a matter of polemics surrounding unconventional families or the popular image of Islam. It is central to all modern theologies, inasmuch as all the scriptural, revealed religions—Judaism, Christianity, and Islam—reflect an inherent male bias. The hardships suffered by women under these patriarchal cultures are longstanding matters of record to which the modern religious institutions have been forced to respond, albeit grudgingly. While it would be unfair to level a critique at Islam without referring to Judaism or Christianity, the Muslim world has its own feminist approach. Authors such as Fatima Mernissi, who voices the issues raised in this ethnography, advance understanding of modern Islamic conversion and its continuing appeal.

Mernissi's work is a contribution to current reformist trends in Islam that date back to the nineteenth-century modernists Mohamed Abdu and Jamal Al-Din al-Afghani. Contemporary exponents of this thinking include scholars such as Bassam Tibi, Mahmoud Arkoun, and the late Fazlur Rahman, though none has waded so boldly as Mernissi into the question of feminism and Islam. In contrast to literalistic tendencies in Islamic thought, the reformers represent those who reject a mythical return to an Islamic past governed by medieval sharia but wish nonetheless to preserve their Muslim identity amid technological change and global culture. To say that one hears about fundamentalism or scripturalistic interpretations of the Quran more frequently than reform in American Muslim communities says more about the ability of various forces that are opposed to a genuine revival of Islam to monopolize popular debate than it does about the way Muslims think and behave. In this sense, Naima Saif'ullah's unsuccessful marriages and her failure at polygamy have not broken her faith in Islam, precisely because she sees herself not as a convert to some monolithic patriarchal Islam but as a serious, professional woman who has chosen to accept Islam as a moral compass for her life. She wishes to participate in a living Islam, one that can change to accommodate her needs and those of her growing son. She views her religion as an organized forum where she can contest the predominant male perspective without having her faith judged by her capacity to conform to it. The network she can establish among other Muslims is the practical means for achieving her dignity and respect as a woman. Her behavior suggests that conversion to Islam is seen by some African-American women as a special vehicle for empowerment, whereas secular feminism has focused almost exclusively on the interests of middle-class women with more societal opportunities to begin with. As contradictory as this may seem, the feminist political contention that a rising tide will lift all boats does not sit well with inner-city women, who cannot even view the ocean.

Mernissi shows this to be precisely the case when she declares her own personal interest in Islam as the focal point for discussions about power and self-empowerment: "Islam makes sense because it speaks about power and self-empowerment."[49]

Her discourse involves mostly examples from the Middle East and North Africa, but her views articulate the modernist positions taken by many women throughout the Islamic world. In terms of their present situation, Mernissi finds that although "polygamy is dying statistically," its legal status remains symbolic of a deeper attitude that permeates traditional Islam—so deeply that it is "still at work even within monogamous households." Word for word, she cites a woman voicing Naima's complaint about Jaffar Muhammad's rhetorical way of prevailing in a domestic squabble by threatening to "take a second wife." Mernissi's informant reports similarly that "[h]e keeps repeating that he will get a new wife. He threatens me every morning."[50]

Polygamy remains symptomatic of the underlying struggle between the sexes as exercised by Muslims. According to Mernissi, the sexual nature of marriage is overemphasized in the traditional Islamic view, leading the Muslim male to objectify his relations with women in terms of his own self-satisfaction. If the woman is unable to satisfy him in marriage or if his desires surpass her natural proclivities, the male sees polygamy as a legitimate option, one that may satisfy his imagination more often than his carnal desire.

The traditional Islamic view, some argue, does not explicitly favor men over women, but it unequivocally reduces marriage and its partners to the essence of their sexuality, their erotic capacity. If there is a concept of sublimation specific to Islam, then its essence lies in polygamy as a way of regulating female sexuality. Citing al-Ghazali, Mernissi writes that "polygamy entitles the male not simply to satisfy his sexuality but to indulge it to saturation without taking the woman's needs into consideration, women being considered simply 'agents' in its process." She also writes: "Polygamy implies that a man's sexual drive might require copulation with more than one partner to relieve his soul and body from sexual tension."[51]

This position assumes the same erotic functions for human sexuality as Western (Freudian) theories of sublimation. In Islam, without the idea that sexual tension can become a creative and not just a procreative force, carnal energy has to be resolved immediately lest disorder prevail. One sees confirmation of this morality in the fundamentalist devaluation of the creative arts.

The problem of repression (and sublimation) within oneself is resolved for the Muslim by projecting that repression onto another. Women's subjugation becomes the very cornerstone of civilization. Where Christian morality contains eros within a personal phantasm of moral transcendence and divinity, Islam constitutes its very morality on the ability to exert external control of the other, and that is done to the degree that symbolic boundaries can be instituted between male and female, Muslim and infidel. Mawdudi, an advocate of this traditional approach when it comes to family values in Islam, depicts marriage and divorce as the primary institutions of Muslim society, the framework for the promulgation and exercise of Quranic morality, with the responsibility existing ultimately with the Muslim individual, for whom sexual satisfaction and moral conduct remains unmediated by either state authority or secular culture.[52] Islam does not render unto the state this kind of power, making it even more necessary to enforce a seeming contradiction between marriage as a private affair between consenting parties and the application of sexual morality as a public matter on which the social order is founded. In this context, Naima's dispute with Bilal over his failure to pay child support became a matter for public concern only because Bilal himself was unable to control her. The situation required the intervention of at least two other men, both imams, to reinforce sexual hierarchy in the face of Naima's threat to solicit the courts—in her words, "to go downtown." Reluctant as they were to become embroiled in domestic affairs, the imams were forced to construct a mediation scenario in the hope of assuaging Naima's anger while really providing Bilal with an escape hatch that would allow the sexual balance of power to remain intact. Mernissi summarizes this dilemma in theological terms.

> The expectation that women will not cooperate, that they will need to be coerced, explains man's religious duty to control the women under his roof. The man is responsible not only for satisfying the woman sexually and providing for her economically, but as a policeman of the Muslim order, also for disciplining and guarding his female relatives.[53]

Historically, men's rights and privileges in the Muslim family stem from the logic of the dowry, used as a contractual link between clans in seventh-century Arabia. Marriage symbolized the formal structural bond between two descent groups; the dowry accompanying the bride to her husband's family represents a material exchange of property, a gift of goods and person from one Arabian patrilineage to another for the duration of the conjugal union. In the generations that followed the rise of Islam, the wealth represented in the dowry became a palpable contract and the material foundation of Muslim social identity. Upon divorce, the dowry returned to the wife's clan to restore the premarital status quo.

Muslim legal rulings concerning marriage, divorce, and the distribution of rights thus presumed the existence of patrilineal segments and the matrimonial exchanges occurring between them in precapitalist societies. Mawdudi echoed these principles in an attempt to reinforce the ideal social structures of Islam. When African Americans assimilated his writings to their own circumstances, however, their new practices were out of context, more ideological than theological. How could it be any other way in a society where religious laws regarding marriage and reproduction have been surpassed by state authority? Where few patrilineal units can claim the necessary stability from one generation to the next? In the absence of an orderly template for reproducing patrilineal kinship patterns, the unmodified application of strict Islamic marriage laws can only reinforce misogyny of the kind that permeates Shaharazad Ali's work.

As for divorce, the archaic right of marital repudiation fell to the Arabian male. It was his duty to return the dowry to his wife's clan as a way to clear the social ledger once the marriage dissolved. This formula for divorce helped to avoid illicit copulation, regarded as a reprehensible sin, if the woman was unable or unwilling to fulfill her sexual obligations. One can assume that the contribution of a woman's dowry to the finances of her husband's clan mitigated the possibility of divorce or restitution if she were unable to conceive a child. In such conditions, polygamy could be an expedient solution to a social problem in its capacity to avoid divorce while reproducing the kin structure. Practiced as an alternative to divorce, polygamy is not so dissimilar from adoption, in the sense that an infertile wife may consent to her husband's marriage to a younger cowife who will bear him a child. The child is likely to inherit some part of the first wife's wealth, so her consent to polygamy is tantamount to adopting the new wife and her children.

Adoption was more than merely a solution to the potential disruption caused by divorce because it was also the foremost paradigm for Islamic politics. Historically, it was a key strategy in early Islamic diplomacy and a dynamic force whereby nonbelievers could be incorporated into the umma. Following conversion, an African, Christian, Jewish, or Zoroastrian tribe was "adopted" into one of several Arab lineages. Much has been written about the status of peoples adopted into the dar al-Islam and the bearing this has on the definition of slavery, in particular.

The precise meaning of the Quranic doctrine that "marriage is half of your religion" resides within the structural unity of polygamous marriage, adoption, and conversion. These customs govern the incorporation of non-Muslims into the Islamic umma. They are eternally codified by the Quran and, for that matter, applicable to the study of conversion in North America. Although one cannot speak of adoption as reflecting most conversions, it has occurred with recent intermarriages between African-American Muslims and members of the West African tariqas, principally the Tijaniyya and Muridiyya. It could be said also that some African-American sects, notably the Moorish Science Temple, the

AAUAA, the African Islamic Mission, and the early Ansaru Allah, claimed descent from Arabian lineages. This fictive reckoning of kinship forms part of the Islamic narrative that is used by converts to assert an "African-Arabic" identity, sometimes referred to as "Sherifism."[54] It begins as a strategy for "passing," eventually becoming a virtual distinction that sets them apart, theoretically, from non-Muslim African Americans.

The corresponding right for a woman to cancel the marriage in traditional Islamic society derives from pre-Islamic systems of Arab kinship. The woman's descent group forfeited their claims on her dowry or repaid any outstanding debts to her husband's lineage as a way to settle accounts. This form of Arab divorce, *khula*, allowed women to purchase freedom by compensating the patrilineage directly.[55] As an instrument for domestic accumulation under the guise of sacred law, it solidifies patrilineal inheritance at the expense of women's rights. It was an important dissuasive factor for repudiation initiated by the wife and contributed to the decline of female power in Arabia. "If a woman could dismiss her husband at will then she possessed substantial independence and self-determination. The Muslim social order was vehemently opposed to self-determination for women and declared that only men could repudiate their spouses."[56]

Among African-American Muslims, the wali has become a very strong institution for curbing "active female sexuality [and] preventing female self-determination" in a secular society that recognizes many rights that are denied to women in Islam. When the wali acts in loco parentis he becomes, in Mernissi's terms, "the policeman" of Islamic social order. The right of a Muslim woman to repudiate her husband can thus be summarized as a form of pre-Islamic habeas corpus that was curtailed by the rise of patriarchal authority. This authority was further reinforced by the *idda*, a period of ninety days' sexual abstinence by the woman to complete the divorce. Mernissi claims that idda furnishes conclusive evidence that "the Muslim god does not expect a woman's cooperation."[57] It should be added that a single woman convert is automatically expected to have a wali, another male who influences her choice of marriage partners. If she converts and then marries, as Naima discovered, she submits her sexual persona to the consensus of the congregation. Naima's decision to divorce, while entirely personal, became an occasion for the community to exercise its power, first when the imam discouraged her from pursuing Bilal in civil court and second when the women of the mosque ostracized her.

The rules of Muslim marriage and divorce reproduce Arab kinship with all its historical contradictions. Once codified in sharia, this formula guided the domestication and conversion of nonbelievers outside Arabia. The Muslim family writ large is the umma (literally, the womb), and it is spatially demarcated through the boundaries between dar al-Islam and dar al-harb. The boundaries separating these social spaces are controversial. They invoke every social and historical controversy faced by Muslims. The boundary is symbolized by a veil (purdah) that separates forces of evil from those of good, public from private space, history from eternity, belief and infidelity, and finally women from men. The problem with the propagation of the faith, or its maintenance under hostile conditions, resembles those faced in sexuality. Marriage and conversion are complementary, and both are strong assertions of patriarchy as the fundamental principle of Muslim society. Adoption and polygamy guarantee its reproduction, while divorce, in contrast, spells total rupture.

10

An Islamic Pedagogy
of the Oppressed?

C AN Islam help an oppressed class overcome social and
economic injustice? African-American Muslims wres-
tle continually with this question, and by investing
their dreams and desires in Allah's law and Allah's order, they respond affir-
matively. A majority view the Quran not only as a divine source of inspiration but also as a practical guide for redressing the deficiencies of inferior
jobs, substandard housing, and unequal education that impose daily lessons of subjugation and violence. Islam strikes them as a liberation theology. It measures ethical conduct according to a sacred ideal and anchors
belief in a knowable tradition whose particular cultural expressions symbolize, quite visibly, an overcoming of the status quo. Those who fail to rise
above their material poverty are prone to human error, for they learn time
and again that Islam is a "simple religion" that requires obedience to a

singular authority who extends a rope that must be clasped tightly and followed along the route to personal redemption. Deviation from a total focus on this authority is the cause of all personal and social problems. The true believer must therefore liberate himself or herself from human dependencies, whatever their nature, unless of course they are sanctioned by Allah through his perfect code, the sharia.

This simile has its strongest appeal in dispirited ghetto neighborhoods where the opportunities for genuine economic advancement are meager and where schools have deteriorated into "maximum security" institutions, all but resembling the surrounding violent and drug-ridden streets.[1] Successful professionals flee these neighborhoods, leaving them dependent on a political order that lacks a clear set of defining principles, open to corruption yet seldom accountable. Schools are usually run by outsiders who have little at stake in bringing the benefits of modern education and sustained economic growth to the inner city. Their classrooms function only to reproduce a pool of unskilled labor, reducing young workers' horizons to a choice among minimum wage jobs, military service, homelessness, and frequently prison. In city after city African-American elected officials have foundered while trying to provide for moral and pedagogical uplift of the type that otherwise fostered success for countless immigrant communities throughout the twentieth century. Even faced with the "new economic" agenda (privatization, vouchers, charters, and corporate sponsorship), big-city mayors, education commissioners, and community activists are excluded for the most part from the grants and endowments that normally flood suburban America to float an independent cadre of forward-looking educators and technicians, who themselves become models for students and young workers.[2] From many perspectives, any semblance of economic and political order has disappeared, along with traditional sources of moral authority. This is particularly evident in the decline of neighborhood "old heads," men who habitually served as resources for employment and civic values.[3] Despite the unprecedented economic boom of the 1990s, the inner city remains nonetheless crisis prone and its future gloomy.[4]

Islam tackles these problems by "reimagining" inner-city existence in much the same way that similarly oppressed communities around the world have "built their own 'welfare states' . . . on the basis of networks of solidarity and reciprocity" and similarly anchored their collective identity in religious movements.[5] Historically, this is very different from either black nationalism or the integrationist civil rights agenda defined by Martin Luther King Jr. almost half a century ago. The Islamic movement does not oppose these ideals as much at it sidesteps them in rejecting the Western agenda, rooted in canon law and individual rights, and disdaining the leftist politics of class consciousness.

The convert embraces a profoundly conservative political outlook that views secular jurisprudence suspiciously as an inadequate, flawed approximation of divine law and justice. By using the Quran and the Hadith to "reconstruct meaning as a global alternative to the exclusionary global order,"[6] the

Muslim exchanges the old ideals of integration and civil rights for an alternative narrative. The ritual of conversion effectively sets new pedagogical goals as the necessary elements for the process of self-rediscovery and social reconstruction. These goals are linked in turn to complete understanding and unwavering obedience to the rule of Allah, given directly in the text of the Quran and indirectly through the Sunna or exemplary conduct of the Prophet Muhammad as reported in the Hadith. These two sources comprise Islamic law, without which one cannot understand Islamic society.[7] A useful corollary might be: to understand Islamic pedagogy is to know that it is the law and nothing else. An examination of the role of Muslim schools, especially their grassroots characteristics, is important to fully appreciate the impact of Islamic pedagogy on African-American Muslims.

The growth of Muslim education in North America has paralleled the demographic expansion of Islam of the past thirty years. Currently there are several hundred elementary religious schools attached to mosques and several regional schools but as yet no accredited colleges or universities. Most elementary schools are locally financed and controlled by the mosque's imam. A few larger schools, such as Toronto's Islamic Community School and Atlanta's unified Muslim school district, have more than one thousand students in grades kindergarten through twelve and their own fleet of yellow school buses. Toronto's director of Islamic education, Abdullah Idris, came from the Sudan and earned a doctorate in International Relations at the University of Toronto. His school serves the approximately one hundred thousand Muslim families in greater Toronto composed of immigrants from Africa, Asia, and the Middle East. African Americans comprise less than 10 percent of Toronto's Muslim population.

Islamic schools are eligible for funding from the Islamic Society of North America through the North American Islamic Trust (NAIT), an endowment that functions according to the principles of the waqf in traditional Muslim society, which sets aside property and income for charitable purposes. Through the trust the ISNA maintains its influence over almost one-third of the approximately 750 mosques in North America by extending them loans in exchange for the power to make appointments to the mosque management committees and boards of trustees.[8]

The ISNA also runs its Islamic Teaching Center and a summer leadership institute at its headquarters in Plainfield, Indiana. Men who have been elected at home to become imams receive stipends and a scholarship to the center, where they can acquire teaching methods and meet friendly authorities whom they may call on for future consultation. Academic scholarships, though limited in number, furnish an opportunity for an elite to study at Islamic universities abroad.

In 1989 the ISNA's national director of education was Ishan Bagby, an African American with a doctorate in Islamic Studies. He explained that he turned to Islam in 1969 following the ghetto uprisings that swept the United States after Martin Luther King Jr.'s assassination the previous year. As a young college student living in Cleveland, he campaigned for social justice as a civil rights activist. "I tried to be a good Christian like Dr. King but gave up when it seemed like no one else was trying." He converted to Islam at Cleveland's Mosque of Islamic Revival (IRM), which was affiliated with the Dar ul-Islam movement under Imam Mutawif Shahid. "From that time on I had a desire to know God, and I thought Islam provided that happy balance of concern for the world, of creating an alternative to the present social, political structure. . . . It was the merging of those two aspects that really drew me to Islam."

Bagby soon became part of the DAR movement, serving as the director of its national education program. When he was drafted by the U.S. army in 1970 he claimed conscientious objector status and performed his alternative service in Atlanta, where he devoted himself to starting the city's first indigenous mosque. All went well at first. Then trouble erupted with constant bickering between the DAR and other groups, particularly the Nation of Islam. In 1973 an orthodox Muslim died in a conflict with the NOI, one of a series of incidents that led Bagby to become disenchanted with the DAR's direction. Although his mosque disintegrated, he remained determined to rectify the mistakes, chiefly the isolation of African Americans from the immigrant Muslim community. A year later he began working with immigrant Muslims to create the Islamic Center of Atlanta and gradually emerged as its leader.

Concluding that African Americans needed the benefits of an Arab-Islamic pedagogy to participate equally in the umma, he began to study for a Ph.D., attending the American University in Cairo on a year-long Fulbright dissertation fellowship. Without a solid foundation in Arab-Islamic pedagogy, he thought indigenous Muslims would remain vulnerable to criticism from the outside, either competing groups or immigrants. To be serious about leadership meant, therefore, returning to school full-time, as few adults can do while they support their families. "I figured that I could handle it . . . that's what propelled me," said Bagby.[9]

Under Bagby's supervision, the ISNA promoted a national curriculum that would theoretically serve the interests of both African Americans and immigrants. The organization's headquarters in Plainfield, Indiana, resembles a small college campus and is built around an ultramodern mosque, with roads and walkways laying out the grid of a future Islamic university. Its informal environment creates an atmosphere of sanctuary and is meant to facilitate encounters between various members of the North American umma. For example, Luqman Abdul Shahid, the acting imam of Harlem's Mosque of Islamic Brotherhood, spent the summer attending the leadership training program along with Muhammad Farah, a Somalian from Toronto's Jami Mosque. Another man in his late thirties, Mikhail Ibrahim, who had converted to Islam only recently, was also part of the summer leadership institute. Although Ibrahim had "looked at Islam" during college at Ohio State, he had opted for Christianity instead and was ordained in the Methodist Church. Sent to preach in the South, he grew dissatisfied with the church's emphasis on institutional fund-raising as opposed to spirituality. "I found myself becoming a very good businessman to raise annual

dues but not to generate money to help poor people. . . . It felt like I was becoming a pawn in someone else's hand." This pushed him to explore the message of Islam more seriously as an alternative that would permit him to become
"a full being and enjoy the here and now."

> I have no problem with Jesus, only with the way he is materially used to
> rob and oppress here and abroad. This doesn't serve the African Ameri-
> can. Christianity does not have the desire to universalize. It alienates in-
> stead. Jimmy Swaggart appeals strictly to whites, for example, and in that
> sense I don't see any genuine response to the problems of race in Chris-
> tianity. It does not try to create a dialogue with other cultures. On the
> other hand, the message of the Islamic world-brotherhood, the umma, is
> what I seek. Although there are sectarian Muslims, if we practice the reli-
> gious ideals of Islam, then there is a real possibility for world peace. The
> Jews don't accept everyone, but anyone can accept Islam.[10]

In practice, however, Ibrahim sensed paternalism from foreign Muslims at
ISNA. Saying that they were "out of touch" with those embracing Islam in the
West, he labeled their behavior "ethnocentric" but carefully avoided offending
his hosts. His main concern was to glean as much knowledge as possible, to "sit
at the feet of sheiks and learn things previously absorbed alone." Still, his learning style often angered these teachers. He challenged established views and
asked too many questions about Muslim heretics—the Ahmadiyyas and Sufis,
for instance. Nonetheless, he held firm to his new faith and rationalized the
divergent views as matters of cultural difference, explaining them in terms of a
dichotomy between din and fiqh. On the one hand, din represents the core tenets
of worship according to the Quran. It contains the concept of tauhid (oneness of
Allah), for example, as the functional principle common to all Muslims. On the
other hand, fiqh represents local adaptations in Arab, Pakistani, or African
traditions codified into the four schools (*madhab*) of Islamic jurisprudence. The
cultural dissonance between Muslims from different parts of the umma often
manifests itself erroneously in challenges to an individual's piety.

Ibrahim's observations lent credence to a frequently expressed idea that
ISNA was more concerned with demographics than with the social and economic conditions of African Americans. Because of this many indigenous
imams want to keep their mosques' schools autonomous, seeing in them the alternative to the public schools championed by conservative politicians such as
New York's Mayor Rudolph Guiliani. They sign on to charter movements, the
voucher system, and even court private philanthropy outside the domain of
ISNA and the NAIT. If they follow certain standards, the state will approve these
schools as the legal equivalent of the public school. In many communities the
quality of public education is so desperate and the public outcry so loud that
local governments and school boards sometimes ignore the axiomatic separation of church and state and certify religious schools in cases where they do not

entirely meet curricular standards. Islamic education thus benefits from the traditional role of parochial education in downtrodden neighborhoods. While managing to bypass curricular issues, the movement toward Islamic education has become part of a foundation and future promise of the ability to assert local control in the face of overreaching school boards and education commissioners. In this way the Islamic school can become a focal point for community activity where children and parents absorb scriptural knowledge and apply it to their everyday lives.

From a historical perspective, mosque-based education could be regarded in the same light as the initiatives for community-controlled schools that began in the late 1960s in the Ocean Hill–Brownsville district of Brooklyn, New York, Oakland, California, and the Eastside of Cleveland, Ohio. African-American parents allied themselves with teachers and activists to take public education into their own hands in order to promote schools and a curriculum more in harmony with black identity and more focused on urgent social issues. In some cases, the model for educational autonomy developed out of revolutionary free breakfast and Project Headstart preschool programs, while elsewhere cultural nationalists introduced a comprehensive Afrocentric curriculum for elementary and high schools. Generally, these developments were an expression of a political struggle for the recognition of African-American culture. They were an extraordinary and underestimated demonstration of communal black power that led to the institutionalization of African-American history and literature within less than a decade.

This innovative pedagogy significantly altered the standards of academic performance, allowing for a more balanced cultural literacy. During this period, for example, *The Autobiography of Malcolm X*, *The Wretched of the Earth*, and *Soul on Ice* became popular and accepted titles on high school and college reading lists. African-American nationalism functioned therefore as a vehicle for the accumulation of cultural capital achieved through the successful struggle for political control of inner-city education. It produced a liberating pedagogy in the sense that black youngsters no longer had to look at themselves and their families as the subjects of white domination. Instead they could draw their identity from an ever-expanding bibliography of cultural, linguistic, and historical meaning. This led to an explosion of creative production in the popular arts and writing and ultimately the canonization of African-American literature. The recognition of African-American vernacular English, or Ebonics, as a legitimate dialect was another indication of this process, itself a codification of tradition and customary semantic usage.[11]

In the larger anthropological perspective, however, ethnicity cannot be sustained solely by reference to secular values that are unstable and may vary widely. Organic solidarity is usually dependent on sacred texts or rituals that link individuals to a central myth or invariable theodicy that anchors identity to purpose. Of the many attempts to forge a black theodicy during the twentieth century, Islam has appeared as the most successful alternative to Christianity. The critical goal, identified by Ishan Bagby, was to achieve a certain consistency of meaning and ritual and to assert an approved pedagogy, as opposed to the teachings and catechisms of many heterodox sects. What complicates matters in this task is the delicate balance between the linguistic priority of Arabic, where all Islamic pedagogy must begin, and the din, where controversy abounds, depending on how much Arab or Asian culture gets introduced into the mix. This explains both the importance of organizations like the ISNA in fashioning a national Islamic curriculum and the sharp criticisms of the "ethnocentric" tendencies of immigrant sheiks.

Active learning and inculcation of the underlying basis for Muslim values begin in the mosques and their small schools, where students are drilled in rote learning, a method all but abandoned by progressive educators but still very much alive in the scriptural traditions. By studying Arabic the student meets a classical language for the first time, and although Quranic recital does not equal foreign language literacy, it can establish a framework for serious education. This offers tremendous potential for Muslim parents and their children if they are willing to pay the price of rigorous discipline.

The Islamic School of the Oasis (TISO) is the focal point of the Universal Islamic Brotherhood community, located in a delapidated ghetto neighborhood on Cleveland's far Eastside. The community and the school grew out of an entity called Black Unity House started by Imam Daud Abdul Malik in the 1970s when he was a radical activist called "Diabolo" and always at the center of controversy in the roiling political sea of race relations. A Project Headstart preschool is still located in the Unity House, originally a Presbyterian church, which also now serves as a neighborhood center for substance-abuse counseling. Black Unity House was the scene of tense standoffs between radicals and the Cleveland police. Residents of the neighborhood still remember barricades, revolutionary banners, and sloganeering conducted over dueling bullhorns.

Imam Daud Abdul Malik remains a popular figure who can spend the entire morning gabbing with people on their way to work. He does not dwell on the past. He sees an Islamic future for this neighborhood. It was once home to a stable working class, kept afloat by a nearby Fisher auto body plant that employed thousands of workers in three eight-hour shifts. Three banks at the intersection of Hayden and Woodworth Avenues testify to this lost prosperity. All are now shut, and the Fisher plant and a large General Electric light bulb factory are both abandoned, leaving very few jobs. Across the intersection of Hayden and Glenside Road is an empty lot that is now part of the community's property. There are similar lots between almost every standing structure along Hayden Avenue running west for a mile toward the intersection of Superior Avenue. In 1987 Imam Daud negotiated a contract with the mayor to fight urban decay by boarding up abandoned real estate. As part of this rehabilitation strategy, the Muslims also did their best to chase away the crack dealers.

Next door to Black Unity House stands a four-story apartment building that the Muslims rehabilitated as part of a municipal sweat equity program. A nominal rent finances maintenance and contributes to the UIB's general funds. Masjid ul-Haqq, next door, is the community's mosque. A former social hall, the building was also rescued by the Muslims from the invasive blight of arsonists and crack dens. Out back is a parking lot with a basketball court and a couple of dilapidated school buses. Across the street sits the large three-story brick building housing TISO, trimmed with green and white paint to conform with the surrounding wooden structures. An "Oasis" sign, depicting a date palm illuminated by Arabic calligraphy, hangs from the second-floor façade. In 1983 TISO opened when Daud and his wife, Hassinah Rance, founded the community by inviting several Muslim parolees and their families to settle in the neighborhood and help establish an inner-city hijra governed by sharia law. In 1991 the school's enrolment was sixty-five children, of whom all but a few were Muslim. As TISO's reputation for providing alternative education grew, it attracted the interest of non-Muslim parents, who, desperate for better schools, were willing to have their children abide by Islamic codes and other rules including mandatory participation in daily prayer at the mosque and a strict halal diet on campus.[12] On occasion, unruly students receive corporal punishment. Imam Daud is not shy in admitting that he has used this method to maintain discipline over the years.

The faculty at TISO was drawn mainly from men and women in the community who work according to their individual capacities to keep the school running. The leading authority in all things Islamic was Sheik Masoud Laryea of Ghana, a hafis of the Quran with a doctorate in education from the royal university in Saudi Arabia. He ruled that anthropologists were welcome to study and even photograph the community because such work was consistent with the Quran's mandate for promoting knowledge in all forms. Although some objected, the study was educational and therefore deemed "acceptable" according to his interpretation of tradition.

Another teacher at the school was Jamiel A. Rahman, a former convict who shuttled between TISO and the Hudson Youth Development Center in nearby Brooklyn, Ohio, where he ran substance-abuse counseling programs for adolescent offenders. "When I was released from prison, Imam Daud hooked up a counseling program, left me in charge, and went on a ninety-day sabbatical to Mecca, South Africa, and Iran. He set me up in Cleveland. It was hooked up so it looked like I had a job while on a nine-month furlough."[13] Jamiel explains that eventually he won over the parole officer, who "stuck his neck out for me." Working together at Black Unity House, Jamiel and Daud opened the detox center and a free breakfast program for the neighborhood children. In 1990 Jamiel received a half-million dollar grant to expand his program and eventually relocated to another mosque in Dayton, Ohio.

A younger parolee, Juba Abdullah Ali, commuted to Cleveland from Akron several days each week to teach martial arts at TISO. His street experience helps Imam Daud bridge a gap to the hiphop generation. "I'm dealing with kids that are hard already," he commented. "I show them the side I came from compared to what I am now in Islam. If it weren't for Islam, I'd have a gun and be ripping off a store somewhere."[14]

There were six more full-time teachers at TISO, two conversant in Arabic; they concentrated on the secular curriculum of reading, science, and mathematics. Uneducated parents solemnly assisted in food service and maintenance.

By 1991 most of the direct external funding resources for TISO had evaporated. Federal money channeled to the school through Black Unity House was also suspended after the local HUD administrator heard about the parochial nature of its curriculum. Daud and Jamiel were more successful in retaining the funds designated for drug-abuse prevention and violence reduction, but this was the tail end of the Reagan-Bush era and there were hardly any spare resources to keep the school functioning. Consequently, TISO set a tuition rate of one hundred dollars per month, used volunteer labor whenever possible, and bartered for some teacher salaries by providing rent-free accommodations in the community apartments. It required much labor and cash to bring the first two floors of the building into compliance with safety codes, and the top floor remained closed because of lack of heat.

Inside the school, the lower grades were located on the ground floor, where two corridors feed into an open central area that serves as the school office. Textbooks and workbooks, the elements of a small library, were piled on a table and crammed into makeshift shelving. There was a photocopier and small array of classroom supplies, including a heap of standardized tests. Teachers and students passed through the area, changing classes while Imam Daud presided over administrative matters, seated behind a large desk equipped with a telephone and fax machine. Papers and notes were scattered everywhere. In the corner closest to the corridor opening onto the second set of classrooms was a water cooler frequented by students. Little children sauntered through the area, offering broad smiles and high-fives to Daud, who greeted them as they descended the steps to his office.

"As-salaam-u-alaikum! What is it now, partner?" questions Daud. A famous poster of Malcolm X surveys the scene over his shoulder.

The small boy extends his hand to shake with the imam and replies, "Wa-alaikum salaam!" A fifth-grader bounds over to the desk, requesting permission to call home to remind his mom what time to pick him up. He uses the same one-line phone where a moment earlier Daud was engaged long distance with a sheik in Africa. The conversation finished, the fifth-grader tries to slide quickly past the imam, who lunges good-naturedly at him with a closed fist. "Gotcha!" he laughs. "Next time don't forget the quarter for your phone call." The child grins broadly and pauses to banter before pivoting back toward the classrooms. Teachers glide through the halls. Sister Hassinah stops to confer with her husband about a field trip later in the afternoon. The departure must coincide with the end of afternoon prayers. A little schoolgirl in hijab and ankle-length dress smiles furtively while trudging by. The phone rings, Daud reaches for the receiver, and a glimmer of light reflects from his massive crescent-and-star ring. It complements his salt-and-pepper beard and large afro where no skullcap would ever sit properly, the emblem of another era when Black Power was hotly debated toe-to-toe, face-to-face on the streets outside.

As the morning progresses a steady stream of activity reveals the way students view the imam, sometimes as an authority figure and other times as an inveterate kibitzer—a playful brother to be respected, a demanding taskmaster to be feared. Kids roam the halls inexplicably, ask for a drink of water when caught, and then stall their return, hoping for a joke from the imam, who answers the phone every few minutes yet still manages to keep tabs on everyone, dispatching the wanderers back to class sternly no sooner than having exchanged greetings. No one comes through the office without a nod or comment of acknowledgment.

On the sidewalk outside school, the imam frequently punctuates his comments to wave hello to a passing motorist. Any pedestrian is fair game for a recitation of acquaintances and local genealogies. "I knew your brother. Say, what happened to that store he opened?" Or "Didn't your sister marry so-and-so? I used to go to school with him. Ask him if he remembers that gym teacher? Well, we're running a full-time school here. Getting by doing Allah's work."

On the telephone, it's the same. By the time the conversation finally gets around to business, Daud has turned from family to politics to morality. He's networking old and new acquaintances, Muslims and non-Muslims, throwing out feelings of trust and benevolence. Then his tone changes to lecture a parent who has defaulted on his child's tuition. He listens attentively but rejects the excuse coming from the other end. He throws it back at the caller, who by now is promoting a riff about brotherhood as a weak defense for not paying his bills to other Muslims. Daud sees this as an opportunity to give the caller a lesson in ethics and economics by making the issue of Islamic morality central to the discussion. An older student appears at the desk asking to use the phone. Daud cups the mouthpiece, learns that it's an emergency, and bring his lecture to a close.

In his typical exchange, Daud's dispensation of advice couched in moral reasoning follows closely on his belief in maintaining proper adab, Islamic behavioral decorum. He can be doctrinaire and pedantic, practical yet idealistic in pursuit of community goals. He wants others to assume responsibilities and management positions, as indicated by his trust in Jamiel and Sheik Masoud. While his jokes may be an offering of grace, TISO equals serious Muslim business.

Upholding the Five Pillars of faith is no laughing matter, and there is ample evidence that Daud can be harsh whenever he senses mischief. He challenges the traditions of political and religious leadership among African Americans. His ideal social order relies on scripture, a perspective clearly displayed on Fridays when it is time for jum'a prayer. One study period after lunch, classes dissolve into the usual adolescent chaos, with young voices striving to outdo each other. Hands swing wildly, and clusters of young girls weave carefully through a gauntlet of wisecracking boys. It is a typical school scene. By the time they exit the building to cross the street, however, the students have sharpened themselves into neat rows. Two ninth-graders direct traffic on Hayden Avenue as the children file into Masjid ul-Haqq. Boys enter by climbing steps to the front door, and girls follow the path around the corner to a side entrance. Inside the students and teachers remove their shoes and quietly align themselves into prayerful ranks.

This includes boys like Philip, who is not Muslim but attends TISO because he has been expelled from public school. Philip looks sloppy in his dirty cotton jellaba, which is actually a hand-me-down graduation gown that zippers up the front. He wears his skullcap cocked forward inappropriately, an act of teenage defiance that is insignificant, given the circumstances into which he has plunged. Earlier in the day he was trying to reach his mother by phone to explain that his schedule had changed. The imam waited impatiently as Philip dialed several different numbers trying to locate her. Daud later mentioned that he had paddled Philip several times. He doubts that he will ever become a Muslim but notes that TISO provides the structure necessary for a boy who has little idea where his mother goes or what she does. TISO is the sort of experience that will resonate in Philip's life to the extent he takes responsibility for his own behavior. Despite his unruly appearance, Philip carried himself with reserve. He was soft-spoken and direct, giving thoughtful answers to questions about his school experiences. Even for non-Muslim students, Daud applies Islamic authority to supplement community values in a place where he knows almost everyone's parents and grandparents, their circumstances and their biographies.

If Daud represents a leader who pushed himself upward from the grassroots, he has also helped his community by importing an African-Islamic qadi (scholar-judge) to help him in guiding the people along the righteous path. The idea occurred to him following his disillusionment with Islamic organizations like the ISNA and the Rabitat-inspired Continental Council. In 1990 Daud appealed for assistance for TISO only to receive a desultory grant of ten thousand dollars that could not even make a dent in the repairs necessary to refurbish the Oasis building. Recalling his negotiations with foreign Muslims, Daud acknowledged the problems faced by Wali Akram in the 1930s. Lacking full command of the Islamic din yet determined to maintain autonomy and indigenous Muslim identity, Daud decided to find a sheik who could supervise an Islamic pedagogy and interpret law to the benefit of the Hayden Avenue community.

"So we went to Mecca," he explained, "and spoke with enough people there to identify a few prospective teachers." A young African scholar named Masoud Laryea emerged as the best candidate, but officials at Rabitat had other plans for the sheik and resisted Daud's efforts to recruit him. "We met Sheik Masoud by accident. We told him, 'We've been looking for you. We don't have money, okay, but we have a community, we're struggling, and we need someone of your caliber.'"

A short while after their chance meeting, Daud invited Masoud to make salat with him and eventually persuaded him to come to Cleveland. They still had to contend with arranging Sheik Masoud's papers. Although they usually provide the necessary travel documents for their dawa workers, Rabitat officials were dismayed by Daud's insubordination and by Masoud's apparent willingness to cooperate. Masoud returned to Ghana and planned to meet Daud at the American embassy in Dakar, Senegal, where, he felt, friendly contacts with the powerful Tijaniyya Sufi movement might facilitate the immigration process. Though he expected a modicum of cooperation there, Daud soon learned that the embassy was indifferent to his visa request. He persisted. When asked to leave, Daud grew angry and threatened to turn the consulate inside out. "If you try to evict me, then we're going to war right here," he declared. "So get your marines together because we're going to fight today. There were four of us and we were ready to create that kind of seriousness so they would know!"[15]

After more wrangling, the American Muslims returned to Ohio without Sheik Masoud. Disappointed yet undaunted, they enlisted their local congressman, whose assistance led to a work visa for the sheik the following year. By that time, Rabitat had relented and agreed to put the sheik on their dawa program, meaning that he was to get a salary paid from the Saudi embassy. Daud believes that this concession was a way to exercise "some control over the process." Nonetheless, all Rabitat funding stopped less than a year later, apparently because of their unease with bold, uncompromising American Muslims like Daud Abdul Malik.

What makes such relationships incompatible in the eyes of foreign benefactors? It would be hard for anyone to take issue with Daud's sincerity and commitment to Islam, especially his drive to create a radically different form of religious community in the heart of an American ghetto. Nor would Sheik Masoud's Islamic curriculum be reason for alarm. It adheres to a standard Sunni pedagogy. Accepted throughout the Muslim world, the curriculum begins with instruction in the Quran and the Arabic language. Children recite the sura as a way to learn pronunciation, then vocabulary and grammar. Fluency in the Quran enables the students to understand the scriptural narrative and relate its parables to the imam's Friday sermons. Hadith is a vast body of literature describing the Traditions of the Prophet, and his wisdom and the authoritative rendering of the Quran. More general studies in Islamic history and geography are also part of this package that anchors the student's historical imagination firmly in the Oriental world. A smattering of African cultural history has also been introduced into the TISO curriculum, as have courses of study in science, math, and English corresponding to the public schools' mandated curriculum. Teachers prep their pupils in standardized tests, and all are expected to complete high school. By contrast with some public schools, the students acquire a substantial respect for the importance of higher education, including the different career paths onto which it can lead them. Some students expressed a desire to emulate the few TISO alumni who traveled to Senegal to study under Sheik Hassan Cissé of the Tijaniyya Brotherhood. Daud's several trips to the Sudan also sparked their imaginations when he returned bearing exotic stories that stimulated their thirst for adventure and opportunity.

The idea of foreign travel is a distant dream for inner-city youths unless it refers to a trip to visit relations in the Caribbean or perhaps military service. Daud and Hassinah nonetheless encourage the spirit of travel by actively recruiting foreign teachers and guests. Daud never travels without bringing a few students along to open their minds to the reality of the umma. This attitude personalizes the Islamic master narrative, and sensitizes the student to a new map and a different conception of geopolitics than he or she is likely to receive in public education or media. Voyages of discovery, *rihla*, were the foundations of dawa and led also to Arab-Muslim ethnography, typified by the works of Ibn Khaldûn and Ibn Battuta. For some, the rihla became the ritual of a vision quest, while for others they attained the form of a premodern literary commerce in the guise of collected tales, maps, and scientific discourse.[16]

Daud selected an excellent foil in Sheik Masoud who comes from a humble background in Ghana, where Muslims comprise a 30 percent minority. "Quality Muslims," he emphasizes. Masoud thinks that ethnic dislocation is responsible for the educational crisis among young African Americans. Islamic pedagogy addresses this problem directly by providing them with theological roots, a way of returning to Africa rather than simply converting to an unfamiliar belief system. African Islam, in turn, differs little from the way Islam is practiced elsewhere, giving Black Americans simultaneous opportunities for spiritual redemption and universal embrace.

The sheik criticizes American public schools for the teachers' inability to command discipline and respect, itself a reflection of the general lack of discipline in most families. To counteract these problems, he offers basic classroom discipline and a steady approach to maintaining order among adolescents raised on violent television shows and junk food. His expertise in English grammar is unparalleled even by most middle-class Americans and is so emphatically precise that the students have no excuses for misinterpreting assignments or his stern admonitions about their conduct. As the faculty member in charge of teaching and interpreting halal behavior, Sheik Masoud reinforces a solemn environment where easy fraternization is discouraged and boys and girls sit on opposite sides of the classroom. The hallways are scrupulously monitored; a dress code includes purdah for the girls; and boys are even instructed to squat when urinating to avoid breaking wudzu between prayers.[17]

Beyond the inculcation of coercive rules, a dynamic moral pedagogy is clearly in evidence at TISO. It comprises a set of practical virtues—a behavioral framework, really—that the student learns as a series of moral choices applied to everyday life. The sheik teaches his students that the Quran measures human deeds along an ethical continuum ranging from those that are "obligatory" (*farz*) to those "strictly forbidden" (*bid'a*). In the middle lie practices that are either "indispensable" (*wajib*); "highly recommended" (*sunna*), because they can be traced to the Prophet's actions; "praiseworthy" (*mustahab*); "permissible" (*mubah*); "questionable" (*makruh-e tahrimi*); "negatively affecting one's state of purity" (*makruh-e tanshihi*); and "prohibited" (*haram*).

Practices that are "praiseworthy," for example, include customs that have not been codified, for example, the cultural practice of venerating saints in celebrating Maulid al-Nabi, the Prophet Muhammad's birthday. Such customs are neither specified in the Quran nor the Hadith but can be considered "tolerable" as long as they do not become obligations, as might be the case if their frequency or intensity acquired the character of a sanctioned ritual like Ramadan, for instance. To make someone think they are obliged to perform such rituals at the risk of feeling excluded would constitute an unjustifiable challenge to the rule of scriptural law.

Islamic pedagogy selectively refrains from censuring many local customs unless their practitioners seek to portray them as part of the divinely inspired din. In reality, the classifications along this continuum vary historically and from culture to culture. What might have appeared questionable yesterday or in one place might be permissible in another time or place. Bending rules within orthodox pedagogy, for instance, allows Muslim immigrants in North America to contract interest-bearing loans to buy homes. One prominent theory considers this to be a flexible social dynamic of Islam, unparalleled in other scriptural religions, which permits dawa toward peoples who would otherwise be forced to abandon cherished cultural traditions.[18]

On the other hand, a student learns how to adjust personal and social behavior according to a logic of virtues, more realistic if not more subtle and complex than the usual "Thou shalt not!" of Sunday school religious training. Anchored to sharia and enforced by the imam and other adult males, this new pedagogy of discipline exercises important social potential. It interprets most social pathology as a form of personal disorder while simultaneously situating the individual within an environment where the consequences of such neurotic actions can be thoroughly explored and tested. This contrasts with the discipline of public schools, where control over irrational or disruptive acts is external and not always recognizably legitimate, in the sense that authority figures—the principal, instructor, guidance counselor—lack the ability to enforce meaningful sanctions except through a sluggish bureaucratic process. Teaching right from wrong may be effective where children already recognize themselves in their actions and judgments. However, teaching very right from very wrong and other shades of ethical semantics helps the child to anticipate consequences and recognize himself or herself in a sacred narrative to which his or her friends and neighbors adhere.

Is this a repressive pedagogy, another form of inner-city vigilantism?

From the perspective of parochial education in general and TISO in particular, the rules, as well as the implicit threats of physical coercion, imply a patriarchal order—not the old, lapsed order that appears as the real source of oppression but one based on new virtues and different meanings. Whether symbolic, as in the threat of eternal damnation (*jahennam*) or realized with lashes, violence here conforms to a system of meaning other than the random statistics of an afflicted ghetto. This is the purgative counterviolence that revolutionaries have often theorized and sometimes employed in pursuit of their agenda. It also resembles diverse forms of ethnic violence, which, the honest observer must allow, are practiced throughout immigrant enclaves to the general complacency of state and local power—a normalized violence, in other words, that only attracts concern when it crosses established boundaries, as when armed gangs trespass into middle-class neighborhoods and schools.

The ends determine the means in the type of creative destruction on which the community has been founded. Dilapidated properties were renovated or completely demolished to make room for an imaginary neighborhood corresponding to Imam Daud's blueprints for an African village where Muslims will live alongside one another under the sharia. Delinquents were recuperated from the street and penitentiary, their bodies reappropriated and redefined through salat. In one ritual, seven young men attended jum'a prayers one hot Friday in late August to accept their kalima shahada from Imam Daud. As they were ushered inside, the intersection of Hayden and Woodworth still echoed from the chanting of the adan over the mosque's public address system. The neighborhood of small houses, poor but calm, shimmered in the intense haze sweeping off Lake Erie. The dwellings on Woodworth give way to Hayden Avenue, which is pockmarked by empty lots and a few abandoned buildings. One was still being used as a crackhouse. Although a local newspaper boasted that the Muslim presence had cleared the area of all dealers, Daud spoke more realistically of a need to reclaim, renovate, and rehabilitate block by block, person by person.

The seven initiates exemplified his reclamation project. They sat cross-legged in the carpeted mosque surrounded by the entire male community. Dressed in varying approximations of Islamic garb, they participated in salat and then listened to a sermon by Jamiel Rahman, who admonished them to "hold onto the rope of Allah." Daud addressed them next, explaining in Five-Percenter lingo that they are about to receive the "degrees of knowledge" that are missing from the Masonic orders, meaning the thirty-two degrees representing universal brotherhood. "No more gangbanging!" he warns. He becomes deeply personal and recalls for the audience the emotional upheaval that brought him to Islam.

> I was a revolutionary, you understand. I wasn't scared of nothing, you understand. I tackled everything. I fought. I closed drug houses. I fought the police. I was in shootouts. I had all this stuff, but one day I woke up and I wasn't winning: even though we closed the drug houses, our people were dying of drugs, and they liked it. They were more or less against us! So I said to myself, Well, I have to do things a little different than shooting it out with the police. I'm going to take eleven people that I think are abominations of evil in this world. I'm going to take them out, and whatever comes, I am going to keep fighting evil until they take me. I don't want to die without having understood the truth![19]

A week later there was further evidence of Daud's concept of moral renovation when the community gathered for the nikka, or marriage ceremony, of Amin, age fifteen, and Zechinah, thirteen, both students at TISO. This was the first of several planned youth weddings at Masjid ul-Haqq. Daud and Hassinah believe that supervised marriages—the couple will live with the groom's parents—will enhance their chances for success at school. In contrast to premarital sexual experimentation, forbidden by sharia as the crime of fornication, this young couple will come of age naturally, knowing how to fulfill their sexual desires without the common distractions of dating, peer pressure, and deviant practices often found in popular youth culture. Daud decries "the banality of seeing children born out of wedlock." He sees it as a hangover from slavery, "because we were raised as oppressed people whose culture has been stripped away, and the only way a young man has to 'get down' is through sex and fascination with the material world." Instead of fighting the trend of teenage sexual activity and suffer the possible risk of losing the moral struggle, UIB accepts adolescence as biologically inevitable and therefore sacred if controlled under the aegis of Islam. Better for the community to nurture these children as a married couple than to repress their desires and drive them away from the religion.

Prior to the meager but festive wedding celebration, Daud counsels the couple publicly. He informs them that there are many good examples and role models at UIB. He and Sister Hassinah have been married for twenty-nine years and the other stalwart adults, including Jamiel Rahman, for an average of ten years. "Procreation is a way of seeing Allah if it occurs as part of the marriage covenant which exists between the couple and Allah . . ." He reveals the Islamic ideals he wishes to instil among his flock.

> In a chaotic world, men have been given a degree over women. It doesn't mean that women are enslaved. Those of us who have lived in the dunya know that it is not true [that Islam enslaves women]. Our job as men is to keep the women and children in check. Your wife must be obedient. If you feel she has done wrong, then you have the right to confine her to your house. If you feel disloyalty, then admonish her gently. The Quran, remember, does not condone beating your wife.

In the context of this kind of marital advice, it is remarkable that the sexual order described in Daud's speech did not necessarily correspond to the reality of a woman's role at UIB. His relationship with Hassinah appeared to be one of equals, of a committed team leading their small community by example. They were married in 1969 when Daud was stationed at an air force base in Omaha. Hassinah had been raised in the Black Church but "left religion altogether" when she left her mother's house. Once married, they traveled extensively. They were exposed to Islam during an extended trip to Morocco but did not convert, returning to Ohio, where Daud threw himself into revolutionary activities. Meanwhile, Hassinah worked on "the other side of the fence" as the first

African-American salesperson for the Xerox Corporation. After realizing that she was a token and could not advance to an executive job—"I was the spook who sat by the door"—she sued the company for racial discrimination, eventually leaving full-time employment. She had also grown restless, leading a "double life" of switching in and out of her husband's world on a daily basis, coming home from a middle-class job to spend time doing radical political work.

She was not interested in Islam after his conversion. "It's not for me," she replied, when he asked her to join him. "First I grow my hair into an Afro, and now you want me to cover my head!" she exclaimed.[20]

"But if you don't try, you'll never know. And if you don't like it, you can always get out," he reasoned. He tried to convince her by calling attention to the positive effects of his religious transformation, the mellowing of his personality and the cooling of his temper.

About six months later, Hassinah realized that indeed they were becoming closer as a couple. She attributed this change to Islam, noting especially that Daud had learned the art of compromise. "I came from a family with deep belief in traditions," she observed. "My father and mother were married for fifty years, we have been married for thirty years, and strong relationships come from compromise." She began to dabble in Islam and then converted.

> I read the Quran a lot now because I have to deal with many of the domestic problems for other women in the community. The important thing is that the African-American woman has a unique place in relation to the past. There are many single mothers in our community. Some of them have met Muslim men who were or are institutionalized. I advise them to check these men out carefully [because] sometimes women have trouble using their spirituality to control their nafs and it presents many problems.
>
> Another problem is polygyny and its impact on the family. The disproportion of available men for women can lead to complicated living situations, but in plural marriages there is justice if both women are treated equally. Therefore, if a man abuses a woman here, we can usually tell from just seeing one or both of them—the way she looks or the way they interact publicly. We expect them to honor scripture and testify before themselves—even if it's incriminating. Then we will intervene and try to help.[21]

Hassinah stated that it would not bother her if Daud wanted to take a second wife asserting confidently that their partnership would always prevail. For his part, Daud was extremely conscious of the shortcomings of the militant nationalists toward women and did not want to reproduce the same mistakes at UIB. He was frequently caught between the dispensing of Islamic dogma and the social agenda he and Hassinah have set for UIB.

There are many other contradictions that affect the application of Islamic ideals among indigenous Muslims. Communities such as UIB experience a gap between law as represented in scripture and the law as lived practice. One scholarly opinion predicts that culture fills whatever discretionary space eludes the principles of the sharia[22] virtually assuring that popular culture and contemporary Islam will continue to dispute both personal and social matters. How much of one's salary goes toward zakat? Is it possible to adhere to interest-free banking procedures? How necessary is it to redefine one's artistic standards away from figuration toward a focus upon scripture where mimetic gestures are minimized in favor of communal values and redemptive theologies? There is a healthy degree of ambivalence about these issues at UIB, prompting Hassinah to say that what goes on behind closed doors is immaterial as long as one's adab is clearly evident in public.

On the other hand, some doctrinal issues and their attendant practices put this community into conflict with authority in other parts of the umma. The standardization of time and the Islamic calendar regulating the ritual cycle, for instance, becomes controversial even in Cleveland, Ohio, where there are several indigenous and immigrant mosques. For many years there were at least three different 'Id al-Fitr celebrations to commemorate the end of Ramadan. This has to do with the politics, science, and theology of sighting the new moon to begin fasting according to the Quran. Moon-sighting is a practice that is customarily directed by community leaders using the naked eye. Given variable atmospheric conditions, following scripture on this account is not always an easy task. Even in good weather, a new crescent moon can be difficult to view with the naked eye. Recently, a number of organizations led by the Rabitat and ISNA began to rely on telephone reports of moon-sightings by religious experts in Saudi Arabia. Another method uses astronomical computer programs that simulate the phases of the moon with great accuracy. Such attempts to standardize the beginning and end of the month-long fast respond to demands by school boards in Muslim neighborhoods for a fixed date when students will need vacation for the 'Id al-Fitr festival. Nonetheless, they run counter to the literal prophetic tradition and risk shirk or a challenge to Allah's absolute control of the heavens. Accordingly, many groups insist on sighting the moon themselves, even if it means being several days out of step with neighboring communities. In Oklahoma, one group of Muslims even sent a plane aloft to get a better view above the clouds.[23]

The difficulties of reckoning dogma in the contemporary world reveal the fault lines of legitimacy throughout Islam. Daud sought to remedy these problems by bringing Sheik Masoud into UIB as the 'alim with a diploma from a highly regarded center of Islamic learning. Although this was an imperfect solution, because it caused TISO to lose one of its funding sources, it was a way to sidestep the considerable tension that exists elsewhere over the issue of influence by Rabitat and ISNA/NAIT. In past years, the ISNA and NAIT sought to control 150 of the estimated 600 mosques in North America, generating an unstable atmosphere for the continued growth of Islam. This was particularly evident at Toronto's central Jami Mosque, where the African-American imam, Sheik Abdullah Hakim Quick, was forced to leave because of his willingness to open the "gates of ijtihad"—the Islamic equivalent of glasnost—to regulate social conflicts in a unique multicultural setting. Calling for greater participation of the jamaat in the mosques affairs, the imam discussed the principles of Islamic leadership and criticized the Jami Mosque's trustees from NAIT for acting like a "Masonic guild" by making decisions in secret.[24]

Far from being a stranger to these controversies, Daud Abdul Malik consciously used them to explore options available for indigenous Muslims. He visited Muslim societies from Africa to the Middle East to confer with religious scholars and political leaders about the dilemma facing Muslims in the West. He disregarded propaganda from both Muslim and non-Muslim camps, keeping for himself an open mind on anything pertinent to UIB. Finally, he managed to avoid the errors of the UISA, where the premature struggle for unity led to the kind of isolation that causes social and cultural stagnation. Instead he realized that Muslim collective identity rests on the judicious balance between one's self-image and the umma.

While adapting his African-American vernacular to the ends of dawa, Daud also actively sampled other sources of legitimacy and power. In the 1980s he established ties to the Tijaniyya, a large transnational Sufi brotherhood based in Senegal, whose hereditary leaders promote a model of confident religious identity to offset encroachments by their own national government and the cryptohegemonic interference of Arab-Muslim powers.

The Tijaniyya have amassed an important degree of economic and political security in a region better known for risk and instability. Their wealth is based on devoted young recruits to an ascetic lifestyle of Quranic study and work. The *talibés* (students) cultivate cash crops on Tijaniyya communal plantations or earn money in European and North American cities. In Africa the Tijaniyya plantation managers negotiate sales for their groundnuts and other crops directly with international wholesalers, bypassing governmental regulations or lobbying key politicians if necessary. With their earnings from legitimate service jobs and peddling in the cities, expatriate talibés subtract bare subsistence wages and remit the difference to their sheiks. In exchange they receive blessings, acts of spiritual empowerment, and sometimes marriage partners. To keep economic capital flowing toward the center of the Tijaniyya movement at Medina Kaolack, sheiks like Cambridge-educated Hassan Cissé expand Tijaniyya dawa through charity, the sponsorship of new schools, pilgrimages, independent missions to other countries, and traditional marriage alliances. Some funds are also contributed to the veneration of deceased sheiks and the upkeep of their mausoleums, which are objects of large annual pilgrimages that fuel new cycles of accumulation and dawa. Sheik Hassan also makes frequent trips to the West to boost morale among the cohorts.

This system represents the ultimate modernization of old West African Sufi brotherhoods who learned to accommodate external powers from eighteenth century onward without surrendering their religious and cultural autonomy.

Symbolized by the proliferation of satellite receivers atop their homes in the holy city of Medina Kaolack, the Tijaniyya leaders can neutralize the Rabitat and similar organizations who compete for dawa with petrodollars but proffer a different image of the umma that is less respectful of local traditions.

For instance, women attain a prominent role in Tijaniyya hierarchy and will not play second fiddle to men in areas of their own expertise. Sheika Mariame Niasse is arguably the most important figure in the "brotherhood" as commissioner of all the religious academies under Tijaniyya direction, mostly in Senegal but also other West African countries. Sheik Ibrahima Niasse, her late father, was regarded by many as the leading *marabout* of the African Sufi orders, a man endowed with heavy charisma through the medium of *wird,* a magical power that appears about once every hundred years. In his extensive travels and many pilgrimages to the Middle East and Holy Lands, Sheik Ibrahima always took his daughter along and never permitted her exclusion because of gender. Today the sheika maintains that while prejudice against women exists in some parts of the Muslim world, this results from local culture and ignorance of the Quran. Emissaries from the Gulf states appear uncomfortable in her presence and seem to prefer meeting with Sheik Hassan, even when it means waiting their turn behind infidels.

Impressed but never committed to following blindly a single model of Black Power, Imam Daud also made several long visits to Sudan after the 1989 declaration there of an Islamic republic. Acknowledging criticism of that government's genocidal war against Christians and animists in the southern part of that vast country, he focused instead on the mechanisms of Islamic power in Khartoum. In a meeting with President Bashir Ahmed he discussed the problem of Africa's original sin—collaboration in the slave trade—and how Africans might redeem themselves vis-à-vis their brothers and sisters in the diaspora. What prospects are there for real economic collaboration between Muslim brothers sharing a common African heritage? Pointing at the Khartoum Intercontinental Hotel, he informed President Bashir that the real estate it sits upon would make an adequate start for reparations. More seriously, he negotiated some scholarships as the basis for a permanent student exchange program.

Daud also parlayed with the eminence gris of Sudan's Islamic revolution, Sheik Hassan al-Turabi, renowned in the umma for his vision of a global Islamic renaissance (though derided in the West as a leading exponent of Islamic revolution). African-American Muslims have figured prominently in al-Turabi's thinking about the general welfare of the umma. He does not regard them as manipulable converts or clumsy newcomers who have a hard time getting things down the right way. In African-American Islam he foresees revolutionary potential.

Daud first encountered al-Turabi's ideas in 1986 when the sheik addressed an ISNA convention in Indianapolis. Pleading with American Muslims to apply their religious fervor creatively, al-Turabi emphasized "the relativity of the forms which Islam would take in a particular situation. In fact," he declared to the shock of many gathered there, "if there were any conflicts of interest, the local interest would prevail and that is [a solution] openly accepted in the Quran: Those who have believed, but have not migrated, who have not joined you in Mecca, they are your brothers in Islam."

Focusing on immigrant Muslims, he advised them to "convey the stock of historical knowledge to new Muslims in America [because] . . . they have the inertia of history behind them, but have to be reminded of the fact that one should not confuse custom and tradition with the values of Islam." He said that this lesson was important for those new in the faith to understand the rise and fall of Islamic civilization. Immoderate attention to the minutiae of ritual and superficial appearance would be a drag on the free pursuit of Islamic values, significantly in attitudes toward women that seem to have chained Muslims almost everywhere to anachronistic values. Finally, he turned directly to the African Americans to describe how their historical circumstances resembled that of the first Muslims in Medina.

> The fact that other Muslims have discovered Islam earlier, is not necessarily to your detriment. I have always said that Islam in America perhaps could be more analogous to Islam in Medina . . . because in Medina people [did] not have to look to hundreds of years of Islam behind them. You are facing the same problems, whether it is in family law or it is in building an Islamic umma, uniting the Muslims in this country.
>
> The input from abroad would enrich Islam in this continent as the input from Europe has enriched the American way of life, so to speak. But there should be no dependency. You have to be original. You can't always look to Muslims overseas to provide you with funds, to provide you with counsel, and to provide you with guidance. . . . The reward for initiation is immensely greater than the reward for emulation, naturally because in initiating, you develop something new.
>
> You have to establish madhab (schools of thought). You can't allow just any Muslim to adopt any point of view whatsoever, freely. This would end in anarchy. We have to have a uniform code for any locality. So the Muslims developed Malik here, the Shafi there.[25]

Challenging Americans to create their own madhab was a radical proclamation, an entreaty for the newest Muslims to open "the gates of ijtihad"—the forbidden paradigm that carries the seeds of reform. Previously, these "gates" have shut out any possibility of an Islamic reformation for the better part of nine centuries, a record solemnly defended by the conservative keepers of the faith who cling to the utmost literalism in Arabic scripture. The *ulema*, or scholarly class, have virtually monopolized fiqh by gerrymandering access to original Arabic texts in the principal centers of Islamic learning and especially by enforcing mnemonics as the standard of intellectual discourse and the capstone of moral reasoning. Within the four madhab of Islamic jurisprudence, the mechanisms for change are limited to *qiyas* and *ijma*, analogy and consensus, respectively, which define a tiny philosophical aperture through which the light of contemporary history and science must pass. Generally, the effects on Islamic civilization have been devastating, in comparison not only to the flourishing early caliphates but particularly with respect to the technological dynamism of contemporary Western capitalism. By limiting access to the arena for modern debate, the ulema succeeded in halting the momentum of classical Islam and reinforcing only the part of the religion that protects Arab culture and its formal linguistic dominance. They have also progressively erased the distinctions among the four existing madhab by the homogenizing power of modern communications, rendering pointless the existence of variant interpretive movements and dampening the internal dialectic of challenge and social reform within the religion.

Islam is not the only religion with similarly reactionary attitudes toward open learning. Indeed, the primary goal of scripture is to constrain its followers to a recitation of invariant rules and fixed meanings. No other religion, however, seems to constrain civil society as extensively as modern Islam. This results in a devastating paralysis of cultural and scientific innovation. Populists like al-Turabi (and Mawdudi and al-Qutb before him) see this dilemma through the prism of anticolonialism and work to destroy the juggernaut of Western hegemony, especially its function in oppressing Muslims. Here, the spirit of internal Islamic revolution meets the ghost of Fanon's purgative, anticolonial violence. This attempt to revive Islam from its dormant classical roots has become the most provocative counterhegemonic ideology since the decline of communism. It scares powerful rulers everywhere.

Imam Daud understands the potential of Islamism to attract gangsters who are as angry today as was Diabolo in his prime, but he is also committed to ending the fratricidal violence that they perpetrate. By harnessing and transforming this rage through dawa, he strives to create advantage where previously there was only failure. On Cleveland's Eastside, this potential was realized after 1996 when TISO benefited from Ohio's experimental school voucher program by attracting scores of parents desperate for an alternative to the public schools. So many new students flooded the school that by 1999 the majority of the student body was non-Muslim, temporarily anyway. This is precisely the milieu in which his dawa will thrive.

His pedagogy certainly addresses the issues of poverty and social inequality, but will it change inner-city society?

The outcome is impossible to predict. Seemingly invariable are the steadily deteriorating conditions that make possible this type of social and cultural experiment. Imagined communities quickly become realities amid the necessity to organize collective subsistence at the very bottom of the socioeconomic ladder. In its haste to abdicate responsibility for the poor, the state has ratified this alternative pedagogy by way of indirect investments as charter grants, local public works, and vouchers, and it subsequently guarantees their viability through religious-charitable tax exemption. The only constraints on autonomous community action in this domain are civil laws that are sometimes ignored in cases of corporal discipline, plural marriage, and vigilantism, where it is more convenient for the state to rationalize violence as the expression of religious freedom than to address it squarely as the result of shameful inequalities.

One could argue, therefore, that Islamic pedagogy serves the interests of the ruling elite by conferring to private and parochial institutions the "management" of public welfare. In addition, welfare-statism has been replaced by no real policy, only a patchwork of church shelters, mentoring programs, private dormitories, soup kitchens, drop-in centers, and any uneasy voluntarism swayed by the minimalist ethics of "compassionate conservatism." In the realm of education, Joe Clark, the notorious high school principal, typified this "tough love" by patrolling his hallways and stairwells armed with a baseball bat. When recently appointed commissioner of the New Jersey department of youth corrections, Clarke opined that there was no genuine difference between his old and new jobs, only a change in title! As this example suggests even more clearly, the elite classes frequently turn their backs on the victims of such violence and sometimes lionize its perpetrators. There is nothing ambiguous about this application of cultural autonomy in the service of indirect class domination. Just as surely as wardens pacify their cell blocks through inmate self-government, the state benignly recognizes this pedagogy in UIB and scores of other orthodox Muslim enclaves because they represent the power of religion to evacuate political militancy from the most oppressed classes. In the face of social isolation and the abdication of all but the most essential public works, an imam can become a spiritual liberator and populist authoritarian simultaneously. This is the double-edged sword of ethnic autonomy in the age of multicultural diversity.

It could also be said, however, that Imam Daud realizes better than anyone how the standard measures of achievement have failed to solve problems of the underclass and succeeded only in reinforcing the boundaries between the ghetto and the middle class. Is it possible or perhaps necessary for those who are stuck inside grim housing projects to adapt different measures of achievement and scholarship, important not in terms of financial rewards but for their moral lessons?

An imam who leads a community similar to UIB once said that he cared not whether any of the students at his school continued their education toward a college degree. What mattered to him was their becoming good Muslims. Other imams across North America have engaged themselves similarly—Muhammad Abdullah in the Southlands of Los Angeles, Imam Siraj Wahaj in Brooklyn, and Derek Ali in Detroit, to mention only a few. They are the faces of transformation in a forgotten but ubiquitous landscape of "savage inequalities" and restricted life chances. Their call to prayer might also be regarded as a prophetic appeal for everyone within listening range to resist the decline of public morality. Only by engaging in tolerance and constructive debate can all Americans practice the politics of recognition and stop paying the awful price dictated by the imperative of personal security. In becoming a minority within a minority, African-American Muslims point the way toward a future of more tolerance, and more diversity. The paradox is that they can guarantee this future only by acting as the vanguard of reform within their own religion.

Conclusion:

African Diaspora and Muslim Umma

The chance that a culture has to put together this complex totality of all
inventions of all orders, which we call a civilization, is a function of the number
and diversity of the cultures with which it participates in the elaboration
of a common strategy. —Claude Lévi-Strauss, "Race and History"

THE steady rise in conversion, combined with ongoing immigration of practicing Muslims into the United States, is a force destined to challenge the spatial and historical paradigms of our religious experience. Especially, though not exclusively, for African Americans, this force addresses issues of religious pluralism that have remained until now beyond the scope of a "national" conscience, entangled, as it were, in the Black Church's spiritual monopoly. It also raises questions that are central to the interpretation of slavery's immoral legacy. Although the Church reformed its practices and became a leading institution in the twentieth century battle for civil rights, its historical accommodations with slavery are still unrepudiated, if not unexamined. In light of this contested narrative and the unresolved ethical problems that remain part of its telling, it would be remiss to conclude without contemplating the historical role of Islam. If Islamic worship and Arab-Muslim pedagogy are to contend for the "souls of black folks," then what are the results of this encounter so far?

Conversion to Islam confronts the chronicler of African-American religion with an unusual dilemma. After digging into the past, he now finds that the present has changed, too. The paradox is that of the traveler who embarks on his long journey from an unpaved crossroads and returns to discover an international airport in its place. Meanwhile, many new routes have become available, and the timetable is filled with destinations at once mysterious and unsettling in their capacity to diminish any pretensions to know the world.

With the question of Islam we find ourselves at one of these intersections. As an inquiry into religious history, it disturbs the old assumption that African-American society is exclusively and fundamentally Christian. It reopens choices about identity and authenticity that appeared to have been resolved in favor of reconciliation with a Christianity that put blacks outside the chapel and then took them in once the carriages transporting white parishioners returned to the plantation. Today, church fathers appear stunned by what they view as a mass defection from their flock, whose steady increase can no longer be guaranteed by promises of redemption in the hereafter. In panic, they have sounded the bells to recruit volunteers in fighting "the most serious threat to the church in America."[1] For all their endorsement, albeit belated, of Martin Luther King Jr.'s courage and martyrdom, religious leaders have witnessed the overcoming of his vision by a defiant cohort of rappers whose mediagenic fantasies resemble the establishment's nightmares, in black and white. Doctrinally correct or not, the gangstas have been "dropping" Islamic symbols for decades and setting the table for genuine conversion once the adolescent's moratorium becomes a serious quest for meaning and values. More generally, and emphatically too, priests, ministers, and rabbis are challenged to adjust their characterizations of the national religious tradition to conform with a Judeo-Christian-*Muslim* ethic.

Politically, Islam is often at odds with the axiomatic pax Romana that is taken to separate church from state while relegating religion to a matter of individual choice and inner faith. Islamic worship is a public ritual; its sharia supplants civil law, theoretically erasing the boundaries between religious obligation and political loyalty with all the contradictions this implies. Islam promises liberation from social problems, yet it makes no similar commitment to legislative freedom. Instead it enumerates degrees of submission and hierarchy, not the least of which is the behavior prescribed for women. By reviving a conservative, patriarchal ethos and simultaneously raising the banner of radical opposition, the Muslim movement displays a tremendous potential to rally traditionalists alongside discontents and to reconcile alienated generations on the basis of a folk culture that, except for its distinctive music, the Black Church has eschewed in favor of its own claims to the grand ecumenical tradition.

Symbolically, Islam deploys the idea of hijra as a self-sustaining representation of Islamic space and time. In choosing Islam, the convert migrates toward the dar al-Islam when she or he joins a mosque or neighborhood community and participates in daily prayer, the annual cycle of rituals, communal feasts, and eventually the pilgrimage to Mecca. Hijra is thus a globalizing force for organizing cultural meaning among Muslims. It is a historically effective platform for self-recognition and a bulwark against secularization. It promotes the translation of one's life experience into the sacred narrative of the Quran and Sunna. By the same token, it functions both as metaphor and ellipsis by managing to subsume the many allegories of spatial mobility rooted in African-American experiences of social transplantation. From Middle Passage, Underground Railroad, and Great Urban Migration to civil rights marches, African-American history equals mass movement whose narrative is always at risk of being assimilated into the secular myths of immigration, "Westward ho," the moonwalk, and upward mobility. Islam rescues these passages from the banality of textbooks and cinematic distortions by recasting them as part of a great, profound struggle—jihad al-akbar—to comply with the will of Allah.

Finally, Islam rewrites biography and even seeks to reinterpret history by claiming African Americans as its own native sons and daughters returned from the wandering of lost souls. Theoretically, the umma erases the color line by re-tracing a circle of inclusion around all humanity. Although fraught by complexities of cultural diversity and socioeconomic status, this rainbow coalition redeems the enforced creolization of slavery, which in one instance the Nation of Islam sought to undo with an impossible ideology of racial separatism (the obverse image of white supremacy) and which in another instance had always given cause to the real possibility of "invisible migration," or passing, as a strategy of personal escape. What, for Christianity, was incontrovertible proof of racial exclusion, the biblical myth of Ham, became for the Muslim of African descent a pedigree of status and pride. The Ethiopian Bilal was the Prophet Muhammad's muezzin and companion, his native Abyssinia an honored place of refuge for persecuted believers even before the hijra. Miscegenation is therefore an empty term within the umma, which disavows racial distinctions and reaffirms its universality in the human swirl that the hajji experiences as evidence of divine euphoria in Mecca. This experience remains literally the touchstone of personal transformation for all pilgrims for months and years afterward when the umma has dissipated into its component nations and tribes. Despite the punctuality of hajj itself, it succeeds over the long haul by resonating through discourse and scripture as the natural order of humanity. It overwhelms the believer as the immanent idea of paradise and affirms the total sovereignty of Allah.

Returning from his pilgrimage in 1964, El-Hajj Malik Shabazz imparted this sense of rapture yet spoke also of challenges concerning black liberation. A double consciousness, persistent as ever, characterized his subsequent actions. He organized two distinct international organizations. In the Organization of Afro-American Unity (OAAU) he meant to unite all New World Africans as a political force analagous to the Organization of African Unity (OAU), comprised of the emerging postcolonial African states. This planned alliance (OAU–OAAU) reflected in turn the politics of nonalignment espoused by men such as Nasser of Egypt, Sukarno of Indonesia, Nehru of India, and Ben Bella of Algeria. There is no question that Malcolm also believed it possible to negotiate a "third way" between Soviet and American hegemony. As a political force representing more than one-third of the planet's population, he envisioned this movement as a powerful voice in the United Nations and other fields of international and humanitarian cooperation. As a social and cultural amalgamation, this movement also aspired to the dreams of Garvey and others who desired to advance the material interests of nonwhite people.

In Muslim Mosques Inc., his second organization, the former Malcolm X aspired not to political or cultural nationalism but to the specific religious internationalism of dar al-Islam, the umma. Here, his dreams were linked to a different kind of social program based entirely on the spirit of Islamic revival.

Expelled from the Nation of Islam because of his opposition to its stubborn insularity, El-Hajj Malik Shabazz became a convert to Islamic revivalism, while simultaneously drawn to the ideals of nonalignment. His subsequent though brief career demonstrated a split or double consciousness between religious and ethnic identity. Did he perceive himself as a Muslim representing a religiously diverse African-American constituency? Or an African American who invested his personal identity in the Muslim umma? These questions concern the dilemma of those who straddle the crossroads of two diasporas, one African, the other Muslim. The loyalties and beliefs of this particular "double consciousness" comprise the idea of a "Black Orient."

THE BLACK ORIENT IN INTELLECTUAL HISTORY   To reflect on the role of the Black Orient in the intellectual history of the African diaspora is to consider the specific ways that Islam and Arab culture influenced nationalist ideologies. Edward Wilmot Blyden set the tone when he claimed that Islam served to uplift African civilization through the force of its monotheistic scripture and its social discipline based on the Quran and sharia. Islam protected Africans, he wrote, from the worst excesses of pagan ritual, alcoholism, and colonial exploitation because it elevated African society on the ladder of social evolution. It created an image of the African as less primitive and worthy of more recognition in the eyes of the European-trained missionary and scholar and provided a framework for African history that was otherwise unthinkable. It gave an international language, Arabic, to the African historical narrative and anchored the individual and communal spirit to a monotheistic religion.

Yet Blyden's exposition of the Black Orient was limited by his avocation of

Protestant missiology. In this Eurocentric view, Africans were potential Christians; Islam was a strategy for distinguishing among those Africans who would be converted to Christianity in the short term and those who might resist the gospel more obstinately. His logic summarized that of abolitionists who sought to prove the African's humanity through concrete evidence of his literacy. As an example of a literate culture par excellence, the Quranic tradition was, in other words, a sign pointing the missionary in the right direction to begin his work.

Upon their arrival in Africa in the fifteenth century, Europeans employed similar distinctions. They set to work building a colonial enterprise for extracting wealth and for managing that process through political and social control. Their work in Africa as colonizers largely depended on learning how to manipulate indigenous political and social organization and belief systems. This knowledge relied in turn on observations that synthesized Arabic and classical texts with empirical data. It concerned a whole range of "human resource" issues such as literacy and numeracy, which gave them as foreigners a functional understanding about Africans and implied the difference between success and failure in their efforts to extract profit from the colonial enterprise. Europeans, for example, remarked carefully on the characteristics separating Islamized from non-Muslim societies, notably the advantages conferred on some people through the agency of Arab-Muslim pedagogy. Such observations were gradually encoded into linguistic and anthropological knowledge, which actually began as the colonizer's shorthand summary of the Other's essential and potentially manipulable features.

For African history, this "essence" is complicated by a view that fails to discriminate between the "precolonial" era (before the fifteenth-century European settlements) and the earlier period of Islamic hegemony (from the tenth century onward) when many African social customs, languages, and religions were influenced, if not wholly determined, by Islamic civilization. This "precolonial" African identity, constructed of Arabic texts written by Muslim chroniclers,[2] contributed largely to the transnational sense of African society that so impressed Blyden. Arabic was the lingua franca for trade and Islam not only a spiritual watershed but also a ritual of exchange. Together these linguistic and religious forces shaped interethnic relations across a wide region and provided a worldview that distinguished between the dar al-Islam and the dar al-harb. Some historians and anthropologists have suggested that one vital function of this paradigm was to distinguish Africans who were potential trading partners from those who were potential slaves.[3]

The subsequent logic of the encounter between Europeans and Africans was therefore mediated, as often as not, by an Arab-Muslim perspective. As a result, the European image of African society was superimposed over a palimpsest of Oriental historiography, creating a double exposure of African time and space, one layer representing European historiography and the other Oriental historiography. Together they composed an emergent picture of medieval Africa as an underdeveloped society with slavery depicted as a somewhat benign, indigenous serfdom. Masters and slaves, it appeared, antedated both Islam and Christianity, so that social relationships of dominance and subordination belonged to the "natural" history of Africa. These were the inescapable, guiltless conclusions of the only rationalization that would absolve the conquerors of their moral responsibility for the brutal slavery they imposed on Africans.

Anticipating the same Pan-African nationalism that excited El-Hajj Malik Shabazz, Blyden saw the positive uses for Islam in rallying the masses to resist European colonial domination. Here, one might contend that he still maintained a utilitarian view of Islam, willing it to act in the service of political liberation instead of spiritual redemption. He was not a sentimental traditionalist but an agent of modernization who tended to think in terms of "progress" and "civilization." The dilemma for all nationalists is to avoid a liberation that returns to traditional forms of social exploitation.

It seems that many early Pan-Africans facing this issue tended to favor an Orientalist perspective, if only for its value in opposing Western colonialism. For example, Duse Mohamed agitated among African students in late nineteenth-century London and mentored a generation of political activists at the *Africa Times and Orient Review*.[4] His apprentice, Marcus Garvey, founded the UNIA and thus fertilized the ground of the Black Muslim subculture in the Moorish Science Temple and the Nation of Islam.[5] In his attempt to fuse Pan-Africanism and Pan-Islamism, Duse Mohamed, like Blyden and eventually El-Hajj Malik Shabazz, ignored the historical antagonisms dividing Arab Muslims from Black Africans, in particular those related to slavery.[6] It is interesting to note, however, that in contrast to his mentor's essentialist conception of Islamic monotheism as the foundation for Pan-African civilization, Marcus Garvey himself would never commit the UNIA to a single religious creed. At one time or another he included disciples of Islam, Ahmadiyyat, Judaism, and Christian orthodoxy under the UNIA tent.[7]

Does the Orient also fail as miserably as the West to promote black liberation, in historical perspective? If so, then how can one explain the continued growth of the African-American Muslim subculture? Any community, real or imagined, will eventually lose its attraction to the social discontent if it automatically ascribes him or her to a servile status. This attitude is borne out in disputes over rituals that pit Muslim immigrants against indigenous converts.[8] Social as opposed to theological antagonisms are also manifest at the organizational level of Islamic centers, in their schools, and in the poorly concealed aversion to interracial marriage in cities with a high percentage of upwardly mobile Muslim immigrants. If the real umma is absent except on a few days every year, then what can conversion ultimately deliver?

I cannot respond without first reconsidering the missionary ideal of conversion as a type of social recruiting in which the convert yields his or her body and soul to a power deemed superior. Unfortunately, this definition has lingered far beyond its utility as an analytical standard because it reinforces the logic of both academic and administrative pedagogues. With the changing reality of both

ethnicity and nationality, however, must come the realization that religious conversion has become one social idiom among others, a modern ritual that facilitates encounter. Much like the exchange of foreign currency in the marketplace,
conversion facilitates crosscultural transactions between different ideologies,
cultures, and religious denominations. It does so for the purpose of elaborating
"common strategies" in pursuit of the elusive goal of civilization, as Lévi-Strauss
explains.[9]

CONVERSION AND THE SYMBOLIC CHALLENGE TO CHRISTIAN HEGE-
MONY   Conversion is a highly personal experience that does not often translate adequately into social discourse. It defies logic and conforms only to that irrational "leap of faith" best articulated by the idea of sacrifice. Jazz musicians
nurtured bebop and impressionism as musical forms by sacrificing their old
songbook to the notes of an unplayed acoustic realm within the symbolic space
of Islam. Muslim prisoners sacrifice their only resource, time, to resist the debilitating effects of the penitentiary regimen. Daoud Ghani and his fellow steel
workers in Buffalo saw in Islam the ideal of realizing land redistribution, an unfulfilled promise of Emancipation. Their efforts to found a community at Jabul
Arabiyya based on the Islamic principles of hijra were successful only to the extent that one can view the exercise of free will as an end in itself. Moral elevation
did not translate into social and economic comfort for Daoud Ghani, who for
over forty years rose from his bed every morning and braved the treacherous
winters of the snowbelt to reach his job twenty-five miles away in Buffalo. Even
after retiring and well into his nineties, Sheik Daoud used his pension and car to
service Jabul Arabiyya's handful of converts, some of whom could not or would
not work but maintained the veneer of pious Muslims. "I guess Allah just keep
me goin' because they need me," he commented, when I asked why the community's sheik sacrificed so much time chauffeuring and running errands for
younger, able-bodied adults. As far as his need to feel useful, it was the dubious
honor of a factory-whistle salute on the day of his retirement from Republic
Steel that brought tears of nostalgia to his tired eyes. Hardship did not matter;
the pleasure was in the imagining and the anticipation of a life that was prophesied to redeem the indignities of slavery.

For Wali Akram, Islamic conversion was the pathway for "a brilliant man, a
good organizer, who always gave good advice" to assert his will against a church
that "had more body movement than brain power," according to his younger
brother, Bertram Gregg, now retired from the CME ministry. "He put so much
into that work on Islam, and I question whether he cheated himself or not? He
would have been much better compensated and reached more people through
the Methodist Church. He could have become a bishop in the church," Bert
summarized.[10]

Unlike the West Valley pioneers or their neighbors at the First Cleveland
Mosque, the individuals and families who migrated to the UIB are part of an un-

derclass characterized by intense anomie, splintered by perpetual cultural frag-
mentation, weakened by poor nutrition, and divorced from vital economic resources such as equity, credit, stable employment, and health care. Their names
are absent from the memory banks of global information networks; some do not
even have telephones and may just as well be living in the favellas or bidonvilles
of the underdeveloped Third World. Above all, their existence has been rendered
virtually invisible as the result of the media's capacity to divert public attention
away from issues of political urgency and toward the demands of consumerism.
Among the UIB residents, the single-parent families, recovering substance
abusers, and parolees fighting for a second chance could never afford to invest
their meager wages in building a rural commune, nor could they envision seemingly distant social and economic goals. Instead, their efforts focused on
survival—a more fundamental (and desperate) struggle to repair and defend an
inhabitable space.

For Imam Daud Abdul Malik and other Eastsiders, conversion meant quite
literally the transformation of ghetto real estate—formerly church property—
into sacred Muslim space. Daud applied a valuable repertoire of countercultural
tools gleaned from the lessons of civil rights and Black Power—squatting, sweat
equity, jawboning, grant-writing, and so on—to foster a relatively stable habitus
that in turn gives adults and children the time and space to develop well-defined
roles and identities rooted in the patriarchal family order. By promulgating
sharia codes and publicly broadcasting the severe penalties administered to vio-
lators, the community erected a set of discernible boundaries to separate themselves from the rest of the ghetto.

Similarly, the Islamic missionary ideal of umma is no longer the unitary
symbol of internationalist Islam that attracted veterans of the Great Migration
to reform their identities on the basis of a Hamitic pedigree according to the example of Professor Muhammad Ezaldeen's AAUAA. The traditionalist vision that
prompted the theory and practice of hijra is nearly defunct itself, having been
replaced during the tumultuous past century by a heterogeneous Muslim world
divided among modernizers anxiously striving to reap the benefits of global development, fundamentalists promoting scripturalism, ethnic discontents who
dispute Arab, Sunni, or Shi'a hegemony, and many others who profess a quietis-
tic stance.

All these tendencies are amplified by modern communications and trans-
portation, thereby attracting cultural entrepreneurs like Imam Daud to explore
alternatives ranging from West African sufism to Sudanese radicalism. Even his
recruitment of a Ghanaian to serve as UIB's resident 'alim reveals a decentralized, nuanced approach, allowing local exigencies in Cleveland to redirect the
priorities of higher echelons in Mecca. Whereas Islamic order once implied
the limits of a particular time and space—hijra, dar al-Islam—those conventions now seem malleable and uncertain. They dissolve as quickly as one can
surf from one internet address to another, blurring the process of Muslim self-
identification in the same way that hiphop recordings compress multiple musi-

cal genres and even random sounds, track layered on simultaneous track, to create a richly textured "sample" of the African-American urban experience.

Accordingly, empirical reality disputes the archaic missionary idea of religious conversion or even sociological theories of revitalization. As a philosophy for negotiating crosscultural identities, Islamic conversion relied on ritual and theodicy to assuage short-term suffering by erecting the promise of true community. Akram's Muslim Ten Year Plan fell short of these goals, as did Professor Muhammad Ezaldeen's AAUAA "units."

Curiously, these programs reformulated the conservative philosophy of Booker T. Washington, who viewed racial segregation as a paradox: a moral tragedy yet also an opportunity to construct a "national" economy and civil society. In the early twentieth century the fraternal lodge was an excellent place for organizing hundreds of corporate associations to fulfill local needs for innovative real estate transactions and insurance and unemployment compensation in the face of racial discrimination. It answered a need to manage socioeconomic risk, guaranteeing, in a time of tremendous distress, the reproduction of the African-American community. It drew strength from an ecumenical position that eschewed religious sectarianism and defended the right to nominate its own leadership without interference from the venerable yet prying Black Church. As the lodge asserted its autonomy vis-à-vis the church, it became a resource for individuals to freely redefine themselves, to revive lapsed folkways, and to acquire new social roles, based on merit and perhaps imagination but never ascription. Some of these roles corresponded to the division of labor in white society—undertaker, dentist, barber, insurance broker, realtor—serving likewise as the bedrock for the local community. Other roles revived traditional identities from the rural South, the Caribbean, and Africa. The hoodoo man, root doctor, midwife, romantic adviser, rebel, griot, and sheik gave the same communities an esthetic texture that was equally indispensable, though it was nonproductive from a bourgeois perspective. On this account, W. E. B. Du Bois admitted grudgingly that the lodge constituted a gigantic if not embarrassing spectacle. He bemoaned its enthusiasm for ritual, believing it to be an example of wasted energy that might otherwise be applied to science and practical arts.

THE CHALLENGE TO ISLAM   Contemporary Islam is an evolving paradox, too. Its revolutionary anticolonialism betrays a reactionary social policy that represses personal freedom while subordinating community development to religious codes that for all their scriptural authority are nonetheless interpretive and historicized. Currently, Islam offers a regime of social control that is unmediated by any form of constitutional deliberation. Reform in Muslim nations is a very difficult process at best. Early Muslim societies correctly understood this problem as one of scriptural literalism and sought remedies in popular movements such as the Kharijite rebellion and the secession of Shi'a. In the latter case, Shi'ism came to represent the Persian cultural backlash against Arab hegemony within Islam. Since then, dozens of autonomous sects have arisen, many in Africa under the guise of Sufism, in which Islamic reform is an active, ongoing process that eludes official fatwa. The reformist spirit accounts for much of Africa's relationship to Islam, evidence of an oscillation, as Gellner calls it, between Quranic scripturalism and African folk traditions. African Muslims have staunchly kept open the doors to ijtihad, mostly because they reside on the economic periphery but also, perhaps, because they have usually been regarded as *mawla*, members of a servile caste. They are the face of the Other, an acknowledged though subaltern component of the umma. African-American Muslims, on the other hand, live at the center of the global economy and politics, where they are still haunted by an oppressive past.

A paradox?

As a civilizational dialogue, Islam portrays a fixed image against which Otherness is measured. This process of authentication differs from that of indigenous African society, where Otherness has generally tended toward relative definitions, making it possible to incorporate all outsiders while simultaneously improbable to establish the nation-state. Concepts of Islamic umma and African diaspora have in common an aversion to nationalism, the former because of the challenge it raises to spiritual unity (tauhid), the latter because of a stubborn refusal to alienate the Other. One sees this in the struggle of African nations to maintain one foot in the Muslim Arab world and another in the global capitalist market. Africans, whether at home or in the diaspora, are torn between global monopolies and local traditions—between development and catastrophe, between orthodoxy and reform, between the Atlantic world and the Orient, between Allah and Jesus, and finally, between their accommodations to other beings and their own becoming.

Finally, what is at stake in the cultural encounter between African Americans and Islam? Though fraught with many difficulties, this is an encounter of world historic proportions that includes pluses and minuses not only for members of the African diaspora but also for the Muslim umma. The story of black pilgrimage to Islam is the story of a contemporary journey. Its outcome is far from predictable.

Glossary of
Arab–Islamic Terminology

ABU. Father

ADAB. Conduct, decorum befitting a pious Muslim

ADAN. Muslim call to prayer, recited by the muezzin

AKHBAR. Officer of communications or public information for the prison mosque

AKIDA. Creed, article of faith

ALMAMI. Prayer leader Contraction of *al-imam* used by West African Muslims

AYAT. Term for a verse of the Quran

'ALIM. Islamic scholar

BABOUCHE. Heelless slipper worn throughout the Middle East and Africa

BARAKA. Good fortune; the charismatic power said to emanate from a Sufi master

BAYAT. Contract; oath of allegiance recognizing the authority of a leader

BID'A. Sinful innovation; deviation from the path of righteousness

DAR AL-HARB. The land of war, territory not under Islamic law and subject to conquest by Muslims; contrasts with dar al-Islam

DAR AL-ISLAM. The land of peace, where Islamic law prevails

DAWA. The summons to acknowledge religious truth and join a religious community; missionary movement

DIN. Religion and religious duties; also judgment at the Last Day There are five pillars of din: witness, prayer, almsgiving, fasting, and pilgrimage

FAJR. Morning prayer before sunrise

FARZ. An obligatory practice

FATWA. An opinion on Islamic law issued by a religious authority

FITNA. The chaos of unbelief; that which constitutes a tests or trial to Islam and Muslims Characteristic of the social chaos (jahiliyyah) prevailing before divine revelation

FIQH. Understanding; jurisprudence, Islamic religious law

HADITH. Traditions reported about the Prophet used to interpret and enhance the laws of the Quran

HAFIS. One who can recite the full text of the Quran from memory

HAJJ. Pilgrimage to Mecca

HALAL. The things, practices, or foods that are pure and permissible in Islam

HARAM. That which is proscribed or forbidden by the Quran or Traditions Derives from the portion of the house for women, from which males are excluded Contrasts with halal

HEGIRA. The emigration of the Prophet from Mecca to Medina in 622, year 1 of the Muslim calendar

HIJAB. Curtain, barrier between a woman and men created by the veil

HIJRA. Migration of Muslims and Muslim communities conforming to tradition

'ID. Muslim festivals; 'Id al-Fitr, the breaking of the fast of Ramadan, and 'Id al-Adha, the sacrificial feast

IDDA. Calculation of elapsed time of a woman's menstrual cycle as part of the ritual of Islamic divorce

IFTAR. Meal consumed after sundown or before dawn during Ramadan

IJTIHAD. Reinterpretation of Islamic law in the absence of specific precedents, creative reasoning

IJMA. Consensus One of two acceptable forms of ijtihad

IQAMAH. Alignment of the body during prayer

JAHENNAM. Hell

JAMAAT. Meeting, assembly, a community of believers

JENAZA. Funeral ceremony; Islamic preparation of the dead and prayers that are recited for burial

JIHAD. Striving for religious perfection, or holy war conducted by Muslims against infidels

JIHAD AL-AKBAR. The great struggle within the human soul to abide divine law

JUMʿA. Friday or Sabbath prayers

KAʿBA. Principal shrine in Mecca, object of the pilgrimage

KEMAR. Traditional head-covering worn by Muslim women to conceal their hair as a sign of sexual modesty

KHAMISA. A loose, sleeved gown worn by men and women

KHULA. Cancellation of a marriage contract Form of divorce granted by the husband at the wife's initiative in which she agrees to give up her dowry

KHUTBAH. Friday sermon, usually delivered in English following prayers and recitation from the Quran in Arabic

MADHAB. Muslim school of law The four principal schools of interpretation of Hanafi, Hanbali, Shafi, and maliki

MAJLIS ASH-SHURA. A gathering, assembly or council A standing committee that adminsters community affairs or a meeting to discuss how to apply Islamic policy in crises

MAKRUH-E TAHRINI. Of questionable value

MAKRUH-E TANSHIHI. Negatively affecting one's state of purity

MASJID *MASAJID* (PL). A mosque or place of prostration and prayer; a center for Muslim communal affairs

MAULID AL-NABI. The celebration of the birth of the Prophet

MAWLA. Client or freedman, servant

MUBAH. Permissible

MUBARI. One who is blessed Next stage of learning after initiation of a convert

MUEZZIN. One who calls the faithful to prayer

MUHAJIRUN. "Those who emigrate," after the faithful who accompanied the Prophet in his exile to Medina

MUJAHID. One who engages struggle in the way of God, on behalf of Islam Signifies a soldier or militant in the cause of Islam but also an individual who exercises inward discipline in pursuit of spiritual well-being

MUJAHIDEEN. Persons who fight a holy war (jihad); guerilla fighters in an Islamic country

MURSHID. Guide, Sufi master

MUSHRIK. Polytheism; sin of elevating idols or humans to the status of Allah

MUSSADIQ. Treasurer or officer of the majlis who manages community finances, including the collection of zakat and Sadaqa

MUSTAHAB. Praiseworthy

MUTA. Contract of temporary marriage, usally practiced by Shi'as.

NAFS. Soul; the animal faculties as opposed to the rational or angelic faculties

NAIBU. Assistant imam and member of the majlis

NIKKA. Islamic marriage ceremony

PURDAH. Quarantine Curtain or veil that screens women from men or strangers

QADI. Judge Interpreter of Quranic law

QIYAS. Reason by analogy; one of two acceptable forms of ijtihad

QUMS. The percentage of one's income that comprises the annual donation to the Muslim community, zakat

RAK'AT. Patterned movements made by worshipers during prayer

RIHLA. Travel for the purpose of acquiring knowlege

SADAQA. Voluntary alms; sometimes a synonym for *zakat*

SADIQUN. Advanced stage of learning in the pedagogy of a convert

SALAT. Muslim ritual prayer performed five times daily A series of obligatory movements, including prostration, symbolic of submission to the will of God

SHAHADA. "Witnessing"; the Muslim profession of faith: by extension, a new convert, one who has recently pledged himself to Islam

SEERA. History of the prophets

SHARIA. The path to be followed; Muslim law, the totality of the Islamic way of life

SHI'A. The group of Muslims who regard Ali and his heirs as the only legitimate successors to the Prophet

SUFFA. Dormitory

SUNNA. The trodden path, custom, the practices of the Prophet and the early community which becomes for all Muslims an authoritative example of the correct way to live a Muslim life

SUNNI. Those who accept the Sunna; the majority of the Muslim community, as opposed to the Shi'a

SURA. Chapter in the Quran

TAFSIR. Commentary and interpretation; the exegesis of the Quran

TAQWA. The fundamental quality of awe before God, piety, duty, devoted avoidance of evil

TARIQA. A Sufi brotherhood

TALIBÉ. Student, follower of a sheik

TALIM. Education, pedagogy Also, officer in charge of education for the community

TAUBAH. Repentance, turning to God

TAUHID. Oneness of Allah, fundamental principal of monotheism

ULEMA. Islamic scholars

UMMA. People or community; the whole of the brotherhood of Muslims The nation or people of Islam in their unity as Muslims beyond ethnic, tribal, local, or other units thereof The Muslim collectivity

UMRAH. A lesser piligrimage; travel to the holy shrines outside the period when the sacred hajj is performed

WAJIB. Indispensable

WALI. A protector, a benefactor, a companion, a governor; a friend of God; the legal guardian of a minor, woman, or incapacitated person

WAQF. Perpetual endowment; land or assets held in trust by religious authorities

WIRD. Mystic or divine properties. Attributed to West African Sufi masters or marabouts

WUDZU. Ritual purification before prayer; the state of sacred hygiene

ZAKAT. A legal alms raised from Muslims; one of the Five Pillars

ZIKHR. Remembrance, memory Sufi recitations of ninety-nine qualities to praise Allah

ZINA. Extramarital relations, illicit copulation

Notes

Introduction

1. Brown, *Manchild*, 327–349.
2. Lincoln, *The Black Muslims in America*; Lomax, *To Kill a Black Man, When the Word Is Given, The Negro Revolt*; Essien-Udom, *Black Nationalism*.
3. See works by Bastide, *Les Religions Africaines au Brésil*, in anthropology; Genovese, *Roll, Jordan, Roll*; Curtin, *The Atlantic Slave Trade, Africa Remembered*; and Freyre, *The Masters and the Slaves*, in history; Thompson, *Flash of the Spirit*, and Kramer, *The Red Fez*, in art history; and Gilroy, *The Black Atlantic*, in cultural studies. Each of these fields owes a tremendous debt to Herskovits's precedent (*The Myth of the Negro Past*).
4. Goldman, "Portrait of Religions."
5. Kosmin and Lachman, *One Nation under God*, 125–137.
6. Barrett et al., in *World Christian Encyclopedia*. 1: 772.

Chapter 1

1. Fenton, "Field Work," 71–85.
2. The red fez is an artifact that frequently points toward Islamic themes in African-American culture. It links the Moorish Science Temple of Islam and Prince Hall Masons; it connects African Americans to West African Sufi brotherhoods, Egypt,

and the Ottoman Empire; it spans a period from the early nineteenth to the late twentieth century. It shows up in the subway, on the street, at jazz festivals, and any grand convocation of those who identify themselves as Muslim.

3 Harding, *There Is a River*; and Mechal Sobel, *Trabelin' On*, have both used the riparian metaphor as a research method in the study of African-American religious history.

4. The epigraph to this section is from Georgia Writers' Project, Works Progress Administration, *Drums and Shadows*, 154.

5. Alford, *Prince among Slaves*; Alho, *The Religion of the Slaves*; Austin, *African Muslims in Antebellum America*; Curtin, *The Atlantic Slave Trade* and *Africa Remembered*; Winters, "Origins of Muslim Slaves,"

6. Curtin, *The Atlantic Slave Trade*, 157.

7. Reis, *Slave Rebellion in Brazil*, 112–136; Genovese, *From Rebellion to Revolution*, 28; Winters, "Islam in Early North and South America."

8. The Brazilian historian J. J. Reis refers to Islam as "a heavyweight contender in a cultural free-for-all that also included the Yoruba orisha cult, Aja-Fon Voodum, the Angolan ancestor spirit cult . . . add[ed] to a creole Catholicism" (*Slave Rebellion in Brazil*, 97).

9. Bolster, *Black Jacks*, 230; Linebaugh and Rediker, *The Many-Headed Hydra*, 334.

10. Grimshaw, *Official History of Freemasonry*, 60–70.

11. Ibid., 75.

12. Ibid., 81.

13. Hall's successor as grand master was Nero Prince, a Jewish emigré from Russia who was denied membership in the white Masonic order.

14. Grimshaw, *Official History of Freemasonry*, 341–342.

15. Davis, *The Scottish Rite*, 7–11.

16. Palmer, "Negro Secret Societies," 207–215.

17. Herskovits, *The Myth of the Negro Past*, 161.

18. Walker, *Appeal*.

19. Delany, *The Condition, Elevation, Emigration; Official Report*; and *The Origin and Objects of Ancient Fremasonry*.

20. Drake, *The Redemption of Africa and Black Religion*; Wilmore, *Black Religion*, and Moses, *The Golden Age of Black Nationalism*.

21. Blyden, *Christianity, Islam and the Negro Race*.

22. Ibid., 11–12.

23. Mudimbe, *The Invention of Africa*, 115.

24. Moses, *Afrotopia*, 26.

25. Particularly interesting is the account of a battle pitting the proponents of "Ethiopian rites" against those favoring "Arabian rites" in the order. It involved a dispute between two claimants to leadership of the Prince Hall Masonic order, one James Cannon, first eminent grand master, and Abdul Hamid Suleiman, who claimed Arabian Masonry as his forte. Indicative of the political bearing of this issue, the matter was brought before a Congressional subcommittee and investigated in 1934 (Voorhis, *Our Colored Brethren*, 51). Abdul Hamid surfaces in Harlem again in the 1930s when he led the first Black Boycott, infamously characterized as the first public manifestation of anti-semitism in Harlem (Sleeper, *The Closest of Strangers*, 49).

26. Odum, *Social and Mental Traits*, 58, 98.

27. Ibid., 111.

28. Palmer, "Negro Secret Societies," 210.

29. Ibid., 211.

30. Odum, 128.

31. Kusmer, *A Ghetto Takes Shape*, 270–274.

32. Ibid., 104.

33. The epigraph to this section is from Bontemps and Conroy, *They Seek A City*, 174.

34. On Noble Drew Ali and the Moorish Science Temple of Islam see Evanzz, *The Messenger*, 62–69; Wilson, *Sacred Drift*, 13–50; Bontemps and Conroy, *They Seek a City*, 173–186; and Fauset, *Black Gods of the Metropolis*, 41–51.

35. The Chicago temple sponsored a Moorish Costume Ball to "remind the descendants of these [*sic*] people of the time when their forefathers were the main people to spread the most progressive ideas of civilization."

36. "The twin pillars of the temple are Islamic religion and Moorish American nationality. 'The word Moorish is a nationality,' Sheik Reynolds-El says. 'People have a tendency to identify us as a religious movement when we inherited our religion along with our nationality'" (Carl Schoettler, "Howard Street Temple," B, 1).

37. Hezekiah-El, audiotape interview by author, Cleveland, 9 April 1992.

38. *Moorish Record* (November 1956). Moorish Science Temple of America Original Documents, Schomburg Center, New York Public Library.

39. Worsley, *The Trumpet Shall Sound;* and LaBarre, *The Ghost Dance*.

40. *Cleveland Plain Dealer*, 24 April 1937.

41. Beynon, "The Voodoo Cult among Negro Migrants in Detroit," 894–907.

42. Rosenwald was the owner of Sears Roebuck and the founder of the philanthropic Julius Rosenwald Fund. Coincindentally, the only book of the period that mentions Noble Drew Ali's Moorish Science Temple of Islam was Bontemps and Conroy *They Seek a City*, a study of the Great Migration, funded in part by the Julius Rosenwald Fund.

43. El-Hajj Heshaam Jabbar, audiotape interview by author, Newark, N.J., 13 June 1990; Evanzz, *The Messenger*, 62.

44. Barry, "In Tax Scheme, a Major Role for Separatists." For an illustration of how the Moors linked antitax strategies to calls for the government to pay reparations for slavery see Schoettler, "Howard Street Temple." A full text of the antitax proclamation appeared in the *Baltimore News American* on 10 August 1978.

45. Bey, "The Clock of Destiny."

46. The Ishmaelites were an important American literary trope first popularized by James Fenimore Cooper in *The Prairie* and prominent in Herman Melville's *Moby-Dick*.

47. Weslager, *Delaware's Forgotten Folk;* and Forbes, *Africans and Native Americans*.

48. Marcus, *Invisible Republic*.

49. "Moor Colony Flourishes in Prince George, Va." newspaper clipping, n.d. Moorish Science Temple of America, original documents, Schomburg Center, New York Public Library.

50. Diop, *Precolonial Black Africa*, 172.

51. See Hakim, "History of the First Muslim Mosque," 153–163.

Chapter 2

1. See Friedmann, *Prophecy Continuous*, for an excellent review of the history and theology of this controversial movement.

2. Ali, *Translation of the Holy Quran.*

3. One cannot escape the striking similarities between Ahmad's doctrines and those popularized in Noble Drew Ali's "Holy Koran," 16–18.

4. Friedmann, *Prophecy Continuous,* 113–114.

5. Chaudry, *Persecution of Ahmadi Muslims.*

6. Turner, "The Ahmadiyya Mission," 58.

7. "Saddiq relentlessly attacked Christian profiteers' role in the slave trade and their role in making blacks forget the religion and language of their forefathers, Islam and Arabic" (Ibid., 60).

8. Ibid., 52–53.

9. Among the converts, Sheik Omar of the Braddock Mosque near Pittsburgh said that "the Bible is not for the Negro [because] it does not belong to him." Several months later a confrontation was reported between one Mrs. Faglee Begum of Youngstown and "a European minister" named Dr. Hammick, who accused her of leading Negroes out of Christianity. "After a very hot discussion, [Begum] brought three people back to the fold of Islam in the person of Brother Ghulam Ahmad and his wife and little girl, Lateefa" (*Cleveland Call and Post,* 3 April 1934).

10. El-Hajj Wali Akram, statement to author, Cleveland, 30 April 1990.

11. Ibid.

12. American Ahmadiyya, *Centenial Souvenir,* 52. Official Ahmadiyya history passes over Muhammad Din's tenure without comment except to call it an "interim period" and to note that the *Sunrise* ceased publication then.

13. Handbill ("Ahmadiyyas"), box 7, bundle 1, folio B, Collected papers of El-Hajj Wali Abdul Akram, First Cleveland Mosque; John Vance, "5 Times Daily 400 Here Salaam One and only Allah," *Cleveland Plain Dealer,* 23 April 1934, 1. Ignoring any details, the Ahmadiyyas say only that "Dr. Muhammad Yusuf continued the missionary work" (American Ahmadiyya, *Centenial Souvenir,* 52).

14. Handbill ("Ahmaddiyyas"), Ibid.

15. The Ethiopian Temples of Islam was founded in 1919 in St. Louis by Professor Paul Nathaniel Johnson, the same man who, calling himself Sheik Ahmad Din, administered Walter Gregg the Ahmadiyya oath of conversion in 1923.

16. Landau, *The Politics of Pan-Islam.*

17. Ferris, "Immigrant Muslims in New York City," 210.

18. Webb's speech,"The Spirit of Islam," is reprinted with a brief commentary in, *The Dawn of Religious Pluralism,* edited by R. H. Seager, 270–280.

19. Webb, *Islam in America,* 67.

20. Köszegi and Melton, *Islam in North America,* 44.

21. Professor Akbar Muhammad of the State University of New York in Binghamton has been researching Webb's biography. There are no publications as yet.

22. Kaplan, *The Arabists,* 7.

23. Zarcone, *Mystiques, Philosophes et Francs-maçons en Islam,* 196.

24. Brown, *The Dervishes.*

25. Zarcone, *Mystiques, Philosophes et Francs-maçons en Islam,* 122. Gramsci also discusses the alliances of mystics and revolutionaries, claiming that religion and other "international organizations—Freemasonry, Rotarianism, the Jews, career diplomacy . . . can be subsumed into the social category of 'intellectuals', whose function on an international scale, is that of mediating the extremes, of 'socializing' the technical discoveries that provide the impetus for all activities of leadership, of devising compromises between, and ways out of, extreme solutions" (*Prison Notebooks,* 182).

26. Wilmore, *Black Religion*, 238.

27. The best summaries of NOI beliefs can be found in Allen Jr., "Identity and Destiny"; Nurridin, "African-American Muslims and the Question of Identity," 267–330; and Turner, *Islam in the African-American Experience*. A complementary perspective traces similar influences historically. For example, see Clegg, *An Original Man*; Bloom, *The American Religion*, 237–271; Lincoln, *Race, Religion*; Goldman, *The Life and Death of Malcolm X*; Wilmore, *Black Religion*; Lomax, *When the Word Is Given*; and Essien-Udom, *Black Nationalism*.

28. Berger, "The Black Muslims," 59.

29. Muhammad, *Message to the Blackman*, 297.

30. See Haines, *Black Radicals*, for analysis of the relationship between Elijah Muhammad's politics and the Civil Rights movement.

31. The Arab American Business Association in Detroit and the Al-Wahid Al-Samad Society in Columbus may be related to Duse Mohamed's dawa efforts in the United States. See Mahmud, introduction to Mohamed, *In the Land of the Pharaohs*, ix–xxxiii; and Letters, Arab-American business association and Al-Wahid Al-Sanad, box 7, bundle 1, folio OO, Collected Papers of El-Hajj Wali Abdul Akram, First Cleveland Mosque, Cleveland.

32. The Islamic Center represented immigrant Muslim interests in New York and Washington, D. C. El-Hajj Wali Akram, interview by author, Cleveland, 25 August 1990.

33. Omar Ali to Akram, 24 August 1943, box 7, bundle 1, folio MM, Collected Papers of El-Hajj Wali Abdul Akram, First Cleveland Mosque, Cleveland.

34. An authoritative review of the alleged wartime subversion of African Americans by Japanese agents can be found in Kearney, *African-American Views of the Japanese*.

35. American Muslim Committee for Defense, Memoranda to the Congressional Military Affairs Committee, 4 July 1941 and 15 March 1943, box 7, bundle 1, folio D, Collected Papers of El-Hajj Wali Abdul Akram.

36. For a general discussion of the status of Muslims living as minorities among infidels see Metcalf, *Making Muslim Space in North American and Europe*; Eickelman and Piscatori, *Muslim Travellers*; Poston, *Islamic Da'wah in the West*; and Lewis, *Islam and the West*.

37. Akram's position was reminiscent of the Ahmadiyya principle of unwavering loyalty to the government in power. See Friedmann, *Prophecy Continuous*, 34.

38. Ezaldeen to Akram, 14 September 1943, box 7, bundle 1, folio A ("AAUAA"), Collected Papers of El-Hajj Wali Abdul Akram.

39. Ibid.

40. The best analysis of the Muhammad Abdu's position favoring modernization as statement of Islamic autonomy is in Tibi, *Islam and the Cultural Accommodation of Social Change*, 21.

41. Akram to Sayeed, 10 November 1943, box 7, bundle 1, folio A ("AAUAA"), Collected Papers of El-Hajj Wali Abdul Akram.

42. They included Abdullah I. Malik of Columbus's Wahid Al-Samad Society for Al-Islam and Karma Jee Karachi of the newly founded AAUAA unit in Detroit, Akram to Malik, 1942–1945, box 7, bundle 1, folios A and OO ("AAUAA"), Collected Papers of El-Hajj Wali Abdul Akram.

43. Laj-Nai (Women's Society) flyers: "The Constitution of the Women's Rights Society," organized 14 January 1946; "A Wig and Fashion Review," sponsored by the

Laj-Nai at Masonic Temple, 8637 Buckeye Road, 26 April 1964; "East Meets West Fashions," 7 May 1972; box 7, bundle 1, folio PP ("Women"), Collected Papers of El-Hajj Wali Abdul Akram.

44. Letters from: Mukhtar Ahmed, 9 September 1944; Sadya Abdaraz 8 October 1945; Rasheeda Khitab al-Deen, 21 Feb. 1945 and 3 March 1945; A. I. Malik, 28 January 1945; 6 and 26 August 1946; box 7, bundle 1, folios MM, OO, PP, Collected Papers of El-Hajj Wali Abdul Akram.

45. Malik to Akram, 28 January 1945, "Wa-hid Al-Samad," box 7, bundle 1, folio OO, Collected Papers of El-Hajj Wali Abdul Akram.

46. Akram to Malik, letter, 6 February 1945, box 7, bundle 1, folio OO, Collected Papers of El-Hajj Wali Abdul Akram.

47. Ashraf to Akram, letter, 9 August 1945, box 7, bundle 1, folio MM, Collected Papers of El-Hajj Wali Abdul Akram.

48. El-Hajj Wali Akram, interview by author, Cleveland, 21 August 1990.

49. The First Muslim Mosque (Pittsburgh); the Braddock Mosque (a Pittsburgh suburb); the Muslim Ten Year Plan; the Adenu Islami (Philadelphia), and the Adenu Allahe (Philadelphia).

Chapter 3

1. Hughes, *Selected Poems*, 246.

2. Gillespie and Fraser, *To Be or Not To Bop*, 490. In his native Cuba, Pozo belonged to the Nañigo sect, one of the several Yoruban secret societies, each of which possessed a distinctive song for its intiation ritual (Thompson, *Flash of the Spirit*, 47).

3. Ibid., 293.

4. Ibid., 291.

5. Many worthwhile insights on the Orientalist movement in modern jazz can be found in Weinstein, *A Night in Tunisia*.

6. Among the putschists who overthrew Egyptian King Farouk in 1952 were many religious activists associated with Ikwan al-muslimun (Muslim Brotherhood). Relations between the military nationalists led by Nasser and the Ikwan deteriorated soon after the revolution, however, and three prominent Ikwan leaders, including Sayid Qutb, were found guilty of treason and hanged in 1966.

7. Muhammad Salahuddin, inteview by author, New York, N.Y., 17 January 1991.

8. Sulaiman al-Hadi, audiotape interview by author, Brooklyn, 22 October 1989.

9. Ibid.

10. Faisal, *Al Islam: The Religion of Humanity*, 11–13.

11. The Ashahadat Tani (Certificate of Acceptance of Islam), Islamic Mission to America Inc., Brooklyn; Muslim Certificate of Identification of Change of Names; Immigration Application. Documents courtesy of Islamic Mission to America, Brooklyn.

12. Muhammad, personal communication.

13. For an excellent history of the Tabligh Jamaat and its influence on Islam in the West, see Metcalf, "New Medinas," 110–127.

14. An adequate though truncated history of the Dar ul-Islam is Curtis, "Urban Muslims."

15. Tawfiq, *The Black Man and Islam*, 15.

16. Y. M. Hamid, audiotape interview by Khalid Griggs, 1 November 1987.

17. Y. M. Hamid, a native of Dominica, West Indies, was very familiar with the

Jamaat-e-Islami Movement, having spent time as a guest in Abul A ʿla Mawdudi's home. On the latter's considerable influence on North American Islam see Poston, *Islamic Daʿwah in the West*, 70–80.

18. Y. M. Hamid, audiotape interview by Kahlid Griggs, 1 November 1987.

19. Dawud Salahuddin, "The Islamic Party and the DAR," 3.

20. Marsh, *From Black Muslims to Muslims*.

21. Saʿid, "Questions and Answers," 18 October 1982, unpublished manuscript.

22. Rumors of connections between the Black Man's Volunteer Army of Liberation and Muslim radicals became public in 1980 when Field-Lieutenant Daoud Salahuddin (David Theodore Belfield) assassinated Ali Akbar Tabatabai in Washington, D.C. The crime bore all the traces of a contract killing because Tabatabai, an Iranian expatriate, was a member of the old regime who had been sentenced to death by Ayatollah Khomeini. Salahuddin knocked on Tabatabai's door, shot him point blank, and then escaped to Tehran, where he now resides. Salahuddin, a graduate of Howard University, converted to Islam as part of Y. M. Hamid's Islamic Party of North America ("The Call of Islam Changed Life of Slaying Suspect," *New York Times*, 8 August 1980 Sec. A, p. 10).

23. Y. M. Hamid, audiotape interview by Khalid Griggs, 1 November 1987.

24. International Islamic Educational Society, *The International Islamic Educational Institute*, 3.

25. Sulaiman al-Hadi, audiotape interview by author, Brooklyn, 22 October 1989.

26. Clines, "U.S. Suspect."

27. Builta, "Al-Fuqra." For a detailed account of Imam Rashad's Islamic heresy and subsequent assassination, see Haddad and Smith, *Mission to America*, 135–168.

28. Gilani, *Quranic Psychiatry*.

29. Boodhoo, "Islamic Fundamentalism in the Caribbean."

30. Dannin, "Ces musulmans courtisés et divisés."

Chapter 4

1. "Imam of Moslems has 10-Year Plan," *Cleveland Plain Dealer*, 20 June 1937, 3.

2. Muraskin, *Middle-Class Blacks in a White Society*, 110.

3. Rev. Bertram Gregg, telephone interview by author, 15 May 1993.

4. Historically speaking, Freemasonry furnished a modicum of protection and shelter from racism, and the Prince Hall lodges became havens for itinerants and migrants traveling through unfamiliar cities. See Williams, *Black Freemasonry and Middle-Class Realities*, 87; and Fauset, *Black Gods of the Metropolis*, 93.

5. Frazier, *The Negro Family in the United States*, 229.

6. Ibid., 231.

7. Din, "Theism," 17.

8. Hameeda Mansur, audiotape interview by author, Cleveland, 25 August 1990.

9. Rasool Akram, interview by author, Cleveland, 26 April 1990.

10. Khan to Akram, 22 November and 3 December 1934, box 7, bundle 1, folio B ("Ahmadiyyas"), Collected Papers of El-Hajj Wali Abdul Akram, First Cleveland Mosque, Cleveland.

11. Akram to Ahmad, 2 January 1935, box 7, bundle 1, folio B ("Ahmadiyyas"), Collected Papers of El-Hajj Wali Abdul Akram.

12. Bengalee to Akram, 12 January 1935, box 7, bundle 1, folio B ("Ah-madiyyas"), Collected Papers of El-Hajj Wali Abdul Akram.

13. Bengalee to Akram, 21 November and 31 December 1934, 19 January 1935, box 7, bundle 1, folio B ("Ahmadiyyas"), Collected Papers of El-Hajj Wali Abdul Akram.

14. Akram to Anonymous, 7 March 1935, box 7, bundle 1, folio B ("Ah-madiyyas") Collected Papers of El-Hajj Wali Abdul Akram.

15. The British raj, for example, which Ghulam Ahmad perceived as more toler-ant than local Indian rulers. See Friedmann, *Prophecy Continuous.*

16. For a critical overview of "post-Christian" doctrinal innovations in American sects, see Bloom, *The American Religion,* 237–255.

17. Hameeda Mansur, audiotape interview by author, Cleveland, 25 August 1990.

18. "Imam of Moslems has a 10-Year Plan," *Cleveland Plain Dealer,* 20 June 1937, 3.

19. Ali to Uthman, 8 February 1937, box 7, bundle 1, folio B, "Ahmadiyyas" Col-lected Papers of El-Hajj Wali Abdul Akram.

20. Hameeda Mansur, audiotape interview by author, Cleveland, 25 August 1990.

21. Hameeda Mansur, correspondence, 10 August 1990.

22. Akmal to Akram, 6 January 1938, box 7, bundle 1, folio B ("Ahmadiyyas"), Collected Papers of El-Hajj Wali Abdul Akram.

23. Akmal to Akram, 29 March 1937, box 7, bundle 1, folio B, Collected Papers of El-Hajj Wali Abdul Akram. The Ahmadiyya Anjuman Ishaat-I-Islam was a breakaway sect of the Ahmadiyyas, commonly referred to as the "Lahoris" for the Indian city where they were headquartered. In opposition to the Qadianis, they denounced the khalifat hierarchy as "a papacy in Islam." The Lahoris functioned like an Islamic Bible-tract publisher by offering incentives to enterprising salesmen (Ilahi to Uthman, 23 March 1937, box 7, bundle 1, folio B, Collected Papers of El-Hajj Wali Abdul Akram). Maulana Muhammad Ali, president of the Lahoris, published a popular English translation of the Holy Quran in 1928. See Muhammad Ali, *Translation of the Holy Quran.*

24. Akmal to Akram, ibid.

25. "A Message to the Dark American," box 3, (Phamphlets and handbills), Col-lected Papers of El-Hajj Wali Abdul Akram.

26. "A Plan of Mosque Organization," box 3, folio G, (Pamphlets and Handbills), Collected Papers of El-Hajj Wali Abdul Akram.

27. Ibid.

28. "Islam and Muslim Prayer," box 3, folio N, (Pamphlets and Handbills), Col-lected Papers of El-Hajj Wali Abdul Akram,

29. Hussain, audiotape interview by author, Cleveland, 9 April 1992.

30. The FBI investigated Elijah Muhammad for subversion beginning in 1932 (Evanzz, *The Messenger,* 105).

31. "Please bring with you the records of said cult, showing the list of members, their Christian names and addresses," the local commissioner demanded. Summons issued by the Cuyahoga County Board of Elections, box 1, folio C, (Letters and Papers) Collected Papers of El-Hajj Wali Abdul Akram.

32. Palmer, "Negro Secret Societies," 207–215.

33. Conscious of the public status conferred by identification cards, Akram de-signed entries for the bearer's armed services registration and discharge numbers, so-cial security numbers, place of employment, automobile license, and registration.

Alongside a photo was the bearer's Arabic name in calligraphy, then spelled phoneti-
cally next to its English translation. The card bore Gregorian and Muslim dates. The
accordion sheet bearing this information with the loyalty statement and a savings account was sheathed in a gold-leaf wallet-size card measuring six by ten centimeters
when folded properly. It was embossed with a red crescent moon and star ("Financial
Membership and Identification Card," box 6, folio A, "Muslim Ten Year Plan," Collected Papers of El-Hajj Wali Abdul Akram).

34. "Muslim Ten Year Plan, Inc.," box 3, (Pamphlets and handbills), Collected Papers of El-Hajj Wali Abdul Akram.

35. Ethmet Hussain, audiotape interview by author, Cleveland, 9 April 1992.

36. Eickelman and Piscatori, *Muslim Travellers*, 3–21

37. Elkholy, *The Arab Moslems in the United States*, 46–47.

38. The Tabligh movement was an evangelical mission dedicated to the rehabilitation of Islamic faith among lapsed Muslims. Its efforts were essentially apolitical and
ecumenical in that it steered clear of controversy by calling for a return to traditional
Islam. While their mission sought to rejuvenate Islam among assimilationist-minded
immigrants, they also heard about the indigenous converts to Islam while visiting
Cleveland. The founder of this reform movement, Muhammad Ilyas, maintained that
tabligh (propagation) was perhaps of greater importance than hajj itself. Their modus
operandi was to enlist travelers for a specific period of tabligh and to sponsor some of
them for the hajj. They deliberately assembled tabligh groups of Muslims from diverse
nationalities as a way of fostering the transnational character of the umma. This
strategy was conceived as a way to remedy the many sectarian divisions of Islam. For a
comparison with the rival Jamaat-e-Islami Movement, see Nasr, *Mawdudi and The Making of Islamic Revivalism*, 65.)

39. Khadija Akram, interview by author, Cleveland, 3 March 1989.

40. Ibid.

41. Imam Abbas Akram, sermon, First Cleveland Mosque, 26 April 1990.

Chapter 5

1. Probably one of the indigenous Ahmadiyya sheiks. "He never did say where
he was from and I never did ask him either," recalled Ghani. The research archives of
the Jabul Arabiyya community contains a notebook of relatively advanced Arabic language studies that belonged to Yusef Hakeem. Each lesson is dated, the earliest date is
July 1933. Records in the Buffalo Historical Society library also indicate that Muslims
from various parts of the world settled in the Buffalo area in the early years of the
twentieth century. A news article in the October 1922 edition of the *Buffalo Times* mentions a coffeehouse on Seneca Street frequented by Yemenite Arabs, but there is no
mention of Islam. The *Buffalo Criterion* newspaper has records of doing business with
the AAUAA as early as 1929 ("50 Years of Islamic Striving," Banquet Program, AAUAA,
Buffalo, N.Y., 17 May 1992, 4).

2. "About three brothers were working at Bethlehem Steel, and I was working in
the Republic Steel, all together six or seven brothers was working. Back then in the
thirties during the depression there wasn't nobody hardly working in Buffalo, but we
happened to be in those mills, and they kept going" (Ghani, audiotape interview with
author, West Valley, N.Y., 17 May 1992).

3. Simultaneous efforts in this direction were made in a rural area of New Jersey
outside Philadelphia (now called Ezaldeen Village) and in Newark. Other prominent

"units" of the AAUAA were located in Youngstown, Ohio; Rochester, New York, Philadelphia; Jacksonville, Florida; and Detroit.

4. Ezaldeen died unexpectedly in 1954.

5. "Black Sunni Moslem Colony Is Tucked Away in Ashford," *Buffalo News*, 15 August 1987, p. 1.

Chapter 6

1. The Ocean Hill–Brownsville teachers' strike was essentially a struggle for neighborhood control of a failing public school system. It also revealed a complicated social confrontation among the teachers' union, an African-American school superintendent, the New York City Board of Education, neighborhood parents of school children, and militant political activists. Local public schools were officially shut for a year while the militants asserted their right to decide who would hire teachers for their schools. Characterized by epithets and racial polarization, the dispute symbolized the generally tense interracial atmosphere in New York City during the late 1960s. See Sleeper, *The Closest of Strangers*, 91–115; Ravitch, *The Great School Wars;* and Kaufman, *Broken Alliance.*

Chapter 7

1. Figures from the Public Affairs Bureau of the New York State Department of Correctional Services in Albany, N.Y.

2. Umar Abdul Jalil, audiotape interview by author, New York, N.Y., 22 January 1992.

3. Ibid.

4. Cloward, *Theoretical Studies in the Social Organization of the Prison.*

5. Foucault, *Discipline and Punish*, 125.

6. Haley, *The Autobiography of Malcolm X*, 157.

7. Perry, *Malcolm*, 114.

8. Haley, *The Autobiography of Malcolm X*, 170.

9. Umar Abdul Jalil, audiotape interview by author, New York, N.Y., 22 January 1992.

10. Mujahid A. Al-Hizbullahi, letter to author, 8 February 1990.

11. "U.S. Tags Club Here Un-American," "FBI Probes Reports of Club Offering Immunity to Draft," "Forbids Draft Dodge Suspect to Drop Lawyer," "Six Cultists Conviced of Draft Dodging," box 7, bundle 1, folio CC ("News clippings"), Collected Papers of El-Hajj Wali Abdul Akram.

12. Fauset, *Black Gods of the Metropolis*; Bontemps and Conroy, *They Seek a City;* Frazier, *The Negro Church in America.*

13. Fauset, *Black Gods of the Metropolis*, 51.

14. Whyte, "Christian Elements"; and Tyler, "The Protestant Ethic."

15. Haines, *Black Radicals and the Civil Rights Mainstream*, 55.

16. The advent of Islam as a "jailhouse" religion was greeted initially with apprehension and rejection. A 1966 survey of wardens and chaplains across the country showed that more than 50 percent of the respondents were totally opposed to accepting the presence of Islam as a legitimate religious endeavor for their inmates (Caldwell, "A Survey of Attitudes toward Black Muslims in Prison," 235).

17. A sampling of the fusion of Islam, the prison experience, and early rap music is heard on tracks such as "Blessed Are Those Who Struggle" (The Last Poets, *Delights of the Garden*, Celluloid Records, New York, CEL 6136, 1987).

18. Mustafa et al.,"Overview."

19. El-Hajj Hassan A. Muhammad, audiotape interview by author, Brooklyn, 15 February 1992.

20. By the late 1970s Minister Louis Farrakhan stepped into the breech to revive the old Nation of Islam, drawing on the power base of older members, a few of whom refused to believe that Elijah Muhammad was even dead.

21. Shuaib Abdur Raheem, telephone interview by author, 26 November 1989.

22. By the late 1960s, SCC (the Student Coordinating Committee) was militant and advocated armed revolution. H. Rap Brown was the alleged author of the famous phrase "Violence is as American as cherry pie." He was hunted down and shot by New York police under the same conspiracy law that produced the famous Chicago Seven trial. Following his conversion to Islam and parole from a New York prison in 1976, Jamil Al-Amin made a pilgrimage to Mecca and then settled in Atlanta's West End to found the Community Mosque of Atlanta. His congregation was the basis for the National Community, a coalition of thirty North American mosques that sought to revive Brooklyn's DAR movement in spirit if not name. Presiding as imam and civic leader for more than two decades, Al-Amin was credited with resuscitating a dying ghetto by ridding the area of drug dealers and prostitutes, making it safe for children and families. His methods provoked intense scrutiny by the FBI and the Atlanta police who skirmished with him intermittently. On 29 March 2000 Al-Amin was arrested as a fugitive in Alabama and extradited back to Georgia, where he faced first-degree murder charges in the death of a police deputy during an alleged gun battle near his Community Store. He remains imprisoned, awaiting trial.

23. Albert Nuh Washington, audiotape interview with author, New York, N.Y., 11 April 1988.

24. Mujahid A. Al-Hizbullahi, letter to author, 8 February 1990.

25. Jalil Muntaqim, audiotape interview by author, Green Haven, N.Y., 4 April 1988.

26. One might argue that the prevalence of advanced electronic detectors, used especially to screen incoming visitors to the prison, mitigates the need to continue the "strip search" unless it is being retained for its general disciplinary effect of symbolic submission and acknowledgement of the state as the ultimate authority over a prisoner's body.

27. Albert Nuh Washington, audiotape interview with author, New York, N.Y., 11 April 1988.

28. Shuaib Abdur Raheem, telephone conversation with author, 11 April 1991.

29. Ibid.

30. Jalil Muntaqim, audiotape interview by author, Green Haven, N.Y., 4 April 1988.

31. Ibid.

32. Caldwell, "A Survey of Attitudes toward Black Muslims in Prison."

33. Shuaib Abdur Raheem, telephone interview by author, 6 December 1989.

34. The watch commander must have a list showing where each prisoner is at any given time during the day, including religious functions and visits. The call-out puts the prisoner on a special status, excusing him from meals or his prison job, for example.

35. In the past many confrontations have arisen between Sunni Muslims and

other groups claiming Islamic affiliations ranging from Shi'a through the followers of Warith Muhammad (the AMM) and members of the Nation of Islam (Louis Farrakhan) to cultural-nationalist sects like the Five Percent Nation, the Zulu Nation, and the Ansaru Allah. When Sankore mosque was established as an orthodox Sunni institution, its founders were conscious of these divisions and designed a pedagogy that would inculcate the principles of common Islamic worship and a practice that would unite all factions into a prison jamaat. The Sunni Muslims even borrowed many of the tested recruiting methods of the Nation of Islam and incorporated them into their prison dawa programs, but they refused any and all association with the heretical teachings of Elijah Muhammad.

Chapter 8

1. El-Hajj Malik Shabazz (Malcolm X), letter to Dr. Said Ramadan.
2. Mernissi, *The Veil and the Male Elite* and *Beyond the Veil*.
3. See Williams, *Crackhouse*, 122–124 for the economy of sex in the cocaine trade.
4. This marriage should be qualified anthropologically as an instance of multilocal polygamy in contrast to a unilocal or a communal household, as advocated by other African-American Muslims.
5. Hameeda Mansur, audiotape interview by author, Cleveland, 25 August 1990.
6. For the widely accepted text on marriage during this period, see Mawdudi, *The Laws of Marriage and Divorce in Islam*.
7. Tawfiq-Toure, "The Marital Life of the Prophet." This position is disputed by others (Mernissi, *Beyond the Veil*, 64; Guillaume, *Islam*, 71; Goldziher, *Muslim Studies*, 1:117; and Smith, *Kinship and Marriage in Early Arabia*, 313).
8. *New York Post*, 6 October 1989, 5; *New York Daily News*, 6 October 1989, 5.
9. Of particular interest is the excellent account of the 1990 murder of Rashad Khalifa in Arizona given by Haddad and Smith, *Mission to America*, 137–168.

Chapter 9

1. Quoted in Bray, "Claiming a Culture," 25–30.
2. Ali, *The Blackman's Guide,* 76.
3. Ibid., 159.
4. Ibid., 169.
5. Mawdudi, *The Laws of Marriage and Divorce in Islam*, 7.
6. Mernissi, *Beyond the Veil*, 53–54.
7. Ibid., 173.
8. Ali, *The Blackman's Guide*, 94.
9. Madhubuti, *Confusion by Any Other Name*; Sinclair, "Shaharazad Ali: 1001 Arabian Lies."
10. Ali, *The Blackman's Guide*, 77.
11. Ibid., 122–123.
12. Ibid., 28.
13. Ibid., 48.
14. Ibid., 159.
15. Ibid., 107.

16. Lévi-Strauss, *The Elementary Structures of Kinship*.

17. Hameeda Mansur, audiotape interview by author, Cleveland, 25 August 1990.

18. Mohamed Kabbaj, audiotape interview by author, Brooklyn, 23 April 1990.

19. Muzaffar Zafar, audiotape interview with author, Dayton, Ohio, 23 August 1990.

20. Aliyah Abdul Karim, audiotape interview with author, Brooklyn, 28 June 1990.

21. "Notable and Quotable," *Wall Street Journal*, 15 August 1997, A16.

22. Foster, *Religion and Sexuality*, 223.

23. Ibid., 139.

24. Ibid., 131, 176, 218.

25. Ibid., 153.

26. Ibid., 245.

27. Foster reports that "one Mormon scholar had noted that in Utah the interrelationships in some families became so complex as virtually to defy analysis. By his death at age eighty-eight, for instance, Benjamin F. Johnson was related by blood or marriage to over eight hundred people. For this persecuted group . . . tribal terms [and] such family ties could make an important contribution to social cohesion" (*Religion and Sexuality*, 151).

28. The sociologist William Julius Wilson describes this demographic factor as a low coefficient of "male marriageability" (*The Truly Disadvantaged*, 83).

29. Sharifa al-Khateeb, letter to the editor.

30. Dannin, "Forms of Huron Kinship and Marriage," 109.

31. There is even some basis to the claim that *muta* (temporary contract marriage), now only practiced by Shi'a Muslims, represents a survival of Arabic polyandry that was diffused as a controversial part of Islamic tradition (Smith, *Kinship and Marriage in Early Arabia*, 88).

32. Foster, *Religion and Sexuality*, 170.

33. Thus "while men could practice polygamy, easy divorce gave women the opportunity for what amounted to serial polygamy" (ibid., 218, n. 109).

34. Ibid., 209.

35. I. Muhammad, *The Goals of a Polygamous Woman*.

36. Sinclair, "Shaharazad Ali: 1001 Arabian Lies."

37. Sheikh Abdullah Hakim, audiotape interview by author, Toronto, 21 July 1989.

38. Foster, *Religion and Sexuality*, 170.

39. Ibid., 145.

40. Mernissi, *Beyond the Veil*, xvi.

41. Kilbride, *Plural Marriage for Our Times*, 20.

42. Ibid., 72.

43. Ibid., 77.

44. Ibid., 77.

45. Ibid., 71.

46. Ibid., 82.

47. Ibid., 81.

48. Ibid., 82.

49. Mernissi, *Beyond the Veil*, xvi.

50. Ibid., 116.

51. Ibid., 47.

52. Mawdudi, *The Laws of Marriage and Divorce in Islam*, 71.
53. Mernissi, *Beyond the Veil*, 82.
54. Diop, *Precolonial Black Africa*, 172; Goldziher, *Muslim Studies*, 1:134.
55. Mernissi, *Beyond the Veil*, 62.
56. Ibid., 54.
57. Ibid., 81.

Chapter 10

1. Devine, *Maximum Security*, 199–221.
2. Lipman, *Race, Class,and Power in School Restructuring*.
3. Anderson, *Streetwise*, 242–243; and Wilson, *When Work Disappears*, 142.
4. Fountain, "Violence Is Down"; and Stewart, "Life in the Killing Zone."
5. Castells, *The Power of Identity*, 62.
6. Ibid., 20.
7. Schacht, *An Introduction to Islamic Law*, 1.
8. The North American Islamic Trust was established in 1971 under the aegis of ISNA's precursor, the Muslim Students of America (*MSA Newsletter*, August 1972).
9. Bagby, audiotape interview by author, Plainfield, Ind. 15 August 1989.
10. Ibrahim, interview by author, Plainfield, Ind., 15 August 1989.
11. Wolfram and Schilling-Estes, *American English*, 151–183.
12. In 1996 Cleveland began an experimental school voucher program that gave needy parents tuition money for private and parochial schools. So many opted for TISO that by 1999 non-Muslim students were in the majority. The program was ruled unconstitutional by the Ohio supreme court, with an appeal pending before the U.S. Supreme Court as of this writing (Wilgoren, "Court Overturns").
13. Jamiel A. Rahman, interview by author, Hudson, Ohio, 16 August 1990.
14. Juba Abdullah Ali, interview by author, Cleveland, 3 April 1992.
15. Daud Abdul Malik, audiotape interview by author, Cleveland, 10 April 1992.
16. Gellens, "The Search for Knowledge in Medieval Muslim Societies"; El Moudden ,"The Ambivalence of *Rihla*."
17. In many quarters Islamic salat is regarded as a tool for behavioral management (Adeyola, "The Islamic Process of Education").
18. Gellner, *Muslim Society*, 1–85. For an ethnographic illustration of this principle see Launay, *Beyond the Stream*.
19. Daud Abdul Malik, sermon, Masjid al-Hagg, Cleveland, 31 August 1990.
20. Hassinah Rance, interview with author, Cleveland, 31 August 1990.
21. Ibid.
22. Rosen, *The Anthropology of Justice*, 39–57.
23. Pearl, "Moon over Mecca, 1"; "Moon Sighting"; "Alhamdullilah, Moon Sighting Unity."
24. "ISNA-Saudi Factor," "Muslims Gradually Waking Up."
25. Hassan al-Turabi, *Address*, 8.

Conclusion

1. Neff, "Answering Islam's Questions," 7.
2. The most important chronicles and travelogues were authored by Al-Jahiz, Al-

Jawzi, Al-Sayuti, Ibn Khaldûn, Ibn Battuta, al-Salawi, Ibn Sina, and Ahmad Baba (Muhammad, "The Image of Africans," 47–74).

3. Willis, *Slaves and Slavery in Muslim Africa;* and Meillassoux, *The Anthropology of Slavery.* Opposing views are given by Diop, *Precolonial Black Africa,* 67; Lapidus, *A History of Islamic Societies,* 220; and Coulon, *Les musulmans et le pouvoir en Afrique noir.*

4. Mahmud, Introduction to *In the Land of the Pharaohs,* xxiv, xxviii.

5. Cronon, *Black Moses,* 15.

6. The image and contradictions of Al-Hajj Malik Shabazz's association with Arabian slave-owners in Mecca have been thoughtfully confronted by Maglangbayan (*Garvey, Lumumba, Malcolm,* 72–73).

7. Burkett, *Garveyism as a Religious Movement.*

8. Dannin, "Understanding the Multi-Ethnic Dilemma."

9. "Race and History," 355.

10. Bertram Gregg, telephone conversation, 15 May 1993.

Bibliography

Abrahams, Peter. "The Meaning of Harlem." *Holiday* (June 1960): 142.

Abun-Nasr, Jamil M. *The Tijaniyya: A Sufi Order in the Modern World*. London: Oxford University Press, 1965.

Adeyola, Dawoud. "The Islamic Process of Education." West Valley, N.Y.: Addeynu Allahe Universal Arabic Association, 1991. Photocopy.

Ahmad, Hazrat Mirza Bashir-ud Din Mahmud. *Ahmadiyyat or The True Islam*. Qadian, Punjab, India: Abul Fazal Mahmud, 1924.

———. *Introduction to the Study of the Holy Quran*. London: London Mosque, 1949.

Ahmad, Hazrat Mirza Tahir. *Murder in the Name of Allah*. Cambridge, England: Lutterworth Press, 1989.

Ahmed, Akbar. *Post-Modernism and Islam: Predicament and Promise*. London: Routledge, 1992.

Ahsan, Abdullah. "A Late Nineteenth Century Muslim Response to the Western Criticism of Islam—An Analysis of Amir Ali's Life and Works." *American Journal of Islamic Social Sciences* 2,2 (1985): 179–206.

Akram, El-Hajj Wali Abdul. "Collected Papers of El-Hajj Wali Abdul Akram and the First Cleveland Mosque," compiled by Robert Dannin and Jolie Stahl. First Cleveland Mosque, Cleveland. Unpublished manuscript.

Alford, Terry. *Prince among Slaves*. New York: Oxford University Press, 1977.

Alhamdullilah, "Moon Sighting Unity," *ISNA Matters* (1 March 1994): 1.

Alho, Olli. *The Religion of the Slaves; A Study of the Religious Traditions and Behavior of the Plantation Slaves in the United States, 1835–1865*. Helsinki: Academia Scientiarum Fennica, 1976.

Ali, A. Yusuf, trans. *The Holy Qur'an*. Brentwood, Md.: Amana Corporation, 1983.

Ali, Maulana Muhammad. *Translation of the Holy Quran*. Lahore, India: Ahmadiyya Anjuman-I-Ishaat Islam, 1928.

Ali, Noble Drew. "The Holy Koran of the Moorish Science Temple of America." Photocopy, n.d.

Ali, Shaharazad. *The Blackman's Guide to Understanding the Black Woman*. Philadelphia: Civilized Publications, 1989.

Al-Khateeb, Sharifa. Letter to the editor, *Al-Umma* 1, 4 (October 1971): 3.

Allen, Ernest Jr. "Identity and Destiny: The Formative Years of the Moorish Science Temple and the Nation of Islam." In *Muslims on the Americanization Path?* edited by Yvonne Haddad and John Esposito, 201–266. Atlanta: Scholar's Press, 1998.

Al-Mansour, Khalid Abdullah Tariq, and Faisal Fahd al-Talal. *The Challenges of Spreading Islam in America*. Chicago: First African Arabian Press, 1980.

Al-Turabi, Hassan. "Address to the 1986 Annual ISNA Convention, Indianapolis, Indiana." *Vision*, 16, 2 (n.d.): 8–9.

American Ahmadiyya. *Centennial Souvenir, 1889–1989*. Washington, D.C.: Ahmidiyya Movement in Islam, 1989.

Amselle, Jean-Loup. *Logiques métisses*. Paris: Payot, 1990.

Anderson, Elijah. *Streetwise*. Chicago: University of Chicago Press, 1990.

Arberry, A. J. *Revelation and Reason in Islam*. London: Allen and Unwin 1957.

Asante, Molefi Kete. *Afrocentricity*. Trenton, N.J.: Africa World Press, 1988.

Ashmore, Harry. *The Other Side of Jordan*. New York: Norton, 1960.

Aswad, Barbara. *Arabic-Speaking Communities in American Cities*. New York: Center for Immigration Studies, 1974.

Austin, Allan D. *African Muslims in Antebellum America*. New York: Garland Press, 1984.

Baker, Ross K. "Inmate Self-Government." *Journal of Criminal Law, Criminology, and Public Science* 55 (1964): 39–47.

Bakhash, Shaul. "What Khomeini Did." *New York Review of Books* 36, 12 (20 July 1989): 16–19.

Baldwin, James. *The Fire Next Time*. New York: Modern Library, 1995.

Balk, Alfred, and Alex Haley. "Black Merchants of Hate." In *Politics, U.S.A.*, edited by Andrew Mackay Scott and Earle Wallace, 59–67. New York: Macmillan, 1965.

Ball, Charles. *Slavery in the United States: A Narrative of the Life and Adventures of Charles Ball*. 1837; reprint, New York: Negro Universities Press, 1969.

Barrett, David B., George T. Kurian, and Todd M. Johnson ed. *World Christian Encyclopedia*. 2nd edition. New York: Oxford University Press, 2001.

Barrett, Leonard. *The Rastafarians*. Boston: Beacon Press, 1974.

———. *Soul Force: African Heritage in Afro-American Religion*. Garden City, N.Y.: Anchor Books, 1974.

Barry, Dan. "In Tax Scheme, a Major Role for Separatists." *New York Times*, 12 December 1997, sec. A, p. 1.

Bastide, Roger. *African Civilizations in the New World*. New York: Harper and Row, 1971.

———. *Les religions Africaines au Brésil*. Paris: Presses Univeritaires de France, 1960.

Batran, Aziz. *Islam and Revolution in Africa*. Brattleboro, Vt.: Amana Books, 1984.

Behrman, Lucy. *Muslim Brotherhoods and Politics in Senegal*. Cambridge: Harvard University Press, 1970.

Benaboud, Muhammad. "Orientalism on the Revelation of the Prophet: The Cases of W. Montgomery Watt, Maxime Rodinson, and Duncan Black MacDonald." *American Journal of Islamic Social Sciences* 3,2 (1986): 309–326.

Bennett, Lerone, Jr. *Before the Mayflower: A History of the Negro in America*. Baltimore: Penguin, 1962.

Berger, Morroe. "The Black Muslims." *Horizon* (winter 1964): 49–64.

Berger, Peter L., and Thomnas Luckman . *The Social Construction of Reality*. London: Penguin Press, 1971.

Bernard, Jessie. *Marriage and Family among Negroes*. Englewood Cliffs, N.J.: Prentice-Hall, 1966.

Bey, C. Mosley. "The Clock of Destiny." Cleveland, 1947. Photocopy.

Beynon, Erdmann Doane "The Voodoo Cult among Negro Migrants in Detroit." *American Journal of Sociology* (May 1938): 894–907.

Bloom, Harold. *The American Religion*. New York: Simon and Schuster, 1992.

Blyden, Edward Wilmot. *Christianity, Islam and the Negro Race*. 1887; reprint, New York: ECA, 1990.

Bolster, W. Jeffrey. *Black Jacks, African American Seamen in the Age of Sail*. Cambridge, Mass.: Harvard University Press, 1997.

Bontemps, Arna, and Jack Conroy. *They Seek a City*. Garden City, N.Y.: Doubleday, Doran, 1945.

Bontemps, Arna, ed. *Great Slave Narratives*. Boston: Beacon Press, 1969.

Boodhoo, Ken I. "Islamic Fundamentalism in the Caribbean: The Attempted Coup in Trinidad," Dialogues, no. 135, Occasional Papers Series. Miami: Florida International University, February 1992.

Boudhiba, Abdelwahab. *Sexuality in Islam*. London: Routledge and Kegan Paul, 1985.

Bourdieu, Pierre. *The Field of Cultural Production*. New York: Columbia University Press, 1993.

Bowker, Lee. *Prison Subcultures*. Lexington, Mass.: Heath, 1977.

Bray, Rosemary. "Claiming a Culture." *New York Times Magazine*, 23 April 1989, 25–30.

Breitman, George, Herman Porter, and Baxter Smith. *The Assassination of Malcolm X*. New York: Pathfinder Press, 1976.

Broderick, Francis L., and August Meier. *Negro Protest Thought in the Twentieth Century*. Indianapolis: Bobbs-Merrill, 1965.

Brody, Stuart. "The Political Prisoner Syndrome." *Crime and Delinquency* 20 (April 1974): 102–111.

Brotz, Howard. *The Black Jews of Harlem*. New York: Schocken 1970.

Brotz, Howard, ed. *Negro Social and Political Thought: 1850–1900, Representative Texts*. New York: Basic Books, 1966.

Brown, Claude. *Manchild in the Promised Land*. New York: Signet, 1965.

Brown, John Porter. *The Dervishes of Oriental Spiritualism*. 1868; reprint, London: H. A. Rose, 1968.

Builta, Jeffrey A. "Al-Fuqra." In John Murray and Richard H. Ward (eds.), *Extremist Groups*. Chicago: Office of International Criminal Justice, University of Illinois, 1998. Internet edition.

Bunyan, John. *The Pilgrim's Progress*. New York: Oxford University Press, 1998.

Burke, Edmund, III, and Ira Lapidus. *Islam, Politics, and Social Movements*. Berkeley: University of California Press, 1988.

Burkett, Randall K. *Garveyism as a Religious Movement*. Metuchen, N.J.: Scarecrow Press, 1978.

Caldwell, Wallace F. "A Survey of Attitudes toward Black Muslims in Prison." *Journal of Human Relations* 16 (1966): 220–238.

Calverly, Edwin. "Negro Muslims in Hartford." *Moslem World* 55 (October 1965): 340–345.

Cannon, J. *Female Networking in a Contemporary Mormom Polygynous Commune.* Tucson: University of Arizona Press, 1993.

Carré, Olivier, and Gérard Michaud, eds. *Les Fréres Musulmans.* Paris: Gallimard, 1983.

Cass, Don A. *Negro Freemasonry and Segregation.* Chicago: Ezra Cook, 1957.

Castells, Manuel. *The Power of Identity.* Oxford: Blackwell, 1997.

Chaudry, Rashid Ahmad, ed. *Persecution of Ahmadi Muslims and Their Response.* London: Ahmadiyya Muslim Association, 1989.

Chrisman, Robert, and Nathan Hare, eds. *Pan-Africanism.* Indianapolis: Bobbs-Merrill, 1974.

Clarke, John Henrik. *Malcolm X, the Man and His Times.* New York: Collier, 1969.

Clarke, Peter B. *West Africa and Islam.* London: Edward Arnold, 1982.

Cleaver, Eldridge. "The Decline of the Black Muslims." In *Eldridge Cleaver,* edited by Robert Scheer, 13–18. New York: Random House, 1968.

Clegg, Claude Andrew. *An Original Man: The Life and Times of Elijah Muhanmad.* New York: St. Martin's Press, 1997.

Clemmer, Donald. *The Prison Community.* New York: Holt, Rinehart and Winston, 1940.

Clines, Francis X. "U. S. Suspect in Bombing Plots: Zealous Causes and Civic Roles." *New York Times,* 28 June 1993, Sec. B, p. 2.

Cloward, Richard A., et al. *Theoretical Studies in the Social Organization of the Prison.* New York: Social Science Research Council, 1960.

Colvin, Lucie Gallistel. *Historical Dictionary of Senegal.* Metuchen, N.J.: Scarecrow Press, 1981.

Cone, James. *A Black Theology of Liberation.* Philadelphia: Lippincott, 1970.

Conway, Flo, and Jim Siegelman. *Snapping: America's Epidemic of Sudden Personality Changes.* New York: Lippincott, 1978.

Cooper, James Fenimore. *The Prairie.* 1827.

Cottman, George S. "Old Time Slums of Indianapolis." *Indiana Magazine of History* 7 (December 1911): 170–173.

Cotton, Samuel. *Silent Terror.* New York: Harlem River Press, 1998.

Coulon, Christian. *Le Marabout et le Prince (Islam et pouvoir au Sénégal).* Paris: Pedone, 1981.

———. *Les musulmans et le pouvoir en Afrique noir.* Paris: Karthala, 1983.

Coulson, Noel J. *Conflicts and Tensions in Islamic Jurisprudence.* Chicago: University of Chicago Press, 1969.

Cragg, Kenneth, ed. and trans. *Readings in the Qur'an.* London: Collins, 1988.

Crawford, George Williamson. *Prince Hall and His Followers.* 1914; reprint, New York: A. M. S. Press, 1971.

Cronon, E. David. *Black Moses: The Story of Marcus Garvey and the Universal Negro Improvement Association* . Madison: University of Wisconsin Press, 1955.

Cruise O'Brien, D. B. *The Mourides of Senegal.* Oxford: Clarendon Press, 1971.

Crummery, Donald. *Banditry, Rebellion and Social Protest in Africa.* Portsmouth, N.H.: Heinemann, 1986.

Curtin, Philip D. *The Atlantic Slave Trade.* Madison: University of Wisconsin Press, 1969.

Curtin, Philip D., et al. *African History.* London: Longman Group, 1995.

Curtin, Philip D., ed. *Africa Remembered.* Madison: University of Wisconsin Press, 1967.

Curtis, R. M. "Urban Muslims: The Formation of the Dar ul-Islam Movement." In *Muslim Communities in North America,* edited by Yvonne Haddad and Jane Smith, 51–73. Albany: SUNY Press, 1994.

Cutler, Donald R., ed. *The Religous Situation.* Boston: Beacon Press, 1968.

Dannin, Robert M. "Ethno-Methodological Approaches to Studying Islam in America." In *The Diversity of the African-American Religious Experience: A Continuing Dialogue.* New York: Schomburg Center for Research in Black Culture, New York Public Library, 1995.

———. "Forms of Huron Kinship and Marriage." *Ethnology*, 21, 2 (April 1982): 101–110.

———. "An Island in a Sea of Ignorance: Dimensions Contours of the Prison Mosque." In *Making Muslim Space*, edited by Barbara D. Metcalf, 131–146. Berkeley: University of California Press, 1996.

———. "Ces musulmans courtisés et divisés." *Le Monde Diplomatique* (February 1993): 17.

———. "Railroad Justice Revisted." *City Sun* 9, 20 and 21 (1991): 6–12.

———. "Understanding the Multi-Ethnic Dilemma of African-American Muslims." In *Muslims on the Americanization Path?* edited by John Esposito and Yvonne Haddad, 331–358. Atlanta, Ga.: Scholars Press, 1998.

Davis, Harry E. "Alpha Lodge No. 11, New Jersey." *Journal of Negro History* 20 (1935): 180–189.

———. "Documents Relating to Negro Masonry in America." *Journal of Negro History* 21 (1936): 411–432.

———. *A History of Freemasonry among Negroes.* Cleveland, 1946.

———. *The Scottish Rite in the Prince Hall Fraternity.* 1940.

deCerteau, Michel. *The Practice of Everyday Life.* Berkeley, Calif.: University of California Press, 1984.

Delany, Martin. *The Condition, Elevation, Emigration and Destiny of the Colored People of the United States, Politically Considered.* Philadelphia, 1852.

———. *Official Report of the Niger Valley Exploring Party.* New York: Thomas Hamilton, 1861.

———. *The Origin and Objects of Ancient Freemasonry; Its Introduction into the U.S. and the Legitimacy among Colored Men. A Treatise Delivered before St. Cyprian Lodge*, no. 13. 24 June 1853.

Denny, Frederick. *Islam.* San Francisco: Harper and Row, 1987.

Denslow, William R. *Freemasonary and the American Indian.* Masonic Service Organization, 1956.

Devine, John. *Maximum Security.* Chicago: University of Chicago Press, 1996.

Dillard, J. L. *Black English.* New York: Vintage Books, 1972.

Din, Sheikh Ahmad. *Theism.* St. Louis, Mo.: Sheikh Ahmad Publishing, 1927.

Diop, Cheikh Anta. *Precolonial Black Africa.* Westport, Conn.: Lawrence Hill Press, 1987.

Disuqi, Rasha. "Orientalism in Moby Dick." *American Journal of Islamic Social Sciences* 4,1 (1987): 117–126.

Drake, St. Clair. "The African Diaspora in Pan-African Perspective." *Black Scholar* 7 (September 1975): 2–13.

———. *Black Folk Here and There.* Los Angeles: Center for Afro-American Studies, University of California, 1990.

———. *Churches and Voluntary Associations in the Chicago Negro Community.* Chicago: Works Progress Administration, 1940.

———. *The Redemption of Africa and Black Religion.* Chicago: Third World Press, 1970.

Drake, St. Clair, and Horace Cayton. *Black Metropolis.* New York: Harcourt, Brace, 1945.

Du Bois, W. E. B. *The Souls of Black Folks.* Chicago: A. C. McClary, 1903.

————, ed. *Economic Cooperation among Negroes.* Atlanta University Publications, no. 12. Atlanta, 1907.

Durkheim, Emile. *The Elementary Forms of Religious Life.* London: Allen and Unwin, 1964.

Ehrman, Albert. "Black Judaism in New York." *Journal of Ecumenical Studies* 8,1 (winter 1971): 103–113.

Eickelman, Dale, and James Piscatori, eds. *Muslim Travellers.* Berkeley: University of California Press, 1990.

El-Amin, Mustafa. *Freemasonry, Ancient Egypt, and the Islamic Destiny.* Jersey City, N.J.: New Mind Productions, 1988.

Elkholy, Abdo A. *The Arab Moslems in the U.S.* New Haven: College and University Press, 1966.

El Moudden, Abderrahmane. "The Ambivalence of *Rihla*: Community Integration and Self-definition in Moroccan Travel Accounts, 1300–1800." In *Muslim Travellers,* edited by Dale Eickelman and James Piscatori, 69–84. Berkeley: University of California Press, 1990.

El Saadawi, Nawal. *The Hidden Face of Eve.* Boston: Beacon Press, 1980.

Essien-Udom, E. U. *Black Nationalism.* Chicago: University of Chicago Press, 1962.

Estabrook, Arthur H.. "The Tribe of Ishmael." *Eugenics, Genetics and the Family.* Baltimore: Williams and Wilkins Co., 1923.

Evans-Pritchard, E. E. *The Sanusi of Cyrenaica.* London: Oxford University Press, 1949.

————. "Social Anthropology: Past and Present." *Man* 50, 198 (1950): 118–124.

Evanzz, Karl. *The Messenger.* New York: Pantheon, 1999.

Faisal, Sheikh Daoud Ahmed. *Al-Islam: The Religion of Humanity.* Brooklyn: Islamic Mission of America, n.d.

Farah, Caesar E. *Islam.* New York: Barron's, 1987.

Farah, Madelain. *Marriage and Sexuality in Islam.* Salt Lake City: University of Utah Press, 1984.

Farwell, Byron. *Prisoners of the Mahdi.* New York: Norton, 1989.

Fauset, Arthur Huff. *Black Gods of the Metropolis: Negro Religious Cults of the Urban North.* Philadelphia: University of Pennsylvania Press, 1944.

Felder, Cain Hope, ed. *Stony the Road We Trod.* Minneapolis: Fortune Press, 1991.

Fenton, William. "Field Work, Museum Studies, and Ethnohistorical Research." *Ethnohistory* 13 (1966): 71–85.

Ferris, Marc. "Immigrant Muslims in New York City." In *Muslim Communities in North America,* edited by Yvonne Yazbeck Haddad and Jane Idleman Smith, 209–230. Albany: SUNY Press, 1994.

Fisher, Allan G. B., and Humphrey J. Fisher. *Slavery and Muslim Society in Africa.* Garden City, N.Y.: Doubleday, 1971.

Fisher, George P. *The So-Called Moors of Delaware.* 1895; reprint, Public Archives Commission of Delaware, Dover, 1929.

Forbes, Jack. *Africans and Native Americans.* Urbana: University of Illinois Press, 1993.

Fortes, Meyer. *Oedipus and Job in West African Religion.* Cambridge, England: Cambridge University Press, 1959.

Fortes, Meyer, and G. E. Dieterlen, eds. *African Systems of Thought.* London: Oxford University Press, 1965.

Foster, Lawrence. *Religion and Sexuality.* Urbana: University of Illinois Press, 1980.

Foucault, Michel. *Discipline and Punish: The Birth of the Prison.* Translated by Alan Sheridan. New York: Pantheon Books, 1977.

Fountain, John W. "Violence Is Down, but Some Areas Still Suffer." *New York Times*, 11 January 2001, sec. A, p. 14.

Frazier, E. Franklin. *Black Bourgeoisie*. 1957; reprint, New York: Collier Books, 1962.

———. *The Negro Church in America*. New York: Schocken Books, 1964.

———. *The Negro Family in the United States*. 1939; reprint, Chicago: University Press, 1966.

Freyre, Gilberto. *The Masters and the Slaves*. Berkeley: University of California Press, 1986.

Friedman, Jonathan. *Cultural Identity and Global Process*. London: Sage, 1994.

Friedmann, Yohanan. *Prophecy Continuous*. Berkeley: University of California Press, 1989.

Geertz, Clifford. *The Interpretation of Cultures*. New York: Basic Books, 1973.

———. *Islam Observed*. Chicago: University of Chicago Press, 1968.

Gellens, Sam I. "The Search for Knowledge in Medieval Muslim Societies." In *Muslim Travellers*, edited by Dale Eickelman and James Piscatori, 50–68. Berkeley: University of California Press, 1990.

Gellner, Ernest. *Legitimation of Belief*. Cambridge, England: Cambridge University Press, 1974.

———. *Muslim Society*. Cambridge, England: Cambridge University Press, 1981.

———. *Post-Modernism, Reason and Religion*. London: Routledge, 1992.

Genovese, Eugene D. *From Rebellion to Revolution*. New York: Vintage Books, 1981.

———. *In Red and Black, Marxian Explorations in Southern and Afro-American History*. Knoxville: University of Tennessee Press, 1984.

———. *The Political Economy of Slavery*. New York: Vintage Books, 1967.

———. *Roll, Jordan, Roll*. New York: Vintage Books, 1976.

Georgia Writers' Project, Works Progress Adminstration. *Drums and Shadows*. New York: Anchor Books, 1972.

Giddens, Paula . *When and Where I Enter*. New York: Bantam, 1984.

Gilani, el-Sheikh Mohy-ud-Din Syed Mubarik Ali. *Quranic Psychiatry*. Lahore, Pakistan: Zawia Books, 1978.

Gilroy, Paul. *The Black Atlantic*. Cambridge: Harvard University Press, 1993.

Gillespie, Dizzy, and Al Frazer. *To Be or Not to Bop*. New York: Da Capo Press, 1979.

Gillespie, V. Bailey. *Religious Conversion and Personal Identity: How and Why People Change*. Birmingham, Ala.: Religious Education Press, 1979.

Gilsenan, M. *Recognizing Islam: An Anthropologist's Introduction*. London: Croom Helm, 1982.

Glock, Charles Y. *Religion in Sociological Perspective: Essays in the Empirical Study of Religion*. Chicago: University of Chicago Press, 1974.

Godfrey, K. "Joseph Smith and the Masons." *Journal of the Illinois State Historical Society* 64 (spring 1971): 66–78.

Goldman, Ari. "Portrait of Religions in U.S. Holds Dozens of Surprises." *New York Times*, 10 April 1991, sec. A, p. 1.

Goldman, Peter. *The Life and Death of Malcolm X*. Urbana: University of Illinois Press, 1979.

Goldziher, Ignaz. *Muslim Studies*, 2 vols. Albany: SUNY Press, 1967.

Gourgi, Abu'l-Qasim. *Temporary Marriage (Mut'a) in Islamic Law*. Tehran Iran: Ansari-yar Publications, 1991.

Grabites, Pierre. "American Negro Mohammedans." *Catholic World* 2 (1933): 559–566.

Gramsci, Antonio. *Selections for the Prison Notebooks*. New York: International, 1971.

Grant, Douglas. *The Fortunate Slave*. New York: Oxford University Press, 1968.

Greenberg, Joseph. "The Deciphering of the 'Ben Ali' Diary." *Journal of Negro History* 25 (1940): 372–375.

Grimshaw, William H. *Official History of Freemasonry among Colored Peoples of North America*. Montreal: Broadway, 1903.

Grosso, Sony, and John Devaney. *Murder at the Harlem Mosque*. New York: Crown, 1977.

Guillaume, Alfred. *Islam*. New York: Penguin, 1956.

Gutman, Herbert. *The Black Family in Slavery and Freedom, 1750–1925*. New York: Pantheon, 1976.

Haddad, Yvonne Yazbeck. "A Century of Islam in America." *Occasional Paper*, no. 4. Washington D.C.: American Institute for Islamic Studies, American University, 1986.

———, ed. *The Muslims of America*. New York: Oxford University Press, 1991.

Haddad, Yvonne Yazbeck, and Adair T. Lummis. *Islamic Values in the United States*. New York: Oxford University Press, 1987.

Haddad, Yvonne Yazbeck, et al., eds. *The Islamic Impact*. Syracuse, N.Y.: Syracuse University Press, 1984.

Haddad, Yvonne Yazbeck, and John Esposito, eds. *Muslims on the Americanization Path?* Altanta: Scholars Press, 1998.

Haddad, Yvonne Yazbeck, and Jane Idleman Smith, eds. *Mission to America*. Gainesville, Fla.: University Press of Florida, 1993.

———. *Muslim Communities in North America*. Albany: SUNY Press, 1994.

Haines, Herbert H. *Black Radicals and the Civil Rights Mainstream, 1954–1970*. Knoxville: University of Tennessee Press, 1988.

Hakim, Jameela A. "History of the First Muslim Mosque of Pittsburgh, Pennsylvania." In *Islam in North America: A Sourcebook*, edited by Michael A. Köszegi and J. Gordon Melton, 153–163. New York: Garland, 1992.

Halasa, Malu. *Elijah Muhammad, Religious Leader*. New York: Chelsea House, 1990.

Haley, Alex. *The Autobiography of Malcolm X*. New York: Ballantine, 1964.

Hankins, Frank. "Fraternal Orders." In *Encyclopaedia of the Social Sciences*, vol. 6, edited by Edwin R. A. Seligman, 423–425. New York: Macmillan, 1934.

———. "Masonry." In *Encyclopaedia of the Social Sciences*, vol. 10, edited by Edwin R. A. Seligman, 177–184. New York: Macmillan, 1934.

Harding, Vincent. *There Is a River*. New York: Vintage Books, 1983.

Hardy, Michael, and William Pleasant. *The Honorable Louis Farrakhan: A Minister for Progress*. New York: New Alliance, 1985.

Heirich, Max. "Change of Heart: A Test of Some Widely Held Theories about Religious Conversion." *American Journal of Sociology* 83,3 (november 1977): 653–678.

Henige, David. *Oral Historiography*. New York: Longmann, 1985.

Herskovits, Melville. "African Gods and Catholic Saints in New World Negro Belief." *American Anthropologist* 39 (1937): 635–643.

———. *The Myth of the Negro Past*. Boston: Beacon Press, 1990.

———. *The New World Negro*. Bloomington: Indiana University Press, 1966.

Higginson, Thomas Wentworth. *Army Life in a Black Regiment*. 1869; reprint, New York: Norton, 1984.

Hill, Robert A., ed. *Marcus Garvey: Life and Lessons*. Berkeley: University of California Press, 1987.

Hly, Ladislav. *Religion and Custom in a Muslim Society*. Cambridge, England: Cambridge University Press, 1991.

Hobsbawm, Eric. *The Age of Extremes*. New York: Pantheon, 1994.

Hobsbawm, Eric, and Terrence Ranger, eds. *The Invention of Tradition*. Cambridge, England: Cambridge University Press, 1988.

Hodgson, M. G. S. *The Venture of Islam*. Chicago: University of Chicago Press, 1974.

Hooglund, Eric. *Taking Root: Arab-American Community Studies*. Vol. 1 and 2. Washington, D.C.: American-Arab Anti-Discrimination Committee Research Institute, 1985.

hooks, bell. *Ain't I a Woman*. Boston: South End Press, 1981.

Horton, Robin. "A Definition of Religion and Its Uses." *Journal of the Royal Anthropological Institute* 90 (1960): 206.

———. "Ritual Man in Africa." *Africa* 34 (1964): 85–104.

Howard, Clark. *The Zebra Killings*. London: New English Library, 1979.

Hughes, Langston. *Selected Poems*. New York: Vintage Books, 1990.

Hussain, Asaf, et al., eds. *Orientalism, Islam and Islamists*. Brattleboro, Vt.: Amana Books, 1984.

Hussain, Fida. *Wives of the Prophet*. Lahore, Pakistan: Muhammad Ashraf, 1983.

International Islamic Educational Society. *The International Islamic Educational Institute*. Lahore, Pakistan, 1977.

Isa, As Sayyid. *The Ansar Cult: Rebuttal to the Slanderers*. Brooklyn: Original Tents of Kedar, 1989.

———. *Are Pictures a Sin?* Brooklyn: Original Tents of Kedar, 1989.

———. *360 Questions to Ask the Orthodox Sunni Muslims*. Brooklyn: Original Tents of Kedar, 1989.

———. *Whatever Happened to the Nubian Islamic Hebrews?* Brooklyn: Original Tents of Kedar, 1985.

———. *Who Was Noble Drew Ali?* Brooklyn: Ansaaru Allah, 1980.

"ISNA-Saudi Factor and the Muslim Community's Struggle for Control of Jami Mosque." *Crescent International* 19, 8 (July 1990): 10.

Iverson, Joan Smyth. *The Antipolygamy Controversy in U.S. Women's Movements, 1880–1925*. New York: Garland, 1997.

Jacobs, James B. "Stratification and Conflict among Prison Inmates." *Journal of Criminal Law and Criminology* 66 (December 1976): 476–482.

———. "Street Gangs behind Bars." *Social Problems* 21 (1974): 395–411.

Jamal, Hakim. *Malcolm and Me from the Dead Level*. New York: Random House, 1971.

James, William. *The Varieties of Religious Experience*. New York: Vintage Books, 1990.

Jenkins, Betty Lanier, and Susan Phillis. *Black Separatism: A Bibliography*. Westport, Conn.: Greenwood Press, 1976.

Jones, Raymond J. *A Comparative Study of Religions Cult Behavior among Negroes with Special Reference to Emotional Group Conditioning Factors*. Washington, DC: Howard University, 1939.

Kane, Cheikh Hamidou. *Ambiguous Adventure*. Portsmouth, N.H.: Heinemann Educational Books, 1963.

Kaplan, Robert D. *The Arabists*. New York: Free Press, 1993.

Karim-Bey, Dhanifu Sayed. "The Fallen Moorish Empire." Long Beach, Calif.: Islamic Moorish Empire in the West, 1989. Photocopy.

Katz, Jacob. *Jews and Freemasons in Europe, 1723–1939*. Cambridge: Harvard University Press, 1970.

Kaufman, Jonathan. *Broken Alliance*. New York: New American Library, 1988.

Kearney, Reginald. *African-American Views of the Japanese: Solidarity of Sedition?* Albany: SUNY Press, 1998.

Keiser, R. Lincoln. *The Vice Lords: Warriors of the Streets.* New York: Holt, Rinehart and Winston, 1969.

Kepel, Gilles. *Allah in the West.* Stanford: Stanford University Press, 1997.

Khaldûn, Ibn. *The Muqqadimah.* 1377; reprint, Princeton: Princeton University Press, 1967.

Khamsin Collective. *Women in the Middle East.* London: Zed Books, 1987.

Kilbride, Philip. *Plural Marriage for Our Times: A Reinvented Option?* Wesport, Conn.: Bergin and Garvey, 1994.

Kierkegaard, Søren. *Fear and Trembling.* New York: Penquin, 1985.

Killian, Lewis M.. *The Impossible Revolution?* New York: Random House, 1968.

Kilson, Martin, and Robert Rotberg, eds. *The African Diaspora: Interpretive Essays.* Cambridge: Harvard University Press, 1976.

King, Kenneth J. "Some Notes on Arnold Ford." In Randall Burkett and Richard Newman (eds.) *Black Apostles.* Boston: G. K. Hall, 1978.

Kiser, Clyde V. *Sea Island to City: A Study of St. Helena Islanders in Harlem and Other Urban Centers.* New York: Columbia University Press, 1932.

Klein, Martin A. *Islam and Imperialism in Senegal.* Hoover Institute. Stanford: Stanford University Press, 1968.

———. "The Moslem Revolution in Nineteenth Century Senegambia." In *Boston University Papers on Africa,* vol. 4, edited by Daniel McCall et al. Boston: Boston University African Studies Center, 1969.

———. "Social and Economic Factors in the Muslim Revolution in Senegambia." *Journal of African History* 13 (1972): 419–441.

Kly, Y. N. *The Black Book: The True Political Philosophy of Malcolm X.* Atlanta: Clarity Press, 1986.

Koehnline, James. "Migration of the Tribe of Ishmael." *Dharma Beat* 10 (1990): 14–27.

Kose, Ali. *Conversion to Islam.* London: Kegan Paul International, 1996.

Kosmin, Barry A., and Seymour Lachman. *One Nation under God.* New York: Harmony Books, 1993.

Köszegi, Michael A., and J. Gordon Melton. *Islam in North America: A Sourcebook.* New York: Garland, 1992.

Kramer, Fritz. *The Red Fez.* London: Verso, 1993.

Kritzeck, James, and William H. Lewis. *Islam in Africa.* New York: Van Nostrand-Reinhold, 1969.

Kroll, Michael. "Counsel behind Bars." *California Lawyer,* (June 1987): 36–99.

Kusmer, Kenneth L. *A Ghetto Takes Shape.* Urbana: University of Illinois Press, 1976.

LaBarre, Weston. *The Ghost Dance.* Garden City, N.Y.: Doubleday, 1970.

———. "Material for a History of the Studies of Crisis Cults: A Bibliographical Essay." *Current Anthropology,* 12, 1 (1971): 3–44.

Landau, Jacob M. *The Politics of Pan-Islam.* Oxford: Clarendon Press, 1990.

Landes, Ruth. "Negro Jews in Harlem." *Jewish Journal of Sociology* 9,2 (December 1967): 175–189.

Langmuir, Gavin I. *History, Religion and Anti-Semitism.* Berkeley: University of California Press, 1990.

Lapidus, Ira M. *A History of Islamic Societies.* Berkeley: University of California Press, 1988.

Launay, Robert. *Beyond the Stream.* Berkeley: University of California Press, 1992.

Leaming, Hugo P. "The Ben Ishmael Tribe." In *The Ethnic Frontier*, edited by M. G. Holli and Peter Jones. Grand Rapids, Mich.: Eerdmans, 1977.

———. "Hidden Americans: Maroons of Virginia and the Carolinas." Ph.D. diss., University of Illinois, Chicago Circle, 1979.

Lefebvre, Henri. *The Production of Space*. Oxford: Blackwell, 1991.

Leibow, Elliot. *Tally's Corner*. Boston: Little, Brown, 1967.

Lévi-Strauss, Claude. *The Elementary Structures of Kinship*. Boston: Beacon Press, 1969.

———. "Race and History," in *Structural Anthropology*, vol. 2, 323–362. New York: Basic Books 1976.

Levtzion, Nehemia. *Conversion to Islam*. New York: Holmes and Meier, 1979.

Lévy, Reuben. *The Social Structure of Islam*. Cambridge, England: Cambridge University Press, 1962.

Lewis, Bernard. "The African Diaspora and the Civilization of Islam." In *The African Diaspora: Interpretive Essays*, edited by Martin Kilson and Robert Rotberg, 37–56. Cambridge: Harvard University Press, 1976.

———. *Islam and the West*. New York: Oxford University Press, 1993.

———. *Islam: From the Prophet Muhammad to the Capture of Constantinople*. New York: Oxford University Press, 1974.

———. "Islamic Revolution." *New York Review of Books*. (21 January 1988): 46–50.

———. *The Jews of Islam*. Princeton: Princeton University Press, 1984.

———. *Race and Slavery in the Middle East*. New York: Oxford University Press, 1990.

Lincoln, C. Eric. *Race, Religion and the Continuing American Dilemma*. New York: Hill and Wang, 1984.

———. *The Black Muslims in America*. Boston: Beacon Press, 1961.

Lincoln, C. Eric, and Lawrence Mamiya. *The Black Church in the African American Experience*. Durham, N.C.: Duke University Press, 1990.

Linebaugh, Peter, and Marcus Rediker. *The Many-Headed Hydra*. Boston: Beacon Press, 2000.

Lipman, Pauline. *Race, Class, and Power in School Restructuring*. Albany: SUNY Press, 1998.

Lomax, Louis E. *The Negro Revolt*. New York: Harper and Row, 1962.

———. *To Kill a Black Man*. Los Angeles: Holloway, 1968.

———. *When the Word Is Given*. Cleveland: World, 1963.

Mackenzie, Norman, ed. *Secret Societies*. New York: Holt, Rinehart and Winston, 1967.

Madhubuti, Haki R., ed. *Confusion by Any Other Name: Essays Exploring the Negative Impact of "The Blackman's Guide to Understanding the Black Woman."* Chicago: Third World Press, 1990.

Maglangbayan, Shawna. *Garvey, Lumumba, Malcolm: Black National Separatists*. Chicago: Third World Press, 1972.

Mahmud, Khalil. Introduction to *In the Land of the Pharaohs*, by Duse Mohamed. London: Frank Cass, 1968.

Makdisi, Nadem. "The Moslems of America." *Christian Century* (26 August 1959): 969–971.

Maloney, Carolyn J. "Anthropologist Sheds Light on Jungle Communities Founded by Fugitive Slaves," *Chronicle of Higher Education*, 22 May 1998, Sec. B, p. 2.

Marcus, Greil. *Invisible Republic*. New York: Henry Holt, 1997.

Marks, Carole. *Farewell—We're Good and Gone*. Bloomington: Indiania University Press, 1989.

Marsh, Clifton. *From Black Muslims to Muslims*. Metuchen, N.J.: Scarecrow Press, 1984.

Marty, Paul. *Etudes sur l'Islam au Sénégal*. Paris: Leroux, 1917.

Mar'uf, A. Muhammad. "The Rescuing of Muslim Anthropological Thought." *American Journal of Islamic Social Sciences* 4,2 (1987): 305–320.

Marx, Gary T. *Protest and Prejudice*. New York: Harper and Row, 1969.

Mawdudi, Abul A'la. *The Laws of Marriage and Divorce in Islam*. Kuwait: Islamic Book Publishers, 1983.

———. *Towards Understanding Islam*. 1932; reprint, New York: Islamic Circle of North America, 1986.

Mbiti, John S. *African Religions and Philosophy*. Oxford: Heinemann, 1969.

McCulloch, Oscar C. "The Tribe of Ishmael: A Study in Social Degradation." *Proceedings of the Fifteenth National Conference of Charities and Corrections*. Indianapolis: Charity Organization Society, 1891.

Mehdi, Mohammad T. *Islam and Intolerance*. New York: New World Press, 1990.

Meier, August. *Negro Thought in America*. Ann Arbor: University of Michigan Press, 1970.

Meier, August, and Elliott M. Rudwick. *From Plantation to Ghetto*. New York: Hill and Wang, 1966.

Meillassoux, Claude. *The Anthropology of Slavery*. Chicago: University of Chicago Press, 1991.

Meirs, Suzanne, and Igor Kopytoff, eds. *Slavery in Africa*. Madison: University of Wisconsin, 1979.

Melton, J. Gordon. *Biographical Dictionary of American Cult and Sect Leaders*. New York: Garland, 1986.

Mernissi, Fatima. *Beyond the Veil*. Bloomington: Indiana University Press, 1987.

———. *The Veil and the Male Elite*. Reading: Mass.: Addison-Wesley, 1991.

Metcalf, Barbara Daly. "New Medinas: The Tablighi Jama'at in America and Europe." In *Making Muslim Space in North American and Europe*, 110–127. Berkeley: University of California Press, 1996.

Michaud, Gérard, and Olivier Carré. *Les Frères Musulmans*. Paris: Collection Archives, 1983.

Miller, Carol Poh, and Robert Wheeler. *Cleveland; A Concise History 1796–1990*. Bloomington: Indiana University Press, 1990.

Miller, Nathan. "Secret Societies." In *Encyclopaedia of the Social Sciences*, vol. 13, edited by Edwin R. A. Seligman, 621–623. New York: Macmillan, 1934.

Mohamed, Duse. *In the Land of the Pharaohs*. London: Frank Cass, 1968.

Monteil, Vincent. *L'Islam Noir*. Paris: Editions du Seuil, 1971.

"Moon Sighting." *Islamic Horizons* (April 1994): 23.

Moore, Kathleen. "Muslims in Prison: Claims to Consitutional Protection of Religious Liberty." In *Muslims in America*, edited by Yvonne Yazbeck Haddad, 136–156. New York: Oxford University Press, 1991.

Morris, Brian. *Anthropological Studies of Religion*. Cambridge, England: Cambridge University Press, 1987.

Moorish Science Temple of America. Original Documents. Schomburg Center for Research in Black Culture. New York Public Library.

Moses, Wilson Jeremiah. *Afrotopia*. New York: Cambridge University Press, 1998.

———. *The Golden Age of Black Nationalism, 1850–1925*. New York: Oxford University Press, 1978.

Mudimbe, V. Y. *The Invention of Africa*. Bloomington: Indiana University Press, 1988.

Muhammad, Akbar. "The Image of Africans in Arabic Literature." In *Islam and Slavery in Muslim Africa*, vol. 1, edited by John Ralph Willis, 47–74. London: Frank Cass, 1985.

Muhammad, Elijah. *Message to the Blackman in America*. Philadelphia: Hakim's, 1965.

———. *The Supreme Wisdom*. Chicago: University of Islam, 1965.

Muhammad, Ifetayo. *The Goals of a Polygamous Woman*. Brooklyn: Oyo Graphics, 1989.

Muhammad, Warith Deen. *An African American Genesis*. Calumet City, Ill.: Muslim American Ccommunity Assistance Publication Fund, 1986.

———. *Focus on Al-Islam*. Chicago: Zakat, 1988.

———. *Imam W. Deen Muhammad Speaks from Harlem, N.Y.* Chicago: W. D. Muhammad, 1984.

Muraskin, William Alan. *Middle-Class Blacks in a White Society*. Berkeley: University of California Press, 1975.

"Muslims Gradually Waking Up to the Dangers Confronting Mosques in North America." *Crescent International*, v. 18, no. 11 (August 1989): 10.

Mustafa, Khalil A., et al. "Overview Revealing the Premeditated Overthrow of the Sankore Masjid at Green Haven Correctional Facility and Those Similarly Situated throughout New York State Correctional Facilities." Green Haven, N.Y., September 3, 1981. Photocopy. Unpublished manuscript.

Mutahhari, Murtada Martyr. "The Human Status of Women in the Quran." *Mahjubah* v.1 (September 1985): 5–9.

Naeem, Abdul Basit. "The Black Man and Islam." *Moslem World and the U.S.A.* (August-September 1956): 4

Naipaul, V. S. *The Middle Passage*. New York: Vintage Books, 1981.

Nasir, Khalil Ahmad. *The Status of Women in Islam*. Washington, D.C.: Ahmadiyya Movement in Islam, n.d.

Nasr, Seyyed Vali Reza. *Mawdudi and the Making of Islamic Revivalism*. New York: Oxford University Press, 1996.

Nasr, S. H. *An Introduction to Islamic Cosmological Doctrine*. Cambridge: Harvard University Press, 1964.

Neff, David. "Answering Islam's Questions." *Christianity Today* 44, 4 (3 April 2000): 7.

Newman, Edwin. "Black Muslims." In *The Hate Reader*, 106–110. Dobbs Ferry, N.Y.: Oceana, 1964.

Nigosian, Soloman. *Islam: The Way of Submission*. London: Antiquarian Press, 1987.

Nu'man, Imam Muhammad Armiya. *What Every American Should Know about Islam and the Muslims*. Jersey City, N.J.: New Mind, 1985.

Nurridin, Yusuf. "African-American Muslims and the Question of Identity." In *Muslims on the Americanization Path?* edited by Yvonne Yazbeck Haddad and John Esposito, 267–330. Atlanta: Scholar's Press, 1998.

Nyang, Sulayman S. "The Dar ul-Islam Movement." Washington, D.C.: Howard University, n.d. Photocopy.

———. "History as a Weapon." *Vision*. 2, 3 (n.d.): 3.

———. "A History of Muslims in North America." *Al-Itihad* (September 1986): 39–47.

———. *Islam, Christianity, and African Identity*. Brentwood, Md.: Amana, 1984.

Odum, Howard. *Social and Mental Traits of the Negro*. New York: Columbia University Press, 1910.

Oliver, Paul. *Savannah Syncopators: African Retentions in the Blues*. New York: Stein and Day, 1970.

Paden, John N. *Religion and Political Culture in Kano*. Berkeley: University of California Press, 1973.

Palmer, Edward Nelson. "Negro Secret Societies." *Social Forces* 23, 2 (October 1944): 207–215.

Parrinder, Geoffrey. *African Traditional Religion*. London: Hutchinson's University Library, 1954.

Paschal, Andrew G., ed. *A W. E. B. Du Bois Reader*. New York: Collier Books, 1971.

Passerini, Luisa. *Fascism in Popular Memory*. Cambridge, England: Cambridge University Press, 1988.

Patterson, Orlando. "Toward a Future That Has No Past—Reflections on the Fate of Blacks in the Americas." *Public Interest* 27 (spring 1972): 25–62.

Peacock, James L. *Muslim Puritans: Reformist Psychology in Southeast Asian Islam*. Berkeley: University of California Press, 1978.

Pearl, Daniel. "Moon over Mecca: It's Tough to Pinpoint Start of Holy Month." *Wall Street Journal*, 7 January 1997, sec. A, p. 1.

Perry, Bruce. *Malcolm*. New York: Station Hill, 1991.

Pesle, Octave. *La répudiation chez les Malékites de l'Afrique du Nord*. Rabat: Félix Moncho, 1937.

Peters, F. E., ed. *Judaism, Christianity, and Islam*. Princeton: Princeton University Press, 1990.

Philips, Abu Meenah Bilal. *The Ansar Cult in America*. Riyadh: Tawheed, 1988.

Poole, Stanley Lane. *The Moors in Spain*. Lahore, Pakistan: Publishers United, n.d.

Poston, Larry. "The Future of Da'wah in North America." *American Journal of Islamic Social Sciences* 8 (1991): 501–511.

———. *Islamic Da'wah in the West*. New York: Oxford Universioty Press, 1992.

Price, Richard. *Maroon Societies*. Baltimore: Johns Hopkins University Press, 1979.

Price, Sally. *Co-Wives and Calabashes*. Ann Arbor: University of Michigan Press, 1984.

Puckett, Newbell. *Folk Beliefs of the Southern Negro*. 1926; reprint, New York: Negro University Press, 1968.

Qutb, Sayyid. *Social Justice in Islam*, translated by John B. Hardie. Washington: American Council of Learned Societies, 1953.

Rahman, Fazlur. *Islam and Modernity*. Chicago: University of Chicago Press, 1984.

Rambo, Lewis R. *Understanding Religious Conversion*. New Haven: Yale University, 1993.

Rashid, Hakim M.. "The Socialization of Muslim Children in America: Toward a Conceptual Framework." *American Journal of Islamic Social Sciences* 5,2 (1988): 205–218.

Ravitch, Diane. *The Great School Wars*. New York: Basic Books, 1988.

Ray, Benjamin C. *African Religions*. Englewood Cliffs, N.J.: Prentice-Hall, 1976.

Raymond, Charles A. "The Religious Life of the Negro Slave." *Harper's New Monthly Magazine* 27 (1863): 479–485.

Record, Wilson. *Race and Radicalism*. Ithaca, N.Y.: Cornell University Press, 1964.

Reed, Ishmael. *Mumbo Jumbo*. New York: Atheneum, 1972.

Reis, João José. *Slave Rebellion in Brazil*. Baltimore: Johns Hopkins University Press, 1993.

Ricoeur, Paul. *History and Truth*. Evanston, Ill.: Northwestern University Press, 1965.

———. *The Symbolism of Evil*. New York: Harper and Row, 1967.

Robertson, Claire C., and Martin A. Klein, *Women and Slavery in Africa*. Madison: University of Wisconsin Press, 1983.

Robinson, David. *The Holy War of Umar Tal*. Oxford: Oxford University Press, 1985.

Robinson, Edward L., and William A. Rafferty. *Morocco Centennial 1851–1951*. Danville, Ill.: Recording and Statistical Corporation Services, 1951.

Rodinson, Maxime. *Europe and the Mystique of Islam.* Seattle, Wash.: University of Washington Press, 1987.

———. *Islam and Capitalism.* Austin: University of Texas Press, 1981.

———. *Marxism and the Muslim World.* New York: Monthly Review Press, 1980.

———. *Muhammad.* New York: Pantheon, 1971.

Rogers, J. A. *From "Superman" to Man.* St. Petersburg, Fl.: Helga M. Rogers, 1968.

———. *Nature Knows No Color Line.* St. Petersburg, Fl.: Helga M. Rogers, 1952.

Rosen, Lawrence. *The Anthropology of Justice.* Cambridge, England: Cambridge University Press, 1989.

Rout, Leslie B. "The African in Colonial Brazil." In *The African Diaspora:Interpretive Essays,* edited by Martin L. Kilson and Richard I. Rothberg, 132–171. Cambridge: Harvard University Press, 1976.

Sabbah, Fatna. *Woman in the Muslim Unconsciousness.* New York: Pergamon Press, 1988.

Sabir, Waliyuddin A. *Reconstruction of the African American Male.* Jersey City, N.J.: New Mind, 1989.

Said, Edward. *Covering Islam.* New York: Pantheon, 1981.

———. *Orientalism.* New York: Vintage Books, 1979.

Sa'id, Muhammad. "Questions and Answers About Indigeous U.S. Muslims." Teheran, October 18, 1982. Photocopy. Unpublished manuscript.

Salahuddin, Dawud. "The Islamic Party and the DAR." Chicago: Jamaat ul-Muslimeen, n.d. Mimeographed.

Schacht, Joseph. *An Introduction to Islamic Law.* New York: Clarendon Press, 1982.

———. "Islamic Religious Law." In *The Legacy of Islam,* edited by Joseph Schacht and Clifford E. Bosworth, 392–403. Oxford: Oxford University Press, 1979.

Schoettler, Carl. "Howard Street Temple Guides Moorish Science in U.S." *Baltimore Evening Sun,* 20 January 1978, sec. B, 1.

Seif-al-Hatimy, Said Abdullah. *Woman in Islam.* Lahore, Pakistan: Islamic Publications, 1983.

Semmes, Clovis. *Cultural Hegemony and African American Development.* Westport, Conn.: Praeger, 1992.

Shabazz, El Hajj Malik [Malcolm X]. Letter to Dr. Said Ramadan, 20 February 1965. Reprinted in *Vision* 6, 2 (March 1987): 4.

Shah, Idries. *The Sufis.* London: Octagon Press, 1964.

Shakir, M. H. *Holy Qur'an.* Milton Keynes, England: Mihrab, 1986.

Sherwin, Marc. *The Extremists.* New York: St. Martin's Press, 1963.

Siddiqui, Mohammed. "Notes on the Muslims of America Conference." *American Journal of Islamic Social Sciences* 5,2 (1988): 319–325.

Sills, David. "Voluntary Associations: Sociological Aspects." In *Encylopaedia of the Social Sciences,* vol. 15, edited by Edwin R. A. Seligman, 362–379. New York: Macmillan, 1934.

Simmel, Georg. *Essays on Religion.* New Haven: Yale University Press, 1997.

Simon, John K. "Michel Foucault on Attica: An Interview." *Social Justice* 18,3 (1991): 26–34.

Simpson, Frank T. "The Moorish Science Temple and Its 'Koran.'" *Moslem World* 37 (January 1947): 56–61.

Simpson, George Eaton. *Black Religions in the New World.* New York: Columbia University Press, 1978.

Sinclair, Abiola. "Shaharazad Ali: 1001 Arabian Lies." *New York Amsterdam News* 81,29 (21 July 1990): 24.

Sivan, Emmanuel. *Radical Islam, Medieval Theology and Modern Politics*. New Haven: Yale University Press, 1985.

Sleeper, Jim. *The Closest of Strangers*. New York: Norton, 1990.

Smith, W. Robertson. *Kinship and Marriage in Early Arabia*. 1907; reprint, edited by Stanley A. Cook, Oosterhut, Netherlands: Anthropological Publications, 1966.

Smith, Wilfred Cantwell. *Islam in Modern History*. New York: Mentor Books, 1959.

Sobel, Mechal. *Trabelin' On*. Princeton: Princeton University Press, 1988.

Solé, Robert. *Le Tarbouche*. Paris: Éditions du Seuil, 1992.

Stack, Carol B. *All Our Kin: Strategies for Survival in a Black Community*. New York: Harper and Row, 1974.

———. *Call to Home*. New York: Basic Books, 1996.

Stampp, Kenneth. *The Peculiar Institution*. New York: Vintage Books, 1956.

Staples, Robert. *The Black Woman in America*. Chicago: Nelson-Hall, 1973.

Stevenson, David. *The Origins of Freemasonry*. Cambridge, England: Cambridge University Press, 1988.

Stewart, Jocelyn Y. "Life in the Killing Zone." *Los Angeles Times*, 7 January 2001, internet edition, http://www.latimes.com/new/state/reports/southeast.

Stoddard, Lothrop. *The New World of Islam*. London: Chapman and Hall, 1921.

Sullivan, Ronald. "In New York, State Prisoners Work or Else." *New York Times*, 27 January 1992, sec. B, p. 1.

Tambiah, Stanely Jeyaraja. *Magic, Science, Religion and the Scope of Rationality*. Cambridge, England: Cambridge University Press, 1990.

Tawfiq, K. Ahmad. "The Black Man and Islam." Brooklyn: Aim Graphics, 1971. Pamphlet.

Tawfiq-Toure, Halima. "The Marital Life of the Prophet: The Misunderstood Subject." Paper presented at the Sixth International Seerah Conference, New York, N.Y., 23 December 1989.

Thayer, George. "The Black Nationalists." In *The Farther Shores of Politics*. New York: Simon and Schuster, 1967.

Thernstrom, Stephan and Abigal Thernstrom. *America in Black and White*. New York: Simon and Schuster, 1997.

Thomas, Charles W., and Samuel C. Foster. "Prisonization in the Inmate Contra-Culture." *Social Problems* 20 (fall 1972): 229–239.

Thompson, Robert Farris. *Flash of the Spirit*. New York: Vintage Books, 1984.

Tibi, Bassam. *The Challenge of Fundamentalism*. Berkeley: University of California Press, 1998.

———. *Islam and the Cultural Accomodation of Social Change*. Boulder, Col.: Westview Press, 1990.

Tolstoy, Leo. *A Confession*. New York: Penguin, 1987.

Trimingham, J. Spencer. *A History of Islam in West Africa*. London: Oxford University Press, 1962.

———. *The Influence of Islam upon Africa*. New York: Praeger, 1968.

Trotter, Joe William, Jr. *The Great Migration in Historical Perspective*. Bloomington: Indiana University Press, 1991.

Turner, Brian S. *Religion and Social Theory: A Materialist Perspective*. London: Heinemann, 1983.

———. *Weber and Islam*. London: Routledge and Kegan Paul, 1974.

Turner, Richard B. "The Ahmadiyya Mission to Blacks in the United States in the 1920s." *Journal of Religious Thought* 44, 2 (winter–spring 1988): 50–66.

——. *Islam in the African-American Experience*. Bloomington: University of Indiana Press, 1997.

Turner, Victor. *Image and Pilgrimage in Christian Culture*. New York: Columbia University Press, 1978.

Tyler, Lawrence. "The Protestant Ethic among the Black Muslims." *Phylon* 27 (spring 1966): 5–14.

Voorhis, Harold Van Buren. *Negro Masonry in the U.S.* New York: Henry Emmerson, 1945.

——. *Our Colored Brethren: The Story of the Alpha Lodge of New Jersey*. New York: Henry Emmerson, 1960.

Wade, Richard C. *Slavery in the Cities*. Oxford: Oxford University Press, 1964.

Walker, David. *Appeal to the Coloured Citizens of the World*. 1829; reprint, edited by Charles Wiltse, New York: Hill and Wang, 1965.

Washington, Joseph R., Jr. *Black Religion*. Boston: Beacon Press, 1964.

Watson, G. Llewellyn. "Social Structure and Social Movements: The Black Muslims in the U.S.A. and the Ras-Tafarians in Jamaica." *British Journal of Sociology* 24 (June 1973): 197–199.

Watt, W. Montgomery. *Islam and the Integration of Society*. London: Oxford University Press, 1961.

——. *Islamic Philosophy and Theology*. Edinburgh: Edinburgh University Press, 1962.

——. *Islamic Political Thought*. Edinburgh: Edinburgh University Press, 1968.

——. *Muhammad at Mecca*. London: Oxford University Press, 1953.

——. *Muhammad at Medina*. London: Oxford University Press, 1956.

——. *Muhammad: Prophet and Statesman*. London: Oxford University Press, 1961.

Webb, Mohammed Alexander Russell. *Islam in America*. New York: Oriental Publishing, 1893.

——. "The Spirit of Islam." In *The Dawn of Religious Pluralism*, edited by Richard Hughes Seager, 270–280. La Salle, Ill.: Open Court, 1993.

Weber, Max. *The Sociology of Religion*. Boston: Beacon Press, 1963.

Weider, Lawrence. *Language and Social Reality: The Case of Telling the Convict Code*. The Hague: Mouton Press, 1974.

Weinstein, Norman C. *A Night in Tunisia*. New York: Limelight Editions, 1993.

Wenck, Ernest A., and Rudolf H. Moos. "Prison Environment: The Social Ecology of Correctional Institutions." *Crime and Delinquency Literature* 4 (1972): 591–621.

Weslager, James O. *Delaware's Forgotten Folk: The Story of the Moors and the Naticokes*. Philadelphia: University of Pennsylvania Press, 1943.

Whyte, W. "Christian Elements in Negro American Muslim Religious Beliefs." *Phylon* 24 (1964): 382–388.

Wilgoren, Jodi. "Court Overturns Use of Vouchers in Ohio Schools." *New York Times*, 12 December 2000, sec. A, 1.

Williams, Loretta J. *Black Freemasonry and Middle-Class Realities*. Columbia: University of Missouri Press, 1980.

Williams, Terry. *Crackhouse*. New York: Penguin Books, 1992.

Williamson, Harry A. *A History of Freemasonry among the American Negroes*. New York: MaCoy, 1924.

——. *The Negro in Masonic Literature*. Brooklyn, 1922.

Willis, John Ralph, ed. *In the Path of Allah, The Passion of al-Hajj ʿUmar*. London: Frank Cass, 1989.

———. *Slaves and Slavery in Muslim Africa*. 2 vols. London: Frank Cass, 1985.

Wilmore, Gayraud. *Black Religion and Black Radicalism*. Garden City, N.Y.: Anchor Doubleday, 1973.

Wilson, Peter Lamborn. *Sacred Drift: Essays on the Margins of Islam*. San Francisco: City Lights Books, 1993.

———. *Scandal: Essays in Islamic Heresy*. Brooklyn: Autonomedia, 1988.

Wilson, William Julius. *The Truly Disadvantaged*. Chicago: University of Chicago Press, 1987.

———. *When Work Disappears*. New York: Knopf, 1996.

Winkel, Eric A. "Remembering Islam: A Critique of Habermas and Foucault." *American Journal of Islamic Social Sciences* 6,1 (1989): 13–35.

Winters, Clyde Ahmad. "Islam in Early North and South America." *Al-Ittihad* (July-October 1977): 57–67.

———. "Origins of Muslim Slaves in the United States." *Al-Ittihad* (September 1986): 49–51.

Wolfram, Walt, and Natalie Schilling-Estes. *American English*. Malden, Mass.: Blackwell, 1998.

Woodson, Carter G. "Insurance Business among Negroes." *Journal of Negro History* 14 2 (April 1929): 202–226.

Worsley, Peter. *The Trumpet Shall Sound: A Study of "Cargo" Cults in Melanesia*. New York: Schocken Books, 1968.

Wye, Christopher G. "The New Deal and the Negro Community: Toward a Broader Conceptualization." *Journal of American History* 59 (December 1972): 621–639.

Yinger, J. Milton. *Countercultures*. New York: Free Press, 1982.

———. *Religion, Society and the Individual*. New York: Macmillan, 1957.

———. *The Scientific Study of Religion*. New York: Macmillan, 1970.

Young, Kimball. *Isn't One Wife Enough?* New York: Henry Holt, 1954.

Zarcone, Thierry. *Mystiques, Philosphes et Francs-maçons en Islam*. Paris: Librairie d'amérique et d'orient Adrien Maisonneuve, 1993.

Zaretsky, Irving, and Mark Leone, eds. *Religious Movements in Contemporary America*. Princeton: Princeton University Press, 1974.

Index